W9-ADE-566

The Dictionary of Confusable Words

The Dictionary of Confusable Words

Laurence Urdang

Facts On File Publications
New York, New York • Oxford, England

The Dictionary of Confusable Words

Copyright © 1988 by Laurence Urdang Inc.

All rights reserved. No part of this book may be reproduced or utilized in any form or by any means, electronic or mechanical, including photocopying, recording or by any information storage and retrieval systems, without permission in writing from the Publisher.

Library of Congress Cataloging in Publication Data: 88-045090

CIP data available on request

ISBN 0-8160-1650-X

Printed in the United States of America

10 9 8 7 6 5 4 3 2 1

Foreword

This book came about because over the many years during which I have compiled dictionaries, encyclopedias, and other reference books, I have often encountered people who mix up more or less ordinary things. They have trouble remembering the difference between *cement* and *concrete*, or between a *fission bomb* and a *fusion bomb;* they wonder about the difference(s) between an *accordion* and a *concertina* and between *perfume, cologne,* and *toilet water;* they cannot keep straight the difference between *fuse* and *fuze* and have no convenient place where they could check the sizes of *magnums, jereboams, methuselahs,* and so forth, let alone a source where they could find them all listed in one place. I must confess that I am among them. But, surrounded by reference books, I can usually find the answer or satisfy my curiosity without much trouble. Most people have a dictionary and, perhaps, an encyclopedia. Although much information is contained in the former, it is rarely pulled together in a useful, contrastive way, and it is not the function of dictionaries to list "sets" of terms: that is, one can find the definition of, say, *jereboam* without difficulty, but the dictionary is unlikely to provide the information that *magnum, methuselah,* etc., also belong to the same category. Besides, the function of dictionaries is to define, not explain, and the kinds of information referred to here often require more background than a dictionary provides or can be expected to provide.

Encyclopedias, it is true, do provide this sort of information, but they are generally large, multi-volume affairs, and I cannot recall the last time I looked something up in one without having to find (and read) articles in at least two different volumes. Also, if one is seeking some basic information, most of the larger encyclopedias provide far more information and background than is needed, and finding a relatively simple fact usually means reading through a lot of verbiage.

Dictionaries and encyclopedias simply have too much in them for the purpose under discussion: their "universes" are much more extensive than needed to distinguish the kinds of information about which most people have questions. I must confess that I have not taken a survey to determine and classify the kinds of information about which "most people have questions," and the content of this book is based largely on my own confusions and needs and those I have observed and noted after only 35 years of working with information. Some information has been intentionally omitted, either because it is too abstruse or, at the other extreme, because it can be easily found in a dictionary. Certainly, notions like *General Theory of Relativity* vs. *Special Theory of Relativity* fall into the former category; and the difference between *autobiography* and *biography* fall into the latter.

Undoubtedly, anyone picking up this book will already know some of the things that are in it, immediately prompting the question, "Why did he include *that!*" and the comment, "Everyone knows *that!*" It is hoped, however, that not everyone is so smugly in control of the distinctions between *which* and *that*, between a *tiger lily* and a *day lily*, and between the *X chromosome* and the *Y chromosome* (which male, which female?), between *the Immaculate Conception* and *the Virgin Birth*. And I must confess that having done the research and written this entire book, I find myself referring to it because I have forgotten something.

I have tried, wherever possible, to maintain a layman's approach to the many subjects treated here. In a few entries, the discussion becomes a little technical; but that is unavoidable. In compiling the material for this book, I have not only tried to select topics that I thought would be useful but to explain them in a way that is easily understandable. The style is informal, almost chatty, except in those (relatively few) entries that seemed quite cut and dried, admitting of little more than contrastive definitions of the components. I was quite surprised when I came to prepare the Index, for, although there does not seem to be much text, the information that is treated required more than 5,000 references. Thus, the user should not be deceived into thinking that the words in bold type at the head of an entry reveal all that lurks within: to make proper use of this book, one should first resort to the Index. If the term or idea being sought is not listed there, then it probably is not in the book.

It is only when the users of this book have gained some experience with it that its shortcomings will become evident. Suggestions for its improvement and comprehensiveness are welcome and will lead, I trust, to an enlarged, even more useful book in a revised, expanded edition to be published in the future.

Finally, I should like to thank Gerry Helferich, Executive Editor at Facts On File, who accepted on faith my rather vague description of the work at its beginnings and who has exhibited sympathetic tolerance with the manuscript as delivered.

Laurence Urdang

Old Lyme, Connecticut
January 1988

A Note on the INDEX

1. Entries in the Index appear in several forms, which ought to be distinguished:
   (a) Entries in *italics* (e.g., *burglary, burro*) are references to definitions, comments, and other information about the term itself.
   (b) Entries in roman (e.g., burglary, Caesar) are used in the text as words or illustrations but are not, necessarily, commented on. Thus, *burglary* refers to the entry **burglary /** where *"burglary"* is defined and discussed. But "burglary" is also mentioned in the entry for **homicide /** though it is not discussed there.
   (c) Entries in quotation marks in the index follow the style in the text.
2. (a) Most of the entries in the text have unique headings (e.g., **European plan / American plan, prefix / infix / suffix.** To save space, these have been shortened to include only the first term, up to and including the virgule, and thus appear in the Index as **European plan /, prefix /.**
   (b) In a few cases, however, the same term may appear as the first element in the heading of more than one entry; to avoid ambiguity, references to such entries have been extended to include the second term. Thus, there are three entries that contain *"acute"* as the first element; these are shown at the left, below, with the form in which they appear in the Index at the right:

acute / chronic	**acute / chronic**
acute / grave / circumflex / umlaut / tilde / cedilla	**acute / grave**
acute / obtuse	**acute / obtuse**

Define Your Terms

A horizon / B horizon / C horizon

These are terms designating three main types of soil layers that occur in nature—that is, they do not pertain to cultivated areas. The uppermost is the *A horizon*, characterized by weathering and by the greatest proportion of organic matter; the middle layer, or *B horizon*, which is not exposed to weathering, consists of humus and other organic materials that are leached into it through the A horizon by rain and other water; the bottom layer, or *C horizon*, consists of partially decomposed rock and, to a limited degree, some of the elements leached through from the B horizon. Below all is the bedrock.

a / an

The standard practice governing the choice between *a* and *an* is very simple:

(1) *a* is used before all words beginning with a consonant sound, including words beginning with *h* when it is pronounced, as in *home, honey, hug,* etc. It is used in Britain before *herb,* but not in the U.S., because in Britain the *h* in *herb* pronounced. The *h* in *herbaceous* is pronounced in the U.S., so *a herbaceous border* is said in both countries. *A* is also used before words that begin with a *y*-sound, like *united, use, Yugoslavian* (whether spelled with a *Y* or a *J*), *yew,* etc.

(2) *an* is used before all words beginning with a vowel sound; that includes words that begin with an *h* that is not pronounced, like *honest, hour,* and, in the U.S., *herb.* Unless the speaker is using some variety of English in which normal initial *h* is not pronounced, like Cockney, the standard preferred form is *a* preceding words like *hotel, history, historical, hysterical,* etc. Saying "an historical novel, an hotel, an hysteresis curve, an hydrangea," etc., on the grounds that the first syllable is not stressed is affected and not in keeping with normal English pronunciation anywhere, nor does it appear in standard writing.

abbreviation / acronym / initialism

An *abbreviation* is any shortened form of a word, phrase, name, title, or other formation, whether formed from the initials of separate words, as *C.O.D.* for 'cash on delivery' or *D.S.O.* for 'Distinguished Service Order', from the initials of parts of the same word, as *Gb* for 'gilbert', from a collapsing of a word or phrase by removing parts, as *mdse.* for 'merchandise' or *pd.* for 'paid', from the retention of only the first syllable, letter, or other part of a word, as *ped.* for 'pedal,' *ave.* for 'avenue', or from any combination of these, as *etc.* for 'et cetera'. As can be seen, the use of periods varies: the practice in England till recently was to omit the period (called "full stop" there) in shortenings that include the first and last letters of the word, as *Mr, St* (for *Saint*), etc.; but that is no longer followed universally, and periods are sometimes used in such abbreviations. *Acronym* has become specialized in common usage to refer to any kind of abbreviation that produces a pronounceable word, like *UNESCO* for 'United Nations Educational, Scientific, and Cultural Organization,' *radar* for 'radio detection and ranging,' or *niacin* for 'ni(cotinic) ac(id) + -in* (a special suffix)'. By that criterion, *U.S.A.* (or *USA*) as an abbreviation for 'United States of America' would not qualify as an acronym because it is not pronounced "oosa" or "yoosa." Conventionally, acronyms are written without periods. *Initialism* is a recent coinage used in referring to any kind of shortening. Since WWII many names have been bestowed on various associations, societies, processes, etc., merely with an eye toward the kind of acronym they would produce or to ensure that an acronym would, indeed, be yielded; for example, *START* for 'Strategic Arms Reduction Talks', *WIPO* for 'World Intellectual Property Organization', *IGFET* for 'insulated-gate field-effect transistor'.

abnormal / subnormal

Normal means 'ordinary; common; regular; typical'; *abnormal* simply means 'not normal; different from normal' and should not be confused with *subnormal*, which means 'below normal.' Thus, a person's behavior might be abnormal without being subnormal.

abridged / unabridged

In the United States, where quality and quantity are often confused, the word *unabridged* as applied to dictionaries has taken on the meaning 'complete.' Although that was not the original intention of the publishers of "unabridged dictionaries," they have thrived on the misunderstanding. The literal meaning of *unabridged* is, of course, 'not abridged,' in other words, 'not cut down from a larger source.' In referring to an ordinary book, it means 'uncut, in its original form'; but it has taken on the meaning of 'the largest of its kind' in reference to dictionaries. Publishers have leapt at the opportunities afforded by this usage: without qualification, if an entirely original dictionary only 100 pages in length were published it could properly be called "unabridged," since it was 'not cut down from a larger source.' (If the "source" considered is the entire language, then there is no such thing as an "unabridged dictionary.") Although they have not gone that far, publishers have labeled as "unabridged" dictionaries containing 260,000 entries, 450,000 entries, and 600,000 entries—none of them, of course, "complete descriptions of the English language"; in fact, the publisher of the 600,000-entry "unabridged" put out the 450,000-entry edition about 35 years later and called that one "unabridged," which emphasizes how meaningless the word has become when applied to dictionaries. Meaningless as it might be in lexical terms, *unabridged* retains a magical cachet in commercial contexts.

abscissa / ordinate

In a plane Cartesian coordinate system, the *abscissa* is the vertical, or Y-axis, the *ordinate* the horizontal, or X-axis.

absorption / adsorption

Absorption in its everyday sense is the noun for the processing of *absorbing,* as what a sponge does to water. In chemical parlance, it refers to the process by which an absorbed substance penetrates the pores and membranes of another substance (the *absorbent*). In biology, it refers to the phenomenon of osmosis by which a fluid or dissolved substance passes through the membrane of a cell. *Adsorption* is a specialized term in physical chemistry for the process by which a layer of a gas clings to a surface, usually of a solid but sometimes of a liquid, as the *adsorption* of a gas by activated charcoal.

abstract noun / concrete noun

> *Abstract nouns* are the names of abstract ideas, like *goodness, evil, beauty, fear, love, health, panic, thought; concrete nouns* are the names of physical objects that can be seen and felt, like *table, apple, moon.*

AC / DC

> *AC,* or *alternating current,* is an electric current generated by a device that causes the current to reverse its direction at a specific rate, in most commercial applications at 50 or 60 cycles per second. The voltage of an alternating current can be increased or decreased by a transformer, with proportional loss or gain in amperage. AC current is in wide use in the world partly because it is easier to transmit, but the amperage and voltage vary from country to country. *DC,* or *direct current,* completes it circuit in one direction only; its voltage can only be decreased by a transformer, not increased. It is the electric current produced typically by a battery.

Acadia / Arcadia

> *Acadia* is the name for the (formerly French) Canadian Maritime Provinces, that is, Nova Scotia, the setting for Longfellow's *Evangeline.* There is evidence that its French name, *Acadie,* is from the name of the river *Shubenacadie,* presumably a local Indian name. *Arcadia* has a more complex history. Originally one of the four main dialect areas of ancient Greece (along with *Aeolia, Doria,* and *Ionia*), it is today a department of Greece. It was associated with pastoral, bucolic ancient Greek poetry and, presumably for that reason, was chosen by Sir Philip Sydney for the title of his pastoral romance (1590), which was based on *Diana,* a pastoral by Montemayor, which, in turn, was based on *Daphnis and Chloe,* the Greek pastoral love story by Longos (A.D. 4th century), which goes back to the idylls of Stesichorus (632 B.C.). According to legend, Daphnis was the originator of pastoral poetry. As a consequence of all this, *Arcadia* was adopted by later writers as the setting for pastoral romances and is still used in that sense.

accent / pitch / tone

> In language, *accent* can mean either the way a person pronounces a language—that is, whether he has a Northern, Southern, Yorkshire,

French, or other accent—or the stress given a particular word or syllable: *The accent is on '-low' in 'below'.* In this latter sense, it may refer to the loudness with which a syllable or word is uttered in relation to the other, surrounding elements or to the fullness of the vowel in the syllable. In some languages, as Chinese, *tone* is a feature essential to the meaning, in the sense that a word spoken with a certain tone pattern may have a meaning completely different from the same word uttered with a different pattern. Tone should not be confused with intonation or inflection. which can be a factor in conveying meaning both in English and in Chinese: a statement like *Are you ready?* said with a rising inflection is usually merely a question, but the tone in which it is said may carry with it a sense of impatience, annoyance, exasperation, or other emotional overtones. Strictly speaking, intonation is connotative in nature, not grammatical. (See also **connotation / denotation.**) Another instance might be the way one says the word *Ready:* with a rising inflection, it is a question; with a falling inflection, it is a confirmation that the speaker is "prepared." *Pitch* is not used in linguistics as a feature, but it nonetheless describes the level at which a sound is made: in speaking of "rising" and "falling" inflection, above, it is the pitch, or number of vibrations per second that determines how "high" or "low" a sound is. A bassoon or bass viol, for example, produces sounds of lower pitch than those of a piccolo or violin.

accordion / concertina

The *accordion* and the *concertina,* both dating from the 1820s, operate on the same basic principle: they consist of a pair of headboards between which is a bellows. When the headboards are pulled apart and pushed together, the air to and from the bellows passes over reeds in the headboards; these reeds, which produce a sound not unlike that of the harmonica, are controlled by a number of buttons in the headboards of the concertina and, in the accordion, by a pianolike keyboard at one end for notes and buttons at the other for chords and other effects. The accordion is rectangular and rather bulky, the concertina hexagonal and more easily portable. The accordion is not generally used in playing serious music, but the concertina, which is said to produce a finer tone, has been used in symphony orchestras, and several modern composers have written passages for it, including Tchaikovsky.

account receivable / account payable

In accounting and bookkeeping, an *account receivable*, informally called a *receivable*, is a record of an amount owed to a company or individual. It may include payment for any kind of transaction, that is, for the goods or services sold by the company, for capital assets sold, etc. An *account payable*, informally called a *payable*, is a record of an amount owed by a company or individual to others for goods or services of any kind.

acute / chronic

In medicine, *acute* describes a disease of sudden onset and short duration, *chronic* one slow to develop and, often, of long duration, though without any implication of incurability.

acute / obtuse

In geometry, these terms describe different kinds of angles, *acute* referring to an angle of less than 90°, *obtuse* to one of more than 90°.

acute / grave / circumflex / umlaut / tilde / cedilla

These are the names of various accents, or diacritical marks, that are frequently encountered on foreign words borrowed by English. In some cases, they may be dropped; whether or not they are retained depends on the extent to which the individual word has been assimilated into English, on the style of the material in which the word is used, and on the availability of the particular character in the typefaces used. The *acute accent*, which angles upward to the right, is found in French over *e* (*séance, soigné, méchant*) to indicate a change in quality of pronunciation or to mark the full pronunciation of a syllable (*risqué*), usually interpreted in English as a mark to pronounce the *e* as AY; in Spanish it is used over vowels to indicate that the syllables in which they appear are to be stressed though they normally would not be (*cimarrón, trópico, tía*). The *grave accent*, which angles upward to the left, is also found in French over *a* or *e* (*à la carte, misère, frère*) to denote a certain quality of the pronunciation and in Italian and other languages over the vowel of a syllable that does not ordinarily bear the stress of the word to indicate that it should be stressed (Italian *cantò, è, città;* English *agèd, belovèd, cursèd*). The *circumflex accent,* which resembles a small inverted "v," occurs in French over *a, e, i,* or *o* (*pâté, être, maître, rôle*) and in other languages to mark a change in the usual pronunciation of the vowel; in French the circumflex often indicates the omission of a sound that has been omitted (as the omission of the *-s-* of Latin *costa* from French *côte* 'coast'). The *tilde* occurs in Spanish over *n* (*mañana, cabaña, señor*) and in Portuguese over vowels to indicate their nasalization (*pão, torrão, verão*). The *umlaut* is used in German over *a, o,* or *u* (*Götterdämmerung, Führer*). *Hacek,* pronounced HAH-check and also written *hàček,* is the name for the inverted circumflex that may appear over *s* or *c* in words from Czechoslovakian. The *cedilla* is used under a *c* to indicate its pronunciation before *a, o,* or *u* as *s* in French (*français, garçon, reçu*) and in Portuguese (*abastança, destroço, roça*). The name for the two small dots, once regularly used in English over words like *naïve* (where it still appears in the original French) and *coöperate,* but now generally abandoned, is *diaeresis* (also spelled *dieresis*); its function is to indicate that two vowels written together are to be pronounced separately, not as a diphthong. The small, *u*-like crescent used in some pronunciation systems over a vowel is called a *breve mark,* often used to indicate a "short" sound like that of *at* in contrast to a long sound like that of *ate.* A small curved line used to link two letters together is called by its typographic name, *ligature;* it may appear above the letters (as in the old-fashioned way of printing ſt) or below the letters (as in the pronunciation systems of some dictionaries in which s̲h̲ indicates that the sound is as in *show* rather than as in *gashouse.* The straight bar over a vowel, as used in transcriptions of Latin and in some pronunciation systems, is called a *macron* or, informally, a *long mark.* The small, hooklike symbol that appears under *a, e,* or *o* in Polish (as in *Częstochowa*) is called an *ogonek* and serves to nasalize the vowel; the mark in Polish that looks like an acute accent but is used over *n* (as in *Gdańsk*) is called a *przecinek* (which actually means 'comma') and serves to indicate that the preceding vowel is nasalized. The diacritics used in Greek have their own names: the one preceding a word beginning with a vowel and resembling an open single quotation mark (ʻ) is called *rough breathing,* or *spiritus asper,* and signals the pronunciation of an *h;* the one preceding an initial vowel and resembling a closed single quotation mark (ʼ) is called *smooth breathing,* or *spiritus lenis,* and signals the absence of an *h.* The *hamza,* or *hamzah,* is a hooklike mark written over a letter in Arabic to indicate that an *alif* is to serve as a consonant (a glottal stop), and not as a vowel. The foregoing are the main diacritical marks encountered in the transcriptions of foreign languages into English. Their uses in the individual languages varies considerably and can only be touched on here. Except for Arabic, Greek, Russian, Hebrew, Yiddish, and, formerly, German, all the other Western European and Middle Eastern languages normally use the Roman alphabet or some version of it.

adagio / allegro / largo

These terms are musical directions for the relative tempos (or tempi) at which a piece or passage is to be played. *Adagio,* which comes from the Italian meaning 'at ease,' is a direction to play the passage so marked slowly; *largo,* from Italian 'large, broad,' is a direction to play the passage grandly and broadly, though somewhat faster than *adagio; allegro,* which means 'cheerful, merry' in Italian, is an indication that the passage be played at a lively, brisk fashion. Further refinements are *adagietto* 'slowly, but not as slowly as *adagio'; larghetto* 'slowly, but not as slowly as *largo'; largamente* 'at a slow, majestic, dignified pace'; *allargando* 'tending towards a slower tempo and in a dignified, more powerful manner'; *allegretto* 'briskly, but not as quickly as *allegro'; andante* 'at a moderate tempo' or *andantino* 'at a modified—quicker or slower—pace than *andante'*; and *agitato* 'at a rapid tempo.'

adapt / adopt

As the spelling indicates, these are two completely different words: *adapt* is a verb (its noun is *adaptation*) meaning to 'conform, adjust, change, or modify to suit different conditions'; *adopt* is a verb (its noun is *adoption*) meaning to 'accept as one's own something (often a child) that belongs to someone else; select and pursue a plan; assume or take on'. Something that has undergone adoption is said to be *adopted: an adopted child;* the person or people who do the adopting are said to be *adoptive parents.*

adenoid / sinus / tonsil

These organs are situated in the throat and head but are sometimes confused because they are somehow associated with upper respiratory ailments. The *tonsils* are small masses of (mainly lymphoid) tissue on each side of the throat; their precise function is unknown, and, in the past, they were removed if they became inflamed or infected; earlier in the 20th century they were thought to be associated with the onset of a number of diseases and were routinely removed from young children whether or not they gave any sign of inflammation or infection. The *adenoids,* properly called the *pharyngeal tonsils,* are situated at the top of the back of the throat, where the throat connects with the nasal passages. These organs can swell and obstruct the flow of air through the nose, especially in children; if they become inflamed or infected, they are sometimes removed. Blockage of the nasal passage can result in an abnormal, muted, nasal manner of speaking. The *sinuses,* properly the *paranasal sinuses,* are air cavities in bones around the nose, between the eyebrows, above the upper teeth, and in the forehead. These may become inflamed and obstructed as a result of any number of disorders, in which case slight changes in atmospheric pressure may cause headache and local pain and tenderness. If the cause is infection, antibiotic medication is usually administered; in other cases, decongestants, analgesics, and inhalants may be prescribed; surgery may be the resort in the event of severe and chronic sinusitis. (See also **upper respiratory tract / lower respiratory tract.**)

adjective / attributive noun

Linguists have classified languages into several types according to their grammar and, consequently, their syntax. (See **grammar / syntax.**) Without going into detail, it is useful to note that in some languages, like Latin, Greek, Sanskrit, Polish, and Russian, the relationships among the words of an utterance are indicated by the various endings that are added (mainly) to nouns, adjectives, and verbs; such endings are called *inflections,* and the languages are classified as *inflecting languages;* some inflecting languages have more inflections than others and are further described as *highly inflecting, inflecting,* or *partly inflecting.* Other languages, like Hungarian, Turkish, American Indian languages, and Finnish, express the relationships of ideas in a sentence by combining strings of meaningful elements (called *morphemes*); such languages are called *agglutinating* *languages;* to some extent, inflecting languages do that also, but not to the same extent. Although English is a Germanic language, it has developed differently from Modern German in the sense that German has retained many of its earlier characteristics of an inflecting language while English, though it has kept some inflections (especially in the personal pronouns), has lost most of them and depends on word position to determine the relationships among words in a sentence. Chinese functions in a similar fashion, and such languages are called *isolating languages,* with, again, various degrees noted among them. A simple illustration of an important difference between inflecting and isolating languages can be seen in a comparison between a sentence in Latin and one in English. In Latin, *Femina puellam videt* means 'The woman sees the girl'; setting aside matters of style (in which emphasis might be affected by word order), these words could appear in any order—*Videt femina puellam; Videt puellam femina; Femina puellam videt; Puellam femina videt; Puellam videt femina*—without any loss of the sense of 'who sees whom.' In English, however, *The woman sees the girl* and *The girl sees the woman* mean entirely different things (and other orders, like, *Sees the girl the woman,* while not entirely impossible if the realm of grammar is to include poetic licence, create gibberish in ordinary English). In Latin, the relationship between *femina* and *puellam,* as to which is the subject of *videt* and which the object, is expressed by the endings *-a* and *-am;* although English had such endings at an earlier stage in its development, about a thousand years ago, they gradually disappeared, and *word order* became the criterion by which the relationships of words came to be expressed. It is true that some inflections remain in English—personal pronouns have been mentioned, and the possessive and plural of nouns, though phonetically indistinguishable from one another for the most part, are still different from the only other form—but their numbers cannot be compared with those in truly inflecting languages; some tenses of verbs, for example, are now expressed almost entirely by auxiliaries, like *will* and *have,* rather than by changes of endings attached to roots. In inflecting languages, adjectives usually agree with the nouns they modify in number, gender, and case. In the Latin illustration given above, if the adjective for 'beautiful,' *bella,* were added, in that form it would modify *femina;* in order to modify *puellam,* it would have to be in the same case, *bellam.* (Although most adjectives in Latin can have three genders and five cases each in singular and plural, for various reasons there are only twelve forms to choose from instead of the expected thirty; still, twelve is quite a few compared with the one available in English.) Theoretically, the Latin adjective could appear anywhere in the sentence given: as long as it was of the form *bella*, it would be understood to modify *femina;* if in the form *bellam*, to modify *puellam.* In English, of course, not only can *beautiful* be placed in only a limited number of places, it generally modifies the noun it precedes, and *The beautiful woman sees the girl* means something different from *The woman sees the beautiful girl.* Because they no longer have their inflections in English, nouns and adjectives have lost their distinguishing characteristics, and it is impossible to tell them apart. For centuries, the style of the language followed along traditional lines, and what had been adjectives in earlier stages remained so and what had been nouns remained nouns. But, as the flexibility of the language came to be felt by its speakers, nouns increasingly appeared in the positions formerly occupied by adjectives—that is, preceding other nouns to modify them. Notwithstanding, most of them remain nouns, for they do not fulfill the criteria of adjectives in that they cannot be compared the way adjectives can and cannot be substituted for adjectives in all contexts. For example, where, traditionally, one might have said *policies of the administration,* the more common expression today is likely to be *administration policies;* where the earlier form was *in the presidency of Eisenhower* or *when Eisenhower was president,* today one encounters, in both speech and writing, *the Eisenhower presidency; a painter of portraits* has become *a portrait painter;* although some people object to the expression, they are far outnumbered by those who report that they *had a fun time,* and so on. If it is important to distinguish an adjective from a noun, it may be easy to identify nouns because, as stated, they do not normally have comparatives or superlatives: standard English does not admit of "booker" or "bookest" or of "more operator" or "most operator." Also, an elementary transformation can be used: nouns cannot usually occur in predicative position, that is, after the verb *to be,* and if one effects a conversion from *the X Y* to *the Y is X,* the noun used as an adjective almost always surfaces as awkward English: *These are administration policies* does not convert idiomatically into "These policies are administration," nor is *the portrait painter* convertible to "the painter is portrait." Yet, the substitution of a "true" adjective, like *administrative, good, bad, indifferent, obscure,* etc., will be shown to work in both contexts. Although such noun transformations do not work for idiomatic English today, perhaps they will in the future.

admission / admittance

Admission covers the 'price charged for entering,' 'acceptance for a position or office,' 'confession of a crime, error, or the like,' and 'acknowledgment that something is valid, legitimate, or true.' *Admittance* is used mainly in the senses 'right of entry' or 'act of letting someone enter.' Thus, NO ADMISSION (usually NO ADMISSION FEE or ADMISSION: FREE) means that there is no charge for entering, while NO ADMITTANCE means that all entry is forbidden (except, perhaps, to "authorized personnel." Confusion can arise because there is one sense that is shared between the two words; both can mean 'right or authority to enter': *She was denied admission* (or *admittance*) *to the men's locker room.*

adverse / averse

Adverse means 'unfavorable; antagonistic, hostile; contrary' and is found in contexts where it modifies a variety of influences: *adverse winds and currents; adverse criticism; adverse ideas.* In idiomatic English, a person cannot be adverse. *Averse* means 'opposed; loath; having a fairly strong feeling of repugnance' and is used with *to: I am averse to inviting George to the party. She was not averse to accepting a bribe.* In idiomatic English, an inanimate object cannot be averse.

aerobic / anaerobic

These terms are applied to organisms that require atmospheric oxygen (*aerobic*) and those that do not (*anaerobic*).

affect / effect

These words are easier to distinguish as verbs: *affect* means to 'have an influence on; bring about a change in' and is usually used in negative contexts: *The boss's attitude affected the efficiency of the employees; The weather should not affect our plans, as billiards is played indoors. Effect* means to 'bring about a result; make (something) happen; accomplish': *The arbitrator effected a compromise; We easily effected the changeover from electric to gas heat.* There is another *affect* with the meanings 'pretend; imitate': *He affects a British accent to try to impress other Americans; Although she knew who had committed the crime, she affected ignorance.* Both are stressed on the second syllable and, because the vowel sound of the first syllable is reduced, they sound very much alike; that seldom causes any problems in speech, but when one puts the pronunciation into writing, the spelling is sometimes wrong. When the words function as nouns, *effect* means 'result; outcome': *I have no idea what the effect might be of adding water; My trying to calm him had no effect. Affect,* stressed on its first syllable, is rarely used as a noun outside its specialized contexts in psychology, where it means 'emotion.' *Affection* is seldom confused with anything: it means a 'liking, fondness' in ordinary language; in somewhat old-fashioned general language (but still current in medical usage), it refers to an ailment in a vague way: *She is suffering from some bronchial affection. Affected* as an adjective means 'unnatural, artificial' and usually refers to behavior that is pretentious or, often, when used of a man, slight effeminacy: someone who is affected is 'putting on airs'; its associated noun is *affectation. Affective* is a relatively rare use (outside of psychology) and means 'emotional; pertaining to or expressing feeling.' *Effective,* on the other hand, means 'having an effect; producing a result or results': *The quarantine was an effective way to stop the spread of the disease;* it can also mean 'operative; in operation; in effect': *The new tax laws become effective next year.* (See also **effective / effectual / efficient / efficacious.**)

aggravate / irritate

It would be difficult to find a book on English usage published in the past 150 years that failed to point out that *aggravate* means to 'exacerbate, intensify, or make worse' and not to 'annoy, irritate, or exasperate,' for which it is often used. After so many years, the observer of language might think the point conceded; but the traditionalists persist, notwithstanding the implication that by the time someone complains that a misbehaving child, for example, has caused much aggravation, it is very likely that the culprit has already created an irritating situation which has already been exacerbated, intensified, or made worse. If the purists are to be assuaged, each of these words should be kept in its own niche.

agnostic / atheist

An *agnostic* (who follows *agnosticism*) is a disbeliever in God who claims to be ignorant of the existence of God or of any god. An *atheist* (who follows *atheism*) is a disbeliever who asserts that there is no God or gods.

airspeed / groundspeed

In an airplane or other airborne vehicle, the *airspeed,* which is displayed on an indicator, is the speed through the air; the *groundspeed* is the speed over the ground, that is, the earth below. To take the simplest cases, if an aircraft were traveling at 300 miles per hour through air that is completely motionless, its groundspeed and airspeed would both be equal to 300 miles per hour; if there were a headwind of 100 miles per hour, the airspeed would still be 300 miles per hour, but the groundspeed would be 200 miles per hour; if there were a tailwind of 100 miles per hour, the airspeed would remain at 300 miles per hour, but the groundspeed would be 400 miles per hour. It can readily be seen that in the first instance, in an hour a distance of 300 miles would be covered, in the second, a distance of 200 miles, and in the third, a distance of 400 miles. It is, of course, the groundspeed that determines how quickly one reaches a destination: the prevailing winds in the North Atlantic are from west to east; therefore, flying at the same airspeed, flights from the United States usually take less time to arrive in Europe than those going in the opposite direction. Vessels at sea use *knotmeters* to determine their speed through the water, which may be itself moving in the same, opposite, or other direction. In all of the above instances, the situation is made more complex in ordinary circumstances, when the medium being traveled through is rarely precisely in the same or the opposite direction of travel. Formerly, various techniques were employed—dead reckoning, radio, loran, sightings of markers (where that was possible), celestial navigation—but today most commercial navigation techniques employ inertial guidance systems, the positions of fixed artificial satellites, or both, to determine the position of an aircraft or ship.

ale / beer / bass / bitter / porter / stout / lager

These are all names for various kinds of alcoholic beverages made from and flavored with various ingredients. Some of them differ depending on British and North American usage. It is easiest to see their similarities and differences in a table:

NAMES	INGREDIENTS / COLOR	ALCOHOLIC STRENGTH
ale	(in Britain) fermented barley, flavored with hops / pale yellow	medium
	(in U.S., Canada) fermented hops at high temperature / pale yellow	medium
beer	malt, sugar, hops fermented with yeast / pale yellow to dark brown	low / medium
bass	(A trade name for beer or ale made by Bass & Co., Burton-on-Trent, England.)	
bitter	draft beer, strong hops flavor, low effervescence / light brown	low
porter	black malt / dark brown	medium / strong
stout	porter more strongly flavored with malt and hops / blackish-brown	strong
lager	young, effervescent beer / pale yellow	low / medium

These vary considerably by country, both in ingredients and strength. Lager brewed in Australia, for instance, has a higher alcoholic content than that brewed in the U.S.

alimentary canal / esophagus / trachea

The *alimentary canal*, also called the *digestive tube*, is the entire neuro-muscular tube, about 9 meters [about 29½ feet] long, that extends from the mouth to the anus through which nutriments are passed. The part between the *pharynx*, at the back of the throat, to the stomach is called the *esophagus*. The *trachea*, or *windpipe*, which conveys air to the lungs, is alongside the esophagus and is about 11 cm [about 28 inches] long.

all right / alright / always / all ways / already / all ready

Although, already, albeit, and *always* are adverbs (sometimes adverbial conjunctions) in English and have been assimilated as solid words spelled with one *l. All right* has not yet been accepted as a one-word adverb, and the form *alright* is considered poor style, frowned upon by teachers of the language; that does not, of course, preclude its appearance in writing or in certain varieties of slang or colloquial English, in which one can encounter expressions like, *He's an all right guy.* But in that context *all right* is an adjective phrase and not an adverb. Except for *although* and the somewhat learned or archaic *albeit,* a distinction has developed between *already,* as an adverb, and *all ready,* as an adjective phrase: *He is here already, and he is all ready to go.* Some think it better style to place the adverb *already* close to the verb it modifies: *He is already here, and he is all ready to go;* but the question may well arise whether the adverb is modifying the verb *is* or the adverb *here.* The *all* of *all ready* merely means 'totally.' Some dialects of English have been influenced by those whose native language was German, in which *jetzt* is taken to be equivalent to English *already* or *now;* in German, *jetzt* frequently appears at the end of a sentence, but that is German, not English, and it is considered poor style to follow German word order in utterances like, *Let's go already,* which is not really English but a translation of *jetzt* into 'already' instead of 'now': there is nothing odd about saying *Let's go now* in English, which is normal. Similarly, *always* has acquired the sense 'forever,' and *all ways* has retained the sense 'in every manner or way.' *Almost* is another word that derived from a two-element form, though *all most* would seem peculiar to most speakers of English today. The same can be said about *alone* and *all one.* (See also **altogether / all together.**)

alligator / crocodile / caiman / gavial

Crocodilia is the name for the order to which these reptiles belong; the other names listed are of varieties of the order and are called crocodilians. Thus, *crocodiles, alligators, caimans,* and *gavials,* while they differ a little in size and physical appearance, are distinguished largely by where they are found: *alligators* in eastern China and the southeastern U.S.; *caimans* in tropical America; *crocodiles* on the Nile and elsewhere; and *gavials* in India and Pakistan. Crocodiles live in the southeastern U.S., but no alligators live on the Nile.

allopathy / homeopathy

Allopathy is a method of treating disease by the administering of drugs intended to produce symptoms and an environment inimical to the pathogens or causes of the disease being treated; for example, if a patient is diagnosed as suffering from iron deficiency anemia, an iron supplement may be prescribed to increase the synthesis of hemoglobin. *Homeopathy,* developed late in the 18th century by Dr. Samuel Hahnemann (1755–1843), is a method in which very small amounts of drugs are administered, the idea being that while large amounts of a drug may cause symptoms of a disease, lesser dosage will allay those symptoms; in practice, only enough medication is administered to treat the symptoms, medications being diluted to one tenth of their potency by mixing them with milk sugar.

allusion / illusion

These words are seldom confused when written, but they sound very much alike in normal speech and should be kept apart. An *allusion* is a reference; it is what is *alluded* to, as in *I wish you would not make allusion to the green streaks in Debbie's orange hairdo,* or *I was insulted when she alluded to my big feet.* It is not usually a direct reference but an oblique hint or suggestion; thus, in the last example, "she" alluded to big feet by saying something like, "You must have difficulty in finding shoes to fit you," or some other brutally subtle comment. An *illusion* is a fancied vision, the appearance of something that is imaginary, a false impression. The verb *illude* does exist, but it is rare. Some magicians, either just to be different, for showmanship, or because they want to acknowledge that no such thing as magic really exists, call themselves "illusionists," maintaining that they create *illusions,* or false images of reality. Another word that intrudes into this set is *delusion,* and its associated verb, *delude.* A *delusion* is a 'mistaken impression or wrong idea': a person may have a delusion that he is Napoleon (or that she is Joan of Arc—or, indeed, that he is Joan of Arc). In a less pathological sense, *delude* simply means to 'fool, hoodwink.' Delusions of a serious nature, that interfere with a person's ability to function normally in everyday situations are largely the domain of psychologists and psychiatrists.

alpha wave / beta wave / delta wave / theta wave

For years the expression *brain wave* was used in a jocular way to mean 'inspiration'; recent medical research has shown that there are at least four identifiable 'brain waves' that are detectable by electroencephalographs, which record differences in electrical potential between parts of the brain. These appear to be rhythmic in nature and have been classified into four types:

TYPE OF WAVE	FREQUENCY	DESCRIPTION
alpha	8–13 Hz high voltage	most commonly recorded; involve parietal and occipital lobes and posterior sections of temporal lobes; person relaxed, with eyes closed, and nonattentive; opening eyes affects patterns.
beta	13 + Hz low voltage	involve frontal and central cerebral areas; person alert, with eyes open; associated with energetic mental activity.
delta	4 Hz high voltage	person deep in dreamless sleep, not easily aroused
theta	4-7 Hz low voltage	temporal lobes; person awake but relaxed and sleepy

These waves are also called *rhythms*, e.g., *alpha rhythm*, etc.

alternate / alternative

Alternative means 'another choice,' and it may be used in the plural to refer to more than two other choices: *He has only two alternatives— he can stay or he can go. The restaurant offers strawberry and raspberry sherbets and a few other alternatives.* It may be used as an adjective: *The alternative selections do not appeal to me.* As an adverb, but used mostly as an adverbial conjunction, *alternatively* means 'as an alternative action': *She can stay and face the music or, alternatively, she can leave now before they find out what she has done.* It may be useful to think of *alternate* as a verb meaning to 'move between (or among) two (or more) choices': *She alternates between playing first violin and acting as concertmaster.* In this sense, the adjective use becomes clear: *The orchestra has an alternate concertmaster.* U.S. and Canadian English use *alternate* as a noun to refer to two or more people or things that have been selected among which one may choose: *She is the alternate I was referring to.* One would *Choose between alternatives,* that is, from a number of objects, people, courses of action, etc., that are possible; in order to *choose between alternates,* the possibilities would have to have been narrowed down to a precious few, each of which would have to be designated, more or less formally, as 'alternates.' The verb *alternate* means to 'go back and forth between two places or conditions': *The weather this summer has alternated between being unbearably hot and unbelievably chilly. We alternated between living in the country and in the city.*

alternator / generator

These terms are commonly encountered in connection with the generation of electrical power in cars, which were formerly universally equipped with *generators,* or *dynamos,* which produced direct current by mechanical connection to the drive shaft of the engine via a belt or, less commonly, a system of gears; most modern cars are equipped with *alternators,* similarly functioning motors that produce alternating current. In both instances, electrical power from a storage battery is used to start the engine; once the engine is running, the generator or alternator replenishes the charge of the storage battery and produces sufficient electric power to operate the electrical systems of the engine as well as lights, radio, fans, windscreen wipers, and other electrical devices. (See also **AC / DC.**)

alto-rilievo / mezzo-rilievo / basso-rilievo

These are Italian terms used in the fine arts to describe the depth to which a relatively flat, three-dimensional sculptured piece projects from its background. In *basso-rilievo,* also called *bas relief* in French or, in English, *low relief,* the figures are only slightly raised from the background. In *mezzo-rilievo,* or *middle relief,* they may project as much as one third of their full dimension from the surrounding material. In *alto-rilievo,* or *high relief,* they may project as much as half of their full dimension. These proportions are vague because there is no well-defined regulation and because the proportions depend to some extent on the scale of the pieces. These various levels of reliefs pertain largely to sculptures that are traditionally used in friezes inside and outside of buildings, typically those built in the classic style.

altogether / all together

Although these are closely related, they are used differently. *All together* means 'everything or everybody in the same place or at once': *I want you all together in the meeting room at noon. All together, now—"Long Live the Queen!"* Altogether is used to mean 'entirely, completely': *It is altogether too late for you to go out. You are altogether too rude.* It also means 'everything included': *Altogether, I paid twenty dollars to the butcher this week.*   And it also means 'generally, on the whole, all things considered': *I thought it was altogether a pretty good exhibition.* There is a jocular use of *altogether* as a noun meaning 'one's birthday suit' since it is, presumably, all in one piece: *At the end of the show, the cast were standing there in the altogether.*

altruism / egoism

Altruism describes a principle, feeling, or practice of selfless consideration and concern for others. An *altruist* is one who does things for others without expecting any return or benefit. *Egoism* is selfish concern for oneself alone, without consideration or care for others. An *egoist* is self-centered, looking after only his own interests. (See also **egoism / egotism.**)

alumnus / alumna

These are terms used mainly in the U.S. and Canada for graduates of a school or college, an *alumnus* (plural, *alumni*) being a male graduate, an *alumna* (plural, *alumnae*) being a female. When the sexes are mixed, *alumni* is used.

AM (VHF) / FM (UHF)

Both of these refer to methods of transmitting radio signals. *AM* is an abbreviation of *amplitude modulation; FM* is an abbreviation of *frequency modulation.* All radio-frequency carrier waves consist of two elements, the height, or amplitude of the wave and the number, or frequency of waves in an interval. In amplitude modulation, the height, or amplitude, of the wave is modified, or modulated, in accordance with that of the input signal, and there is no change in the frequency; in frequency modulation, the frequency is modified in accordance with that of the input signal, and there is no change in amplitude. AM transmission, also called *very high frequency* (*VHF*), is used for both local and long-distance broadcasting, much of which is received at frequencies of between 520 and 1600 kilohertz: its medium waves can bounce between the ionosphere and the earth for transmission over long distances. FM transmission, also called *ultrahigh frequency* (*UHF*), which is generally static-free and is used for the transmission of the sound and picture in television as well as for ordinary broadcasting, cannot pass beyond the horizon: therefore, its signal must be relayed by transmission towers (or transmitted by cable) in order to reach receivers situated over the horizon. (See also **long wave / medium wave / short wave.**)

amaze / surprise

Amaze means to 'astonish'; *surprise* means to 'meet with suddenly or without warning,' though they are used interchangeably in some of their other senses. An anecdote relates how Dr. Samuel Johnson, the great English author and lexicographer, was found by his wife with a wench on his knee. "I am surprised," quoth the wife. "No," responded the good doctor; "I am surprised, you are amazed."

amend / emend

Amend means 'add to (a text)'; something that is so added is called an *amendment.* and it is usually added to some sort of formal document: the provisions added to the Constitution of the United States are called amendments, for instance. *Emend* is a rather formal word that means 'make corrections or changes (in a text)'; a change or correction so made is called an *emendation.*

amiable / amicable

Generally, one would characterize people and other living beings as being *amiable*, relationships, documents, and things of that sort as being *amicable: Jensen is an amiable fellow. We reached an amicable agreement.*

amid / amidst / among / amongst

Amidst is a rather formal or poetic variant of *amid,* and means the same thing. *Amongst,* a variant of *among,* is considered formal, literary, or poetic in the United States, but is often the choice in Britain: *We walked amongst the flowers.* The difference between *amid /amidst* and *among /amongst* is that the former refers to things that are not or cannot be counted: *I searched amid the gravel for my contact lens.* The latter is usually reserved for use when countable objects surround: *The seaweed gathered among the pilings. We searched among the books for the dictionary. Amongst the possibilities we may have to include suicide.* (See also **among / amongst / between.**)

among / amongst / between

Among and *amongst* are variants of one another, the former being more common in the U.S., the latter in Britain. The distinction between either of these and *between* is that *among /amongst* is used when three or more items are under consideration, *between* when only two are involved: *Among* (or *amongst*) *the three of us; amongst us four; between the two of us; between you and me.* It is unlikely that one would encounter "among the two of us," but a sentence like, *The four nations settled the differences between them* is often heard or read if the emphasis is that the settlement was between any given pair of them: country A settled its differences separately with countries B, C, and D; country B separately with countries C and D, and so forth. If that is the case, then *between* is the proper choice; otherwise, it is good practice to avoid confusing the two. (See also **amid / amidst / among / amongst.**)

amoral / immoral

The prefix *a-* in English comes from Greek *a-*(used before a consonant, except *h*) or *an-*(used before a vowel) meaning 'not, lacking (in), without': *asymmetry, amorphous, aphasia; anomaly, anhydrous, anechoic.* It is not among the most productive prefixes in the language, but it does occur. It is related to Latin *in-,* which is, aside from *un-,* probably the most frequent negative prefix in English. *In-* appears in many guises, depending on the word it is attached to; for example, *impossible, irreplaceable, illogical.* But there are several *in-* prefixes in English, with different meanings, and it is not always easy to identify them. Scholars call the negative elements *privatives,* because they deprive the word they modify of its meaning: in other words, *asymmetrical* means 'not symmetrical,' *anechoic* means 'not echoing,' and so on. Some of these negative compounds have come into English intact; others were coined in English from the elements available. According to the citations provided in the *OED, immoral* came into use during the 16th century, *amoral* during the 19th, from which one might be tempted to draw the conclusion that morals had reached a truly parlous state in Victorian times. It seems clear that the newer word was coined because the older did not convey the nuances of meaning needed at the time; the newer, with a different meaning, did not replace the older, and both survive, side by side, each serving its semantic function. *Immoral* means 'not moral' and carries the strong sense of 'possessed of bad morals'; thus, an immoral person is one who is deliberately so, one who is familiar with moral behavior but chooses to act otherwise. *Amoral* means 'lacking in or without morals' and is used of a person who has not the slightest idea of what others would consider to be moral behavior: a person devoid of moral sense or sensitivity. The distinction is useful and convenient, and each of the words should be sustained in its own orbit of semantic usage.

amuse / bemuse

Amuse means to 'entertain; make smile or laugh': *She was amused at the suggestion that she might be a spy. He told an amusing anecdote. Bemuse* means to 'confuse, bewilder': *She was bemused by his suggestion that she should change the tire.* The words are not synonyms, obviously, hence are not interchangeable. Some people, including the editors of *The Sunday Times Magazine* [London], seem to think that *bemuse* is a 'fancier' variant of *amuse;* in an article about Sally Jones [18 October 1987, p. 72], the catchline read: ".. [L]ife seemed rather quiet so Sally and her partner Karen Whalley .. become the Sparkle Sisters in the evenings and weekends, strutting their stuff before a variety of bemused audiences."

anadromous / catadromous / diadromous

These terms relate to the migration of fish. *Anadromous* fishes are those that migrate from the sea up a river to spawn, like the salmon; *catadromous* fishes are those that migrate from a river to the sea to spawn, like the eel; *diadromous* fishes are those that migrate between fresh and salt waters, like the salmon and the eel.

analog / digital

Computer Technology. Although *analog* (also spelled *analogue*) appears in other contexts, it is used contrastively with *digital* in reference to computers and their means of processing information. In a digital computer, data is converted into a mathematical code, usually in binary representation, for processing on the principle that an electrical circuit is either ON or OFF. In the simplest pattern, a single lamp when lit conveys the information that electricity is flowing through the filament of the bulb and dark that it is not. Alternatively, one might assign "Yes" to the ON state of the lamp and "No" to the OFF state. If this principle is applied to a large number of such lamps, more complicated states can be represented. For example, in a bank of nine lamps each may be assigned a value in the **binary system** (*q.v.*) of numerical representation, establishing a pattern like the following:

LAMP	1	2	3	4	5	6	7	8	9
BINARY VALUE	2^0	2^1	2^2	2^3	2^4	2^5	2^6	2^7	2^8
DECIMAL VALUE	1	2	4	8	16	32	64	128	256

If lamps 1, 3, 5, 7, and 9 are lit, then the numerical value represented would be $1 + 4 + 16 + 64 + 256 = 341$, which, in a particular programming scheme would have an assigned meaning. If 2, 4, 6, and 8 were lit, the value would be $2 + 8 + 32 + 128 = 170$, which would mean something different. Information could likewise be assigned to the pattern of lamps lit or off: since nine lamps offer the possibility of 512 different patterns, it is possible to represent that many different information states, though with only nine lamps, the actual total numerical value that could be achieved is 511 (which eliminates the condition of all lamps being off). Digital computers use electronic diodes, not lamps, and have much greater capacity than nine such circuits; but the principles are generally the same. They are called *digital* because they employ digits. An *analog*, properly, is something that is similar to something else—that is, the two things are in some way proportionate. There are many examples of analog devices in everyday life: a bathroom scale; a thermometer; a yardstick. It can be seen that on a bathroom scale, for example, the weight of the person presses down on a platform which, through some arrangement, causes a dial with numbers on it to move past a pointer; in some scales, the pointer is moved along a dial; in others, numbers may be read off a display, an electronic circuit may actuate a voice synthesizer which tells the reading aloud, and so forth. All of these methods for reading off the weight are not the weight itself but analogous representations of the weight, whether it be in pounds, kilograms, stones, or some other system. *Analog computers* also operate on a physical basis, whether it be the voltage, amperage, or resistance of an electric current, the pressure, volume, or temperature of a fluid, or any other measurable physical characteristic. In the late 1960s, some *hybrid computers* were made which made use of analog information but processed it (far more rapidly and accurately) by digital means. These were generally abandoned when the development of high-speed digital computers of enormous capacity made it possible to simulate analog information digitally. Besides, analog computers prove difficult and expensive to program and operate, though systems employing them are in use in places where physical states must be monitored and interpreted continuously, as in hydroelectric generating stations, nuclear power facilities, and so forth.

analogous / homologous

Homologous features of organisms are those that were originally the same in evolutionary development but have adapted differently, as the arms of human beings, the wings of birds, the forelegs of cats, and the flippers of whales or the hair of mammals, the scales of fishes, and the feathers of birds; *analogous* features are those that resemble one another in function but are traceable back to completely different origins, as the wings of birds and of insects or the tails of cats and of birds. (See also **convergent evolution / divergent evolution.**)

analysis / synthesis

The breaking down or taking apart, bit by bit, of a complicated structure or idea is the process of *analysis;* the procedure is called *analytical,* and the verb is *analyze* (spelled *analyse* in Britain). The bringing together of many different pieces or parts to create something that is *synthetic*—an integrated whole—is the process of *synthesis;* the procedure is called *synthetic,* and the verb is *synthesize* (sometimes spelled *synthesise* in Britain), less commonly *synthetize* (or *synthetise*). *Synthetic* is also applied to the things that have been created: we call synthetic cloths (made up of many different chemicals) *synthetics.* Also, *synthetic* carries the meaning of 'fake, phony' because synthetic things are *artificial.*

androgen / estrogen

The *androgens* are the male sex hormones, the most important of which is *testosterone,* and the *estrogens* (spelled *oestrogens* in Britain) are the female sex hormones, the most important of which is *estradiol* (spelled *oestradiol* in Britain).

animal / vegetable / mineral

Although microbiologists have in recent years thrown some doubt on where the line between *animal* and *vegetable* can be drawn with precision, these three categories are nonetheless felt to be convenient for the purposes of most people, who are not, after all, microbiologists. *Animals* are generally thought of as including organisms that are mobile in their search for food, that have nervous systems, and that feed on other organisms. There are plants that exhibit—or seem to exhibit—a certain amount of mobility (like the Venus's-flytrap, which closes around an insect that disturbs the trigger hairs that line its leaf apex), some feed on other organisms (like the Venus's-flytrap and the jack-in-the-pulpit), and some (the Venus's-flytrap again) may seem to have nervous systems; but no one, including biologists, would consider those plants to be animals. The borderline cases can be found, for the most part, among microorganisms, which, by definition, cannot be seen by the naked eye and are not susceptible of classification by people with normal vision. *Minerals* may seem simple enough to classify—they are, after all, merely rocks—but it must be noted that they include metals and, indeed, all substances that do not grow or reproduce. It cannot be denied that living organisms may eventually become minerals (witness the formation of coal, the petrification of trees and bones, etc.), but these are details that are concocted for the sake of argumentation and attempt to take the very informal, general notion of *animal-vegetable-mineral* beyond the realm of ordinary conversation, which is where it belongs, away from the encroachments of pedantry.

anorexia / bulimia / bulimorexia

In the context of psychological disorders, these terms describe problems that manifest themselves in some way in connection with food and are generally termed "eating disorders." *Anorexia* means 'loss of appetite'; *anorexia nervosa* is a technical name for abstinence from food to the point where the patient literally wastes away and, in some instances, dies. *Bulimia* describes a condition in which the patient compulsively overeats, becoming obese in the process, for the food taken in is rarely nutritious and consists mainly (or entirely) of "junk food" and sweets. *Bulimorexia*, also called *bulimia nervosa*, is a disorder in which the person overeats, as in bulimia, then forces himself to vomit; the result is similar to that brought about by anorexia. All of these are considered to be psychogenic, not organic.

anterior / posterior

Anterior means 'front' or 'situated at the front, (usually) where the abdomen is'; *posterior* means 'rear' or 'situated at the rear, (usually) where the spine is.' Although these are a matched pair, the second has a much greater frequency in the language, being used, somewhat facetiously, for 'behind, bottom, derrière, butt, arse, ass, buttocks', etc. Another word for *anterior* is *ventral;* both are used in scientific contexts (zoology and botany, mainly) where they carry the senses of 'abdominal' as well as 'front' but also, in a general way, of the "business" side of an organism, particularly a plant. Another word for *posterior* is *dorsal.*

antipasto / hors d'oeuvre

These are different terms, the first Italian, the second French, for the same thing: what are called appetizers or, informally, starters in English. *Antipasto*, which is not Italian for a 'man who dislikes pasta,' comes from *anti-*, a variant of *ante-*, meaning 'before', and *pasto*, a word meaning 'food'; *hors d'oeuvre* is French *hors de* 'outside of' + *oeuvre* 'main course.' Both consist of light, spicy snacks intended to spark the appetite, and they differ as do their national cuisines. *Anti-*

pasto is used as a collective: the word refers to the entire collection and people do not speak of 'an antipasto'; *hors d'oeuvre*, on the other hand, may be singular or plural (*hors d'oeuvres*), referring to one or more individual appetizers. A *canapé* is a small cracker or decoratively shaped piece of bread or toast spread with cheese or some other topping, sometimes applied with a pastry tube for ornamentation. Canapés are usually served with apéritifs or other drinks that are not necessarily a precursor to dinner.

antiques / collectibles / memorabilia

Generally speaking, an *antique* is any artifact that is a relic of a bygone era. That does not include archaeological finds and is usually restricted to items of furniture, textiles, furnishings, bibelots, objets d'art, and the like; although a painting or other graphic or sculptural work of art may be an antique, it is rarely referred to as such in the trade. According to the customs regulations of some countries, something must be at least 100 years old before it can qualify as an antique, in which case in certain countries it may be imported without payment of duty (because works of art are not taxed). Genuine antiques are often quite expensive, out of the reach of many who wish to collect them. Thus there sprang up, after World War II, a market for objects, jewelry, and furnishings that could not qualify as antiques but were nonetheless coveted and, consequently, gained in value. At first, these were largely Victorian and other late-19th-century items, many of them of the German and Viennese *Jugenstil*, or *Wienerwerkstätter* school, which later developed into the French *Art Nouveau*. More recently, collectors took a fancy to *Art Deco*, represented by designs from the 1920s and '30s. None of these could properly be termed antiques, so the 'marketing term' *collectible* (also spelled *collectable*) was coined in order to give them the cachet needed to help them sell in shops and at auction (and in the numerous "flea markets" that sprang up everywhere). Gradually, with the passage of time, *collectibles* do become *antiques*, especially if they fetch prices that allow them to compete with the real article, which they can often do if they are of some artistic quality. *Collectibles* is also used of items that are merely collected by people because they like them (like apostle spoons), or because they are outstanding examples of *kitsch* (like china nudes with clocks in their stomachs), or because people covet them as representative mementos of a time past (like old film posters and other advertising). In some applications, the term used for these last items is *memorabilia*. Hobby items, like coins and stamps, are not usually included in these categories.

anvil / hammer / stirrup

These are the names of the tiny bones, called *ossicles,* of the middle ear that transmit sound vibrations from the outer ear, as received by the *eardrum,* or *tympanum,* to the inner ear, where various nerve endings transmit the signals to the brain via the *auditory nerve.* The vibrations of the eardrum are picked up by the *hammer,* or *malleus,* which transmits them to the *anvil,* or *incus,* and thence to the *stirrup,* or *stapes,* which transmits them through the *fenestra ovalis* or *fenestra vestibuli* to the *cochlea.*

anxious / eager

Language purists become fanatical about the separation of these words, but the fact remains that on the colloquial level, they have become virtually interchangeable. In writing, which at once presupposes a more formal level (except, of course, in dialogue), the distinction between *anxious* and *eager* should be maintained—as, indeed, in careful speech. *Anxious* means 'filled with anxiety': *I was anxious about her walking through the park alone at night. We anxiously awaited the names of those killed in action.* On the literal level, people are not (usually) *anxious* to go to a party or to find out who played a role in a play. *Eager* means 'earnestly longing; keen': *We were eager to learn if Mother had enjoyed herself. She eagerly requested an application.*

apogee / perigee

Both terms refer to points in an orbit around the earth, *apogee* being the point where the orbiting body is at its farthest from the earth, *perigee* the point where it is at its closest.

apologetics / irenics / polemics

In Christian theology, these terms refer to the relationship of the church to other churches. *Apologetics* concerns itself with the defense of the Christian faith; *irenics,* or *eirenics,* with the securing of Christian unity; and *polemics* with the refutation of errors.

appraise / apprise

Appraise means to 'provide an appraisal, or an estimate of the value of (something)'; *apprise* means to 'inform or advise': *The auction house appraised the painting at twice what I paid for it. They apprised me of their appraisal. I was apprised of the situation by my informants.* A spelling variant of *apprise,* sometimes encountered in British but rarely in American writing, is *apprize.*

arachnoid membrane / pia mater / dura mater

The three membranes that enclose the brain and spinal cord are called *meninges.* The innermost is the *pia mater,* which contains blood vessels that nourish the nerve tissue. The *arachnoid* encases the pia mater and the *subarachnoid space.* The most fibrous of the three, the *dura mater,* encloses these and the *subdural space;* the part that covers the brain is called the *dura mater encephali,* that which covers the spinal cord, the *dura mater spinalis.*

archaic / obsolete

These terms are encountered most frequently in the labels of definitions of words in dictionaries. Take, for instance, *yclept,* a word used by Shakespeare. Were no one to use it today, under any circumstances, it would be labeled *obsolete* in the dictionary; as it happens, the word is used occasionally in order to give a flavor of olden times to the text in which it appears, hence is labeled *archaic* in the dictionary. Any obsolete word can be used to achieve such an effect: if it is so used frequently, then the dictionary label is likely to be *archaic.* Many dictionaries do not list obsolete words at all: even a word like *phlogiston* 'a substance formerly thought by chemists to be present in all substances and released when they are burnt' is not labeled obsolete because it is felt to be used today, albeit as a historical term. *Argentum,* on the other hand, is an obsolete name for the element silver and is likely to be so labeled in any modern dictionary that lists it.

Arctic Circle / Antarctic Circle

The *Arctic Circle* is an imaginary ring around the earth, parallel to and about 66° north of the equator, that marks the southern boundary of the north frigid zone; above the Arctic Circle and in this zone, the sun is not visible (at sea level) between the autumnal (about September 21st) and vernal (about March 21st) equinoxes. The *Antarctic Circle* is an imaginary ring round the earth, parallel to and about 66° south of the equator, that marks the northern boundary of the south frigid zone; below the Antarctic Circle and within this zone, the sun is not visible (at sea level) between the vernal and autumnal equinoxes. (See also Tropic of Cancer/Tropic of Capricorn.)

aria / recitative / chorus

An *aria* is any solo singing performance, usually so referred to when part of an opera, but also sometimes so called when forming part of an oratorio or cantata (*q.v.*). Preceding the aria in an opera and serving more or less as a setting for it is the *recitative*, essentially a form of dialogue or narrative that is not sung but said on a fixed note without meter or rhythm: the *recitativo secco* 'dry recitative' is accompanied by an occasional strum on a cello or harpsichord; the orchestra plays during the performance of a *recitativo accompagnato* or *recitativo stromentato* 'accompanied or instrumental recitative.' The operatic *chorus* consists of a number of singers singing the same music; they may sing the chorus of a song, with soloist singing the verse, or they may sing an entire composition.

arithmetically / exponentially / geometrically / harmonically

People are often heard to use these terms in an informal way when referring to the rate at which things change (usually, increase): *There has been an exponential increase in the wealth of mideast oil producers. The number of illiterates seems to have increased geometrically.* One rarely hears, outside of technical—and technically accurate—discussions, the phrase *arithmetic increase*. These are expressions that have specific meanings in mathematics and ought not be bandied about lightly, since each has its own descriptive function and might as well be used accurately, even in metaphors or in hyperbole. In an *arithmetic series* or *progression* (in which the change or increase is said to be *arithmetical*), each successive element is the result of adding a quantity to the preceding number; these progress in a fashion like 1, 3, 5, 7, 9, . . . , or 1, 8, 15, 22, . . . , etc., in the first of which the common difference is 2 and in the second, 7. In a *geometric series* or *progression* (in which the change is said to be *geometric*), numbers progress in such a way that the ratio between successive terms is the same, as in 1, 5, 25, 125, . . . , or 1, $^1/_5$, $^1/_{25}$, $^1/_{125}$, $^1/_{625}$, . . . , etc., in the first of which the factor is 5 and in the second $^1/_5$. In an *exponential series* or *progression* (in which the change or increase is said to be *exponential*), numbers progress in accord with a factor affecting their exponents, as in 3, 27, 729, 531,441, . . . , etc., in which the exponent is 3. In a *harmonic series* or *progression*, there is a constant difference between the reciprocals of the terms, as in 1 + $^1/_3$ + $^1/_5$ + $^1/_7$ + ... Clearly, an exponential progression or increase is the most dramatic.

arraignment / indictment

In terms of criminal law, an indictment is a formal written charge "handed down" by a grand jury against an individual who is to be tried for the crime. *Arraignment* is the process of bringing a prisoner before a court in order to answer an *indictment*. After the prisoner's plea, a trial date is usually set and the prisoner is remanded into custody or, depending on the disposition of the court, freed on bail.

arteriosclerosis / atherosclerosis

Although both of these terms refer to arterial disorders resulting in a decrease in the blood supply to parts of the body fed by the artery or arteries involved, *arteriosclerosis* is brought about by a thickening or calcification of the arterial walls and a consequent loss of elasticity; *atherosclerosis* is brought about by deposits of plaques of cholesterol and cellular debris, which has the effect, also, of thickening the arterial walls.

artery / arteriole / vein / venule / capillary

An *artery* is a blood vessel that conveys blood from the heart to other parts of the body; a *vein* is a blood vessel that returns blood from various parts of the body to the right atrium of the heart; a *capillary* is one of billions of tiny blood vessels that supply blood from the arterioles to local areas of the body; as the skin, the organs, and so forth. *Arterioles* are smaller branches of arteries that feed blood to the capillaries; *venules* are vessels that return blood from the capillaries to the veins. The blood in arteries is bright red; that in veins and capillaries is somewhat darker, almost purplish, which is seen as bluish in those areas where the veins are close to the surface of the skin, as at the insides of the wrists and at the sides of the feet. There are two coronary arteries, the right and the left, each of which divides into two main branches; these divide into fifteen other arteries, which divide further into twenty-six large arteries, and so forth. The veinous system is divided into the *portal veins*, which drain blood from the viscera and convey it to the liver, the two *pulmonary veins*, which return oxygenated blood to the left atrium of the heart, and the *systemic veins*, which return deoxygenated blood to the heart.

artichoke / Jerusalem artichoke

These are two entirely different plants, both used as food. The *artichoke*, also called *globe artichoke*, is, as its name suggests, globular in shape; the part that is eaten is the flower of the plant, which consists of a large, budlike arrangement, from two to four inches in diameter, with tightly overlapping fleshy leaves. When cooked, the leaves are peeled off one by one and the edible part is scraped off the inside. The heart of the artichoke is sometimes pickled or marinated for use in salads. The *Jerusalem artichoke* is a plant the root of which is eaten as a vegetable. It is in the family of sunflowers, and the *Jerusalem* part of its name is a corruption of the Italian word for 'sunflower,' *girasole*.

ascender / descender / x-height

In typography, these terms describe the various forms of lower-case characters. *Descenders* are the parts of characters that extend below the base line on which type is set (or the real or imaginary line on which text is written); thus, the letters *g, j, p, q,* and *y* have descenders. The term *x-height* refers to the vertical depth of the characters *a, c, e, i, m, n, o, r, s, u, v, w, x,* and *z;* such characters are called "x-high." *Ascenders* are the parts of characters that extend above x-height, as in *b, d, f, h, k, l,* and *t.* In some typefaces, these terms may be applied differently; that is, a *z* might have a descender (as it might in handwritten text). These terms are not usually applied to numerals or capital letters.

Ashkenazi / Sephardi

These are the two main strains of Jews in Europe. *Ashkenazi* refers to the Jews of Germany and eastern Europe; as a noun, *Ashkenazi* has a Hebrew-style plural, *Ashkenazim,* alongside the less frequent English plural, *Ashkenazis. Ashkenaz* was a "son of Gomer [Gen. x,3; I Chron. 1, 6], son of Japheth, son of Noah, typifying a race of people identified with the Ascanians of Phrygia and, in medieval times, with the Germans," according to the *OED. Sephardi* refers to the Jews of Spain and Portugal; as a noun, *Sephardi* has a Hebrew-style plural, *Sephardim,* alongside the less frequent English plural, *Sephardis.* According to the *OED,* the name derives from the name of a country, *Sepharad,* mentioned only in Obadiah 20 and associated with Spain. During the Middle Ages and, later, the Spanish Inquisition, many Sephardim (as well as Moors) became baptized as Christians and changed their names to escape persecution and death. Some genuinely embraced Christianity, others only outwardly, continuing their adherence to Judaism secretly. These latter became known as *Marranos,* a Spanish word which, at the time of compilation of the letter M of the *OED* (1905), was marked as "not naturalized." *Merriam-Webster Third Unabridged* etymologizes *Marrano* as "lit., pig, prob. fr. Ar *maḥram* something prohibited; fr. the fact that the eating of pork is outlawed by the Jewish and Muslim religions." If that is the case, the name must have been an opprobrious one, used by the Spanish in derogation or contempt, for, certainly, neither the Jews nor the Muslims would have referred to themselves in such terms.

ass / donkey / mule / hinny / burro

There are two animals of the horse family, the African wild ass, *Equus asinus,* and the Asiatic wild ass, *Equus hemionus.* Both resemble small horses, are strong, sure-footed, docile, have long ears, and are proverbial for their stubbornness; both are properly called *asses,* though, in the United States, where *ass* is also a taboo word meaning 'bottom, buttocks' (British *arse*), the word is often avoided in favor of *donkey.* The *donkey* is a descendant of the African variety and has long been used as a beast of burden. A *mule* is the offspring of a male donkey and a female horse; a *hinny* is the offspring of a female donkey and a male horse. Both, which are used as beasts of burden, were formerly thought to be sterile, but there is recent evidence of female mules (if not hinnies) giving birth. *Burro* is a Spanish word for a donkey.

assemblage / collage

In fine art, an *assemblage* is a collection of various objects, scraps, etc. fixed together to a flat surface or to create a three-dimensional structure by an artist. A *collage* is (usually) a collection of photographs, papers, fabrics, and other two-dimensional objects, especially symbolic in spirit, affixed by an artist to a flat surface (usually a canvas) and often integrated into a painting or other graphic representation.

associative law / commutative law / distributive law

These "laws" apply to ordinary mathematics and in certain schools of logic and have so thoroughly penetrated the consciousness as to appear "natural." They are, nonetheless, arbitrary, as mathematicians and logicians are aware. The *associative law* states that when an equation consists of a set of elements on each side, the grouping of the elements shall have no effect on the equivalence; in other words, $a + (b + c) = (a + b) + c$. The *commutative law* states that the ordering of the elements in certain operations shall have no effect on their value; in other words, $x \times y = y \times x$. This law is valid for addition $(4 + 2 = 2 + 4)$, but it cannot be applied to subtraction $(5 - 3 \neq 3 - 5)$, nor to division $(6 \div 2 \neq 2 \div 6)$. The *distributive law* states that in expressions where two or more operations are to be performed, the order in which they are to be done will not affect their value; in other words, $a(b + c) = ab + ac$.

assume / presume

The meanings of these words are quite close, but *assume* is used to mean, simply, to 'come to a conclusion on the basis of what is known or felt to be true', while *presume* means almost the same thing but connotes an arrogation of boldness and of unwarranted inference (which might well be unjustified): *After talking with you yesterday, I assumed you were going to the party. I saw them together and pre-sumed they had reconciled their differences, but, from what you tell me, I was wrong. His psychiatrist presumed to advise me how to behave towards him. Let us assume, for the moment, that the moon is made of green cheese.* It is in their associated nouns, *assumption* and *presump-tion*, that the distinction is most prominent. Both verbs and nouns have specialized meanings in law, not treated here. (See also **pre-sumptive / presumptuous.**)

-ate / -ite

In the naming of chemical compounds, *-ate* is commonly used to dis-tinguish salts or esters of acids with a name ending in *-ous*, as *nitrate* (from *nitrous*) from those with a name ending in *-ic*, as *nitrite* (from *nitric*); *sulfate* (from *sulfurous*) and *sulfite* (from *sulfuric*); or *chlorate* (from *chloric*) and *chlorite* (from *chlorous*). (See also **-ic / -ous.**)

atlas / caryatid

An *atlas* (plural, *atlantes*) is an architectural support, as for a roof, pedestal, etc., carved in the form of a man; the same functional piece carved in the shape of a woman is called a *caryatid* (plural, *caryatids* or *caryatides*). The word *telamon* is a variant of *atlas*, but is not as common. Caryatids are relatively rare in classical architecture, their best known use being as supports for the roof of the porch of the Erechtheum, a temple on the Acropolis in Athens. More recently, they were employed in Art Deco designs that were influenced by Egyptian motifs from French Empire styles, and they appear as column decora-tions in architecture and, especially, furniture.

atoll / island / guyot

If one takes *island* to mean 'any body of land surrounded by water,' then all of the continents are islands; in the broadest sense, *island* is usually understood to mean 'any (such) body of land excluding conti-nents', which may not be much more useful. Yet, there are islands that are parts of the continents with which they are associated—that is, they are more or less prominences on the continental shelf that project above the surface of the sea—and there are islands that are formed on the tops of mountains that are at the bottom of the sea;

examples of the latter are the Hawaiian Islands and many other such chains or individual islands in the Pacific Ocean. (Such mountains are not properly called *seamounts*, which do not project above the surface of the sea. A seamount with a flat top is called a *guyot*, pronounced "ghee-OH," to honor Arnold Guyot, a 19th-century geologist and geographer.) *Atolls* are ring-shaped coral reefs formed when a submarine volcano erupts, ejecting sufficient material over a period of time to build its cone high enough to protrude above the surface of the sea; after the volcanic activity ceases and the top cools, it is gradually eroded till the ringlike base of its cone is below the surface; this ring becomes the home of billions upon billions of tiny animals the skeletons of which form coral; after a long time, these skeletons build up above the surface of the sea, forming a lagoon surrounded by a calcareous ring. From that time onwards, chance plays a role in the future of the atoll: dust, debris, floating vegetation, and the deterioration of the coral may contribute to giving the ring a landlike solidity, where airborne, seaborne, and birdborne flora and fauna might find a home; if so, the atoll is gradually built up to the status of an island, though, technically, it is still an atoll. If the atoll fails to accrete sufficient material, it may remain awash at sea level or, depending on a number of other factors, be eroded down to a lower level to become a guyot. In the Mediterranean area, in the North Atlantic (near Iceland), but, particularly, in the Pacific Ocean, where the earth's crust is thinner and its movement is more active than elsewhere, volcanoes do not, necessarily, become "extinct": rather, after a dormant period during which the earth's crust on which the cone of the volcano rests may move several miles, the volcanic activity beneath the crust again begins, breaking through the crust to form a volcanic cone at some distance from the previous one. It is believed that a chain of volcanic islands, like those of Hawaii, was so formed. Although, according to currently accepted theory, the continents drift about, they are far too massive to allow movement of the crust as readily as elsewhere, which partly explains why volcanoes like Etna and Vesuvius are not seen to be drifting about the countryside. On the other hand, it is only about 1900 years since the major eruption of Vesuvius that destroyed Pompeii and Herculaneum, and over that minute interval (in geological terms) the drift would have been a few inches only. Most of the active volcanoes in the world are situated along identified faults in the earth's crust.

atom bomb / hydrogen bomb / neutron bomb

An *atom bomb* or *atomic bomb* is a *fission bomb,* in which the explosive force is created by the conversion of mass into energy when the nuclei of a fissionable material, like uranium or plutonium, are split. The more powerful *hydrogen bomb* is a *fusion bomb,* in which the explosive force is created by the release of energy when light nuclei, as of hydrogen, are fused together in a thermonuclear reaction. A *neutron bomb* is a nuclear bomb that creates wide devastation but little radioactive fallout and residue, leading to its having been nicknamed a "clean bomb." (See also **fission / fusion.**)

atom / molecule

An *atom* is the smallest unit of matter that retains the characteristics of an element; a *molecule* is the smallest unit of matter that retains the characteristics of a compound. Atoms of elements clump together to form molecules of the element, but it is meaningless to speak of an "atom of a compound" because compounds are made up of molecules that are combinations of different atoms. There are various kinds of compounds that display special characteristics, e.g., *macromolecular compounds,* which include crystals, which are not made up of discrete molecules but in which covalent bonds serve to link the atoms together to form, in effect, giant molecules, each a crystal; and *ionic compounds,* in which the molecules are bonded together by ionization.

austral / boreal / septentrional

These could scarcely be said to be common, everyday words, yet they refer to common, everyday concepts: *austral* is a formal word for 'southern' (whence *Australia*); *boreal* a technical word for 'northern', most often encountered in *aurora borealis* (its southern counterpart being named *aurora australis*); and *septentrional,* a relatively rare word meaning 'northern': its origin is Latin *septem triones* 'seven oxen', in reference to the seven stars that form the Big Dipper in the constellation Ursa Major, near the north celestial pole, hence visible only from the northern hemisphere. Those familiar with French may know *septentrional* 'northern' has a somewhat greater frequency, albeit in formal contexts, than its counterpart enjoys in English, the common French for 'northern' being *du nord.*

authoritarian / authoritative

Both of these words are derived from *authority: authoritarian* means 'submissive to or exercising authority; dominating; bossy'; *authoritative* means 'supported, approved, or validated by authority; official'. Thus, a government or person might be authoritarian, or domineering, a reference book or information authoritative.

autogiro / helicopter

Both of these are what are called *rotating-wing aircraft*. The *autogiro*, or *autogyro*, has wings, like an ordinary airplane, a propeller for driving the craft forward, and rotating blades atop the fuselage that enable it to take off and land vertically. *Autogiro* was originally a trade mark in the United States, but its present status has not been determined; its name means 'self-rotating.' Autogiros were far more common in the 1930s and are rarely, if ever, seen today. *Helicopters* are very common today. They do not usually have wings, but larger models may have horizontal stabilizers in the form of short, stubby, winglike projections from sides of the fuselage. They also have rotating blades, or "wings," mounted above the fuselage and a small propeller set vertically into the tail of the craft and with a spinning axis parallel to the fuselage to prevent the aircraft from being driven about horizontally by the force of the rotating blades. For additional power, larger helicopters often have two sets of rotating blades on different axes, one near the front, the other near the rear; in such designs a vertical tail propeller is unnecessary. The helicopter—the name comes from the Greek words *helico-* 'spiral' + *pter-* 'wing'—can lift off and land vertically; to gain forward motion it must tilt forward so that the rotating blades can catch the air slightly ahead of the craft. Both the helicopter and the autogiro can hover.

auxesis / merisis

In biology, two kinds of plant growth are recognized, one, in which the size of individual cells increases, is called *auxesis;* the other, in which the number of cells increases, called *merisis.*

avoirdupois weight / troy weight / apothecaries' weight / metric weight

Avoirdupois weight is the most common, being used generally in measuring weights of food, people, and merchandise. In weighing people, the British use the unit of the *stone,* or 14 pounds (6.350 kilograms), which is not used elsewhere; a person weighing 185 pounds would be said to weigh 13 stone 3 (pounds). The unit of all three systems is the *grain,* which is equal to 0.0648 gram—that is, 15.432 grains equal one gram. The three systems are shown below with their metric equivalents. *Apothecaries' weight* is used by apothecaries, and *troy weight* by jewelers.

AVOIRDUPOIS WEIGHT
1 dram = 27.34 grains (1.772 grams)
16 drams = 1 ounce (28.3495 grams)
16 ounces = 1 pound (453.59 grams)
14 pounds = 1 stone (6.35 kilograms)
112 pounds = 1 hundredweight (in the U.K.)
100 pounds = 1 hundredweight (in the U.S.)
2000 pounds = 1 (long) ton (907.18 kilograms)
2240 pounds = 1 (short) ton (1016.05 kilograms)

TROY WEIGHT
3.086 grains = 1 karat (200 milligrams)
24 grains = 1 pennyweight (1.5552 grams)
20 pennyweights = 1 ounce (31.1035 grams)
12 ounces = 1 pound (373.24 grams)

APOTHECARIES' WEIGHT
20 grains = 1 scruple (1,296 grams)
3 scruples = 1 dram (3.888 grams)
8 drams = 1 ounce (31.1035 grams)
12 ounces = 1 pound (373.24 grams)

It may be useful to note that because gold is weighed using troy weight, an ounce of gold is equivalent to 31.1035 grams troy but only 28.3495 avoirdupois. For comparison, here are the metric units:

METRIC SYSTEM
1000 milligrams
  or 10 decigrams   = 1 gram (15.432 grains)
1000 grams
  or 10 hectograms = 1 kilogram (2.2046 pounds avdp.)
  10 hectograms = 1 kilogram
  10 quintals   = 1 metric ton (2204.6 pounds avdp.)

The *metric system* is increasing in use in many parts of the world, though those that formerly used the Imperial System show both avoirdupois and metric weights on packaged products in Britain, where everyday weighing of foods is usually done using the Imperial System, even though the Metric System has been officially adopted. In the United States, although the virtues of the Metric System have been extolled for many years, attempts at making it official through legislation have been unsuccessful.

backwardation / contango

These are common terms associated with dealings on the London Stock Exchange. *Backwardation* describes the percentage paid by a seller of shares to the buyer in return for the right to postpone their delivery till a future date agreed with the buyer, usually the next following settlement period. Its opposite is *contango*, which is a percentage paid by a buyer of shares to the seller in return for delaying their delivery till a day agreed with the seller, usually the next *settling-day*. In Stock Exchange terminology, *settling-day* is the day, which occurs fortnightly, on which accounts are paid up.

bacteria / virus / microbe / germ / bacillus

Germ and *microbe* are words in the general language for any single-celled microorganism—that is, an element of a living plant or animal that cannot be seen without the aid of a microscope—usually one that causes disease in plants or animals. People sometimes distinguish between *germs* and *viruses*. *Viruses* are too small to be seen by an optical microscope but can be viewed with the aid of an electron microscope. Viruses consist of a nucleic acid (which is involved mainly in the processing of energy and in the determination and transmission of genetic characteristics; see also **DNA / RNA**) with a coating of protein; because they are incapable of independent metabolic activity, they can reproduce only within a cell of a living plant or animal, and their reproduction can be extremely rapid—as much as 100,000 an hour. Viruses, which may be introduced into the body through a break in the skin, respiration, or ingestion, are the cause of the common cold and of many of the most dangerous diseases of human beings, including poliomyelitis, certain kinds of pneumonia and hepatitis, herpes, and, possibly, AIDS (acquired immune deficiency syndrome). *Bacteria* (singular *bacterium*) are single-celled microorganisms, much larger than viruses; many cause diseases in plants and animals, being responsible for such afflictions as anthrax, tuberculosis, rickettsial diseases like typhus, certain forms of endocarditis, leprosy (Hansen's disease), etc. Bacteria (from the Greek word meaning 'little rod' because those first identified were all rod-shaped) are available in three varieties: *cocci* (singular *coccus*), which are spherical, are typified by the genus *Streptococcus* or *Staphylococcus*, varieties of which cause scarlet fever and osteomyelitis; *bacilli* (singular *bacillus*) which are rod-shaped and cause gangrene, botulism, tetanus, etc.; and *spirilla* (singular *spirillum*) which are spiral and cause ratbite fever, etc.

bad / badly

As the number of speakers who are concerned about preserving traditional grammatical concepts dwindles, so the number of those who fail to distinguish between *bad*, the adjective, and, *badly*, the adverb, increases. On observation, it would appear that the former is crowding the latter out of existence: far more people are likely to say, *I need to go bad* than *I need to go badly.* Moreover, one rarely, if ever, hears *a badly boy;* thus, the contamination does not travel in the opposite direction, and some might argue that English is generally under a shortening influence, evidenced by *real* for *really* and *beat* for *beaten* in addition to *bad* for *badly* and other high-frequency examples. Those who wish to maintain a puristic style in language try to ensure the use of *bad* as an adjective and of *badly* as an adverb, modifying not only verbs but also adjectives and words (like participles) that act like adjectives: *a badly done painting.* The greatest concentration of misapplication seems to focus on utterances that employ very common verbs or copulas, that is, linking verbs like *feel:*

> We don't do too bad for ourselves.
> We don't do too badly for ourselves.

> I felt badly about losing my ring.
> I felt bad about losing my ring.

In both pairs of the preceding examples, the second is preferred in standard English. (See also **good / well; thin / thinly.**)

baking powder / baking soda

Baking soda is sodium bicarbonate (also called bicarbonate of soda), widely used as an antacid medication, in fire extinguishers, and as an ingredient of *baking powder*, to which an acid, as cream of tartar, is added to create a substitute for yeast in baking: baking powder, when moistened, yields carbon dioxide, which causes the dough to rise.

balcony / terrace / deck / porch / veranda / patio

In general, a *balcony* is a rather small, flat projection from the side of a building, with a stone or metal railing, allowing occupants to go out onto it; it is usually small, perhaps having enough space for a table and a chair or two, and may be on a private house or an apartment building. A *terrace* is, etymologically, a paved area on the ground, usually alongside a building; terraces typically occur in numbers of two or more, resembling steps. *Terrace* now also refers to a paved, flat area over a building setback; as this is generally more grandiose than a balcony, balconies are today often called terraces, regardless of their size. In Britain, *terrace* has the special sense of a row of (usually) identical houses (*terraced houses*) having common dividing walls—what, in the U.S. and Canada would be called *row houses*. A *deck*, in the U.S., is a relatively large balcony of a house, usually built of wood, supported by columns that are fixed into the ground; decks first appeared as a feature of summer houses and beach houses to afford private or semiprivate accommodation for outdoor recreation, lounging, sunbathing, barbecuing, etc., but their popularity has extended to ordinary, albeit more luxurious housing. A *veranda*, also spelled *verandah*, and a *porch* are the same thing in the U.S. and Canada, namely, a roofed gallery along an exterior wall of a house, enclosed with a railing and often screening (to keep away insects), with access from the outside; it is used for lounging. In Britain, a *porch* is a structure outside a house that provides a covered entrance for a doorway, what in the U.S. and Canada would be called a *portico*. A *patio* is a paved area adjoining a house, forming either a partially or totally enclosed inner courtyard or, like a terrace, situated alongside an outside wall; usually open to the sky, it is used for lounging and entertaining al fresco.

band / orchestra / ensemble / combo

Band is applied mainly to a collection of musicians playing wind and percussion instruments, as in a *military band* or a *brass band.* Since the 1930s, in particular, when the term *dance band* came into being, bands have sometimes included stringed instruments, as well. Some of those dance bands, which were quite large, became known as *big bands.* An *orchestra* usually has a number of instrumentalists playing wind, percussion, and bowed stringed instruments, the number and makeup depending usually on a variety of factors, such as where they are playing (an orchestra pit in a theater cannot accommodate a full symphony orchestra) and what they are playing (Wagner wrote music requiring a large brass section). A *chamber orchestra* is a small orchestra, but still one having more than one musician for each part. An *ensemble* is a small group playing a limited number of instruments that are selected for specific effect or in keeping with the requirements of the composer. A *jazz band,* or *combo* (short for *combination*), is a group of jazz musicians playing instruments that usually include at least a piano and double bass, to which may be added a reeded wind instrument, like a clarinet or saxophone, a reedless horn, like a trombone or trumpet, and virtually any other kind of instrument, as a violin, vibraphone, banjo, guitar, etc. A *rock band* is usually made up of a variety of electronic instruments, as a synthesizer, electric guitar, etc., as well as percussion instruments, the sounds of which are modified through a complex of electronic echo chambers, amplifiers, and other devices.

bar mitzvah / bat mitzvah

In Judaism, a *bar mitzvah* (sometimes capitalized) is a youth of thirteen who is said to have attained the age at which he is inducted into the faith to assume the mantle of full religious obligations of an adult. A *bat mitzvah* (sometimes capitalized, sometimes spelled *bas mitzvah*) is a girl of twelve who is considered as having attained the age at which she is ready to assume the full religious obligations of an adult. The terms are from Hebrew, in which they mean, respectively, a 'son [daughter] of the law, or commandment.'

barometer / thermometer / hydrometer / hygrometer

A *barometer* is a device for measuring atmospheric pressure and may work on any of a variety of principles. The most common types are the *aneroid barometer* and the *mercury barometer.* The aneroid barometer consists of a partially evacuated chamber with a flexible side, like a diaphragm; changes in the surrounding atmospheric pressure cause the flexible side to move, actuating a control of some sort, an indicator in the form of a pointer to a graduated dial, or both. The mercury barometer consists of an evacuated tube; sealed at one end, it is filled with mercury and inverted so that the open end is immersed in a dish of mercury; the top of the column drops down the tube, leaving a vacuum above; changes in atmospheric pressure on the surface of the mercury in the dish affect the column of mercury in the tube, the height of which is read off against a graduated scale. This is also called a *Torricellian tube* or *Torricellian barometer.* A *thermometer,* a device for measuring temperature, may also work on any of a number of principles. The most common are the *mercury* or *alcohol thermometer,* in which a column of mercury or (colored) alcohol in a sealed tube expands or contracts in accordance with the temperature, and the position of the end of the column relative to a scale is read to determine the temperature, and the *bimetallic thermometer,* in which strips of different metals (usually two) expand and contract at different rates in response to changes in the temperature to actuate a pointer which moves relative to a scale from which the temperature is read and to a control device for switching heat or air conditioning on or off. This latter type is found especially in thermostats used to control the temperature in homes and other places that are artificially heated or cooled.

baroque / rococo

Originally applied to styles of jewelry, particularly to irregular pearls, *baroque* was later extended to architectural and other designs characterized by elaborate, often grotesque ornamentation, typical of the late 16th and 17th centuries, especially in France. The origin of the word *baroque* is uncertain; some authorities think it comes from Spanish *barrueco* 'irregular pearl,' but others trace it to Federigo Barocci, a 16th-century Italian who painted in a grotesquely ornate manner, though it seems likely that his name would have yielded a word more like '*baroche*' in French. *Rococo* describes the excessively florid, ornate style of architecture and furniture, originally incorporating shell and scroll designs—the word comes from French *rocaille* 'pebblework or shellwork'—that was typical of the 17th- and 18th-century Louis XIV and Louis XV periods. Applied to music, *baroque* refers to the compositions of the 17th and 18th centuries character-ized by a departure from Renaissance modal principles and the con-centration on giving equal emphasis to all the individual parts with a focus on the melody and bass as the two principal means of expres-sion. Its chief exponents were J. S. Bach, Monteverdi, Corelli, Vivaldi, Lully, Handel, and Purcell. *Rococo music,* delicately light and elegant in character, was developed in the 18th century and is typified by the compositions of J. C. Bach, Couperin, Telemann, and Mozart. The transition between the two is noted in the *galant style* of the earlier keyboard works of the Bachs and of Couperin and Telemann, charac-terized by ornamentation and a lack of profundity in reaction to the ponderous and elaborate style of the preceding baroque period. In general metaphoric use, both words are used to describe anything that is old-fashioned and over-ornamented, including *baroque ideas.*

barrister / solicitor

In Great Britain, those who practise law are divided into two groups, *barristers,* who represent clients in open court and may appear at the bar, and *solicitors,* who are permitted to conduct litigation in court but not (with some minor exceptions) to plead cases in open court. In practice, individuals who bring an action or are under indictment deal with a solicitor, and when a barrister's services are required, may never actually meet him (or her) face to face. There are indica-tions, however, that these roles may change during the coming years.

base metal / noble metal

The *noble metals* are so designated both because they are more valua-ble and because they are more resistant to corrosion, *base metals* being more common and more subject to rust and disintegration when exposed to weather and some corrosive agents. In applications where corrosion is an important (and prevalent) factor, as in sea water, a plate of zinc (a base metal) is often fastened to the hull of a vessel near the bronze propeller and drive shaft: bronze is not a noble metal, but it is "less base" than zinc, and the corrosive effects brought about by the electrolytic action of sea water act on the cheaper zinc, destroying it, rather than the more expensive bronze fixtures. The "nobility" of a metal is relative in that it depends on the oxidizing power of the medium; yet, gold and silver are usually considered as the noble metals; in some instances, copper is included.

bass / baritone / tenor / alto / contralto / soprano / mezzo-soprano

These are the names of the major registers of singing voices. The lowest male voice is the *bass,* which ranges from middle C to E one and a half octaves lower; next is the *baritone,* which ranges from the A flat above middle C to the A flat two octaves lower; the highest male voice register is the *tenor,* which ranges from the C an octave below middle C to the C an octave above. *Falsetto* is more a manner of voice production than a register and is used by tenors or baritones to sing in the *alto* range, from the G below middle C to the C an octave above. The male *alto* voice is used mainly in choral singing, especially of liturgical music. The lowest of the female voice registers is the *contralto,* ranging approximately from the E below middle C to the D more than an octave above; next is the *mezzo-soprano,* with a range between A below middle C to the F more than an octave above; the highest female voice is the *soprano,* which ranges from about middle C to C two octaves higher. The voices with these registers are also characterized by their main focus and their power. A *basso profondo* is a bass with a very low range, suited to dramatic roles (in opera, for example); a *basso cantante* is a bass suited to lyrical roles. Among female sopranos, the *dramatic soprano,* with a rich, powerful voice, is suited for roles in Wagnerian operas; the *lyric soprano,* with a somewhat lighter resonance, is often heard in operettas or light operas; and the *coloratura soprano,* for which much of Italian opera was composed, is characterized by lightness and agility. Vocal music is generally composed for four parts—bass, tenor, contralto (or alto), and soprano—with those whose registers fall into the middle ranges singing the parts above or below.

beam / joist / rafter / stud / column / post

In building construction, a *beam* (also called a *girder* when of heavy steel) is a main horizontal member that is supported by walls, by *columns,* or *posts.* Fixed horizontally between the beams of a structure are the *joists,* at closer intervals; these serve to support the floor above or a flat roof. If the roof is pitched, the slanting supports between the main framing members are usually called *rafters*. *Studs* are vertical members set between columns or posts for supporting a wall. In a modern commercial structure, columns and beams of steel may be 30 or more feet apart; if wood is used, as in much residential construction, the distance is less, perhaps 16 or 20 feet. Commercial buildings may not have any joists if reinforced concrete is used for the floors. Depending on their size and the weight they are expected to support, joists in other construction are set from 12 to 16 inches apart. Wall studs, similarly, are generally set 16 inches apart in modern construction, though older buildings may have them set 20, 24, or as much as 30 inches apart. In Britain, a steel beam having a cross section of a capital I is called an *RSJ* (for *rolled steel joist*).

belvedere / gazebo / summerhouse

Belvedere is the oldest word of the three, dating from the 16th-century Italian meaning 'pretty view'; *gazebo*, an 18th-century term, may be macaronic Latin for 'I shall see,' formed by adding the Latin first person singular future suffix, *-ebo*, to the English word *gaze*; *summerhouse* is an ordinary English compound meaning a 'house for use in the summertime.' All refer to a small, usually wooden, roofed, often decorative structure set in a garden, where those possessed of a garden-cum-belvedere can take their ease. As there is nothing to distinguish them, the three terms are used interchangeably.

bergère / fauteuil

In the most general applications of the words, these are types of armchairs, the *bergère* being one with the sides closed between the arm and the seat, the *fauteuil* the type with an open space. The styles originated in France in the 18th century and in the context of the furniture of that period may be applied quite specifically to earlier upholstered pieces and to later chairs and settees with seats, backs, or both made from cane. The origin of *bergère* in the French word for 'shepherdess' leads one to believe that the style might have been developed from French Provincial designs; on the other hand, the reference might be facetious, in reference to amatory shepherdesses. *Fauteuil* is traced back to a word meaning 'folding stool.'

beside / besides

Both of these words serve as prepositions and as adverbs, and the only way to keep each in its own place may be by checking them in the dictionary (or here) when doubt arises. Idiomatically, they appear in contexts like the following:

beside (preposition)   *She walked beside me.*
                              That is beside the point.
                              I was beside myself with grief.

beside (adverb)   *Whenever I went out, my dog went along*
                              beside.

besides (preposition)   *Besides French, she knows German.*

besides (adverb)   *I didn't want to go; besides, I wasn't asked.*
                              He won a house in the competition and a
                              car besides.

best / better

1. There is a "rule" in English, often violated (like most rules), that holds that when a comparison is made between two things, the comparative of the adjective (or adverb) should be used and that the superlative must be reserved for a statement about three or more: *The trophy went to the best hockey player.* In colloquial usage, however, one usually hears, at the end of a recital of the rules in a boxing match, *" . . and may the best man win!'* Similarly, *May the best team win* when there are only two. The idiomatic expression calls for *put one's best foot forward,* where there is not likely to be any ambiguity about the number of feet involved. In more formal contexts, the preferred form would be *better: She was the better of the two finalists. Let the better man win.* If the number of finalists is not specified but might be presumed to consist of three or more, then: *She was the best of the finalists.* But idiom must prevail, and no normal speaker would ever say, "Put your better foot forward."

2. In Britain, it is customary to use *best* in constructions like, *You had best leave now if you want to be early,* though *better* also occurs. Americans are more likely to say *You had better leave now if you want to be early,* and *best* is almost never heard in this context. In both, *you had* is commonly contracted to *you'd.*

better than / more than / over

Some precisians maintain that the substitution of *better than* for *more than* is poor style in constructions like *The book contains better than 2000 pages. There are better than 6000 inmates in that prison.* Those are "absolute" constructions; in comparative constructions, the issue does not arise: *This book contains more pages than that one. There are more inmates in this prison than in any other.* It will be noted, too, that the word order changes between absolute and comparative constructions. Notwithstanding the objections of purists, *better than* occurs so frequently in absolute constructions that it has become an acceptable part of the language and merits no special attention. Another complaint of the purists is focused on the use of *over* for *more than*, as in *This book contains over 2000 entries.* An enterprising researcher has traced the origin of this criticism to Ambrose Bierce, who, in other respects, was better known for his frivolities with language. There is nothing formally wrong with using *over* for *more than*, and the only objection might be in defense of style. Those who do not like it need not use it, but they should be aware that the usage is well established in the language.

bi- / semi-

For various complicated reasons, English contains some irresolvable ambiguities, one of which is the prefix *bi-*, which can mean either 'occurring every two (specified periods)' or 'occurring twice in the course of one (specified period).' Thus, *biweekly, bimonthly, biennially,* etc. can mean either 'every two weeks, months, years, etc.' or 'twice a week, a month, a year, etc.' There is only one thing that can be done about this situation: avoid using the prefix altogether and, to eliminate misunderstanding, simply spell out clearly what is intended in each instance. Some people substitute *semi-* in those contexts where 'twice a week, month, year, etc.' is intended, but it should be emphasized that the result of so doing is not always accurate: *semi-*properly means 'half'; although it is true that an event that takes place, say, every half year occurs twice during that year, there is a difference between saying that something happens 'once in each half-year period' (which might be once during January-June and once again during July-December) and 'twice in each twelve-month period' (which might be on March 21st and March 22nd). In some instances, the distinction will make no difference, but where it does (or might), it is worth noting the difference. (See also **bisect / dissect**.)

big bang theory / steady-state theory

The *big bang theory* holds that the universe was created in a primordial explosion, from the center of which its constituents are still expanding outwards, and that it will contract into a singularity, pulsating in this fashion cyclically every 80 billion years. According to the *steady-state theory,* the universe is constantly expanding and will continue to do so, without contracting.

billiards / pool / snooker

Billiards is the name for any of a variety of games played with from two to fifteen balls plus a cueball on a rectangular table (twice as long as it is wide) having a raised, cushioned edge. In some games, as *carom billiards,* the table has no pockets; in others, as *snooker,* there is a pocket at each corner and one midway along each of the long sides. *Pool,* also called *pocket billiards,* is the name for several kinds of billiard games the object of which is to drive fifteen numbered or colored balls into pockets by means of the cueball which the player strikes with a cue. *Snooker* is a game played with a cueball, fifteen red balls, and six balls of other colors in which the object is to drive into any pocket any red ball (which scores 1 and remains off the table), then pocket one of the other colored balls (which score from 2 to 7, depending on the color, and, if potted, are placed back on the table), a player continuing till he misses or has pocketed all the balls. To gain a competitive advantage, a player may maneuver the cueball into a position behind another ball so as to block his opponent's shot; the player is then said to have *made a snooker,* and his opponent is said to have been *snookered,* an expression that has carried over into the general language; it is analogous to the word *stymied,* borrowed from golf.

billion / milliard

Articles in U.S. newspapers and in usage books and dictionaries that touch on the subject uniformly state, categorically, that 'one thousand million' (1,000,000,000) is called a *billion* in America and a *milliard* in

Great Britain. Although that information was once true, the American *billion* has pretty much taken hold in Britain, where *milliard* has fallen into disuse. Those British speakers who cannot quite bring themselves to say *billion* say *thousand million*. *Trillion*, which in the U.S. means 'a million million' (1,000,000,000,000), has been somewhat slower to change in Britain, where it denotes 'a million million million' (one followed by 18 zeros). As these figures come into greater prominence with the growth of national debts and other monetary designations, it seems likely that the British usage of *trillion* will also follow the American.

bisect / dissect

Bisect means to 'cut in two'; it is a familiar word in geometry, where one bisects an angle by cutting it into two equal parts or trisects an angle into three equal parts. *Dissect* means to 'cut open and examine' and is usually used literally in connection with the work done in a laboratory. Plants and animals are cut open in classrooms to study their anatomies and in scientific laboratories to aid in the identification of injury and disease; medical examiners and pathologists dissect human cadavers to determine the cause of death, especially if there is any doubt about how or why a person died. The *-sect* part of these words is from the same Latin word, meaning 'cut,' that appears in *section* 'division.' The prefix *dis-* comes from the Latin element meaning 'apart' and is seen in many English words—*discrete, discontinue, disengage,* etc.; it is not the same as the prefix *di-*, which has two existences, one as a variant of *dia-*, meaning 'passing through,' 'completely,' 'moving apart,' seen in *dialect, diorama, diagnosis,* etc., the other meaning 'two,' 'twice,' 'double,' as in *dichotomy, dioxide, dissyllable,* etc. The prefix *bi-* is common in English with the meaning 'two, into two', appearing in words like *bifocal, bilabial, binomial,* etc. (See also **bi- / semi-.**)

bit / byte / baud

In computer technology, a *bit,* (an acronym formed from *bi*nary dig*it*), is the smallest basic unit of information, consisting of either a 0 or a 1, the symbols representing values in binary notation. A *byte* (an artificial coinage) is six or eight bits, whichever is required in the context of the system to represent a character. A *baud,* (named after a French inventor, J.M.E. Baudot, 1845–1903), is a unit of speed by which data is transmitted electronically between computers, or one unit per second; thus, a device might be said to transmit data at the rate of 1900 baud.

black bile / blood / phlegm / yellow bile

These are the *humors*, the name given by medical practitioners in medieval times to the four bodily fluids that were believed to control health and temperament. *Black bile*, secreted by the kidneys or spleen, was said to be responsible for gloominess; *blood* was regarded as the seat of the emotions and passion, and it remains in the language in expressions like *bad blood* (between enemies), *in cold blood*, etc.; *phlegm*, or mucus, a cool, moist fluid, caused sluggishness, whence we get modern *phlegmatic* 'cool, unemotional'; *yellow bile*, a product of the liver, was said to produce anger or irascibility.

Blackshirts / Brownshirts

So named because of the color of the shirts they wore as part of their uniforms, the *Blackshirts* were European fascists, especially in Italy under Mussolini; the *Brownshirts* were also European fascists, especially the storm troopers in Nazi Germany under Hitler. Both terms are occasionally used as epithets for any organized militant fascists.

Blue / Gray

Named for the color of their uniforms in the War Between the States (otherwise called the U.S. Civil War (1861–65)), the Union army of the North wore blue and the Confederate army of the South wore gray. (See also **Confederate States of America / U.S. Federal Union.**)

blue collar / white collar

These are metaphors for workers whose jobs involve physical labor (*blue-collar workers* or *jobs*) and those whose work is in an office or of a managerial nature (*white-collar workers* or *jobs*). The images drawn on are the blue workshirts supposedly characteristic of the former and the traditional white shirts (in former times with detachable collars, often of Celluloid) of the latter.

boat / ship

In the Navy, a *boat* is defined as a 'vessel that can be hauled aboard a ship,' a *ship* being somewhat larger, though a submarine is always referred to as a boat, possibly because the early ones were quite small. This distinction is rarely made by ordinary users of the language who might refer to a larger vessel as a "boat" as often as a "ship"; yet, for some unexplainable reason, reference to a small vessel, especially a rowboat, dinghy, or even a medium-sized yacht as a "ship" would be taken as being facetious. Certain clichés have become idiomatic with one word or the other: *boat house; bull boat; bumboat; crash boat; dreamboat; go boating; lifeboat; miss the boat; right off the boat; rock the boat; in the same boat; on a slow boat to China; love boat; ship of fools; wait for one's ship to come in; shape up or ship out; rat leaving a sinking ship; sister ship; jump ship; space ship; run a tight* (or *taut*) *ship; ship of state; ship of the desert; shipshape; ship oars; ship water; ship's company; ship's papers; ships that pass in the night.*

Bolshevism / Menshevism / Leninism / Trotskyism / Marxism / Stalinism

These terms, which relate to political factions in the Soviet Union in the period of 1917–20, are seldom used today (except historically). The *Bolsheviks*, adherents to *Bolshevism*, believed in gaining complete control of the government and in the violent overthrow of all institutions that interfered with that aim and with the establishment of full socialism and of a workers' state; it was the Bolsheviks who overthrew the tsarist regime of Russia and established the Union of Soviet Socialist Republics. The *Mensheviks*, adherents to *Menshevism*, believed in the gradual and mainly peaceful replacement of the tsarist government by a socialist state. As a political movement, Menshevism goes back to 1903; essentially, when it became clear that Menshevism was not succeeding quickly enough, Bolshevism arose, and it was the Bolsheviks who led the revolution of 1917. The names *Bolshevik* and *Menshevik* mean, respectively, 'major party' and 'minor party.' Because they were closely associated with the period of political upheaval around 1917, the names of *Nikolai Lenin* (real name: Vladimir Ilyich Ulanov (1870–1924)) and *Leon Trotsky* (real name: Lev, or Leib Davidovich Bronstein (1879–1940)) are important. *Leninism* advocated a form of communism characterized by a dictatorship of the proletariat, that is, those workers who have no capital assets and depend for their livelihood on working with their hands; *Trotskyism* concerned itself with the immediate overthrow of all noncommunist states by the proletariat. Most of the modern theories of communism are directly descended from the economic philosophies of Karl Marx (1818–83) and Friedrich Engels (1820–95), both of whom were German socialists who lived in England. The only major political figure who was active during the revolution of 1917 and survived well into the 20th century was *Josef V. Stalin* (real name: Iosif Vissarionovich Dzhugashvili (1879–1953)), who, as premier of the U.S.S.R. from 1922 to 1953 (following the administration of Lenin), practised what has become known as *Stalinism*, which advocated the vesting of all power in an individual leader, the utter suppression of any political or ideological views except those of his government, and a foreign policy marked by aggressive behavior.

bolt / screw

Although they are manufactured in endless varieties, *bolts* and *screws*, made for fastening things together, differ in that the former have the same diameter the entire length of their shaft while the latter come to a tapered point at the opposite end from the head. Both are threaded for all or only a part of their length, depending on the application. A *bolt* may fit into a threaded hole or insert or it may be passed through a smooth hole in two or more pieces to fasten them together by a nut or some other separate, threaded piece. *Screws*, which are used mostly for fastening to wooden objects, are also made for attaching to sheet metal, in which case they are called *self-tapping screws* which cut their own threads into plain holes. Both screws and bolts are made in many sizes and with a number of different kinds of heads that may be slotted (for standard) or cross-slotted (for Phillips) screw drivers, hexagonal or square (for wrenches of different types), etc. The profiles of the heads may differ, too, depending on whether the head is to be flush to the surface, countersunk, or protruding.

bond / debenture / share / stock / security

A *bond*, also called a *debenture*, is a formal acknowledgment of a debt incurred by a public company or a government; bonds specify a date by which they are to be redeemed and usually carry a rate of interest to be paid that is fixed at the time of issue, the amount depending

on the reliability of the issuer to repay, the terms for which the
bonds are issued, and the market conditions at the time of issue.
Bonds may be called in—that is, redeemed—by the issuer at any time
before the final date; an owner of a bond may sell it if a purchaser
can be found. In most cases, government bonds are redeemable by a
purchaser at any time before the final date, though at some penalty.
Some bonds have coupons attached that must be clipped off at specified times for redemption of the interest payment then due. In the
United States and Canada, *stock certificates* (called *share certificates* in
Britain) are acknowledgments of investment in a company. If there is
a sufficient market for the shares, they may be traded on one or
more of the stock exchanges, of which there are several in the world,
by placing orders to buy or sell them through brokers licensed to
deal on the respoective exchange(s). Shares may pay *dividends*, that is,
periodic (usually quarterly) distributions of a portion of the profits
made by the share-issuing company; also, depending on the success of
the issuing company, the market value of the shares may increase or
decrease. *Security* is another term for *share* (or *stock*) or *bond.* (See
also **common stock / ordinary shares / preferred stock / preference shares / A shares.**)

book value / market value / par value

The *market value* of something is the amount of money it is said to be
worth if it is offered for sale; it may have nothing whatsoever to do
with its intrinsic value (as in the case of gold, for which an artificial
value may be set by governments, banks, or their representatives, but
which still reflects the effects of market forces). *Book value* is a term
used in business to describe the value placed on a company asset by
the company itself; it may also refer to the difference between the
company's assets and liabilities as reflected in its books, which is
called the *net capital value;* the book value of a share of stock is calculated by dividing this net capital value by the number of shares
issued. *Par value,* used of shares issued by a company, refers to the
value printed on the share certificate; also called *face value,* it may
bear no relation at all to the market value of the shares. Thus, a company may start in business and issue one million shares at a par value
of $1 each in order to acquire the capital required to hire staff, buy
raw materials, rent office and plant space, and so forth. If the company is successful, the market value of the shares may rise in time to

five, ten, or more dollars each; if it is unsuccessful, the market value may decrease to below par value. Book value is taken into consideration mainly in assessing the success of the operation of a company and in taxation.

bound form / free form

Although these are technical terms from linguistics, they are nonetheless useful in referring to words or parts of words. A *bound form* is a meaningful linguistic element, like *pre-*, *-ish*, or *-ing*, that occurs only attached to another form (which may be free or bound); that is, we do not normally find such elements standing alone in speech or writing, they are always part of a word: *preliminary; predestine; childish; daring.* A *free form* is one that can and frequently does stand by itself but need not, necessarily; thus, *under, anti,* or *like* may appear as individual forms in English or they may appear in combinations with other free or bound forms: *understand; underneath; anticyclone; antidote; ringlike* (also, *ring-like*).

bradycardia / tachycardia

In medicine, *bradycardia* refers to an abnormally slow beating of the heart, *tachycardia* an abnormally fast beating.

brandy / cognac

Brandy is the name given to a drink distilled from wine made from grapes or other fruit, for example, *peach brandy. Cognac,* spelled with a capital letter, is the name of a region of France that includes the Charente and Charente-Maritime departments; it is where Cognac, a brandy, is made from the wine of the grapes that grow there. The proprietors of the Cognac-producing region zealously maintain, notwithstanding the loose tongues of those who refer to all brandy as cognac, that while all Cognac is brandy, only very little (and that, of course, the best) brandy is Cognac.

brass / bronze

Brass is an alloy of copper and zinc, *bronze* a somewhat more durable alloy of copper and tin.

braze / weld / solder

Braze is to unite two pieces of metal using a solder containing brass
or another material with a high melting-point. Weld is to unite two
pieces of metal by fusing them together at a high temperature, sometimes with the help of another metal, often by means of the flame of
an acetylene torch. Arc welding differs from welding in that the heat
is generated by the electric arc created between the work and an
electrode connected to a generator. Solder is to unite two pieces of
metal, bonding them together by using another metal (called solder)
that has a melting point lower than that of either metal to be joined;
it is usually accomplished by means of a tool (called a soldering iron)
with an iron point, heated by electricity or by other means.

breeze / gale / storm / hurricane

For the convenience and uniformity of classifying and recording air
movement and meteorological phenomena while at sea, British admi-
ral Sir Francis Beaufort (1774–1857), devised this scale, which is still
in use:

BEAUFORT FORCE NUMBER	STATE OF THE AIR	WIND VELOCITY IN KNOTS
0	calm	0-1
1	light airs	1-3
2	slight breeze	4-6
3	gentle breeze	7-10
4	moderate breeze	11-16
5	fresh breeze	17-21
6	strong breeze	22-27
7	moderate gale	28-33
8	fresh gale	34-40
9	strong gale	41-47
10	whole gale	48-55
11	storm	56-65
12	hurricane	above 65

It should be borne in mind that one knot = one nautical mile per
hour; a nautical mile is approximately equal to 1.15 statute (ordinary,
land) miles. Therefore, if a yachtsman reports that a race was held in

a 25-knot breeze, that would be equivalent to a wind of about 29 miles per hour ashore. Most people ashore pay little attention to wind velocity till it reaches the damaging proportions of a storm or hurricane, and, except for log records, velocities of winds at sea are not a prime topic of conversation till they, too, reach gale proportions. For modern motor-driven vessels, any wind below a Force 8 or 9 has little effect, though small craft warnings may be issued when the strength reaches Force 6 or 7. Wind is not the only element to affect vessels, of course: in the open sea, while a moderate gale (Force 7) might not prove hazardous to a 40-foot sailing yacht, the action of the sea, depending on the sailing direction, may create a danger; and areas closer to shore and estuaries in certain parts of the world may create conditions in which wind and wave action combine with currents, tidal activity, and shallow water to render smaller craft unmanageable. (See also **cyclone / hurricane / tornado / typhoon.**)

bring / take / fetch

These three words are used differently in connection with the conveying or conducting of a person or thing in relation to a place. *Bring* means to 'carry along with one, accompany to a place or event': *Please bring a bottle of wine if you come to my party. You may bring Nicole and Alexandra if you like. Bring my slippers here. Take* means to 'carry or conduct away from a place or event': *The man came to the rubbish. I want to take you away from all this. Take all you want. Take my shirts to the laundry. Fetch* means to 'go and get and bring back': *Fetch my shirts from the laundry. At noon I have to fetch my son from school.*

Buddhism / Hinduism

At the most superficial levels, *Hinduism* may be regarded as a religion based on the *Upanishads*, sacred writings of about 800 B.C., which developed from earlier ritual as set forth in various hymns. Hinduism takes a realistic view of the universe as a cosmological system in which the ultimate principle of unity is the notion *brahman*, which underlies everything. It holds that *atman*, the spiritual essence of man, is caught in a material frame and passes through an endless sequence of rebirths from which liberation can be sought only through meditation and other means to achieve *brahman*, which then

merges with *atman*. In the 5th century B.C., Siddhartha Gautama
(referred to as *buddha* 'the enlightened one'), taught ethics and
meditational practices that rejected the scriptures, social system, and
ritual of Hinduism. According to *Buddhism*, which holds that empiri-
cal phenomena are transient and lack essence, the ultimate *nirvana*,
or release from endless rebirth, can be achieved only by trancelike
meditation. This fundamental teaching later gave rise to a large number of derivative schools; one that developed in Japan, called *Zen*, has
become popular in the West where it is interpreted as focusing on
perception through meditation, yielding religious experience without
the encumbrances of dogma or the ritual of established Western religions. (See also **Hinayana Buddhism / Mahayana Buddhism.**)

budgerigar / parakeet

Budgerigar is the common name in Britain for what Americans would
be more likely to call a *parakeet* (also spelled *parrakeet*), the small,
brightly colored parrot capable of imitating human speech and other
sounds, often kept as a household pet. *Parakeet* is the more general
name for the bird, varieties of which are native to North America and
other areas of the world, *budgerigar* being a native Australian word
properly applied only to the species found there. In both countries
budgie is a popular nickname for the bird.

buffalo / bison

Both of these members are of the cattle tribe. Although it is properly
called the *American bison*, Americans and Canadians call the species
found in North America (formerly in great profusion on the plains,
today seen only in reserves) *buffalo;* taxonomists prefer that the name
buffalo be reserved for species found in Africa, like the *Cape buffalo.*

bug / insect

The word *bug* is loosely applied not only to any small creature with a
lot of legs but also to any microorganism, as a virus or bacterium.
Technically, a *bug* is a particular kind of insect, specifically those
belonging to the order *Hemiptera*, which are characterized as having
forewings that are tough and leathery where they are attached to the
body and membranous at the tip, like ladybugs and other beetles.

Insects, generally, belong to the class of *Insecta,* which have bodies that are divided into three parts, (usually) two pairs of wings, and three pairs of legs, like bees and mosquitoes. *Spiders* are not, technically, insects, for they have four pairs of legs; they belong to the *Arachnidae,* which also include *mites, ticks,* and *scorpions.* The *centipedes* and *millipedes,* which have bodies consisting of many segments, each having one or two pairs of legs, belong to a class called the *myriapods (Myriapoda).* All of the above belong to a phylum called *arthropods (Arthropoda),* which includes all invertebrates with segmented bodies and jointed legs. In addition, the arthropods comprise the *crustaceans—lobsters, shrimp, crabs, barnacles, horseshoe crabs,* etc.—which have ten legs *(Decapoda).* (See also **phylum / class / order / family / genus / species, centipede / millipede.**)

bull / bear

In stock-market parlance, a *bull* is one who buys shares because he believes that their price will increase and that he will be able to sell them at a later date at a profit; his purchasing policies, generally fed by optimism, cause the prices of shares to rise; a market that is tending to rise is said to be *bullish* or a *bull market.* A *bear* is one who is generally pessimistic about prices, expecting them to go down; thus, he sells his holdings in anticipation of being able to buy them after an interval at a lower price, thus keeping the difference as profit; his policies tend to drive prices down as a result of his selling efforts, and such a market is called *bearish* or a *bear market.*

burglary / robbery / theft

Theft is a general word meaning 'the taking of another's property illegally'; it is perpetrated by a *thief.* In criminal law, *burglary* means 'breaking and entering premises with the illegal intention of committing a felony'; it is perpetrated by a *burglar. Robbery* is 'the illegal taking of another's property by force or intimidation, either personally or from his immediate vicinity.' (See also **grand larceny / petty larceny.**)

bush / shrub / tree

Bush and *shrub* are used interchangeably to refer to a relatively low, woody perennial with many stems and branches that grow from a complex quite close to the ground. A *tree* is a woody perennial, usually taller than a shrub, having a longish stem emerging from the earth with branches that start higher up.

butterfly / moth

Both of these creatures belong to the order *Lepidoptera* (from the Greek meaning 'scale-winged'), of the class *Insecta.* Their main distinguishing features are that *butterflies* have clubbed antennae while *moths* do not, and *butterflies* fly about during the day (being *diurnal*) while *moths* fly about in the evening, at twilight (being *crepuscular*) or at night (being *nocturnal*). Varieties of both often have beautifully colored wings and have long been the object of specialized collectors, called *lepidopterists.*

calorie / Calorie

The *calorie* (with a small "c"), also called the *gram calorie* or *small calorie*, was formerly used in science to describe the amount of heat necessary to raise the temperature of one gram of water from 14.5° to 15.5°C at sea level. The *Calorie* (with a capital "C"), also called the *great calorie, large calorie,* or *kilocalorie,* was the quantity of heat equal to 1000 (small) calories. Although the term *calorie* is still used in physiology, nutrition, and certain other applications, in scientific use it has been replaced by the *joule,* which is equivalent to 0.2390 calories.

can buoy / nun buoy

In the context of navigational marks, a *can buoy,* which is cylindrical and always painted black, marks the port, or left side of a channel when proceeding towards a port, a *nun buoy,* which is always painted red and is so called because of the somewhat conical shape of its top, marks the right, or starboard side of a channel when proceeding towards a port, whence the navigational rule, *Red Right Return.*

canvaswork / needlepoint / tapestry

Canvaswork, which is sometimes misleadingly called *tapestry* or *needlepoint,* is properly a pattern sewn onto a piece of open-work canvas with a threaded needle. *Needlepoint* is properly handmade lace, or *tatting.* *Tapestry* is a design woven into a cloth backing and resembles a *rep,* or ribbed piece of fabric; it is variously called *arras, Flemish drapery,* and, after well-known factories where it was produced for centuries, *aubusson* or *gobelin.* (See also **gros point / petit point.**)

cape / isthmus / bay / cove / peninsula / gulf

All of these terms relate to the features of a coastline. A *cape* is a relatively large body of land, or *promontory,* that juts out into a body of water: *Cape Horn; Cape of Good Hope; Cape Cod.* It may also go under the general term, *headland,* especially if it is elevated to some extent above sea level. An *isthmus* is a narrow stretch of land that connects two relatively large land areas: *The Isthmus of Panama connects North and South America. Peninsula* is reserved for a narrow body of land, longer than it is wide, that juts out into a body of water; it may be used of quite large areas: *the Iberian Peninsula; A nickname of Florida is "the Peninsular State." Neck* is a general term describing a thin, necklike strip of land, like a peninsula or, sometimes, a cape. *Ness* is an old-fashioned term for a cape. A *gulf* is a relatively large arm of the sea that is partly enclosed by land areas: *the Gulf of Mexico; the Persian Gulf. Firth,* sometimes *frith,* is a Scots term for a narrow inlet of the sea: *the Firth of Clyde; the Firth of Forth.* A *bay,* larger than a *cove,* is the name given to a partly enclosed arm of the sea forming an indentation in the shoreline; it is similar to a gulf but somewhat smaller: *the Bay of Biscay; Cape Cod Bay.* A *cove* is merely a smaller bay; it is a term used to refer to such configurations along the shore of a sea or lake or on the bank of a river.

carat / karat / caret

In British English, *carat* has two main senses: as a unit of weight for precious stones, chiefly diamonds, it is equivalent to 0.20 grams, and one such *carat* equals 100 points; it is also used to refer to the proportion of gold in an alloy, *24 carats* signifying pure gold. (Partly because of its value but mostly because gold is such a soft metal, pure gold occurs in theory only; in jewelry its purest form is usually 22 carats, and it is seen more often as 18-carat, 14-carat, and 9-carat gold.) It is abbreviated "C" or "c." In the U.S. and Canada, this unit is spelled *karat* and is abbreviated "K" or "k." In both Englishes, a *caret* is a small mark, like an inverted "v," made at a place in written matter where something has been omitted and should be inserted: the omitted text is then written above the caret if there is enough space or, if not, in the margin alongside the line where the caret appears. Although they are pronounced exactly the same way (along with the vegetable, *carrot*) there is no relationship between them.

cardigan / pullover

A *cardigan* is a sweater with buttons down the front. A *pullover* is a sweater that is donned and doffed by pulling it over the head.

cardinal / ordinal

In speaking of numbers, those that denote quantity or value without designating their place in a set, as *one, two, forty, hundred,* are called *cardinal.* Names for numbers that determine their order in a series, as *first, second, fortieth, hundredth,* are called *ordinal.*

carnivore / herbivore / omnivore

Carnivores eat meat, *herbivores* plants, and *omnivores* just about anything. There are also *insectivores,* which eat insects. Many carnivores also eat plants, but their main diet is the flesh of other animals; few herbivores have the dental and gastric equipment needed to eat meat; in a sense, insectivores are carnivores. These terms refer to the natural characteristics of animals, not to their desired preferences as, for instance, might apply to vegetarians.

carpet / rug

Generally, a *rug* is smaller than a *carpet;* also, one would refer to *wall-to-wall* (or, in the U.K., *fitted*) *carpet,* not "rug." Yet the usage is not consistent, for reference is made to *flying carpets. Rug* prevails in the idiom *pull the rug out from under someone* 'undermine, betray, or destroy someone's plans, expectations, etc.,' *cut a rug* 'dance,' *area rug* 'one that is fitting for a particular floor space,' etc.; *carpet* in *on the carpet* 'summoned for reprimanding,' *carpet knight* 'noncombatant soldier,' *red carpet* 'royal treatment,' etc.; they seem to be interchangeable in *sweep under the rug / carpet* 'conceal surreptitiously.' The information that *rug,* being of Germanic origin, is older in the language than the Romance *carpet* reveals little of use in determining genuine distinctions between the terms.

carvel-built / clinker-built

In the context of the construction of the hulls of wooden vessels, *carvel-built* designates a design in which the planks are fastened (always horizontally) to the frames edge to edge, giving a smooth appearance to the hull; in *clinker-built,* or *clincher-built* construction, each plank is lapped over the one below, giving a clapboard effect. Another name for *clinker-built* is *lapstrake, strake* (also *streak*) being a word for the horizontal planking pieces in the hull. It is not clear why smooth-sided hulls should be called *carvel-built: carvel* comes from *caravel,* a kind of sailing vessel, the characteristics of which did not specify the construction method or design of the hull.

casting / injection molding / extrusion molding / forging

These terms describe various ways in which three-dimensional objects can be formed. In *casting,* a mold is made and the substance of which the object is to be made is poured into it; when the substance hardens, the mold is removed and the cast object is either in its final state or may be subjected to further treatment, as polishing, painting, etc. The material from which the mold is made is determined by the substance to be cast: if the substance is molten metal, the cast must be of sand, of some ceramic material, or of an alloy with a melting point higher than that of the substance; if the substance is plaster, the cast might be made of rubber, wood, or some other such material. In *injection molding,* a molten substance is forced into a small hole in a mold, which is opened after the substance has set to remove the object; injection molding is often employed in the making of plastic objects. In *extrusion molding,* a (usually) solid rod of the substance to be formed is forced through a die which gives it an external shape, as in the forming of continuous trim made of plastic or metal; extrusion molding differs from *drawing,* which is used in making wire, in that drawing involves the pulling of a ductile substance through a die rather than forcibly pushing it through. In *forming,* a piece of metal—usually sheet metal—is placed over one side of a mold and the other side of the mold, or die is forced down on it under enormous pressure. *Forging* is the shaping of a piece by striking it repeatedly with a hammer (as a blacksmith would in forming an object or a farrier might in making a horseshoe); in mechanical systems, a heavy, hammerlike part serves the same function. In *drop forging*, a similar method is employed except that the upper half of the mold is held in a very heavy piece which is raised and dropped onto the lower, sometimes striking the piece repeatedly. *Die stamping*, which is the method used in striking coins, is similar to drop forging.

cathode / anode

In an ordinary battery, or dry cell, technically called an electrolytic cell, the *cathode* is the positive terminal—that is, the negatively charged electrode which is marked with a " + ." In a *cathode-ray tube*, this terminal emits electrons which are focused into a narrow beam, or ray, and directed toward a screen, where they excite the fluorescent coating and appear as a spot of light. By controlling the electrical charge of a number of plates through which the beam passes, its direction can be modified with great speed and precision, creating an image on the face of the glass tube which can be viewed from the outside. The screens in ordinary television receivers are cathode-ray tubes, which also find application in oscilloscopes, computer monitors, etc. The *anode* is the negative terminal—that is, the positively charged electrode in an electrolytic cell—which is marked with a "–."

centipede / millipede

Although the *centipede* (the name of which comes from Latin meaning 'hundred feet') has more body segments, generally, than the *millipede* (the name of which comes from Latin meaning 'thousand feet'), the former has only one pair of feet on each segment, while the latter has two pairs. Centipedes have from 15 to 170-odd segments, millipedes from 20 to 60-odd. Both are members of the group called *Myriapoda*, which comes from Greek 'ten thousand feet' and which includes other arthropods.

centerboard / daggerboard / leeboard

Among smaller sailing vessels, especially those that have no keel, a "removable" or "adjustable" keel is provided by a *centerboard*, which is a strong, flat board, usually triangular and hinged at one corner so that it can be swung down into the water under the boat through a waterproof slot, called a centerboard trunk, in order to serve the function of a keel; it is used when the craft is sailing in any direction but downwind, where it would accomplish little but to increase drag. Centerboards may be very heavy, requiring them to be raised and lowered by mechanical means. A *daggerboard* is a narrower, lighter centerboard, as used in a dinghy, and may be lifted entirely out of its housing, like a dagger from its sheath. Some commercial coastal sailing vessels, especially those built by the Dutch, are equipped with large boards on each side of the outside of the hull, called *leeboards*; the one on the leeward side of the boat is lowered into the water to reduce drift, serving the same purpose as a centerboard.

centrifugal force / centripetal force

Centrifugal force acts in a direction away from the center of rotation or curvature of a rotating or orbiting body; that is, it is the force that keeps a string taut if one is swinging a ball around at the end of it. *Centripetal force* acts towards the center of rotation or curvature; that is, it is the force of the string in the preceding example that counteracts the centrifugal force. If the centrifugal force is greater than the centripetal force, the string breaks.

centum / satem

In a useful phonological classification of Indo-European languages for certain purposes, a distinction is made between the *centum languages*, those belonging to the Anatolian, Celtic, Germanic, Hellenic, Italic, and Tocharian branches, which retained the earlier pronunciation of velar stops (like *k*), and the *satem languages*, those belonging to the Albanian, Armenian, Baltic, Indic, Iranian, and Slavonic branches, in which the velar stops became palatal continuants (*k* changed to *s* or *š*). They are so called because the Latin word for 'hundred,' *centum*, typifies the former, while the Avestan word for 'hundred,' *satem*, typifies the latter.

cerebrum / cerebellum

The *cerebrum*, which is involved in sensory and motor functions, as well as the intellectual functions of memory, speech, writing, and emotion, is the main part of the brain, divided into the left and right cerebral hemispheres by a central sulcus, or groove. The hemispheres are connected at the bottom of the sulcus by the *corpus callosum*. The *cerebellum*, which is involved in the coordination of voluntary muscular activity and the maintenance of balance, is a smaller part of the brain situated at the rear and below the cerebrum.

champagne / Asti spumante / sparkling wine

Sparkling wine is the generic term for any wine that is either naturally or artificially effervescent. *Asti spumante—spumante* means 'sparkling'—is an artificially effervescent wine from *Asti,* a town in Italy. *Champagne* is, strictly speaking, a white wine from the Champagne region of northeastern France that is made naturally effervescent by a method called double distillation; against the approval of those who control the making of champagne in France, similar sparkling wines of other areas of the world, notably those of Spain, New York State, and California, are also marketed under the name *champagne*. Another effervescent wine is *sparkling burgundy*.

characteristic / mantissa

In logarithms, the whole number part, to the left of the decimal point, is called the *characteristic;* it is not usually given in tables of logarithms because it can readily be determined mentally. The decimal part, to the right of the decimal point, is called the *mantissa*.

chickenpox / cowpox / smallpox / pox

Pox is rarely used today in its former sense, 'any disease that causes pock-marks to appear on the skin,' *pox* being an alternative spelling of *pocks,* the plural of *pock. Great pox, French pox,* and *Spanish pox* were formerly used to denote syphilis, indicating that at one time *pox* had acquired the sense 'any serious, often fatal disease,' whence the curse, *a pox upon you* (or *him, her, it, them*) or, as some wags would have it, *Pox vobiscum. French pox,* also known as *the French disease,* terms obviously used by the English at a time when much loving but little love occurred between the two, had its counterpart in French *la maladie Anglaise. Chickenpox,* or *varicella,* is a disease caused by a herpesvirus, varicella zoster virus, which is accompanied by a low fever and the outbreak of pustules on the chest and back, later spreading to the face and other parts. These pustules itch and, if they are scratched, may leave permanent scars, or pox (pocks), especially on the face. The disease is not serious in young children but in adults may be severe, leading to complications. One attack confers immunity. It is not transmitted by chickens or other fowl and is named either for its mildness or because the skin with pockmarks resembles that of a plucked chicken. *Cowpox,* on the other hand, is transmitted by cows infected with the *vaccinia* virus. It is also a mild disease, the main significance of which is the discovery, by Edward Jenner, in 1798, that infection by cowpox confers immunity to smallpox. *Smallpox,* also called *variola,* is a highly contagious disease; *variola minor* causes a mild form of smallpox called *alastrim; variola major* causes a severe form which can be fatal. Smallpox is not known to occur naturally, and man is the only known transmitter. With worldwide immunity conferred by vaccination with cowpox vaccine (Latin *vacca* means 'cow'), the World Health Organization announced some years ago that smallpox had been eradicated entirely from the face of the earth.

chicory / endive / escarole

In the United States, *endive* is the oblong vegetable with flat, tight, white leaves, edged with pale green, somewhat resembling a small, elongated cabbage; eaten raw in salads or braised as a vegetable, it is sold in markets as imported from Belgium and is often called *Belgian endive.* In Britain, it is called *chicory* or *succory.* Another variety of this plant, having broad, loose leaves with crinkled edges and used in salads, is called *chicory* or *escarole* in the U.S. The name *escarole* is not used in Britain, where what the Americans call *chicory* is called *endive.* The root of the (British) chicory (or American *endive*) is roasted and dried for use as a flavoring in or substitute for coffee.

china / porcelain / ironstone / stoneware / earthenware

These are names for various grades and kinds of what can generically be referred to as ceramic ware. *China,* without a modifying word (as in *bone china*), is the general term for tableware and decorative pieces

made from certain kinds of clay that has been glazed, usually decorated, and fired in a kiln at high temperatures. *Ironstone* is a hard, usually white ceramic ware, developed as a cheap alternative to
expensive *bone china,* which is a fine, translucent material, so called
because it contains bone ash, which is made from calcined bones.
Stoneware, which is often used glazed for larger pieces, as serving
platters, ewers, basins, tile, etc., falls intermediate in quality between
porcelain, a strong material fired at a low temperature before glazing
and at a high temperature after, and *earthenware,* a relatively weak,
coarse, porous material fired at a low temperature and sometimes
glazed, sometimes not (as in making bricks, certain storage vessels,
etc.).

circadian / diurnal / nocturnal / tidal / menstrual / annual

These are terms used by biologists to describe the periods of various
functions that have been observed in organisms. *Circadian* means 'at
twenty-four hour intervals'; it is used when a neutral word is needed
to distinguish from *diurnal* events that take place "each day" and *nocturnal* events that take place "each night." Thus, *circadian* is used to
refer to a human being's "biological clock," a pattern of normal
rhythms established by functions like bowel movements, meal times,
sleep periods, and so forth, that are independent of solar or lunar
events. *Nocturnal* is used of animals that are better adapted for functioning at night, like owls, of plants that exhibit changes at night, like
night-blooming cereus or night jasmine, which bloom at night, and of
other organisms, like plankton, the depth of which below the surface
of the sea varies between daytime and night-time. *Diurnal* describes
the very large number of species of plants and animals that display
adaptation to the sunlit hours, like morning glory and four-o'clock,
which bloom at those times, and many reptiles, which, being poikilothermal (*q.v.*), depend on the warmth of the sun. Flora and fauna of
the sea are affected by tidal influences, chiefly those that inhabit littoral (that is, shoreline) regions; sea grasses, sand crabs, and certain
fishes are examples. Although, technically, *menstrual* means, simply,
'monthly,' its frequency of application to the menstrual cycle in wom-
en has loaded it so with that connotation that the more neutral
monthly is generally used in its place. The most common application
of *menstrual* is to the process of readjustment that takes place in the
females of primates following ovulation, which occurs, more or less,

at monthly intervals. *Annual* cycles, regarded also as seasonal, are observable in almost all species in connection with estrus, flowering and the production of seeds, hibernation (*q.v.*), the habitual search for food by herds of grazing cattle, the migrations of birds (which may also be regarded as semi-annual), and many other phenomena. Not all species exhibit periodicity of a year or less: the periodical cicada, or seventeen-year locust of the eastern United States, remains underground in its nymphal state for seventeen years in the northern states and thirteen in the southern; and the Mexican agave, called the century plant because it was formerly thought to bloom once every hundred years but is now known to bloom more often, still propagates itself at unusually long intervals.

city / town / borough / municipality / village

In common use, the over-all term, in Great Britain and the United States for any region or collection of residential and commercial buildings that has its own government is *municipality.* In the U.S., a *hamlet* is any tiny collection of houses; in Britain, it refers, often specifically, to such a community that has no church. *Village* is used in a very general, nontechnical way in both countries for a small group of dwellings that is larger than a hamlet. In the U.S., the term has been applied to areas within a city that might once have been separate villages (or hamlets) but have been absorbed into the larger entity, as *Greenwich Village,* in New York City. *Town* is used in a great variety of ways in Britain and the U.S., mainly to denote a place that is bigger than a village but smaller than a city. In some states, *town* is a legal designation for a municipal corporation that constitutes a political unit, but elsewhere in the U.S. the term is used generally for anything smaller than a city that is a subdivision of a county; elsewhere in America, *town* and *township* are interchangeable. *Town* is also widely used to refer to a city, often a large one that is nearby; this usage was probably jocular originally, but is not usually felt to be so any longer. The words *downtown,* which refers to the main commercial part of a city, *uptown,* to a district of the city at some remove from downtown and marked chiefly as a residential area, and *midtown,* the sections between in cities large enough to allow a distinction, are common in Canada, the U.S., and to some extent in other English-speaking communities, are not heard in Britain. *Borough* is a relatively simple term in the U.S., where it is used for any town or township having a municipal charter; it is also the designation of the five constituent parts of New York City, also called *counties* (but, to complicate things, with different names), the names of which are, with their borough names in parentheses, Richmond (Staten Island), Kings (Brooklyn), New York (Manhattan), Queens (Queens), and (the) Bronx (Bronx). In Britain, a borough is so designated if it has a royal charter (till 1975 called a *burgh* in Scotland) or if it is the constituency of a Member of Parliament; along with the City of London, thirty-two boroughs make up Greater London, e.g., Chelsea, Westminster, Lambeth, etc. (In the U.S., the Board of Geographic Names required all municipalities with *-burgh* in their names to change the spelling to *-burg;* all complied save Pittsburgh, which refused, and today it is the only city in the U.S. to spell its suffix in that fashion.) In Britain, in order to be officially called a *city,* a place must be so designated by the Crown and was, at least formerly, the seat of a bishop. In the U.S. and elsewhere, a city is any (proportionately) large collection of commercial and residential buildings, a municipal corporation that is a political entity. In recent years, the newer word *conurbation* has been coined to describe an urban sprawl created by the merging of contiguous towns and their suburbs. In the U.S., the term *megalopolis* has become popular in reference to the "conurbation of cities," particularly in describing the apparent disappearance of any separation between communities between Boston, Massachusetts, and Washington, D.C.

civil law / criminal law / common law / case law / international law / statute law

Civil law, also called *municipal law,* is the body of rules of conduct enacted by the government of a nation to deal with the rights of its citizens and remedies they can take to ensure that their rights are not violated. It is contrasted with *international law,* which governs the legal intercourse between nations, and with *criminal law,* which concerns itself with the identification of illegal acts as harmful to society and with the punishment of offenders, which itself may constitute a subdivision termed a *penal code.* Distinct from *statute law,* which is the result of acts of legislature, *common law* is the law resulting from court judgments and decrees that recognize usages and customs, often quite ancient. *Equity law* is the body of jurisprudence based on what is considered to be fair (and *equitable*), what would be thought of as "natural justice," *Case law* refers to interpretation of law based on previous judgments rendered by precedent in earlier litigation. *Constitutional law,* which exists only in countries that have a constitution, like the United States, deals with the relationship between a state and its citizens, especially in regard to their rights as provided for in the constitution.

claret / burgundy / beaujolais / bordeaux / port / sherry

These are various common names for French wines. *Burgundy* is a medium red or white wine produced in eastern France, in the district named *Bourgogne,* west of the Saône river, near Dijon. *Beaujolais* is a relatively light variety of burgundy made from grapes cultivated in the southern regions of Bourgogne; it is most commonly red and is often drunk fresh in November, after the annual harvest, when it is called *Beaujolais nouveau;* a sparkling (mildly effervescent) variety is also available. *Bordeaux* wines, among the finest, full-bodied red and white wines in the world, are grown in southwestern France, along the river Garonne, near the city of Bordeaux, whence the region gets its name; a rosé, or pink wine is also made in the region. *Claret* is a name used, mainly in Britain, for red wines from Bordeaux. Although the slang term *plonk* is used in Britain, Australia, and New Zealand for any cheap alcoholic drink, the word comes from French *blanc* 'white,' in reference to white wine, which it presumably once denoted. *Port* is a strong, fortified red wine from Portugal, so named because it was originally shipped from the city of Oporto; a heavy, after-dinner wine, port is aged in the bottle, and the older ports, the so-called *vintage ports,* can be extremely expensive. *Sherry,* usually drunk as an apéritif, is also a fortified wine; it is blended in many ways to produce wines that are light, medium, or heavy in a variety of sweetnesses and drynesses; the heaviest, sweetest, is called *cream sherry,* the medium is called *milk sherry. Sherry* is named for the Spanish city of Jerez (originally Xeres), whence the wine is shipped. All of these wines have been widely imitated by vintners throughout the world, particularly in the western United States, partly through blending, partly by growing strains of the grape varieties locally. Although wines made in California, Australia, England, and other areas have much to recommend them, some aficionados who can readily identify the source of a wine insist that continental European wines are the best. Italy produces many good red wines (e.g., *chianti,* also available as a white) as well as whites (e.g., *orvieto* and *frascati*), as do Spain, Austria, Switzerland, Rumania, Yugoslavia, and Bulgaria. Germany is known for its white dry *hock* and *riesling,* for the sweeter *liebfraumilch,* and for other white wines produced in the region of the Rhine. (See also **brandy / cognac.**)

classic / classical

Classic means 'of the best or highest class; in keeping with a traditional (high) standard of principles; of enduring importance or significance; simple and basic.' Thus, one may speak of *the classics,* that is, well-established works of art or literature that are regarded as forming the basis of modern culture, or of a *classic dress,* that is, a simple garment, of solid color, unadorned, and of moderate length—one that remains fashionable regardless of changes in fads and that may be accessorized by accents of jewelry, etc. *Classical* refers, particularly, to the ancient cultures of Greece and Rome and to the things associated with them. Thus, one speaks of *Classical Greek* (in contrast to Modern Greek—both *Classical* and *Modern* being capitalized because they are part of the proper names of languages), *Classical Latin* (in contrast to *Church Latin*), *Classical Arabic* (in contrast to that spoken today), and so forth. There are also *classical art,* marked by conservatism, *classical music,* referring generally to almost any music that cannot be otherwise classified as popular or folk music, *classical education,* in which the study of Latin and Greek and the humanities is emphasized, etc. In a common expression, people refer to a *classic example* of something, meaning a 'perfect example that epitomizes exactly what is being exemplified.'

club soda / seltzer

At one time, these terms were entirely interchangeable, both referring to any water that is effervescent by virtue of the presence of carbon dioxide in solution, whether naturally present or artificially introduced. Lately, however, a distinction has arisen in the U.S. between *club soda,* which is fizzy water that may contain salt or other sodium compounds, and *seltzer,* which is the same thing but has no salt. The reason is that many people in the U.S. have been advised by their doctors to avoid the intake of sodium because of its association with heart disease, and others, who have not been so advised, believe that a reduction of salt in their diet will stave off cardiac problems. The name *seltzer*, itself, usually spelled *Seltzer* in Britain, comes from the name of a place near Wiesbaden, in West Germany, called (*Nieder*) *Selters*, where there is a mineral spring producing (naturally effervescent) water called, in German, *Selterser Wasser*. In Britain, *club soda* is usually called *soda water* or just *soda* for short, terms which are also used in the U.S.

cold front / warm front / occluded front

These terms describe typical meteorological phenomena. The leading edge of an advancing mass of air that is cooler than the mass it is replacing is called a *cold front*, and it is characterized by a wedgelike slipping of the cooler, denser air beneath the warmer, forcing it to rise and causing rapid wind shifts, a drop in temperature, and, often, rainfall. When the cooler air forces the warmer air upward and the atmospheric pressure is low, the entire system may stall, and that is termed an *occluded front*. A *warm front* is the leading edge of a mass of warmer air advancing on and rising over a mass of cooler air, resulting in a variety of cloud conditions. The systems rarely occur in as clearcut a way as here described, and, among other conditions, the differences between the temperatures of the masses, their relative sizes, cyclonic and anticyclonic wind patterns, humidity, and other factors play an important role in the way the phenomena manifest themselves.

cold-blooded / warm-blooded

The scientific word for *cold-blooded* is *poikilothermal*, that for *warm-blooded*, *homoiothermal* (which has the variants *homeothermal*, *homothermal*, *homoiothermic*, and *homoiothermous*). In general, mammals and birds are warm-blooded, reptiles, amphibians, fish, and crustaceans cold-blooded. The term *cold-blooded* is a bit of a misnomer, for the blood of such creatures merely takes on that of their environment; some land animals, for instance, regulate their body temperature by basking in the sun, or, if they overheat, by burying themselves or taking refuge in the shade. On the other hand, warm-blooded creatures maintain a fairly constant internal body temperature. In human beings, steady body temperature is governed by the thermotaxic nerve mechanism, and variation of more than a degree

or two from the normal temperature of 98.6° (Fahrenheit) may indicate the presence of infection or other disease; an increase or
decrease of as much as six degrees can be fatal.

coliseum / Colosseum

Colosseum is the name of the amphitheater, built in Rome in A.D.
75–80, the ruins of which can still be seen there. The name spawned
the variant, *colisseum,* which, in turn, yielded the variant *coliseum,*
which is today used to refer to any large amphitheater or stadium
used for entertainment, sports, etc.

college / university

In its sense of an 'association or fellowship of colleagues,' *college* survives in both British and American English in *College of Physicians and
Surgeons, electoral college,* etc., and in Britain in *College of Arms,* etc.
This notion of "society, guild" was applied to groups of scholars organized within a university for any of a variety of reasons, including the
support of indigent students, the pursuit of specialized studies, etc.
The term *university* is applied to the entire organization of scholars in
many disciplines associated in an institution of advanced learning.
Typically, a university, as the University of Paris, Oxford, Cambridge,
etc., was made up of a central administration under which several
colleges were organized. The University of Paris, for example, includes
the College of the Sorbonne and others, Oxford University, Balliol College and others. These were originally largely clerical, but secular education soon followed. Later, if all but one of the colleges at a university
ceased to exist, the university and college became one and the same.
The present system of colleges and universities in Europe was established in the Renaissance. When systems of higher education were
organized in America, they followed the European pattern. More
recently in the United States, state institutions of higher learning have
been organized with branches in a number of places (within the state),
each named for its site, as the *University of California at Los Angeles,
State University of New York at Buffalo,* etc., each a unit of the larger
state system. In some instances, a secondary school originally associated with a university was given the name *college,* hence, *Winchester College, Eton College.* In other cases, there was no connection with a
university and the name *college* was merely appropriated, as in *Dulwich*

College, Sarah Lawrence College. In Britain, generally, the several colleges at a university are more or less autonomous, with separate administrations, budgets, and endowments, resulting in some of the (especially newer) colleges at the major, older universities being much poorer (financially) than others. In the United States, an institution of higher learning may be established with the status of a *college,* acquiring *university* status (which is conferred by the individual states) only when it has been demonstrated that it is constituted of more than one faculty and, especially, that it is qualified to confer advanced degrees. (See also **public school / private school.**)

colloquial / informal

In many contexts, these two words mean the same thing. Many years ago, lexicographers chose *colloquial* as a label to describe the level of a word or a particular sense of a word that was used in *colloquy,* that is, in ordinary conversation, or, to put it differently, in *informal* usage. As dictionary users became more familiar with the labels on words and definitions, because they had their own opinions about whether a word or sense was standard, formal, informal, or slang, *colloquial* came to be interpreted in a variety of different ways. It was often taken to mean 'slang,' which was not what had been intended by the lexicographers. Consequently, many of the dictionaries published after the 1950s reflect a change from the label *Colloquial* to the label *Informal.* It is probably only a matter of time before users who consider a word so labeled to be slang, thus corrupting the intention of the lexicographers, who may return to *colloquial* after a generation or two. (See also **informal / slang / taboo, standard / nonstandard.**)

colophon / logo(type)

Traditionally, a *colophon* is a statement, published at the end of a book, that contains the kinds of information included on the title page. Because title pages are used in virtually all books published today, *colophon* has lost that sense except in antiquarian contexts. In modern books, some publishers include a note at the back describing the typography, paper, and other information about its design and production, and this note has been referred to in later times as the *colophon.* It is also used, though loosely, for the publisher's name or trademark as it may appear on the title page, copyright page, end sheets, or spine of the book or its dust jacket. Those who insist on being technical use *logotype* or, more often, its shortened form, *logo,* for the publisher's mark.

colt / filly / foal / pony / mare / stallion / gelding

Generally, a *colt* is any young male horse; technically, especially in racing parlance, it is a male horse not more than four years old. A *filly,* generally, is any young female horse; technically, in racing parlance, it is a female horse not more than four years old. A *foal* is any young horse, male or female. A *pony* is a breed of small horse. A *mare* is a full-grown female horse. A full-grown male horse is called a *stallion* or, if it has been castrated, a *gelding.*

comet / meteor

The name *meteor* is given to any meteorite or meteoroid that passes through the earth's atmosphere to become luminous and visible. A *comet* is a heavenly body consisting of a mass of dust, ice, rock, or debris and a gaseous envelope, which streams out from it creating a tail sometimes millions of miles in length, that orbits the sun. Its orbit is usually eccentric and sometimes quite large: Halley's comet takes 75 years to complete its orbit. The tail, or *coma,* from which the comet gets its name, is diaphanously light and is blown by the force of the solar wind so that it always extends away from the sun. (See also **meteorite / meteoroid.**)

common stock / ordinary shares / preferred stock / preference shares / A shares

These terms refer to the kinds of equity shares held by owners of a company. The U.S. term *common stock* or *share,* the same as the British term *ordinary share,* is a certificate acknowledging part ownership in a company which has issued such share certificates in return for capital investment; if there is a sufficient market for the shares in such a company, they may be traded publicly on one or another of the several stock exchanges around the world. The owners of such shares are entitled to receive a share of the profits of the company and have a claim on its net assets after payment is made to holders of *preferred stock,* or *preference shares.* In the U.S., such a company is called a *corporation,* and its shareholders are not liable for its debts. In Britain, a company may issue *A shares,* which return a higher rate of dividend that preference shares but are subject to limited voting rights and certain other restrictions. British shareholders' liability may be limited, as in a *limited company* or *public limited company.* In Britain, a *public company* is a limited company that issues shares for public subscription which are traded freely and may be purchased by anyone; a *private company* is a limited company the shares of which are closely held and may not be transferred freely by their owners. In Britain, a *public corporation* is a state-run organization that controls the operations of an industry, utility, or other enterprise that is owned by the government and for which shares are not issued. What is called *preferred stock* in the U.S. goes under the name *preference share* in Britain; both refer to a kind of equity ownership in a company that entitles the shareholder to a share in the net profit and net assets of the company greater than that of the holders of common stock (that is, ordinary shares) but at some sacrifice in the dividend rate paid. The terms *limited* (*ltd.*) and *incorporated* (*inc.*) are used in the U.S. interchangeably to designate a corporation of limited liability; in Britain, the term *limited* is used to designate what is described above as a *limited company,* and *plc* is used to designate what is described above as a *public limited company.* The terms *incorporated* and *corporation,* while well known in Britain, are not used in the titles or names of companies. (See also **corporation / partnership.**)

common / mutual

In one of its main senses, *mutual* means 'reciprocal; exchanging or interchanging between two or more people or things; shared by two or more people or things': *mutual respect; mutual distrust; mutual agreement; mutual acquaintances; mutual enemies.* Thus, if two people respect one another, they have mutual respect for each other; if three nations concur in a treaty, they have reached mutual agreement. The important part of the meaning is that the parties to being mutual are involved with each other, however many there might be, not with any person or thing outside their circle. In one of its most frequent meanings, *common* is used to mean the same things meant by *mutual,* but some people insist that the emphasis is on activity or feeling directed at an outside party. In other words, they hold that two people could be said to have a friend *in common,* or to have a *common friend,* but that it is wrong to say that they have a *mutual friend.* Speakers of English are very reluctant to use the phrase *common friend* because *common* has a high-frequency sense of 'ordinary, average; low-class, vulgar, coarse,' and people do not wish to refer to their friends that way. There is not much resistance to referring to a *common enemy,* however, nor is there any objection to saying that two people have a friend *in common.* As a result of the resistance against *common friend,* the not unreasonable *mutual friend* has come into use; it has been about for almost a century and a half, for Charles Dickens, who was no mean stylist in the English language, seemed equally reluctant to use *common friend* because of the undertones and overtones of *common* and entitled one of his novels *Our Mutual Friend.* One might think that what was good enough for Dickens might be good enough for the ordinary (though not 'common') speaker of English, but the purists, whose prejudices are contagious, persist in their efforts to disallow *mutual friend.* They should be paid no heed.

compare / contrast

Students in the United States are familiar with the kind of question that begins, "Compare and / or contrast . . ," followed by specifics in any of the social sciences or liberal arts. *Compare* emphasizes the similarities between or among things, though not losing sight of the differences; *contrast* emphasizes the differences. When similarities are emphasized, especially between or among items that are not on the same plane or in the same class, the usual preposition is *to: Shall I compare thee to a summer's day? Compared to Donald's poetry, mine is doggerel.* When the items compared are felt to be on the same level, more or less, the usual preposition is *with: How can you compare your writing with Santayana's? Compared with oranges from Florida, I think those from Jaffa are better.* Sometimes, the preposition is omitted altogether, especially when the idea is negative: *Wines from Italy and from France cannot compare. Constance's voice is beyond compare.* Sometimes, where juxtaposition is not at issue or is denied, *and* may be used: *Comparing Whistler and Dali is like comparing apples and bananas.* These usages carry over to the nouns, *comparison* and *con-*

trast. Contrast is commonly followed by *with, between,* or *to: People insist on stressing the contrasts between British and American English. The character of Hector contrasts nicely with that of Achilles. In contrast to her earlier novels, her latest is a gem.*

compensatory damages / punitive damages / liquidated damages / nominal damages

In United States law, *compensatory, actual,* or *general damages* is a legal term for money or other compensation paid by a defendant to a (successful) plaintiff for an injury suffered as a result of the defendant's negligence, willful act, or failure to act; the injury need not be literally a physical one, as in the case of an accident; it may be any form of injury, whether to the plaintiff's person, property, or rights. *Punitive,* or *exemplary damages* are those awarded to a successful plaintiff, to be paid by a defendant, as punishment for careless or evil behavior, fraud, violence, or deliberate intent in causing the injury suffered; such damages are paid if the defendant has been deemed responsible for the degradation, shame, anguish, or other aggravation of the wrong perpetrated, and are considered also to be exemplary so as to set an example for others. *Liquidated damages* is the term for the compensation paid to a successful plaintiff by a defendant in accordance with the terms of an agreement that stipulates the amount to be paid as damages in the event of failure to perform or other conditions provided for in the agreement. *Unliquidated damages* refers to a situation in which the specific amounts are not provided for in an agreement and it is not feasible to determine either what payment should be made or the monetary value of the injury sustained. In some instances, a plaintiff may be awarded token damages in recognition that the injury sustained was the result of the defendant's negligent or wicked behavior but that the injury, though he has a right to compensation for it, resulted in no substantial loss; such judgments, which recognize the plaintiff's legal right, are for *nominal damages,* which, in some cases in Britain, have been for no more than a shilling. In contrast to *nominal damages* are *substantial damages,* which refer to much larger sums, sometimes amounting to hundreds of millions of dollars, especially when a number of people are affected.

complex / complicated

In ordinary usage, no meaningful or idiomatic distinction can be made between these words, though some may maintain that *complex* is a slightly more "learned" word than *complicated*. The noun forms, *complex* and *complication*, are another matter, the former being reserved for applications associated with psychology, mathematics, and other specialized applications, the latter with any involved or intricate matters of a general nature. Only *complicate* occurs as a verb—at least at present.

compliment / complement

These two words sound exactly alike, and it is easy to get them confused. *Complement* is perhaps a bit less frequently used; it carries the sense of 'complete; completion'. A useful device for remembering which word is which might be that *complement* and *complete* have the same first six letters; also, *complement* is related to *supplement*, and both have that *-e-* in the middle. In addition to 'complete; completion' is the implied sense of 'whatever is necessary for completion; set off to advantage': *The window treatment complements the decor perfectly. We have a full complement of editors on our staff at the moment.* The word *compliment* has the sense of 'admire; praise; respect' or an expression of these: *I compliment you on your taste in reference books. I don't know if I can take any more compliments without blushing.* Its spelling is rarely compromised unless *complement* crops up in the vicinity to cause confusion.

compose / comprise

Many critics express their dislike of the use of either of these words for the other, insisting that one "cannot say" *be comprised of* as in *The list was comprised of property-owners only.* Because *comprise* means 'include, contain,' the "proper" form would be *The list comprised property owners only* or *The list was composed of property owners only.* Regardless of the adverse advice of self-appointed guardians of the language, all these forms are used by perfectly respectable speakers and writers.

concave / convex

In the field of optics, it is sometimes difficult to remember which of these terms applies to which kind of lens. A *concave* lens is one that is thinner at the center than at the edges: if it is concave on one side and flat on the other, it is called *concave* or *plano-concave;* and if it is concave on both sides, it is called *concavo-concave.* A lens that is curved on both sides and of uniform thickness from edge to center, is called *concavo-convex.* A *convex* lens is one that is thicker at the center than at the edges: if it is convex on one side and flat on the other, it is called *convex* or *plano-convex;* if it is convex on both sides, it is called *convexo-convex* or *biconvex;* and if it is convex on one side and concave on the other, resembling a crescent in profile, it is called *convexo-concave* or a *meniscus.* In all cases, the curvatures are sections of a sphere or a paraboloid.

concertmaster / leader

A *leader* of an orchestra, called a *concertmaster* in the United States, is the first violinist, who assumes certain administrative functions under the direction of the *conductor.* The conductor is ultimately responsible for the tempo and changes in tempo at which a piece is played, for the timing of the playing by soloists or groups of players, for the relative volume at which the various instruments are played, for phrasing and emphasis, and, perhaps most individually, for the interpretation of the composition.

conductor / semiconductor / insulator

These are materials that are categorized according to their ability to conduct electricity. At normal temperatures, metals are the best *conductors* because they have free electrons, that is, according to the theory that energy is transmitted through a solid in *bands* (called *band theory*), the *conduction* and *valence bands* in metals are either not packed with electrons or overlap, allowing the electrons to move freely through the material. *Insulators,* at the opposite extreme, have full valence bands and, between those and conduction bands, *forbidden bands,* which prevent the free movement of electrons, making insulators virtually opaque to electrical conductivity. *Semiconductors* are materials, usually solid crystals of germanium or silicon, in which the orbits of the electrons overlap, creating a network of energy bands

that can be controlled by changes in the electrical field or in temperature; these are called *intrinsic semiconductors*. The patterns of electron movements in some semiconductors are subject not only to the
states of the bands but also to empty states in the valence band,
called *holes*. The introduction, called *doping*, of an impurity like boron
or gallium, which has lower valence atoms, creates a state in which
there is an "unsatisfied" electron per atom, creating a hole. Such semiconductors are called *p-type conductors*. Doping with impurities like
antimony or arsenic, which have a higher valence, makes additional
electrons available for conduction; these *extrinsic semiconductors* are
called *n-type conductors*. Semiconductors used in electronic devices to
regulate the flow of electrons are typically *diodes*, that is, they are
crystals that have been doped so that they are half *p*-type and half
n-type, and the flow of electrons between them can be controlled by
changing the charge that separates them. This enables the diode to
act as a rectifier, which changes the characteristics of the current or
signal passing through it: a single diode acts as a half-wave rectifier;
two act as a full-wave rectifier. Because they are not as fragile as
thermionic valves (the formerly ubiquitous radio tubes), are not as
sensitive to shock and changes in temperature and humidity, and are
far more compact, *transistors*, which consist of semiconductors with
the added capability of amplification, are now widely used, allowing
for the greater durability and miniaturization of almost all electronic
devices.

Confederate States of America / U.S. Federal Union

The *Confederate States of America*, also called *the Confederacy*, or *the
South*, consisted of eleven southern states of the United States that
seceded from the Union in 1861 over the issue of slavery. They were
Alabama, Arkansas, Florida, Georgia, Louisiana, Mississippi, North
Carolina, South Carolina, Tennessee, Texas, and Virginia. They were
defeated in the War Between the States, or American Civil War
(1861–65), by the forces of the *United States*, or *Federal Union*, also
called *the Union*, or *the North*, which consisted of the sixteen north-
ern states of Connecticut, Delaware, Illinois, Indiana, Kentucky, Maine,
Maryland, Massachusetts, Missouri, New Hampshire, New Jersey, New
York, Ohio, Pennsylvania, Rhode Island, and Vermont. (See also **Blue /
Gray.**)

conjugation / declension

In the jargon of grammar, the forms of nouns, pronouns, and adjectives can be arrayed in *declensions* ('are declined'), or *inflections* ('are inflected'); for example, the declension of the personal pronoun *I* looks like this:

	SINGULAR	PLURAL
SUBJECTIVE	*I*	*we*
POSSESSIVE	*my, of me, mine*	*our, of us, ours*
OBJECTIVE	*me*	*us*

The forms of verbs are said to arrayed in *conjugations* ('are conjugated'); the conjugation of the present tense of *see* is the following:

	SINGULAR	PLURAL
FIRST PERSON	*I see, am seeing, do see*	*we see, are seeing, do see*
SECOND PERSON	*you see, are seeing, do see*	*you see, are seeing, do see*
THIRD PERSON	*he, she,* or *it sees, are seeing, do see*	*they see, are seeing, do see*

The forms of adjectives may be further described in *comparisons* ('are compared'), listing the forms of the degrees expressed:

POSITIVE	COMPARATIVE	SUPERLATIVE
good	*better*	*best*

In some languages there are far more forms than there are in English. (See also **positive / comparative / superlative.**)

connotation / denotation

In the context of the meanings of words, *connotation* refers to meaning that is influenced by personal experience, one's culture, or both, which tend to color the sense of a word by the way a person feels about it; *denotation* refers to the generally accepted meaning of the word, independent of emotional influence. Thus, for example, the denotative definition of *cancer* is a description of the word as the

name of an affliction; but because many people have had personal
experience with the disease, either directly or because a loved one
might have succumbed to it, *cancer* connotes 'pain, anguish, great
expense for treatment, the dread of terminal illness' and other associations that are not, strictly speaking, inherent in the (purely clinical)
denotation of the word. *Ice cream* and *chocolate,* which have the same
denotation for all speakers of English, might have different connotations, depending on whether the speaker likes them or breaks out in
spots after eating them. In the same vein, *Hitler* is, denotatively, merely the name of a German dictator; but those who suffered under his
regime have quite a subjective emotional reaction to reading, hearing,
or uttering his name because it carries with it so many unpleasant
associations, whether they be personal or, because so many Western
countries were adversely affected by his actions, cultural. Traditionally, the definitions in dictionaries are supposed to be denotative and
free of all connotative influence. But in his *Dictionary,* Dr. Samuel
Johnson, who had little respect for the Scots, occasionally allowed a
subjective, or connotative definition to overwhelm his otherwise objective view, as is evidenced by his definition of *oats:*

a grain that is fed to horses in England but supports the people
in Scotland.

consonant / vowel

A *vowel* is (usually) a voiced speech sound in which the passage of air
from the lungs is unobstructed by closure of the larynx or pharynx
or by the tongue, teeth, lips, or other organs of articulation being in
contact or near contact. (In some languages, like Portuguese, linguists
have identified unvoiced vowels, which accounts for the "usually,"
above.) Different vowel sounds are made by changing the shape of the
mouth, or oral cavity, and, in some languages, by lowering the velum
to allow the air to resonate in the nasal passages and produce a nasal
vowel. French, for example, has several nasal vowels which contrast
with non-nasal counterparts:

NASAL	EXAMPLE	NON-NASAL	EXAMPLE
[ã]	*entré*	[a]	*attrait*
[œ̃]	*jeûn*	[œ]	*jeu*
[ɔ̃]	*pompe*	[ɔ]	*pop*
[æ̃]	*lin*	[æ]	*laine*

(Although, in each of the above examples, the spelling of the word containing the nasalized vowel includes an *-n-*, the *-n-* merely marks the preceding vowel as a nasal and is not articulated as an *-n-* is in English; and although the presence of an *-n-* does not invariably signal a nasalization of the vowel—e.g., *fine* (vs. *fin*), *pleine* (vs. *plein*), etc.— nasalized vowels do not occur in French unless an *-n-* or *-m-* follows the vowel.) In some languages, phoneticians identify voiceless vowels, that is, vowels articulated without laryngeal vibration, but such sounds are not a feature of the English sound system. Of the approximately 40 distinctive speech sounds (*phonemes*) in English—the number varies from dialect to dialect—about 9 or 10 are "pure" vowels, that is, not diphthongs or triphthongs. (See also **monophthong / diphthong / triphthong.**) They are distinguished by two main characteristics, the position of the lips (rounded, as in *awe, pool*; neutral, as in *up, end, at*; or spread, as in *east*) and the position of the tongue and which part of it is used (e.g., low / back unrounded, as in *cot, alms*; low / front unrounded, as in *act, cap*; high / back unrounded, as in *foot*; high / back rounded, as in *cool*). All vowels are *continuants*, that is, one can continue to say them as long as one's breath lasts. If the air flow from the lungs is blocked completely or partially by any of the speech organs, the sounds produced is said to be a *consonant*. Thus, a consonant may be either a *stop*, in which completely blockage occurs (albeit temporarily), as in *b, p, d, g, t, k*, etc., or a *continuant*, in which partial blockage occurs but the air is allowed to pass through, as in *f, v, s, z, th*, etc. Just as the vowels can be distinguished by the position of the lips and that of the tongue, the consonants can be differentiated by their place of articulation (e.g., *p*, pronounced with the lips, vs. *k*, pronounced with the back of the tongue against the palate), whether they are stops or continuants (e.g., *t*, a stop pronounced with the tip of the tongue against the back of the upper tooth ridge, vs. *th*, a continuant pronounced in the same way), whether they are nasal or non-nasal (e.g., *n*, a nasal stop which is otherwise articulated the same way as *d*, a non-nasal stop), and whether they are voiced or unvoiced (e.g., *t*, which is the unvoiced version of which *d* is the voiced). There are other sets of characteristics that have been proposed by various schools of linguistics. These four characteristics, these minimal contrastive units, are called *distinctive features* by linguists, and they enable them to arrange some of the non-nasal consonants into a pattern like the following:

	BILABIALS	LABIO-DENTALS	INTER-DENTALS	DORSO-DENTALS	DORSO-PALATALS	VELARS
UNVOICED:						
STOPS	*p*	—	—	*t*	—	*k*
CONTINUANTS	—	*f*	*th*[1]	*s*	*sh*	*kh*[2]
VOICED:						
STOPS	*b*	—	—	*d*	—	*g*
CONTINUANTS	—	*v*	*th*[3]	*z*	*zh*[4]	—

[Notes: [1]As in *thigh, nothing, path.*
[2]As in the Scottish pronunciation of *loch.*
[3]As in *this, mother, lathe.*
[4]As in *azure, mirage.*]

As can be seen, this pattern does not allow for the inclusion of all of the consonant sounds of English. Some of the sounds, like *l* and *r*, do not fit into this scheme; others, like *w* and *y* (as in *wit, you*) are designated semivowels. The sound *h* (as in *host*) is a voiceless continuant (fricative) that is pronounced far back in the throat (in the glottis) for which no column appears here. There are differences of opinion regarding the classifications of some sounds: is the initial sound of *check* a distinctive sounds, or is it composed of *t* + *sh*? Is its voiced counterpart, the consonant sounds in *judge*, a distinctive sound or composed of *d* + *zh*? There is no doubt that these are legitimate sounds of the language, but are they *phones*, that is, pronunciation variants or composites of "basic sounds" (similar to diphthongs for vowels), or are they *phonemes*, that is, among the 40 or so minimal phonetic units that are used to distinguish words? (See also **phone / phoneme.**)

constant / variable

In mathematics, a *constant* is a quantity that remains unchanged throughout a mathematical operation or a universal, or *fundamental constant*, like the speed of light or the gravitational constant that appears in Newton's law of gravitation. It may be represented by a symbol (*G*, in the case of the gravitational constant) in a symbolic formula or as a numerical value for the purposes of calculation. A *varia-*

ble is a quantity that changes depending on the set of values in a specific situation. For example, in the formula for converting temperature from Celsius to Fahrenheit, $F° = (9/5 \times C) + 32$, (or Fahrenheit to Celsius. $C° = 5/9 \times (F - 32)$), the constants are $9/5$, $5/9$, and 32, the variables, C and F.

contact landing / instrument landing

These aeronautical terms refer to a landing made with the landing-place in full view (*contact landing*) and to one in fog, rain, snow, darkness, or other obscuring interference in which the landing-place cannot be seen (*instrument landing*). Pilots also speak of *contact flight*, in which the land or water remains in sight.

contagious magic / imitative magic / sympathetic magic

Contagious magic is that based on the assumption that a lock of hair or something else physically associated with a person, as a garment, can affect that person when removed, so something done to the artifact will have a direct effect on the person. *Imitative*, or *homeopathic magic* is based on the belief that if an action is performed that imitates a desired event, the event will come about, as that the insertion of pins in a doll made in a person's image will cause the person pain or may result in his death, or that a dance in which the falling of rain is imitated will cause rain to fall. In *sympathetic magic*, as in contagious magic, a supernatural connection is assumed between something that is or was closely associated with a person, but not necessarily physically, and it is believed that action taken on the object will affect the person.

contemptible / contemptuous

It should be easy to keep these apart: *contemptible*, formed from *contempt* 'hatred' and *-ible* the combining form of 'able', means 'hate-able; meriting contempt'; *contemptuous* means 'hateful; hating; full of contempt' (for something or someone).

continuous / continual / constant

Constant means 'unceasing; unremitting; permanent'; *continual* means 'repeatedly; again and again at close intervals'; *continuous* means 'without interruption.' Thus, one speaks of *continual nagging, continual travel,* or *continual work stoppages;* of *continuous hiccuping, continuous development of technology,* or *continuous breathing;* of *constant ringing in one's ears, constant percentage of unemployment,* or *constant disagreement over the issues. Constant* is used somewhat loosely: one may refer to *constant interruptions,* for example. But *continual* and *continuous* are discriminated in good style. (See also **spasmodic / sporadic.**)

contract bridge / auction bridge / duplicate bridge / rubber bridge / honeymoon bridge

These are all varieties of *bridge,* a card game derived from whist. The most common form of the game for social play is *contract bridge,* in which one pair of partners, bidding against an opponent pair in the first part of the game, undertake to win a specific number of tricks (the number they have bid when winning the contract), with the resultant score determined by their relative success or failure. The most common form of the game played in tournaments is *duplicate bridge,* a form of contract bridge in which hands are dealt for each of a number of tables, and teams of players move about among the tables in such a way that each team has played one pair of hands at each table, thus competing among them for the best score played with a given hand; the form of play and scoring are the same as in contract bridge. *Auction bridge,* a variety of the game that has been largely superseded, is similar to contract bridge, differing mainly in the scoring: in contract bridge, tricks taken by the declarer in excess of those contracted for are scored "above the line" and do not count towards game; in auction bridge, such extra tricks are counted towards game. *Rubber bridge* is similar to duplicate bridge except that a fresh hand is dealt for each round and the aim is to be the first to score a rubber, or two games. *Honeymoon bridge* is contract bridge played by two people in which each bids on the cards held, speculating on the cards dealt to the hands opposite which are not seen till a contract is reached.

convergent evolution / divergent evolution

Convergent evolution refers to the coincidental similarity of development in totally unrelated species under environmental influence, as in the wings of insects, bats, and birds or the body shapes of dolphins and fish. *Divergent evolution*, also called *adaptive radiation*, refers to different development owing to environmental influence, as in the adaptive development of the same structure into scales on fish and feathers on birds, and into discrete species of what were once closely related species, as in Darwin's discovery on the Galàpagos of fourteen species of finches, each of which is adapted to exploit a different food source, unlike those on the mainland, where competition for alternative sources is too keen. Recent research has revealed that mutations in the mitochondrial DNA molecule (See **DNA / RNA.**) occur at a rate of from two to four percent every million years, which is five to ten times faster than in nuclear DNA. This has enabled scientists to establish a timetable for the divergence of different species from one original species, as, for example, human beings from apes, the domestic cat from the lion or tiger, and the donkey from the horse. It is within the nuclear DNA molecule that such characteristics as body shape, hair type and color, skin and eye pigmentation, etc., are determined; but nuclear DNA contains several hundred million *restriction sites,* each of which contains from four to six *bases,* and it is thus far more difficult to analyze this molecule than that of the mitochondria, which contain only about sixteen thousand base pairs. All of which is to say that analysis of nuclear DNA has not yet revealed the period required to effect body changes within species.

convergent series / divergent series

In mathematics, a *convergent series* is a numerical series in which the increments between successive terms decreases and its sum approaches a limit as the number of terms increases. For example, in the series $1/2 + 1/4 + 1/8 + 1/16 + \ldots + 1/2n$ the sum approaches a limit of 2 as n approaches infinity; in the series $1/2 + 1/3 + 1/2 + \ldots + 1/n + 1$, the sum approaches 1. In a *divergent series,* the sum has no limit and may oscillate or may approach minus or plus infinity, as, for example, in the series $1 + 2 + 3 + \ldots + n.$

convince / persuade / induce

If one is successful in *persuading* someone to take some course of action or accept a belief or principle, then he has *convinced* the person, and they share the same *conviction* (or *convictions*). Thus, to *persuade* is to 'try to convince, urge, influence, or otherwise make an effort to win another over,' and one could not be said to have *convinced* another till that person has accepted. Both *persuade* and *convince* can be followed by *of*, *to*, or a *that*-clause: *She persuaded me to consider the proposition seriously. They persuaded me that I should resign. I was persuaded of the wisdom of his advice. She was convinced of the need to sleep. He convinced her that his was the only way to do it* (or *of doing it*). *We convinced him to stay.* Into this affray comes *induce*, which, perhaps because it shares the second syllable with *seduce*, perhaps because the noun, *inducement*, carries the meaning of 'reward,' means to 'influence another to a course of thought or action' to which its connotations have added, 'with the anticipation of some gain.'

cooperative / condominium

Although these terms describe different conditions under which people have interest in real property in the United States and Canada, these kinds of ownership have increased in popularity elsewhere. In a *cooperative*, the property in question, usually consisting of more than one dwelling unit, is owned by a corporation, and a buyer purchases shares in the corporation. Technically, the buyer is not purchasing more than those shares and is not entitled to any other rights, but in practice the quantity bought is relative to the value of the apartment, house, or other property in question, which the purchaser (presumably) occupies. Each of the shareholders in a cooperative makes periodic (usually monthly) payments, in proportion to the value of the shares held, to a central fund from which are disbursed expenses for property taxes, charges (as for water, which might not be separately metered), the maintenance of common property, the salaries of the personnel that may be required for service, etc. It is the corporation, not the individual, that owns the property, and there are often restrictions on how many people may live in it, how it may be used (for example, whether it may be occupied by a doctor for professional use), whom it may be sold to, and so on. In a *condominium*, the buyer purchases the property from its owner (just as he would in any property transaction), and he owns the apartment, house, or other property in question. The owners in a condominium unite to form an association to which each makes a periodic (usually monthly) payment to cover expenses for the maintenance of common property, which is owned jointly. Taxes are paid by the individual owner, who receives a deed to the property he has purchased (unlike the cooperative owner, who receives no such document). There are fewer restrictions in general on a condominium owner, as regards, for example, sale of his property; but as a tenant in common of the whole property, he must abide by the regulations that are (democratically) set forth by the association.

copyright / patent

In principle, both these terms refer to the award of a legal monopoly to the originator of a unique and original creation for a specified period of time. A *copyright* is virtually automatic on the registration of a piece of art, writing, music, etc.; entire magazines can be copyrighted, as can individual poems or short stories, stage dramas, television plays, motion pictures, musical compositions (both music and lyrics), paintings, photographs—almost anything that is classifiable as an artistic creation. The governments of major countries maintain copyright offices, which, on submission of application with the required number of copies of a work, issue a certificate acknowledging the date of application; the term of copyright varies from country to country, but most major nations extend new copyrights to the fiftieth year after the death of the creator; governments issue certificates of copyright registration on request, without considering the validity of the applicants' claims to originality. In recent years, most governments have joined in agreements to honor the copyrights, severally, of their citizens. *Patents* are issued by certain governments for the unique application of principle to specific devices or processes. They are not issued automatically, as are copyrights, but undergo rigorous analysis and comparison with existing patents to determine their originality. Patents may cover not only devices and processes but also chemical compounds, unique hybrid plants, and many other categories of invention. In the United States, the Patent Office also issues registration certificates for trade names and trade marks as well as "design patents," which may cover anything from an unusual way of writing or spelling the name of a product to the actual appearance of a car, airplane, railway engine, etc. The governmental agencies that issue patents or copyrights do not undertake to prosecute their infringement: such matters must be undertaken by the copyright or patent holders, in a civil action; the appropriate agency merely serves as a confirmation of the registration date in the event of prior claim.

corporation / partnership

A *corporation* is the name used in the United States for a form of business association established by one or more persons who sell units of ownership (called *shares*) in their enterprise to investors who believe that they will succeed and make profits, which they will later share in. The word *corporation* is known and used in this sense in Britain, but has wider implications, and the term *company* is more commonly employed. A *close, closely held,* or *closed corporation* in the U.S. is one that has a small number of shareholders; in Britain, the term for a similarly constituted business entity is *close company.* The terms *company* and *firm* are used in both countries for any structured business enterprise; in the U.S., however, it is occasionally used to identify a business association that is a *partnership* in contrast to a corporation. In a *partnership* or *proprietorship,* there may be one or more owners who share, in proportion to their agreed equity, in the profits, liabilities, and, in the event of sale, assets of the business. Because the partners in partnerships are personally liable for its debts, etc., such companies are usually small: once they become larger, the owners consider it prudent to limit their personal liability by changing over to a corporation, or limited company. (See also **common stock / ordinary shares / preferred stock / preference shares / A shares.**)

council / counsel

Counsel is 'guidance, advice'; a *counsel,* also called *counselor-at-law,* in the United States is a lawyer, in Britain a *barrister.* (See also **barrister / solicitor.**) A (U.S.) *counselor* (British *counsellor*) is one who gives advice, or counsel; additionally, in the U.S., it is a person who has charge of a group of youngsters or of a particular activity at a summer camp. A *council* is a deliberative body of people assembled for some purpose, usually one that acts in an advisory capacity or with specifically designated authority. Members of a council are (British) *councillors* (U.S. *councilors*).There is an older form of *councilor,* now in disuse, spelled *counsellor;* to avoid even further confusion, it is best avoided.

count noun / mass noun

These are terms in grammar to help to distinguish between different kinds of words used for naming things, the purpose being to be able to describe how they behave grammatically. *Count nouns* are those for physical objects that can be counted, like pictures, people, razor blades, fingers, and so on. *Mass nouns* are those for physical things that are not usually counted, like water, rice, air, steel, and so on. These nouns behave differently: for example, one says *I bought a picture,* but *I bought some rice.* A full discussion of these classes can be found in a grammar. (See also **abstract noun / concrete noun.**)

cranial nerves

There are twelve cranial nerves, recalled by medical students through the memorization of the following mnemonic (or variation thereof), in which, as will be seen, the twelve initials correspond to the initials of the names of the nerves: *On Old Olympus Tiny Tops, A Finn And German Viewed Some Hops.* They are identified by Roman numerals. Their functions may be recalled by the following mnemonic (or variation thereof): *Some Say Marry Money But My Brothers Say Bad Business Marry Money,* a somewhat cryptic, if not inscrutably oriental saying in which the words beginning with *S* indicate sensory functions, those beginning with *M* motor functions, and those beginning with *B* both sensory and motor functions.

I Olfactory	—Smell (Sensory)
II Optic	—Vision (Sensory)
III Oculomotor	—Eye (Motor)
IV Trochlear	—Eye (Motor)
V Trigeminal	—Head and Face; Chewing (Sensory / Motor)
VI Abducens	—Eye (Motor)
VII Facial	—Face and Mouth (Sensory / Motor)
VIII Acoustic	—Balance; Hearing (Sensory)

IX Glossopharyngeal—Tongue; Swallowing; Saliva Secretion;
              Reflex Control of Blood Pressure and
              Respiration (Sensory / Motor)
X Vagus   —Organ Senses and Movements; Slows
              Heart; Increases Peristalsis; Voice
              (Sensory / Motor)
XI Spinal Accessory —Shoulder, Head, Viscera Movements;
              Voice (Motor)
XII Hypoglossal   —Tongue Movements (Motor)

crayfish / shrimp / lobster / krill

All these marine animals are ten-legged (decapod) crustaceans, and all resemble one another physically, having, typically, the front legs modified into a pair of pincers, a shell-like carapace, and long antennae. The smallest, called *krill*, occurs in Antarctic waters in enormous quantities and forms a staple part of the diet of whalebone whales, penguins, and other animals. The *shrimp* is somewhat larger, ranging in length from about an inch to about five inches; in the U.S. this larger shrimp is sometimes called *crayfish, crawfish,* or *crawdaddy* (dialectal variants), or, in Europe, by the French name, *langoustine.* The *lobster* is the largest and may reach a length of 18 inches and a weight of 15 pounds; a smaller variety, called the *spiny lobster,* is much prized in Europe, where it is often called by its French name, *langouste,* not to be confused with *langoustine.*

criticism / critique / review

A *criticism* is an evaluation or judgment of something, usually a work of art or literature. *Critique* is a somewhat elevated term for the same thing, though it is often used to refer to the piece of writing itself that expresses the criticism. *Review* is used interchangeably with both these words, but it may also imply a rather more comprehensive study of the category of writing, painting, music, or performance that is the subject under discussion. Although neither *criticism* nor *critique* necessarily implies unfavorable or adverse comment, it is often construed as such, while *review* carries no such connotation and is neutral. That is especially true of the verb *criticize,* which is usually taken to mean 'comment on adversely; find fault with.' A *critic,* who writes criticism, is understood to view things either neutrally or unfavorably, depending on the context. *Reviewer,* on the other hand, is considered a neutral term.

cromlech / dolmen / menhir

These terms for ancient stone assemblages, some of them of gargantuan proportions, have separate origins. *Cromlech,* from two Welsh words meaning 'bent or curved stone,' usually refers to the kind of arrangement seen at Stonehenge, that is, a circular pattern of stones stuck vertically into the ground. *Dolmen,* returned from a sojourn in French whither it went from the original Cornish form *tolmen,* is the name given to a flat stone resting horizontally on three or more vertical supporting stones; it is said to have been a tomb. *Menhir,* traced to two Breton words meaning 'long stone,' is the term used for any upright stone, whether standing alone or used in combination, as in a dolmen. The true purpose of these constructions can only be guessed at; because of their orientation with respect to the positions of the sun at various times of the year, they are generally thought to have some religious and agricultural significance.

crow / raven / rook / jackdaw

All these birds are really crows, in that *crow* is the term for any bird of the genus *Corvus,* family *Corvidae,* and all have black or mostly black plumage and a yellow beak. *Rooks* inhabit Eurasia and are not known in North America. *Ravens* are known on all continents; a famous colony of six ravens lives at the Tower of London. *Jackdaws* are Eurasian. Although they also eat carrion, because of their voracious appetite for seeds, all crows are pests to farmers, who have been putting out scarecrows probably since the beginning of agriculture.

crystal / glass

Properly, *crystal,* also called *rock crystal,* is the name given to a clear form of crystallized quartz found as such in nature. It is used for ornamental pieces and, especially, cut into spherical shape, in magic and fortune-telling, when it is called a *crystal ball.* This application has yielded the expression *crystal-gazing* 'looking into the future,' which is what fortune-tellers purport to do. Certain forms of *glass* occur in nature, but it is almost entirely a manufactured substance—classified as a fluid—made from silica and silicates and other additives to produce desired characteristics. In commerce, fine glass, especially when cut or etched, is called crystal; it very rarely consists of real crystallized quartz but is of high quality and contains lead, hence is called *lead crystal*.

cuckold / wittold

A *cuckold* is a man whose wife carries on sexual relations with another, without implication that it is with or without his knowledge; although it is generally assumed that the other is also a man, that is not necessarily inherent in the meaning of the word. A *wittold* is a cuckold who knows that his wife is being unfaithful (though not, necessarily, with whom).

cum dividend / ex dividend

These terms refer to the status of a dividend payment to shareholders of a company, usually with respect to whether or not a prospective purchaser of shares will receive the dividend in question. Dividends are declared by companies as payable to shareholders of record on a certain date. *Cum dividend* means that the purchaser will receive it; *ex dividend* that he will not. The price of the shares usually reflects whether the current dividend has been missed or not.

cum laude / magna cum laude / summa cum laude

In the U.S. college and university system, these terms designate the relative academic standing of a graduate upon completion of (usually) four years of study for a baccalaureate degree, and they appear on the diploma. *Summa cum laude* is Latin for 'with highest praise,' *magna cum laude* for 'with great praise,' and *cum laude* 'with praise.' Depending on the institution granting the degree, the percentage of the graduating class given any of these honors varies, but in no event is the aggregate of all three levels likely to exceed a small number of the candidates.

cyclone / hurricane / tornado / typhoon

Depending on where they occur, storms and stormy winds have been named by the people whom they affect. Travelers for centuries have brought back to English-speaking countries these names, more or less corrupted from their original languages. English contains a number of synonyms and some that are near-synonyms, depending on the area where the term is used. Meteorologists recognize the phenomenon of *cyclonic activity*, which is the name given to a circular movement of air on a large scale with lower pressures at its center than at its perimeter. Virtually all weather systems are the result of such activity, which (looking down from outer space) are counterclockwise in the Northern Hemisphere and clockwise in the Southern. As the pressure difference between the center and the perimeter becomes greater, the air rotates faster and faster, and the system becomes a storm. Generally called a *cyclone*, such a storm is given various names, depending on the part of the world where it occurs. In the Atlantic, it is called a *hurricane;* in the Far East, a *typhoon;* in the Philippines, a *baguio;* along the Pacific coast of Central America, a *cordonazo;* in Australia, a *willy-willy* (not to be confused with a *williwaw* 'violent squall'); in the midwestern United States, a *tornado.* Such a storm, if over water, may create a *waterspout.* Hurricanes are not officially designated as such by the meteorological offices in the United States till their winds reach a velocity of 73 mph, a little below the 75 mph figure into which the Beaufort Scale designation of "above 65 knots" would translate. Such designations may seem arbitrary and without purpose, but they become important because coverage provided by insurance companies often depends on the official description of a storm. (See also **breeze / gale / storm / hurricane.**)

Cynic / Stoic

Because their resultant behavior was similar, the *Cynics* and *Stoics* are sometimes confused. But their philosophies are different. The Cynics, a Greek philosophical school of the 4th century B.C., held that the only good in the world is virtue, the essence of which is self-control, and that yielding to any mundane influences is beneath the dignity of man. The Stoics, who came a generation later, under the influence of the philosopher Zeno (of Citium), believed that man should accept whatever necessities may come along and submit to them without passion or emotion. Today, when we use the term *cyni-*

cal in referring to a person's attitude, we usually mean that he regards others as insincere and driven by motives of self-interest or gain. The *Cynics* were so called by the Greeks after *kyon* 'dog'—in other words, they were even then criticized for their "dog-in-the-manger" attitudes. In modern usage, being *stoical* (or, less commonly, *stoic*) means accepting whatever may come as one's fate, about which nothing can or should be done, with calmness and without feeling (or, at least, without exhibiting any emotion).

dado / wainscot

In general use, as applied to the paneling of an interior wall, these terms are often interchanged; in technical use, however, *dado* is taken to refer to wooden paneling or other decoration only on the lower part of a wall, *wainscot* (or *wainscoting*) to wooden paneling that covers all or nearly all of the wall. In Britain, wainscot is also used for a fine grade of oak. *Dado* is said to come from Italian, where it designates a part of the base of a column, a use carried over into English; the exact origin of *wainscot* is uncertain, but probably comes from *wain* 'wagon' + (Old English) *scot* 'a partition or other part.'

dagger / asterisk / slash

These are terms for typographic symbols that have a variety of uses in printed works, often to mark references to footnotes. As the name suggests, the *asterisk* is a small starlike symbol, printed in superior position—that is, at the top of the line of type on which it belongs—and at the right end of a word, in order to draw attention to some comment about the word or idea it expresses, the comment, also marked at the beginning with an asterisk, being at the foot of the page, at the end of an article, or at the end of a chapter of a book, etc. Asterisks are sometimes put to other uses: a few of them, spaced across a printed page, may indicate a break of some sort; in linguistics, the placement of an asterisk at the beginning of a word may conventionally mark it as a hypothetical form, that is, one for which there is no evidence. In 19th-century typesetting (in particular), in order to draw attention to certain information or to identify it in a special way, typographers preceded it by three asterisks in a triangular pattern (base either up or down), which was called an *asterism*. The *dagger* and *double-dagger*, the latter resembling a dagger with two cross guards (like a cross of Lorraine), are used in a manner similar to the asterisk and are similarly placed, though not in superior position: in situations where two or more footnotes occur on a page, the first is usually marked by an asterisk, the second by a dagger, the third by a double-dagger; if more than three are required, two asterisks might be used, but, because that becomes typographically cumbersome, the use of superior numbers is usually resorted to. The formal name for the dagger is *obelisk*. The *slash*, the formal name of which is *virgule* or *solidus*, is used variously to indicate a choice between two or among three or more alternatives by appropriate placement between each succeeding pair; it occurs typically in the legalistic expression "and / or." As used in this book, the virgule might go under its other name, *separatrix*, which is the name applied to the diagonal line written between the text and the marginal corrections in proofreading.

data / datum

In Latin, from which the word was borrowed, *data* is the plural of *datum*. Curiously, the only evidence found in Latin for the use of the word as a noun occurs in contexts where it means 'debt'; in Latin, *datum* is a form of the past participle of *dare* 'to give,' and it meant 'given,' probably in much the same way that "a given (fact)" is used in English. It was borrowed in the 17th century in that sense but has evolved, mainly in its plural form, to mean a 'set of facts,' usually referring to a verifiable collection of figures, as one would encounter in statistics. In recent years, contaminated by the usage of computer specialists, it has come to be almost synonymous with *information*, as in *data processing*, originally the manipulation (by computer) of numbers, latterly of any kind of information. *Datum*, however, has remained a technical term that is used in surveying for a 'reference point' and in philosophy in a similar sense; it is not used in general language as a singular of *data*. Inevitably, the question arises whether *data*, which is formally a plural, can be properly used with a singular verb and a singular pronoun of reference: the answer is that it can (and is, probably more frequently than with a plural). Outside the realm of scholarly, scientific, and pedantic usage, the use of *data* as a plural sounds very awkward; normal usage is singular: *Please study this data and, when you have finished, take it back to the library.* In scientific writing and, occasionally, speech, *data* can be a plural: *These data show that victims of crime have frequent nightmares.* In casual use, it is used in the same way as the word *information: The data on the election has not yet come in.*

deciduous / evergreen / permanent

Deciduous plants are those that shed all of their leaves at the end of their growing season; *evergreen* plants are those that appear to retain their leaves (or, as they are called on conifers, needles) permanently but, in fact, shed some of them periodically, usually after two or three years. *Deciduous teeth* are those 20 "baby teeth" that are later replaced by the 32 *permanent teeth* in adulthood (often later replaced by dentures).

decry / descry

These words do not have similar meanings in contemporary English. *Decry* means to 'deprecate; express disapproval of openly; denounce': *The parents decried physical punishment in schools. Descry* means to 'catch sight of; see, especially from a distance': *Over the horizon we descried a huge galleon sailing in our direction.* Neither word is among those used with great frequency and both are best kept for literary applications.

definiens / definiendum

The *definiendum* (plural, *definienda*) is a term to be defined. The *definiens* (plural, *definientia*) is the definition given for a term. Thus, in a dictionary entry, the word or phrase appearing (usually) in bold-face type at the beginning is called the *definiendum,* the words used in the definition constitute the *definiens.* Both terms are borrowed from Aristotelian logic.

demi- / hemi- / semi-

These prefixes have the same meaning in English, though they are of different origins: *hemi-* 'half' comes from Greek; *semi-* 'half' comes from Latin. *Demi-* 'half' also comes from the Latin, from *dimidius* 'cut in half,' made up of *dis-* 'apart' + *medium* 'middle.' They all appear together in *hemidemisemiquaver,* a (chiefly) British term for a sixty-fourth note. The distributions of these prefixes differ in English, *demi-* appearing in the smallest number of words, many of French origin (*demibastion, demicannon, demiculverin, demilune, demimonde,* etc.); *hemi-* is used mainly in technical words (*hemianopsia, hemicrania, hemiplagia, hemizygote,* etc.) but also in the common word *hemisphere; semi-* is by far the most popular and productive of the three in English, yielding scores of words (*semiannually, semimonthly, semiweekly, semiautomatic, semiconscious, semicircle,* etc.). Another prefix, *sesqui-* 'half again, one and a half times,' has also been borrowed from Latin, mainly for use in describing anniversaries as *sesquicentennial* '150th.'

deodorant / antiperspirant

A *deodorant* is a cosmetic chemical sold in a dispenser for application, usually to the underarms, for neutralizing or masking body odors with any of a variety of scents. An *antiperspirant* is a cosmetic chemical intended to inhibit perspiration; it also contains substances that neutralize body odors or mask them with a scent.

depository / repository

In many contexts, these words are used interchangeably: both mean a 'place where something is put for safekeeping.' There are, however, some specialized senses where they are not idiomatically interchangeable. The safe box in a bank where one might place deposits after hours is invariably called a (*night*) *depository;* a sepulcher is invariably called a *repository. Depository* has a variant spelling, *depositary,* which is the preferred form used in referring to a person acting as a trustee (with whom important documents and responsibilities are deposited), though *depository* also appears in this context. *Repository* is also used in this sense of a 'trustee.' In Britain, both *depository* (or *depositary*) and *repository* are used to denote a warehouse.

deprecate / depreciate

Because *appreciate* is such a common word in the language and *depreciate* is a readily available antonym for it, the latter has exhibited a tendency to replace *deprecate,* even though they do not mean the same thing. *Depreciate* means to 'devalue, minimize the value of' and is most frequently heard in the context of finance: *The depreciating dollar has made travel abroad more expensive for Americans. Deprecate* means to 'disapprove of, object to': *She treated me in the most deprecating way.* As both words carry the sense of 'belittle, diminish,' it is easy to see how they have become confused, and it appears unlikely that they will ever again be unraveled, with *depreciate* coming to the fore.

descriptive modifier / restrictive modifier

In grammar, a *nonrestrictive* or *descriptive modifier* (usually in the form of a clause) merely describes the word it modifies, while a *restrictive* or *determinative modifier* limits the information it contains to the specific subject. In accordance with accepted practice for good style, nonrestrictive modifiers are usually set off from the word or words modified by commas, and restrictive modifiers are not. The easiest way to show the distinction is by examples:

NONRESTRICTIVE MODIFIER:

My brother, who joined the Navy, was rarely home.

RESTRICTIVE MODIFIER:

My brother who joined the Navy was rarely home.

In the first of these, the information "who joined the Navy," is incidental to the information "My brother was rarely home"; in the second, "who joined the Navy" is being used to distinguish the brother in question from any other brother the speaker might have—those who joined the Army, the Foreign Legion, the Rotary Club, or those who might just have frequented the local pub.

NONRESTRICTIVE MODIFIER:

All of the councilmen, who were present, voted for me.

RESTRICTIVE MODIFIER:

All of the councilmen who were present voted for me.

The distinction should be clear in these sentences: the first suggests that all of the councilmen were present and that all of them voted for "me"; the second suggests that some councilmen were absent, but that all who did attend voted for "me." As can be seen, the nonrestrictive modifier adds nonessential information, while the restrictive modifier identifies the condition under which the predication of the sentence is true. Those who insist on the difference between the usages of

which and *that* believe that the former should be reserved to introduce nonrestrictive clauses, the latter restrictive clauses:

NONRESTRICTIVE:

The house, which is white, is mine.

RESTRICTIVE:

The house that is white is mine.

Although this distinction might be observed by the best writers and
speakers and by others who do so out of habit, it is seldom maintained by most users of the language, who are largely unaware of it.

diagnosis / prognosis

The Greek verb (*gi*)*gnoskein* means 'to know.' It was used in Classical
Greek for compounding, and one of the compounds was the noun
diagnosis (from *diagignoskein* meaning 'to distinguish, identify'). English
borrowed *diagnosis* and retained the essential sense; it is used generally but occurs most often in medical contexts, in reference to identifying a disease. *Prognosis* has a similar history, but its meaning is
'foreknowledge'; it is used mainly in medical contexts in the sense of a
'prediction of the course of a disease,' especially with overtones of the
chances of a patient's future condition or even his survival. Thus, *diagnosis* refers to the identification of a disease, *prognosis* to the likely
future course of the disease and the patient's reactions to it. The verb
for the former is *diagnose;* for the latter it is *prognosticate,* which,
oddly enough, is more often encountered in general language with
the meaning 'prophesy' than in medical contexts.

dialectal / dialectic

Although these words are sometimes interchanged, on a formal level
they have completely different meanings: *dialectal,* with the variants
dialectical and, sometimes, *dialectic,* means 'referring to dialect'; *dialectic,* which is also used as a noun, is a term in philosophy meaning
'relating to the art or practice of logical argument' or, as a noun, 'the
art or practice of logical argument itself.' (There are other technical
senses that pertain to the way the word is used by specific
philosophers.)

diandrous / monandrous / polyandrous

The root *-androus* means 'male'; applied in botany, it refers specifically to the male organ of a plant, the filament and anther, which bear the pollen by which plants fertilize. *Monandrous* describes a plant having one anther, *diandrous* one with two, and *polyandrous* one with an indefinitely larger number. *Monandrous* and *polyandrous* are also used in another context: a woman who has had one husband is said to be *monandrous*, while one who has had many is characterized as *polyandrous*. There is no evidence available to sustain a sense of 'a woman who has had two husbands' for *diandrous*.

diastole / systole

The muscles of the heart contract and relax, alternately, to pump blood through the system. The contraction is called *systole*, the relaxed period between contractions, *diastole*. At systole, the normal blood pressure of a healthy young adult is 120 mm of mercury; at diastole, it is 70 mm. Systolic pressures generally increase with age because of a loss in the elasticity of the blood vessels. The entire circulatory system has a measurable blood pressure, and the pressures usually taken are those at the large arteries. The pressure of the pulse is about 50 mm.

dictionary / encyclopedia

Those who are involved in the preparation, publication, and use of reference books find it convenient to distinguish these terms on a relatively superficial level: a *dictionary* is a book containing, usually in alphabetical order, information about words or words and phrases, either of a general or specialized nature. Thus, we talk about general dictionaries (which contain many words and their definitions) and about specialized dictionaries (which contain words dealing with the vocabulary of a particular field, like chemistry, astronomy, etc.). *Encyclopedias* are reference books, either general or specialized as to subject matter, in which people, places, objects, and ideas are explained at some length, more often than not in such a way as to give the reader some understanding of the subject of the entry by considering it as an element in a skein of information. Among professionals who compile reference books, especially dictionaries, the distinction is sometimes made between *dictionary* and *encyclopedic* definitions: the former are said to be briefer and denotative, the latter somewhat lengthier and usually couched in larger conceptual frames. Thus, the dictionary definition of, say, *horticulture,* would merely define what the *word* means, while the encyclopedic definition would consist of an article on the *subject* of horticulture. Both dictionaries and encyclopedias may be general or specialized. (See also **dictionary / glossary / lexicon / thesaurus.**)

dictionary / glossary / lexicon / thesaurus

In their most general applications, *dictionary, glossary,* and *lexicon* refer to a list of words, or phrases, or both, usually in alphabetical order, followed by (at least) their definitions. *Dictionary* is often reserved for the more comprehensive kind of word book, one that provides entry words separated into syllables in order to show where they can be hyphenated (and, sometimes, as an aid to pronunciation), pronunciations (especially in English dictionaries, usually shown in a pattern of symbols for the sounds of the language in order to avoid ambiguities created by spelling), identification of part of speech, and definitions of the one or more senses of the words as they are used in the language. More elaborate works may also label definitions as to subject field, dialect, or language level; in addition, illustrations of the word in use may be included, either contrived by the editors or in the form of actual citations from published works; synonyms and, in some instances, antonyms may be listed for given senses; usage comments may also be added for selected entries; depending on its size, purpose, and degree of completeness, a dictionary may also contain more or less elaborate etymologies as well as other kinds of linguistic information. Some dictionaries contains pictorial illustrations. *Lexicon* is little more than a formal word for *dictionary. Glossary* usually describes a dictionary in a specialized subject area, consisting only of entry and definition; glossaries are often found in books dealing with subjects that are not well documented, the vocabularies of which have not been published in dictionaries of general application; in many cases, glossaries are used to define jargon or terms of art in narrow fields, especially when it is likely that the book in which they are included may be read by people unfamiliar with the subject. *Thesaurus* means, literally, 'treasury,' but it has come to be used to describe reference works arranged by thematic category; the word was first used by Peter Mark Roget (1779–1869) in the title of his work (1852) on English synonyms (and antonyms), which was arranged in several hundred categories that reflected the author's view of the hierarchical, philosophical structure of the universe of human thought. Today, although *thesaurus* is still used in that way and, particularly, in reference to succeeding editions of Roget's work, it is also used in information theory, in *thesaurus of descriptors* to describe a thematic index for use in accessing structured data stored in a computer. (See also **dictionary / encyclopedia.**)

diesel engine / gasoline engine

These are the two main kinds of internal combustion engines. In a *gasoline engine,* under the control of a carburetor and a system of valves, vaporized fuel is sprayed into two or more cylinders where it is ignited by an electric spark (from spark plugs) under the control of a distributor; when the gasoline vapor explodes successively in the cylinders, pistons are driven out of the cylinders and, connected to a crankshaft, cause it to turn, creating power which is transmitted to wheels, propellers, gears, or other machinery for doing work. In some gasoline engines, the carburetor has been replaced by a fuel injection device and the distributor by an electronic system, but the principle is the same. In a *diesel engine,* a less volatile fuel than gasoline is injected into the cylinders where it is subjected to enormous pressure; the heat generated by the compression causes the fuel to ignite, exploding and causing pistons to turn a crankshaft; the diesel engine has no spark plugs, and starting it requires a powerful electric motor and, often, electric coils for preheating the fuel. In a *diesel-electric engine,* used mainly in railway locomotives, a diesel engine is used for driving an electric motor, which imparts power to the drive wheels.

different from / different to / different than

Virtually all of the usage books published in the United States insist that *different from* is good and proper English and that *different than* is not. Because few there say *different to,* that issue seldom arises. In Britain, on the other hand, the more common form is *different to.* The form *different than,* which would be acceptable in contexts like *Her spike hairdo is more different than yours* (*because it is tinted purple and green*), is frowned on by critics in the U.S. more than in Britain when used in place of *different from* or *different to* in contexts like *Our problems are different to* (or *from*) *theirs.*

dilatation / dilation

These are variants of one another, *dilatation* being generally preferred to *dilation* if only because it is the older, better established form. Both are noun forms of the verb *dilate* 'expand or cause to expand' and are used in various medical and engineering senses. *Dilation* is a modern coinage, made from *dilate* + the noun-forming suffix *-ion; dilatation,* which goes back to Latin, arrived in English via Old French and Middle English.

dioecious / monoecious

Used chiefly of plants, *dioecious* describes those in which male and female organs (*stamens* and *pistils,* respectively) occur in separate individuals, as in willows and poplars, which produce what are called *imperfect flowers;* flowers with pistils but no stamens are called *pistillate,* those with stamens but no pistils, *staminate. Monoecious* describes those that have both male and female organs on the same individual, as in oaks and squashes, which produce what are called *perfect flowers.* Another term for *dioecious* is *diclinous;* another term for *monoecious* is *monoclinous.*

diphthong / triphthong / monophthong

A *diphthong* is a complex vowel sound that can be analyzed into two major sets of sound characteristics, like that of *cow, file, low, boil,* or *cane;* in English spelling, it may be represented as one character (as in *file* and *so*) or as two or more (as in *sow, sew, though, beau,* etc.). In some contexts, consonantal clusters like the *ch* of *church,* the *sh* of *show,* etc., are included. A *monophthong* is a single vowel sound, like that of *hat, calm, pen, pin, lean, fall, good, food,* or the pronunciation of the vowel in *the* when in unstressed position; English spelling being what it is, the representation in writing might be almost anything. In some contexts, consonants like the *b* of *boy,* the *g* of *girl,* etc., are included. It is worth noting that *diphthong* and *monophthong* derive from the Greek *phthong(os)* 'sound, voice' preceded by the common prefixes *di-* 'two' and *mono-* 'one,' which might help in remembering their spelling. A third term, *triphthong,* refers to a complex vowel sound analyzable into three components; such sounds are not common but may be described as that heard in certain pronunciations of *our* in which the *-r* is not pronounced (as in Southern British speech and in that of certain southern and northern dialects in the U.S.). The terms *monophthong, diphthong,* and *triphthong* are occasionally used to describe one, two, or three written characters (and not, necessarily, vowels), but this usage is frowned on by those who would keep the meanings "pure." The preferred terms for written symbols are *digraph* and *trigraph,* the former referring to a sound (diphthong or triphthong) written as two characters, as in, respectively, *boil, good, tool,* etc., and *beau, quay, buoy,* etc. Technically, the *-ough-* of *thought* would perhaps constitute a *"tetragraph,"* but the term is unrecorded. *Digraph* is also used, in printing, to designate two characters sometimes (especially formerly) designed as single pieces of type, for example, æ, œ, etc.

direct mail / mail order / telemarketing

These are popular methods for selling in many parts of the Western world. *Direct mail* is a method by which a business or charity sends a catalogue or other promotional material to a fairly large list of prospective purchasers, who order the wares offered or make a donation by mail or by telephone, paying either by cheque or by charge to a credit card. *Mail order* refers to any business conducted largely or entirely through the mails, often by companies that maintain no retail shops, and usually designates advertising in periodicals soliciting orders which can be obtained by mail or, in recent years, by telephone. *Telemarketing* describes the relatively new practice of telephoning large numbers of potential customers to solicit orders for merchandise or services; in some instances, telemarketing employs not only automatic dialing of prospects' numbers by computer but a recorded solicitation, as well. (See also **hard sell / soft sell.**)

discover / invent

One *discovers*—that is, 'uncovers'—something that is already there, something that has existed but is generally unknown. A chemical element, a planet or star, a creature long thought extinct are discovered. One *invents* things that have never before existed: the transistor, the

wheel, the screw. An invention is a unique application of known principles and, according to the laws of countries where inventions can be
patented, must be embodied in a specific device—that is, ideas cannot
be patented, only devices or processes. (See also **copyright /
patent.**)

discreet / discrete

Because these words are pronounced identically, their spelling is
sometimes confused, and the confusion is not relieved by the fact that
they both come from the same Latin word and have both been in the
language since Middle English times (12th–15th centuries). *Discreet*
means 'prudent; careful in exercising judgment; tactful' and is frequently used to refer to keeping quiet information that is private,
secret, or for some reason best not revealed: *You don't have to worry
about her telling anyone, for she is very discreet.* The nouns it has
yielded are *discretion* 'judgment' and *indiscretion* 'lack of judgment;
action or behavior that demonstrates a lack of judgment; error in
common sense; peccadillo or minor transgression': *She would make a
good diplomat—she is the soul of discretion. Jacquelyn forgives her husband his many indiscretions. Discrete* means 'separate; distinct': *History
must be regarded as an integrated continuum of cause and effect, not as
a sequence of discrete events. The psychology of the mob is different
from the psychology of discrete individuals.* If a noun is needed for
discrete, it is *discreteness*, not often met with.

disinterested / uninterested

These two words have very convenient differences. *Disinterested*
means 'without personal prejudice or bias'; thus, it is proper for a
judge to be disinterested, for a person in that position should not be
making decisions that are influenced by personal gain or motive.
Uninterested means 'not interested; bored'; someone who is uninterested in the outcome of an event simply does not care how it turns out.
One can be both uninterested and disinterested: for instance, a tennis
umpire who is disinterested (as he should be) may also be bored
(which he should not be).

distaff side / spear side

These old-fashioned terms, which occasionally reappear in contemporary writing, refer to the female side (*distaff side*) or the male side (*spear side*) of a family. A *distaff* is a stick with a cleft end, used for holding the yarn when spinning flax, wool, etc., strictly woman's work when the terms were coined.

distraught / distrait

These words are close in the sense that both refer to states of mind. But *distrait* is still felt to be a French loanword, both because of its pronunciation, "di-STRAY," and because it follows the French grammatical rule of changing its pronunciation (and spelling) when referring to a female: it becomes *distraite*, pronounced "di-STRET." Thus, it is less common than the somewhat better assimilated *distraught*, pronounced "di-STRAWT." *Distrait / distraite* means 'absent-minded, especially as a result of worries, apprehension, and the like'; *distraught* means 'bewildered; distracted; agitated.' The effect of the words is so close that an effort to maintain a precise distinction would be pedantic.

distrust / mistrust

For all practical purposes, there is no semantic or grammatical difference between *mistrust* and *distrust*, although some would argue that the prefix *dis-* has merely a negative meaning while *mis-* carries the sense of 'wrong.' Thus, *distrust* would carry a sense like 'not to trust' and *mistrust* the sense 'wrong to trust.' Because *mis-* also has a plainly negative meaning in many words, such a distinction is spurious.

DNA / RNA

DNA, the abbreviation for *deoxyribonucleic acid*, is a complex molecule, the prime constituent of chromosomes, that controls the hereditary characteristics and the synthesis of proteins within the cells of virtually all living creatures. In form, it is described as a "double helix," or a structure of two ribbonlike spirals side by side with ladderlike "rungs" between them: the spirals are *nucleotides*, organic compounds containing nitrogen (*purine* or *pyrimidine*) that are linked to a sugar, in this case the sugar *deoxyribose;* the "rungs," which are called *bases*, are made up of the nucleotides *adenine, cytosine, guanine,* and *thymine* bonded together by hydrogen. Present in the chromosomes inside the nucleus of each cell, DNA replicates itself when the cell divides: the strands unwind when the hydrogen bonds break, and the two new DNA molecules are completely reconstructed, exact duplicates of the original. Within the cell are bacterial enzymes, called *restriction enzymes*, the function of which is to destroy or inhibit any foreign DNA that might invade the cell; they accomplish this by identifying a *restriction site*, or sequence of four to six bases, and splitting the DNA molecule at these points. Each such enzyme is specialized to identify a unique pattern of bases, and more than two hundred have so far been identified. DNA molecules that reside within the cell nucleus are designated *nuclear DNA*; those that reside within the cell but outside the nucleus, in the cytoplasm, are designated *mitochondrial DNA*. There is evidence that there are about sixteen thousand base pairs of mitochondrial DNA and several hundred million base pairs of nuclear DNA. To compare molecules of DNA from different sources or species, the strands are unwound, with their bases, and single strands from each source are placed together; those that form bonds establish similarities between the two, those that do not confirm distinctions. Because mitochondrial DNA is inherited only from the mother, possibly because only the nucleus of the sperm enters the egg in fertilization, the rest being destroyed, mitochondrial DNA cannot be changed by a sexual recombination of genes from each parent. For this reason, though the nuclear DNA of an individual is different from that of its parents, the only change that can be made in mitochondrial DNA is effected by mutation, which is estimated to occur at the rate of from two to four percent every million years. In the technology known as *genetic engineering*, new strains have been produced by artificially combining characteristic bases from different DNA molecules to create a new molecule, called *recombinant DNA*. *RNA*, or *ribonucleic acid*, is a complex nucleic acid present in cells and involved in the synthesis of protein. The RNA molecule resembles a chain of nucleotides with *ribose* as the sugar, to which are bonded the same bases as in DNA except that *uracil* replaces *thymine*. Various RNA molecules have been identified as to their function: *messenger RNA* (*mRNA*), which transmits the genetic code of the DNA molecule to *ribosomes*, specialized areas in the cell; within the ribosome, *ribosomal RNA* (*rRNA*) synthesizes protein and *transfer RNA* (*tRNA*) controls the structuring of amino acids in the synthesis of protein chains. (See also **convergent evolution** / **divergent evolution.**)

dock / *pier* / *wharf* / *jetty* / *quay* / *mole*

These terms denote various structures associated with facilities for boats or ships. *Wharf* and *pier* are variant names for the same thing, a 'long, fixed structure of wood or concrete that is fixed to the shore and projects into a body of water so as to allow vessels to come alongside for loading, unloading, and so forth.' Usually, a wharf is built with its longer sides parallel to the shore, allowing vessels access to only one side. *Quay* (pronounced "KEY") is another word for the same structure, especially if it is built of stone or concrete. A *jetty*, or *mole*, is a '(usually) massive construction of stone or other immovable material that projects from the shore into the water to serve as a barrier for the protection of a harbor or to change currents so as to affect the deposit of sand along beaches'; sometimes, concrete cal-trops are used; sometimes an enclosure of wooden bulkheading is built to be filled with boulders, rocks, etc. Some insist that the word *dock* be reserved for the watery space between wharves, quays, or piers, that is, the area occupied by a vessel. But usage shows that it is also used to refer to the wharves, quays, or piers themselves, hence is ambiguous. Yacht clubs and marinas for private yachts in parts of the world where the tidal differences are relatively great—about three feet or more—often offer the convenience of what may be properly called *floating wharves* or *piers*, but are universally known as *floating docks*.

dominant / *recessive*

In genetics, of a pair of alleles present in the cells of a heterozygous organism, the one that functions is said to be *dominant*, the other, *recessive*. For example, in human beings in which both genes occur, the allele controlling brown eye color is dominant, that controlling blue is recessive.

donor / *recipient*

In blood transfusions and organ transplants, the person who donates

the blood or organ is the *donor,* the one who receives it is the
recipient.

dot-matrix printer / ink-jet printer / daisy-wheel printer / laser printer / chain printer

These are the main types of printers used for creating graphic images
of the data within a computer. The *dot-matrix printer* has a printing
head that consists of the ends of a number of tiny stiff wires
arranged in a rectangular pattern, usually nine rows of five wires
each; the code for a given character in the computer is translated in
the printer into a code that causes the appropriate wires in the print
head to move forward and then strike an inked ribbon which prints
on the paper the image of the desired character, essentially made up
of a pattern of dots set close together. In an *ink-jet printer,* a number
of fine nozzles is actuated by the coded signal to squirt ink onto
paper in the desired pattern. The *daisy-wheel printer* has a disk with
radiating, fingerlike flexible type bars each with one or more characters at the outer end; when actuated by the appropriate code, the
disk turns, bringing the proper type bar into a position before the
inked ribbon so that a hammerlike device can tap it, causing the
image to be transferred to the paper. In a *laser printer,* the paper is
dusted with a powdery ink and the image codes of characters are
projected onto it by a laser, which causes the ink to fuse to the paper,
reproducing the images. In a *chain printer,* a continuous chain, made
up of links that consist of raised type characters, is passed before an
inked ribbon; the computer formats the data in such a way that the
position of each character in each line is predetermined; as the type
character in the chain reaches its proper position in the line, a hammerlike device, situated behind each of the (96 or 132) possible positions, strikes the piece of type causing it to strike the ribbon and
transfer the image to the paper. Earlier printers driven by computers
consisted of (96 or 132) disks set side by side, each with all of the
characters to be printed in raised form on its periphery, each disk
positioned to print a character in one position along a line. As the
codes for the characters and their positions were actuated, the disks
spun to bring the desired characters into position and, when all were
in line, the images were transferred to paper through a ribbon.
Advances in such devices have led to printers that can produce huge
amounts of printed matter in a very short time at some sacrifice of

quality or, conversely, at somewhat slower speeds, reproduction of sufficient graphic-arts quality to permit the preparation of text and illustrations for publication.

doublet / cognate

In linguistics, a *doublet* is a pair of words in the same language that ultimately come from the same source but have different meanings or distributions. For example, *coy,* which comes via Old French, and *quiet,* which comes via Middle English, both derive from the original Latin word *quietus,* the past participle of *quiescere* 'to be quiet.' Although *doublet* implies a 'pair,' doublets can occur in threes: English *dais, dish,* and *disk* (or *disc*), or *discus* are all traceable ultimately to Latin *discus; dais* arrived in Middle English via Old French, *dish* in Middle English via Old English, and *disc* or *disk* and *discus* directly from Latin. The term *cognate* is usually reserved for two or more words in different languages that share a common ancestor, as English *foot,* Latin *ped-,* Greek *poud-,* French *pied,* Italian *piède,* German *Fuß* or English *father,* Latin *pater,* Greek *pater,* Spanish and Italian *padre,* French *père,* German *Vater.*

downbeat / upbeat

In music, the *downbeat* is an accented beat or the first beat of a measure, so marked by the downward stroke of the conductor's arm; the *upbeat* is the unaccented beat, usually occurring just before the downbeat. The metaphors *downbeat* 'discouraging, depressing; dejected, sad' and *upbeat* 'happy, cheerful, optimistic; encouraging' are often used in informal contexts; although they might have been reinforced by their currency in music, they were probably not borrowed from music specifically, for *down* and *up* are common enough words for 'unhappy' and 'happy' in many other contexts in the language.

dramatic poetry / epic poetry / lyric poetry

These occasionally prove to be convenient descriptive terms for different forms of poetic expression, though they are by no means exclusive or universally adopted as categories by critics and commentators. *Dramatic poetry,* in general, is that which relates a story; it may be exemplified by Robert Browning's "My Last Duchess" and "Pippa Passes" or by Samuel Taylor Coleridge's "The Rime of the Ancient Mariner." *Epic poetry,* which also tells a story, conforms to rigid models of style and form; it is exemplified, typically, by Homer's *Iliad* and *Odyssey,* and, in Old English, by *Beowulf.* *Lyric poetry* is characterized by an expression of the poet's personal feelings; originally descriptive of songs accompanied by the lyre, it is descriptive of the emotional romantic poets' works, especially those of John Keats and Percy Bysshe Shelley.

druggist / pharmacist / chemist / apothecary

These terms are here considered in their context of 'one who prepares medical prescriptions.' The common term in the United States is *druggist,* that in Britain, *chemist,* a chemist in the U.S. being a person who is trained in chemistry and usually works in a laboratory doing research. *Pharmacist* is a formal term, known and used in both countries. *Apothecary* is an old-fashioned word for *druggist / chemist* and is also the name of his place of work; druggists work in *drugstores,* chemists in *chemist's shops* or just *chemist's.*

dryad / hamadryad / nereid / oread / psammead

In classical mythology, these are all names of the various nymphs, lovely young female demi-deities who populated the meadows, woodlands, seas, etc., of the ancient world. They are, alas, no longer with us, but at one time the *dryads* inhabited the forests, the *hamadryad* being the spirit of a particular tree; *nereids,* who occupied the sea, were originally among the fifty daughters of the sea god, Nereus; the *oreads,* attendants on the goddess Artemis, enchanted the mountains. There were no *psammeads* in classical mythology: depicted as rather ugly and spiderlike (though friendly), this creature, a sand fairy, was the creation of E. Nesbit, who wrote popular children's books early in the 20th century.

due to / owing to

Examination of books on English usage published in the 19th century reveals consistent cautions against the use of *due to* in place of *owing to* in constructions like, *Due to the rain, the picnic was canceled. I was late due to the fog.* Technically, grammarians analyze *owing to* as a preposition and *due to* as the adjective *due* + *to,* and those commentators on usage remark that this latter construction is to be avoided. The combination *due to,* however, has been well established in the language for centuries, hence the argument is lost on the grounds of age as well as frequency; because *due to* is—at least today—analyzable as a compound preposition (like *owing to, irrespective of, regardless of, consistent with,* and many others), the argument is lost on technical grounds as well. All this aside, the use of *due to* in the sense of 'because of' is today perfectly normal in English, and those usage books that fail or refuse to accept it are simply old-fashioned.

dwarf / midget

A *midget* is a person (of either sex) who is diminutive in stature and well-proportioned; adult midgets may be as little as 30 inches in height. A *dwarf* is a diminutive person, too, but one whose head or other extremities are disproportionately large. Dwarfism is a medical condition brought about by any of a variety of causes, glandular, nutritional, and so forth, and one medical dictionary lists seventeen kinds of dwarf, each kind attributable to another cause. The plural of *dwarf* is either *dwarfs* or *dwarves,* though the former is more frequent.

dynamism / mechanism / organicism / vitalism

Dynamism is the name given to the philosophical theory that everything in the universe functions on the basis of an interplay of forces and energies. It is contrasted with *mechanism,* also called *materialism,* the tenets of which are that all of nature is explainable in terms of the laws of physics and chemistry. Both contrast with *vitalism,* the doctrine that there is a vital principle, called the *élan vital,* inherent in all living organisms and distinct from the physical and chemical functions. And both *mechanism* and *vitalism* contrast, in another dimension, with *organicism,* the theory that organisms are autonomous and that the entire organism, rather than its individual parts, determines vital activities.

each / either / both

The substitution of *either* for *each* or *both* can create unnecessary

ambiguities: *The two guards stand on either side of the king.* Does this
mean 'they stand (together) on one side or the other of the king' or
'one stands on one side and one stands on the other'? The simple
resolution is: *A guard stands on each side of the king* or *The (two)
guards stand on both sides of the king.* Although it is true that in some
contexts only the wildest imagination could discern ambiguity
between *either* and *each* (witness *The playing field has a goal at either
end*), the best policy is to avoid unnecessary ambiguity—there is
already enough opportunity for misunderstanding in the language.
Besides, *The playing field has a goal at each end* is one syllable shorter,
a convincing argument for those who are of an economical bent.
Both, like *either* (and *neither*), can be used to refer to two only; it is
often used for emphasis, where the sense does not require it: *The boy
and girl (both) left the room. I have to work (both) on Sundays and
Mondays.* But: *I am busy both days.* As for their grammar, *each* and
either, being singular, require a singular verb; *both,* always referring
to two, requires a plural verb. (See also **either . . or / neither . .
nor.**)

East Germany / West Germany

These are the everyday names of the two nations which were established by the division of Germany (1949) after the defeat of the Nazi
forces in World War II. The official name of *East Germany,* which
came under the control of the U.S.S.R., is the *German Democratic
Republic.* The official name of *West Germany,* which is an independent
nation, is the *Federal Republic of Germany.*

ebb tide / flood tide / neap tide / spring

Tides on earth are caused by the gravitational attraction of the moon
and the sun; because the moon is closer, it has a somewhat greater
effect. Therefore, the tides are governed by the position of the moon,
and there are two *high,* or *flood tides* and two *low,* or *ebb tides* each
lunar day. Those who live by the sea know that the times of the tides
shift slightly each day, so that if flood tide occurred in the morning
on a certain day, it occurs in the afternoon a week later. That is
because the lunar day, which determines the period of the tides, is
shorter than the solar day, which has an average of 24 hours. When
the sun and the moon are either on the same or opposite sides of the

earth, the highest tides result, called *spring tides;* these take place twice during each lunar orbit of the earth—which is about 29½ days (a lunar month—the interval in which the moon appears as full at one end and as a new moon at the other). When the moon and the sun are not in alignment, the lowest, or *neap tides* result.

ecology / environment

Ecology is the scientific study of the interrelationships between organisms and their environment; another word for it is *bionomics. Environment* is the sum total of the conditions and the surroundings, especially in relation to the organisms of a given area. Possibly because *ecology* is a fashionable word, some people use it to mean 'environment,' but the two do not mean the same thing and they offer the opportunity for useful distinctions.

economic / economical

Economic means 'concerning or relating to economics or finance or to the economy of a business, country, etc.'; *economical* means 'in keeping with a reasonable outlay of money, effort, or other expense; thrifty.' Neither has anything to do with how much something costs, and something might cost a great deal and still be economical if it can be shown to save money in the long run. Thus, an expensive car might be more economical because it lasts longer than a cheap one and costs less to maintain and operate; in that context, one could say that buying it is economical and makes economic sense as well. A writer or speaker who does not waste words is said to have an 'economical style.' In Britain, *economic* has acquired the sense of 'profitable; making good business sense': an *economic rent* charged by a landlord is one that allows him to cover his costs and realize a reasonable profit besides. *Economic zone,* or *exclusive economic zone,* is the offshore area regarded by a nation as its exclusive domain for fishing, oil and mineral exploration, and other exploitation to its economic advantage and that of its citizens.

ectoderm / endoderm / mesoderm

These are the names for the three primary cell layers of an embryo. The innermost, the *endoderm,* or *entoderm,* develops into the linings of the bodily cavities and passages, as the trachea, lungs, bronchi, gastrointestinal tract, and various glands and other organs, and the covering for most of the internal organs. The enclosing layer, the *mesoderm*, develops into bone, connective tissue, blood, muscle, and vascular and lymphatic tissues, as well as the pleurae of the pericardium and peritoneum. The outermost layer, the *ectoderm*, develops into the nervous system, the skin, hair, and fingernails, the mucous membranes, and special sense organs, particularly the eyes and ears. (See also **endothelium / epithelium / mesothelium.**)

ectomorph / endomorph / mesomorph / asthenic / athletic / pyknic

All these terms are used by psychologists, clinically or descriptively, to identify what have been seen as the three *somatotypes*, or main human body types. The first three have reference to embryonic influences: a person with a slender build (an *ectomorph*) is so called because it is thought that the embryonic ectoderm proved dominant in development; predominance of the embryonic endoderm (or entoderm) gives rise to the *endomorph*, a person with a heavy body; the stocky, muscular body of the *mesomorph* results from prominence in development of the embryonic mesoderm. A less formally derived and more general characterization of body structure is seen in the classifications *asthenic*, for the person having a slight, slender build, *athletic*, for one with a well-proportioned, muscular body, and *pyknic*, for the person with a fat, somewhat squat figure. A person with an asthenic build is also called a *leptosome*. In certain psychological contexts, these various body types are said to influence their possessors' personalities.

edition / printing / issue

In book publishing usage, *edition* refers to a particular version of a book that differs from other versions of the same work. The difference might be substantial, as in the case of editions of the Bible based on the work of different translators or on an effort to modernize its language, or nonexistent insofar as text is concerned, as in the case of a novel like Herman Melville's *Moby Dick*, which might be available in a number of editions distinguished by design, illustration, quality of paper and binding, and so forth. When a given edition of a book is first published, it is in its first printing; subsequently, if that printing is sold out and the publisher's expectation of continued sales sufficiently optimistic, it may be reprinted; some popular editions of certain books (especially the Bible, but also novels, reference books, and other works) are reprinted many times, each constituting a *printing* or *impression.* Daily newspapers may be published in several editions, each differing from the preceding in some respect. Sometimes these are given nicknames in the trade: the first edition of a daily or Sunday newspaper, often placed on sale the evening before, is called the *bulldog edition.* In some large cities, like New York and Los Angeles, an edition may also be made up of different sections each carrying local news and advertising appropriate for a particular area where the entire newspaper is to be distributed; *The New York Times,* for example, publishes its Sunday editions with a selection of different sections, a given "package" of sections being delivered for sale in Connecticut, another in Westchester County, another on Long Island, etc. Because of time constraints, newspapers rarely, if ever, publish more than one printing of the same edition, so the term *printing* or *impression* is seldom encountered in journalistic contexts. Periodicals—weeklies, biweeklies, semimonthlies, monthlies, quarterlies—vary somewhat in practice. Monthlies and quarterlies are almost invariably available in only one edition, though certain of these, especially those monthlies that have significantly high circulations in foreign countries, may publish one edition for the country where its main circulation resides and one or more for distribution abroad. That is a common practice among periodicals of greater frequency, though the differences between editions may, as in the case of newspapers, be limited to differences in advertising rather than editorial content. Magazines of very high circulation, like *Time* and *Newsweek,* typically publish regional editions within their countries of origin. Both newspapers and magazines use the term *issue* to describe the edition(s) published under a given date; thus, one speaks of the January issue of a monthly, the issue of a newspaper (or periodical) identified by a specific date, but the Sunday edition of a newspaper.

educator / educationist

Educator is another word for 'teacher,' though it carries with it the connotation of a person whose teaching has resulted in the presence of people who have not only been taught but educated, that is, people who demonstrate a level of culture and knowledge that is above the average. It is largely a term of respect, usually attained after many years. *Educationist* is a more recent coinage, though not as recent as some have been led to believe: the *OED* shows citations from the early 19th century for both *educationist* and *educationalist.* In Britain, where the preferred form is *educationalist,* these terms describe someone who is an authority on the theory and techniques of education, though not, necessarily, an educator (or a teacher). In the United States, where *educationist* is the usual form and *educationalist* is rarely encountered, its denotation is the same as that in Britain. But in recent years, because educationists, who are often administrators and theoreticians with little practical experience, have wrought changes in the systems of education which many believe to be demonstrably for the worse, the name *educationist* has assumed ugly connotations in some circles and is sometimes used disparagingly in the U.S.

effective / effectual / efficient / efficacious

Of these, the most frequent and least likely to be used out of context is *efficient,* which means 'functioning properly and economically': *My employer told me that talking to my friends on the telephone is not the most efficient use of my time. Effective* means 'having a (desired) result (or effect)': *The sales campaign was most effective in urban areas. I am looking for an effective way to break off with my boyfriend.* Both *effectual* and *efficacious* are rarer, relatively more learned words: the meaning of *effectual* is quite close to that of *effective,* 'succeeding in producing a desired result (or effect)': *She found a more effectual way to tell him she no longer loved him;* in legal contexts, it means 'binding; valid.' *Efficacious* means 'serving as an effective solution or remedy; successfully producing or having the sought-after result (or effect)': *This medication should prove efficacious against the Malay waste-away. She has an efficacious plan for the reorganization of the company.* To avoid confusion, *efficacious,* a relatively rare word, and *effectual,* only slightly more common, can be avoided, for the senses of *effective* have spread to include them quite adequately. (See also **affect / effect.**)

effeminate / effete

Effeminate is used of males who display feminine characteristics of behavior and attitude; it is rarely, if ever, used of women, about whom one might say feminine (or, as the case may be, *masculine*), depending on the attributes they exhibit. *Effete* suggests a weak person, decadent as a result of the loss of sexual, intellectual, or moral drive or power; it can be applied to either a man or a woman but, possibly because of cultural conditioning that expects strength from a man, is more often used of men, invariably in an uncomplimentary sense.

egoist / egotist

An *egoist* is a person who practises *egoism*, that is, 'obsession with oneself'; it is used to describe someone who is entirely wrapped up in himself and behaves in a selfish manner. An *egotist* is also self-centered, but his failing is a consuming conviction that he is superior to everyone else; he engages in *egotism*. *Ego* is the Latin word for the vertical pronoun, "I."

either . . or / neither . . nor

We know from Coleridge's "The Rime of the Ancient Mariner" as well as other examples from poetry and archaic usages that *nor* can occur without *neither:*

Water, water everywhere, and all the boards did shrink,
Water, water everywhere nor any drop to drink.

But this is regarded as poetic license and should be avoided in ordinary usage, which requires preceding *neither,* as in this adaptation from Herodotus:

Neither snow, nor rain, nor heat, nor gloom of night stays these couriers from the swift completion of their appointed rounds.

Care should be taken to avoid *neither . . or,* and because *nor* means 'and not', *either . . nor* makes no sense. The usual forms are:

Either she or I should go.
They wanted either her or me to lead the parade.
Neither she nor I should go.
They wanted neither her nor me to lead the parade.

Either and *neither* function as pronouns or adjectives (both grouped under the classification "determiner" in some modern grammars):

ADJECTIVE: Neither side can win.
Neither one side nor the other can win.
Either team can win.
Either one team or the other must win.
I want chocolate, neither strawberry nor vanilla
(. . nor any other flavor).
You may have either strawberry or vanilla (. . or
raspberry . .).
PRONOUN: Of the two horses, neither could win.
Of the two horses, either could win.

In the foregoing, *neither* means 'not one or the other,' and *nor* means 'and not'; *either* means 'one or the other,' and *or* means something like 'alternatively' but is almost impossible to define. Both may be used as conjunctions in the forms *either . . or* (. . *or . .*) and *neither . . nor* (. . *nor . .*), and they need not be restricted to two choices:

Either he, (or) she, (or) I, or all of us must go.
Plant either ivy, (or) clematis, (or) alyssum, or any good cover here.
Neither the navy, (nor) the air force, nor the marines came to help.

The brackets indicate that intermediate *or* and *nor* are optional: they may be omitted but are often added for emphasis or rhythm. See the quotation from Herodotus, above, for a similar example of the use of *neither.* Any following verb should agree with the alternative closest to it:

Either the marines or a squad of soldiers is needed.
Either a squad of soldiers or the marines are needed.
Neither company nor its employees accept responsibility.
Neither the employees nor the company accepts responsibility.
Neither John, nor George, nor Mary accepts responsibility.

(See also **each / either / both.**)

electric / electrical / electronic

In some contexts, it is useful to distinguish between *electric*, which means 'relating, pertaining, derived from, or producing electricity,' and *electrical*, which means 'involving or concerned with electricity.' Thus, an appliance or other device operated by or producing electricity would be an *electric chair, electric clock, electric current, electric eel, electric eye, electric fence, electric furnace, electric generator, electric guitar, electric iron, electric knife, electric lamp, electric light, electric refrigerator, electric shock,* etc.; a person, study, phenomenon, etc., that involves electricity would be an *electrical engineer, electrical storm, electrical transcription,* etc. In the metaphoric sense of 'exciting, thrilling, electrifying,' the choice is always *electric: The atmosphere in the room was electric after he confessed to espionage. Electronics* is the application of the controlled flow of electrons, as in an evacuated radio tube, a semiconductor, transistor, or similar device. *Electronic* pertains to such devices or to the appliances and other contrivances that employ them. The choice between *electric* and *electronic* usually depends on which is the dominant characteristic: for example, though all electronic devices are also electric (in the sense that they operate by electricity), a radio, record player, video cassette recorder, television set, computer, etc., that relies mainly on transistors would be called *electronic;* one might distinguish between a battery-operated clock that uses a quartz crystal as *electronic* and one that used ordinary household electricity to drive a small motor as *electric.* Sometimes, what was formerly an ordinary electric appliance, like an electric iron, has been redesigned to include transistors for the control of certain features, in which case the latter might be called an *electronic iron,* to contrast it with the former. *Electric typewriters,* in which various functions like carriage return and backspacing are performed by electricity, are in some applications being replaced by *electronic typewriters,* in which liquid crystals may be used to display a line of text before printing and in which printing is performed by a matrix of electronically controlled wires that form the patterns of the desired characters before striking a ribbon for transfer of an image to paper.

element / compound / mixture / admixture / alloy / amalgam / solution / colloid / suspension

All these terms except the first refer to combinations of substances. An *element* is a substance consisting of atoms that uniformly contain the same number of protons, or positively charged particles, in their nuclei; it may be a metal (like iron) or a nonmetal (like iodine), a gas (like oxygen), a solid (like copper), or a liquid (like mercury). One of its essential characteristics is that it cannot be changed by chemical means. There are 105 such known substances, 93 of which occur naturally; the others have been produced artifically by changing the constituency of the nuclei of the natural elements. A *compound* is a substance produced when the atoms of two or more elements combine to form a molecule, as water (H_2O), which consists of two atoms of hydrogen chemically bonded to one atom of oxygen. A compound may be a liquid (like water), a gas (like nitrous oxide, HNO_3, or laughing gas, used as an anesthetic), or a solid (like sodium chloride, NaCl, or common table salt). Many elements lose their characteristics when combined into compounds. Hydrogen and oxygen, both flammable gases, combine to form water, a liquid used for putting out fires; sodium, a yellowish, poisonous, highly active metal that burns (that is, combines with the oxygen) when it comes into contact with water, and chlorine, a greenish-yellow, highly poisonous gas, combine to form common table salt, which is white and crystalline. A *mixture* is a combination of two or more elements or compounds or of one or more elements with one or more compounds in which chemical bonding has not taken place, though the characteristics of the ingredients may be changed, and most mixtures have been developed because they have desirable properties suitable for a particular application. An *alloy* is a mixture of metals or of a metal with some other substance. The alloy brass consists, typically, of copper and zinc; another alloy, phosphor bronze, is a mixture of copper, tin, and phosphorus, widely used for bearings, gears, etc. The proportions of the ingredients in a mixture are essential to achieve the desired characteristics. The desired characteristics might be reduced or enhanced electrical conductivity, increased resistance to rust or corrosion, more or less elasticity, color, and so on. Gold is usually alloyed with other metals in jewelry because it is too soft in its pure state to resist wear. *Admixture* is a less common synonym for *mixture* but may also refer to an ingredient added to a mixture, as *an admixture of beaten eggs to the flour.* An *amalgam* can be any blend or combination but may refer specifically to a mixture of mercury with another metal, usually silver, as used in dental fillings. A *solution* is a mixture of one or more substances—elements or compounds or both—in a liquid so that the ingredients are completely and evenly dispersed. It may consist of a solid in a liquid (like salt in seawater), two liquids (like vodka and tomato juice in a Bloody Mary), or a gas and a liquid (like carbon dioxide in water with flavoring to make tonic). A *colloid,* also called a *colloidal solution* or a *suspension,* is a liquid with particles of another substance—solid or liquid—suspended in it, as olive oil and vinegar when they are shaken (not stirred). The heavier of the admixtures in a colloid usually settle out after it has been allowed to stand for a while.

elevation / plan / section

These terms refer to different methods and scales of mechanical drawing. In architectural and other drafting, a *plan* is a two-dimensional scale drawing showing the view of an object or building as if one were looking down on it from above, in the case of a building showing the positions of walls and other fixed structures in a view one might have if the roof or ceiling were removed. An *elevation* is a two-dimensional scale drawing showing an object, building, etc., as if one were viewing it from one side, in the case of a building, as if one wall were removed. A *section* is a two-dimensional scale drawing of one part or detail of an object, building, etc.; it might be either a plan or an elevation and appears as though viewed from an imaginary plane cut through vertically or horizontally to reveal some particular detail or dimensions. (See also **isometric / perspective.**)

embassy / consulate

Both terms concern the representation of a government in a foreign country. There is only one *embassy* maintained in any foreign country by each nation, though not all nations maintain embassies in all countries. The function of the embassy staff, under the direction of the *ambassador,* is to establish and sustain diplomatic and political relations with the government of the country in which the embassy is situated and, in general, to look after the welfare of any of its nationals who may be in that country. A *consulate,* on the other hand, may be situated in a number of cities of a foreign country—in which ones and how many depends on the extent of the interests being pursued. Headed by a *consul,* the function of each consular staff is essentially to establish and maintain commercial relations between the country it represents and the host country and, in certain matters, to aid its nationals.

embolus / thrombus / thromboembolism

A *thrombus* (plural *thrombi*) is a clot of platelets, fibrin, and other blood debris that collects within a blood vessel and becomes attached to its interior wall. *Thrombosis* (plural *thromboses*) is the name for any condition resulting from the presence of a thrombus. An *embolus* (plural *emboli*) may be made up of the same matter or may be a bubble of gas that travels through the bloodstream till it becomes lodged in a valve or other narrow place and causes an obstruction. *Embolism* is the name for any condition arising as a result of the presence of an embolus; although some people use *embolism* for *embolus*, that is not technically accurate. *Thromboembolism* is the name for any condition resulting from obstruction of a blood vessel by an embolus. Any of these conditions can be fatal, depending on where in the body the obstruction occurs.

emigrate / immigrate

A person departing from a country permanently or for a longish period *emigrates* from the country; if forced to do so, by war, political oppression, or other circumstances, he may be called an *emigré;* if he simply leaves, he is an *emigrant.* He then *immigrates* to the country where he plans to live, where he becomes an *immigrant.* There is in New York City an "Emigrant Savings Bank," presumably so named in order to attract the deposits of *immigrants;* where it went wrong is not easy to determine.

enclave / exclave

These terms refer to the same thing, and the choice between them is determined by the point of view of the user. Berlin, for example, properly a part of the Federal Republic of Germany (West Germany), lies entirely within the territory of the German Democratic Republic (East Germany). From the standpoint of the former, it is an *exclave;* from the standpoint of the latter, it is an *enclave.*

encyclopedia / cyclopedia

The form *cyclopedia* (also spelled *cyclopaedia,* especially in Britain) is merely a shortened form of *encyclopedia* (also spelled *encyclopaedia*), and there is nothing more significant to be said about it. The word *encyclopedia,* however, was originally a mistaken formation from Greek *enkýklios paidéa* 'well-rounded education' and was coined in the

18th century by Diderot, d'Alembert, and others who were engaged in the preparation of the *Encyclopédie,* the great French work the purpose of which was to contain and codify all human knowledge.

endemic / epidemic / pandemic / epizootic

In their application to disease, these terms allow for important distinctions to be made. It may be useful to note that they share a common element, *-demic,* which comes from the Greek word *demos* 'people (of a certain region).' An *endemic* disease is one that is associated with a particular group of people or with a particular region: *Sickle cell anemia is endemic among blacks; Tay-Sachs disease is endemic among Jews; Filariasis is endemic in the tropics.* It does not mean that all blacks get sickle cell anemia or all Jews Tay-Sachs disease any more than it means that everyone in the tropics contracts filariasis; it means, simply, that whites rarely contract sickle cell anemia, that the predominant number of people who are afflicted with Tay-Sachs disease are Ashkenazic Jews, and that filariasis is a hazard of being in the tropics—Eskimos are unlikely to get it. An *epidemic* disease is one that affects a large number of people; it may affect a large number in a particular area at the same time, it may affect a large number of people of a certain age, of a particular sex, of a certain occupation, etc.: *Measles, brought to the New World from Europe, reached epidemic proportions among the American Indians, many of whom died from it.* A *pandemic* disease is one that affects a high proportion of the people of a given region, country, or of the world: *Influenza was pandemic in the eastern United States during 1918.* If a condition is epidemic among certain animals, it is termed *epizootic;* if among plants, *epiphytotic.* Of the first three words, *epidemic* is by far the most common in ordinary language, and people tend to use it even though, technically, it would be more accurate to say *endemic* or *pandemic.* The 1918 outbreak of influenza, for instance, has almost invariably been referred to as an *epidemic,* though, properly, it was a *pandemic.*

endocrine / exocrine

Endocrine glands, which are ductless, are those that secrete hormones directly into the bloodstream and serve to control the functions of various organs; *exocrine glands,* which have ducts, secrete directly to the surface of an organ or a tissue. Endocrine glands include the *pitu-*

itary, which governs a large number of bodily functions; the *thyroid,* which controls growth during childhood and the metabolic rate; the *parathyroids,* which affect blood composition and clotting, cellular permeability, and normal neuromuscular reaction to stimuli; the *adrenals,* which trigger the secretion by the liver of *testosterone* and *estrogens* and control the vasoconstrictors, *epinephrine* and *norepinephrine;* the *islands* (or *islets*) *of Langerhans,* which control sugar metabolism; the *Graafian follicle* and *corpus luteum,* which control ovarian functions; the *testes;* and the *gastric* and *intestinal mucosa.* The *pineal gland* is considered an endocrine gland because it is ductless, but its function is unknown. The *thymus gland,* formerly thought to be a part of the endocrine system, is now considered to be in the lymphatic system.

endogenous / exogenous

Endogenous means 'arising from within an organism or system,' as a disease, like cancer, or the growth of a plant root system; *exogenous* means 'arising from outside the organism or system,' as certain essential vitamins which must form part of the diet because they cannot be synthesized by the body, or the growth pattern of plants that add an annual external layer of cells beneath the bark.

endoskeleton / exoskeleton

An *endoskeleton* is a skeleton that is contained entirely within the body of an animal, like the skeletal structures of mammals, those of the sponge, etc. An *exoskeleton* is one that is entirely outside the animal, like the skeletal structures of insects, the shells of clams and oysters, and the shells of snails or tortoises.

endothelium / epithelium / mesothelium

These are the names of various bodily tissues, single layers of plate-like cells. Developing from the *mesoderm,* the *endothelium* lines the heart and the inner surfaces of the lymph vessels and the blood vessels, and the *mesothelium* lines the thorax and abdominal cavity and forms the serous membrane. The *epithelium,* which develops from the *ectoderm* and *endoderm* (or *entoderm*), forms a covering for the internal and external organs and may consist of one or more layers of cells which may be of different types. (See also **ectoderm / endoderm / mesoderm.**)

enervate / innervate

These words, which are close in sound, are opposite is meaning: *enervate.* means to 'make weak, enfeeble' and is most often used as a past participle, as in *We were completely enervated by the climb up the hill; innervate* means to 'stimulate, energize' and is more often used literally, in reference to some part of the body, than metaphorically, as in *The congregation was fully innervated by the enthusiasm of the preacher.*

England / Scotland / Wales / Ireland / Britain / United Kingdom / Commonwealth

England is the name for the part of the British Isles south of Hadrian's Wall, which separates it from *Scotland,* to the north. It is separated from *Wales,* to the northwest, by a demarcation roughly outlined by Offa's Dyke. Till 1921, the term *United Kingdom* referred to these three countries and *Ireland,* which was ruled as a dependency from its conquest by England, early in the 17th century, till 1801, when it became part of *Great Britain.* In 1921 Ireland was divided into *Northern Ireland,* which remained a part of Great Britain, and the *Irish Free State,* which was later declared a republic (1949). Today, the *United Kingdom of Great Britain and Northern Ireland* includes England, Scotland, Northern Ireland, the principality of Wales, and a number of small islands. Care should be taken to distinguish England, Wales, Scotland, and Northern Ireland. The *Commonwealth of Nations,* informally known as *the British Commonwealth,* formerly the *British Commonwealth of Nations,* is a loose association of independent nations most of which were formerly colonies or dependencies of the United Kingdom. All recognize the Queen as their symbolic head and are united in their determination to consult and cooperate to further the interests common to their citizens, international understanding, and world peace. It consists today of 49 states, namely, Antigua and Barbuda, Australia, the Bahamas, Bangladesh, Barbados, Belize, Botswana, Canada, Cyprus, Dominica, The Gambia, Ghana, Grenada, Guyana, India, Jamaica, Kenya, Kiribati, Lesotho, Malawi, Malaysia, Malta, Mauritius, New Zealand, Nigeria, Papua New Guinea, St. Kitts-Nevis, St.

Lucia, Seychelles, Sierra Leone, Singapore, Solomon Islands, Sri Lanka, Swaziland, Tanzania, Trinidad and Tobago, Tonga, Uganda, the
United Kingdom, Vanuatu, Western Samoa, Zambia, and Zimbabwe.
Included are special members whose heads of government do not
attend meetings of the Commonwealth heads of government, namely,
the Grenadines, Maldives, Nauru, St. Vincent, and Tuvalu.

equable / equitable

Although these are not very common words, they are sometimes confused. The February 1987 issue of *Natural History* (p. 31), an otherwise carefully edited publication, contains the following:

> [W]e can interpret the fine grain sizes . . . as indicating a warm
> equitable climate . . .

> [T]he earth was characterized by a warmer and more equitable
> climate . . .

Both of these are not standard in their usage: *equable*, meaning 'relatively uniform, characterized by evenness, and stability, and lack of
substantial change,' is the word intended. *Equitable* means 'fair,
unprejudiced.' Though the Third Edition of the *Merriam-Webster
Unabridged* shows "characterized by evenness (as in temper or climate)" as its third definition, without any sort of label, we can only
assume from that listing that *equitable* is (mistakenly) substituted for
equable often enough to warrant recording that sense. The *OED* and
other dictionaries are silent on the matter, leading one to question the
volume of evidence available to Merriam-Webster.

equinox / solstice

Equinox, as the word suggests, refers to a time when the day and the
night are of equal duration, an event that occurs twice a year when
the sun is directly overhead at the equator, on or about March 21st
and September 22nd. March 21st is called the *Vernal Equinox* in the
northern hemisphere and the *Autumnal Equinox* in the southern
hemisphere; September 22nd is the Autumnal Equinox in the northern and the Vernal in the southern hemisphere. The *solstice* also
occurs twice a year, when the sun is directly overhead over the Tropic of Cancer, about December 22nd, or the Tropic of Capricorn, about
June 21st, respectively the northernmost and southernmost extents of

the sun's apparent motion. (See **Tropic of Cancer.**) December 22nd is called the *Winter Solstice* in the northern hemisphere and the *Summer Solstice* in the southern hemisphere; June 21st is the Summer Solstice in the northern and the Winter Solstice in the southern hemisphere. In the northern hemisphere, December 22nd is the shortest day of the year and June 21st the longest, called *Midsummer* in Britain; in the southern hemisphere, December 22nd is the longest day of the year and June 21st the shortest.

erythrocyte / leukocyte

Leukocytes (spelled *leucocytes* in Britain), also called *white corpuscles* or *white blood cells*, are the white or colorless blood cells the main function of which is to detoxify the blood and prevent the encroachment of bacteria, fungi, viruses, and other invasive foreign agents of infection. They are classified into five types on the basis of the presence or absence of granules, those with granules (*granulocytes*) being *basophils*, *eosinophils*, and *neutrophils*, those without granules (*agranulocytes*) being *lymphocytes* and *monocytes*. *Erythrocytes*, also called *red corpuscles* or *red blood cells*, contain hemoglobin, a complex compound of protein and iron the main functions of which are to carry oxygen to the cells from the lungs and carbon dioxide from the cells to the lungs, for expiration. There are about 4.5 to 5.0 million erythrocytes per cubic millimeter in the blood of normal men and about 4.0 to 4.5 million in that of normal women, depending on such factors as age, activity, altitude, etc. There are from 5,000 to 12,000 leukocytes in the normal blood of both sexes. Leukocytes range in size from 8 to 20 microns in diameter.

estivate / hibernate

As many people know, bears *hibernate*, that is, they enter a deep, comatose condition at the onset of winter from which they do not emerge till the spring signals a new season. They are not the only animals that hibernate, a word coined from Latin *hibernāre* 'spend the winter.' Some animals spend the summer in a sleepy, retired state; this is called *estivating* (also spelled *aestivating*) and is noted in certain snails and other mollusks. Both terms are used, with a touch of humor, in reference to people: *The Wilsons hibernate in Sardinia and estivate in Vermont.*

euphemism / euphuism

Euphuism is quite a rare word outside the realm of literary criticism and is unlikely to cause much confusion among general speakers of English; but students occasionally encounter it, especially in the context of 16th-century literary works. *Euphues* is a character in writings by John Lyly (1554?–1606), *Euphues, the Anatomy of Wit* (1579) and *Euphues and His England* (1580), which were characterized by their ornate, flowery style that made use of elaborate figures of speech in pursuit of elegance. This style came to be called *euphuism. Euphemism*, on the other hand, is the substitution of bland, inoffensive words for those that might be considered blunt, indiscreet, or vulgar. The cultures of the United States and Great Britain, for example, exhibit an almost fanatical avoidance of reference to death and dying, hence the English language is filled with euphemisms that allow speakers the opportunity to substitute different words and phrases for those thought harsh: for *die*, some prefer to say *go to meet one's maker; pass on* or *away; go West; bite the dust; shuffle off this mortal coil; go to the Great Beyond or the Happy Hunting Ground*, and a large number of other choices. While it is conceded that it would be rather indelicate to advise a woman whose husband had just been killed in a car crash that he *croaked, kicked the bucket*, or was *pushing up daisies*, it would be equally silly to describe him as having *gone to that place in the sky*. The opposite extreme of *euphemism* is *dysphemism*, by which is meant the replacement of ordinary words and phrases by those that are deliberately offensive, disparaging, or pejorative. Such replacement may be for the sake of humor, propaganda, sarcasm, or merely out of malice. An example might be a description of Buckingham Palace as *that shack in the park.*

European plan / American plan

These are terms used in the U.S. for hotel rates, *European plan* being a rate that includes no meals (except, sometimes, a light breakfast), *American plan* being a rate that includes at least breakfast and an evening meal and, sometimes, a midday meal as well.

exact science / pure science / social science / natural science / physical science

These and other terms used to describe *sciences* are not conventionally agreed and are not even of great importance; but they frequently crop up in attempts at description of the ways in which university courses are organized and may therefore prove useful; they also arise from time to time in conversation and sometimes, if not imposed too stringently, offer convenient distinctions. The *exact sciences*—physics, chemistry, astronomy, etc.—are so called because they involve measurements that can be made with precision. *Pure science* is that which is regarded as essentially theoretical, in contrast with *applied science*, which is practical; strictly speaking, there is no such thing as a pure or applied science, in the sense that disciplines can be listed under such categories: rather, one discusses the *pure* or *applied* aspects of a science. Thus, considered in the abstract, mathematics is a pure science; but in the context of, say, engineering, it becomes an applied science. The *social sciences* are generally those that deal with human beings and their interrelationships, insofar as those two can be distinguished. History is a social science, so are anthropology and psychology. The term *physical science* is applied to the study of inanimate matter and phenomena, as geology, meteorology, astronomy, vulcanology, etc.; the *earth sciences* are those physical sciences that deal with the earth only, mineralogy, for example. The term *earth sciences* is a bone of contention for some; a letter-writer to *The Times* (24 September 1987) remarked:

> . . [A] debate recently . . argued that the name "geology" should be replaced by "earth sciences" . . . [I]t was felt that "geology" incorporated all study of the Earth; yet on the other hand, "earth sciences" showed beyond all doubt how the subject has been widened by the incorporation of physics, chemistry, biology, meteorology, climatology, astronomy, environmental studies, mining, and so much more . . .

The *natural sciences* include biology and all its branches—botany, zoology, etc.—as well as others, like chemistry and physics, that concern themselves with matter and energy and their interaction. Some people would classify medicine as a science, and, to a certain extent, there is a great deal of science in medicine; but imaginative, philosophical medical practitioners generally consider the practice of medicine to be an art, not a science. It is often useful to distinguish between science and technology, which are frequently confused; technology is the application of science to practical purposes. The principle in physics of the inclined plane, for example, yields in technology (among other things) the screw; devising practical techniques for manufacturing screws also falls into the realm of technology. The terms *science* and *scientific* are bandied about rather loosely, partly out of careless use of the terms, more often because they are powerful attractants of money and power and any association with them lends cachet. In this context one encounters "scientific hairdressing," "scientific approaches to problems," and so forth, where the first might involve merely the intervention of some sort of machine, the latter nothing more than systematic thinking. To be sure, there is nothing wrong with either, but neither is properly scientific.

exotic / erotic

Erotic means 'arousing sexual desire' and can refer to pictures, the actions of another person, and so forth. *Exotic* means 'foreign, out of the ordinary run of things' and can be applied to foods, attire, and other things that seem unusual (to the person using the word). In most contexts, confusion between the two does not arise, but those in the business of entertaining people by the dancing and gyrating of scantily clad or nude women, enjoined from calling them "erotic dancers," dubbed them, euphemistically, *exotic dancers*. *Exotic dancing*, rarely reflecting the choreography practised in cultures alien to the West, has become a weak euphemism for what is otherwise called *striptease*.

explode / implode

Explode is to blow up from a confined area outward; when a balloon is pricked, the pressure inside being greater than that outside causes a violent outward rush of air (or other gas), which is what causes the noise. Similarly, dynamite and other *explosives* explode by forcing matter outwards from a small volume. *Implode* means to 'blow inward': for example, if an ordinary light bulb (in which the pressure inside is lower than that of the surrounding air) is broken, it will implode.

extemporaneous / impromptu

Up till relatively recently, an attempt was made to keep these words, which describe circumstances in which speeches are delivered, separate in meaning: *extemporaneous* was taken to mean 'prepared in advance and carried out with few or no notes'; *impromptu,* 'totally unprepared, performed on the spur of the moment.' In practice, however, the distinction has been all but lost, the two senses having fallen together with the meaning 'done or performed on the spur of the moment.'

extrovert / introvert

These terms, from the field of psychology, are often used rather loosely, merely to describe a person who is generally affable and outgoing (*extrovert*) and one who is thoughtful, quiet, and tends to keep himself and his thoughts to himself (*introvert*). To a great extent those attributes may apply, but to psychologists the terms are more specific: an *extrovert* (also spelled *extravert*) is a person whose attention and interests are entirely outside of himself, while an *introvert* is one whose concerns and interests are entirely in himself. To borrow terms from psychiatry, the introvert internalizes everything, the extrovert externalizes everything. It must be emphasized that these terms recognize a wide spectrum of degrees in both concepts and both are neutral in regard to mental health.

Fahrenheit scale / Celsius scale / Kelvin scale / Rankine scale / Réaumur scale

All of these are temperature scales. The *Réaumur scale,* formerly used in Europe, is no longer in use; in it, the freezing point of water is considered to be 0°, the boiling point 80°. The *Kelvin scale,* used largely for scientific and engineering purposes, is defined so that the triple point of water (that is, the temperature and pressure at which the three phases of water are in equilibrium) is 273.16°K, usually written "273.16°K." The *Rankine scale* is an absolute scale employing the Fahrenheit system and assigning a value of −459.67°F to the temperature at which all molecular activity ceases, called *absolute zero.* In the widely used *Fahrenheit scale,* the freezing point of water is at 32°, the boiling point at 212°. The *Celsius scale,* formerly called the *centigrade scale* but renamed to honor the Swedish astronomer who devised it, uses 0° for the freezing point of water and 100° for the boiling point; this scale is considered the basic metric unit of temperature and is generally replacing the Fahrenheit system. It is often useful to convert from Fahrenheit to Celsius and vice versa. To do so, these formulas may be used:

$$\text{Celsius} = (\text{Fahrenheit} - 32) \times {}^5/_9$$

$$\text{Fahrenheit} = {}^9/_5 (\text{Celsius}) + 32$$

farther / further

Farther is generally used to denote greater distance in literal senses: *A bit farther down the road you will come to a crossing. The sun is farther from the earth than the moon.* *Further* is said to be reserved for figurative, metaphoric uses; it means the same as *farther* but has the additional sense of 'greater extent; more': *I wouldn't take the subject any further if I were you. I hope there will be no further delays. Further comment on the subject would be pointless.* In practice, *further* is often substituted for *farther* in many, if not all contexts; the substitution of *farther* for *further* is considered nonstandard in constructions like "farther delays; farther comment." *Further* is also used for *furthermore: I said I didn't like his behavior; further, I told him he had to leave at once.*

faze / phase

Though pronounced identically to *phase*, the Americanism *faze*, which has a counterpart in British dialectal *feeze*, means to 'disconcert, daunt,' while *phase* means to 'change gradually from one stage to another' and is usually found followed by *in* (or *out*), meaning to 'introduce (or discontinue) gradually.' *Phase* also occurs as a noun meaning a 'stage, period, or interval, especially one during which a change is taking place.'

feminine / masculine / neuter

In the context of grammar, the unfortunate names of these gender terms have probably caused more difficulty for speakers of English than of most other languages. Essentially, they are the names of subclasses of nouns and pronouns in English and, in other languages, of adjectives and verbs. Modern English nouns no longer have grammatical gender themselves, in that their forms (subjective, possessive, objective; singular and plural) are not marked as to gender: the gender of an English noun is reflected in the pronoun used to refer to it.

With certain exceptions, notably references to ships and, sometimes, other vehicles, as well as some animals of unidentifiable sex, the gender of an English noun is the same as its sex. In effect, it is unlike Latin, German, French, and many other languages in which the gender of a noun does not, necessarily, have anything to do with the sex of the person denoted by the word. In Latin, for example, the word for 'farmer' is *agricola*, which happens to be of the feminine gender; but gender is a grammatical category, and it does not mean that Roman farmers were females or even effeminate, any more than German 'girl' (*das Mädchen*), denoted by a neuter noun, is without any sexual attributes. (In the Latin example, *agricola* happens to belong historically to the first declension, which, as it happened, yielded the set of endings that in later Latin were used for the feminine gender.) Natural sex and grammatical gender are different things, and confusion between them has occasioned much controversy, particularly as stirred up by feminists. In a language like English, when the natural sex of a noun is either unknown or immaterial, convention usually dictates the use of a *masculine*—that is, the term of gender, not the sexual attribute *male*—pronoun of reference. Thus, it is common and traditional in English to say:

> A voter must register his name at the town hall.
> Anyone requesting an appointment should leave his name with the receptionist.

If the sex of the subject is known or can be surmised, then *he* or *she* (or their appropriate forms) is used:

> Someone who is breast-feeding should be careful of her diet.
> Anyone who has had a prostatectomy should see his doctor once a year.
> It is a good idea for everyone to see her doctor once a year for a Pap test.
> The eunuch resumed his place at the door of the harem.

The exceptions are few:

> I was aboard the *Titanic* when she went down.
> The lookout on the whaler shouted, "Thar she blows!"
> "She's a grand old flag, She's a high-flying flag . . ."

It is the contention of many feminists that the English language is inherently sexist, that by virtue of its use of a masculine pronoun of reference in ambiguous situations, women are slighted. Various suggestions have been put forth in attempts to rectify the situation, some of them (like introducing a new word, "hisher") quite silly. Although there is little that can be done about changing the grammar of English, feminists have succeeded in making everyone sufficiently aware of their sentiments to ensure that much greater care is taken today to avoid any unintentional prejudice in all kinds of writing—the drafting of legislation, the preparation of documents like insurance policies, and in the general usage of language in newspapers, magazines, radio, television, and other media. The alternatives to the masculine— not the "male"—pronoun of reference are to use either *he or she* (or *his or her, him or her,* etc.) or to resort to *they* (or *their, them,* or *theirs*) as the pronoun of reference. The difficulty with the former choice is that it is awkward, cumbersome, and unacceptable except in legal and semilegal documents, where it has long been used and has little effect one way or the other because they are already so boring and badly, if carefully, written; the use of *they* (etc.) as a pronoun of reference for a singular referent has long been considered a solecism and anathema to good style and grammar. At least, such is the case in the U.S.; in Britain, the use of a plural pronoun for a singular referent is heard far more frequently among educated speakers and has less of a stigma associated with it. There is no easy way round the problem; sometimes, a passage can be rewritten to make the subject plural, thus making a plural pronoun more acceptable:

> Voters must register their names at the town hall.
> People requesting appointments should leave their names with the receptionist.

Either of these, on formal grounds, would be preferable to:

> A voter must register their name at the town hall.
> Anyone requesting an appointment should leave their name with the receptionist.

But that is not always possible. In all events, care should be taken not to offend.

feminine rhyme / masculine rhyme

In prosody, *feminine rhyme* can be either double or triple: if double, the rhyme is of two syllables in which the first is stressed and the second unstressed, as in *fable /table, season /reason,* or *cosy /rosy;* if triple, it is of three syllables in which the first is stressed and the other two unstressed, as in *national /rational, cosily /rosily /Rosalee,* or *terminal /germinal. Masculine rhyme* occurs between words that rhyme in one stressed syllable only, as in *confer /defer, reduce /induce,* or *beware / aware.*

fence / wall / ha-ha

A *wall* is an enclosing structure that is thought of as being more solid than a *fence,* which may be made of wire, rails, or other, usually lighter materials. Contradicting this thesis, it must be added that there are board fences (in which the boards may be set without spaces between), and that people are heard to talk about stone fences, too. But a stone fence is likely to be a flimsy affair, thrown up to divide land by piling up rubble and loose stones found by clearing a field: certainly, a stone wall, like a brick wall, is felt to be a more substantial piece of work, constructed with mortar, and the verb *stonewall* has recently reappeared to mean to 'thoroughly and effectively block,' especially by presenting an adamant, opaque barrier. It is conceivable that the combination *wooden wall* might be heard, but it would probably occur in a context in which it was contrasted with a *plaster wall,* inside a house. It is sometimes convenient to dig a ditch rather than build a fence to enclose an area from which horses and cattle cannot stray; although that is not, strictly speaking, a structure, it is called a *sunken fence* and has been given the name *ha-ha,* not often encountered outside the realm of crossword puzzles. The name comes from the fact that such fences cannot be seen till one is quite close upon them, especially if they are covered with grass, and the surprise on finding one is said to elicit the exclamation, "ha-HA!"

ferret / polecat / skunk

These are different names for various members of the weasel family. Several varieties of *skunk* are native to the New World and are not found in Europe; the *marten* is found in several varieties both in Europe and North America. *Polecat,* a Middle English word which may be derived from French *pol, poul* 'cock' + *cat,* named for its habit of attacking poultry, is the name given in the United States to the skunk; in Great Britain it is usually applied to a variety of marten that can emit an offensive odor, like that of the skunk, and is known also as the *foumart,* from *fou(l) mart(en),* another kind, emitting a somewhat less noxious smell, being called the *sweet marten.* In Great Britain, an

albino variety of polecat called a *ferret* has for centuries been domes-
ticated and bred for hunting rats, rabbits, and other small game; the
black-footed ferret is native to the western plains states of the U.S.
Polecat has long been used in English as an insulting term, the noi-
someness of the animal having become proverbial. Although Shakespeare used *polecat* (three times, all in the same scene in *The Merry
Wives of Windsor*), it seems likely from the context that his was a
punning use, playing on the metaphor of *pole* 'male organ' + *cat* as a
term of abuse for Falstaff, who was dressed as a woman: " . . you
witch, you hag, you poulcat [*sic*], you ronyon!" *Ferrets* are so successful at what they do (chase animals from their burrows) that as both
noun and verb the word *ferret* has become metaphoric for the notion
of digging out something that has been concealed. *Skunk* has long
been used as a mephitic metaphor for anyone who behaves badly,
treacherously, and, particularly, in a manner that leaves a residual
stink that is difficult to be rid of.

fewer / less

These words are often confused, *less* being habitually substituted for
fewer: for some reason, the reverse substitution is seldom encountered. *Less* is the comparative of *little;* the superlative is *least. Fewer* is
the comparative of *few;* the superlative is *fewest.* (See also, **positive /
comparative / superlative.**) In referring to any quantity that can
be counted, *fewer* is the word of choice; if the quantity is a mass
noun, that is, the name of something the elements of which cannot be
counted, then *less* is preferred:

> There is less fuel than I thought.
> There are fewer barrels of fuel than I thought.

> There is less rice on my plate.
> There are fewer grains of rice on my plate.

> Give me less mashed potato, please.
> Give me fewer [individual] potatoes, please.

Less also serves as an adverb, a function not shared by *fewer:*

> I found it less easy than I had expected.
> Please paint the sky a little less blue.

fibula / tibia

Although people may know that these are the names of the two bones in the leg, between the knee and the ankle, they often forget which is which. The *tibia* is the one in front, the *shinbone;* the *fibula* is the one slightly to one side.

FIFO / LIFO

These are acronyms used in business to describe systems of inventory control. *FIFO* stands for *first-in, first-out* and describes the practice by which older products in inventory are sold first, with their value established as if they had been recently acquired in order to take advantage of any increase in price. *LIFO* stands for *last-in, first-out* and describes the practice by which the books of a company should reflect the current market price of the costs of manufacture of a product; it should be noted that *LIFO* does not suggest that the products most recently taken into inventory should be sold before those that are already in stock.

filet / fillet

In the sense of a 'piece of boned meat or fish' or the verb to 'remove the bone from (a piece of meat or fish),' these are variant spellings. The spelling *filet* is preferred in the United States, where it is usually pronounced "fi-LAY"; the form *fillet,* which is older in English, is preferred in Britain, where it is usually pronounced "FILL-it," though the special loin cut of beef is called *filet mignon* in both countries, pronounced "fi-LAY meen-YAWN" (with a final nasalized vowel, not a real *n,* in the U.S. and "FEE-lay MEEN-yon" in Britain. *Fillet* is used in both countries for 'any narrow strip, band, ridge, or the like' and is pronounced "FILL-it" in all instances.

first mortgage / second mortgage

A *mortgage* is a loan granted by a financial institution to a property owner who pledges the property as security for the loan. The *first mortgage* is a mortgage in which no prior claim against the property for security has been made. In a *second mortgage* an additional loan, usually from a different lender, is taken by a property owner, or *mortgagor;* because the second *mortgagee*—that is, the lender—must take a security position subordinate to that of the first mortgagee, the interest rate is usually higher than that charged by the first mortgagee. Traditionally, homeowners sought second mortgages only in cases of need or to raise capital for some enterprise; in recent years, however, the rapidly escalating value of residential and other properties in certain areas has tempted many, particularly those with only small balances owing on their first mortgages, to avail themselves of the equity they hold in the property by taking out second mortgages, provided that interest rates were reasonable, regarding the funds realized from the loan as assets that could appreciate in value faster than the homes to which they had been tied and the costs of interest.

first / firstly / second / secondly

First, second, third, etc. are adverbs in their own right and it is unnecessary to add *-ly* to them.

fish / fishes

On a more or less formal level, a useful distinction is maintained between *fish,* which is used as a plural to refer to fish in general or a quantity of fish of the same kind, and *fishes,* which is also used to refer to a quantity of the finny tribe but emphasizes their variety. Thus, if referring to two trout he had caught, a fisherman would say "two fish"; were one a trout and the other a bass, he might say "two fishes." On the informal level, the distinction is often lost: *There are lots of good fish in the sea.*

flatware / hollowware

Flatware is the name given to metal utensils such as knives, forks, spoons, serving pieces, etc. *Hollowware* (sometimes spelled as two words) refers to metal cups, bowls, and other utensils of sufficient volume to contain food or other substances. Both terms are used in reference to tableware, usually silver or silver plate.

flaunt / flout

If one considers the meanings of these words, their misapplication, which is not unusual, becomes all the more ludicrous. *Flaunt* means to 'display proudly, show off jauntily'; *flout* means to 'treat with mocking disdain or scorn; scoff at.' Thus, one may *flaunt his money* and *flout authority;* although one might, conceivably "flout money," human nature being what it is, he is more likely to "flaunt money"; on the other hand, the "flaunting of authority" has been demonstrated only too frequently through history: those who do not have it, flout authority, those who do, flaunt it. Morality aside, the semantics of the two words require that they be kept apart. Curiously, it appears that *flaunt* is more often substituted for *flout* than the other way round.

flotsam / jetsam / lagan

We often hear *flotsam and jetsam*—that is, these two terms used together—as if they were simply redundancies like *part and parcel, cease and desist,* etc. But they are technically used to refer to different things, both having to do with the remains of a wrecked ship: *flotsam* is the wreckage found floating in the water; *jetsam* is stores, equipment, or other materials found aboard a vessel and thrown overboard during an emergency, either to gain stability or to avoid sinking: jetsam either sinks or is washed ashore. A much more rarely encountered term, *lagan* (also *ligan*), refers to anything that has been jettisoned overboard deliberately and to which a buoy has been attached for later siting, identification, and recovery. All these words have a long history in the legal aspect of seafaring.

fluid / liquid

Although these might normally be thought of as nouns for states of materials, they are defined as adjectives by most dictionaries, the noun senses being covered by definitions like, "a fluid [or liquid] substance." That kind of treatment is a customary ploy among lexicographers whenever they encounter difficulty; in this instance, the problem lies in describing what a *fluid* or a *liquid* is, as contrasted with what it does. As physicists sometimes encounter difficulties in describing the nature of a substance, lexicographers might be forgiven; in fact, one source comments, " . . there is still no comprehensive theory of the liquid state." Ordinarily, it is a simple matter to differentiate between a liquid, a solid, and a gas; but the simplicity vanishes when considering a substance like glass, called "an amorphous inorganic . . substance . . " in one well-known source. Glass is a noncrystalline solid; on the other hand, it is sometimes convenient to regard it as a "supercooled liquid." In scientific terminology, the term *liquid* is preferred to *fluid* (except when discussing the technology of *fluidics*, which is described in terms of *fluids*—but *fluid* remains undefined). If it is important to know the difference(s) between a *fluid* and a *liquid*, one is unlikely to acquire that information from any ordinary work of reference. *Fluid* is the generic term: a fluid is something that flows, like a *liquid* or a *gas*; it is the flowing state of something (like iron or glass) that, at other temperatures or pressures, might be in another state. A *liquid* is a kind of fluid. Glass, for example, may be a fluid at certain temperatures, but it is not a liquid. Generally, liquids flow at normal temperatures but, like water, may solidify at lower temperatures and vaporize at higher.

focal-plane shutter / leaf shutter

These are the names of the two main kinds of camera shutters in use today. The *focal-plane,* or *roller-blind shutter* is a system for creating a slit that allows light to pass from the subject to the film in such a way that the image moves across the section of film to be exposed. The mechanical operation can be most easily described by imagining a window covered by two continuous vertical blinds, one behind the other, each with a roller at each end and each with a horizontal slit, set a few inches apart: when both are closed, no light passes through; when they are drawn upwards so that the slit of the outside one aligns with that of the inside blind, light passes through the slits and falls on the opposite wall, which is analogous to the film in the camera; drawing them up at the same speed would allow the most light through; varying the speed of each allows control over the amount of light that passes through (by narrowing or widening the resulting slit, or aperture) and the amount of time that the light is allowed to enter (slower speed allowing for longer exposure and vice versa). In a camera, the blinds, which may be of metal or opaque cloth, are set much closer together, of course. The *leaf shutter* consists of a number of petallike metal leaves which, when closed, interlock to shut out all light; controlling the amount of time they remain open controls the amount of time that the light is allowed to reach the film (exposure); a diaphragm controls the amount of light that passes through. Shutter speeds are typically available for 1 second and for $1/2$, $1/4$, $1/8$, $1/15$, $1/30$, $1/60$, $1/125$, $1/250$, $1/500$, and $1/1000$ of a second. Exposures depend on the kind of lens used, but are generally available for settings in what are called *f/stops* (for "factorial-stops") at $f/32$, $f/22$, $f/16$, $f/11$, $f/8$, $f/5.6$, $f/4$, $f/2.8$, $f/2$, and $f/1.4$, each successive setting in this series letting in twice as much light as the preceding. It can be seen that certain combinations of speeds and f-stops yield the same exposure: for example, $f/2.8$ at $^1/_{250}$ second is the same as $f/4$ at $^1/_{125}$ second. But there is another factor that enters here, namely, *depth of focus*, or the sharpness of the image produced on the film by objects closer to and farther from the lens: the wider the lens opening (the lower the $f/$stop setting), the shallower the depth of focus; that is, the less likely it is that distant objects will be focused on the film with the same clarity as closer objects. For this reason, in photographing subjects that are closer to the camera in which the background is less important a smaller $f/$stop may be used (with a faster shutter speed), while the converse is true in photographing subjects that are farther away. Many cameras offered for sale to the public have printed on their cases the suggested ratios of shutter speed to aperture opening to produce the best depth of focus.

folio / quarto / octavo / duodecimo

In the art and technique of bookbinding, these are the main book sizes that were once referred to; though they survive in the terminology employed by antiquarian book dealers, they have generally fallen into disuse among commercial publishers and binders, largely because they imply printing and binding methods that are passé and are no longer sufficiently conventionalized as sizes to be serviceable in the book publishing business. A *folio* is a large sheet of paper folded in half to form two leaves, or four pages; a number of such folios produce what is called a *folio binding*, or *edition*, and the oldest printed copies of Shakespeare's plays, for instance, are of this type and usually measured more than 30 centimeters (just under 12 inches) in height. A *quarto*, for which the symbol is $4°$, is a sheet folded twice, to form four leaves, or eight pages; an *octavo*, also called *eightmo* and written *8mo* or $8°$ is folded three times, forming eight leaves, or sixteen pages; and a *duodecimo*, also called *twelvemo* and written *12mo* or $12°$, is folded to form twelve leaves, or twenty-four pages. It can be seen that if paper sizes are not standard, then these designations as book sizes cannot be uniform; yet, in practice, a duodecimo is about $5 \times 7\frac{1}{2}$ inches (width $\times$ height), an octavo about 6×9 inches, and a quarto about 9½ × 12 inches; folios vary widely in their dimensions. There are other sizes, achieved by different folding patterns, e.g., *trigesimo-secundo,* or *thirty-twomo, forty-eightmo,* and *sixty-fourmo;* but the preceding are the most frequently encountered. There are physical and practical limits to the number of times a sheet (depending on its thickness) can be folded—six or seven times being the most; the sixty-fourmo, for instance, produces a book about 2 × 3 inches, and there are not many books smaller than that; very small books are usually produced by cutting or by cutting and folding rather than folding alone. Many of the high-speed presses on which modern books are printed do not use sheets but huge rolls of paper, called *webs.* The standard sizes of paper vary somewhat—the U.S. doggedly retains measurements in inches while Europe long ago switched to metric paper sizes—and if a base measure of, say, 11 × 17 inches is used, the octavo produced from it would be nominally 5½ × 8½ inches and not the conventional 6 × 9 inches.

forgo / forego

Forego means to 'precede, go before'; *forgo* means to 'give up, do without.' A *foregone conclusion* is one that has been assumed without much deliberation because it seems obvious; in other words, it is an end or solution that has virtually come before the stating of the problem. These distinct forms are so often confused that some dictionaries show them as variants of one another; but careful writers keep them apart. Both use the various forms of *go—goes, going, went, gone*—to express changes in tense: *She forwent any reward for her heroism. Please follow the foregoing advice.*

former / latter / first / last

When two items have been mentioned and are to be referred to later on in the same sentence or in a sentence immediately following, in formal written English—and in rather pompous spoken English—the first can be referred to as *the former* and the second as *the latter.* It is useful to keep in mind that *latter* and *last* are, respectively, the comparative and superlative of *late.* If there are three or more items, these references cannot be used, for they make no sense. If three or four items are mentioned, they can be referred to either as *the first (of these), the second (of these), the third (of these),* and, for the last one, either *the last* (*of these*) or *the fourth;* or, if the comments about the items become lengthy or appear somewhat removed from the items they refer to, for the sake of clarity it is best to repeat their names, the words, or whatever the items were, making certain that the references appear in exactly the same wording and order as the originals to avoid confusion. If there are more than four items, it is imperative that the names be repeated, even in writing

> If I had to choose between Doc and Grumpy, I would choose the latter.
> If I had to choose between Grumpy and Doc, I would choose the former.

> Among Grumpy, Doc, and Sleepy, I always preferred the first.
> Among Doc, Sleepy, and Grumpy, I always preferred the last.
> Among Doc, Grumpy, and Sleepy, I always preferred the second.
> Among Sleepy, Grumpy, and Doc, I always preferred Grumpy.

> Among Grumpy, Doc, Sleepy, and Sneezy, I always preferred Grumpy.

The names are almost always repeated in speech, even if only two are involved, because people do not always listen very carefully and redundancy becomes important. If the list is four or longer, requiring even a reader to look back at the earlier sentence and actually count through to the item referred to would present a burdensome annoyance.

fraternal twin / identical twin

Fraternal twins, which do not, necessarily, resemble one another, are two children of the same or different sexes, born at the same time, from two fertilized ova. *Identical twins,* which resemble one another closely, are two children of the same sex, born at the same time, from a single fertilized ovum.

freehold / leasehold

In Britain, a *freehold* is a property owned outright by a tenant, in contrast to a *leasehold,* a property held under a lease, usually for a fixed period. The practice of *leasehold* goes back to a time when it was customary for those who held enormous tracts of land to lease portions to people for building their homes, the landlord collecting ground rent for the term of the lease, often as long as 99 years; the rent charged was subject to periodic review. At the end of the lease period, if the agreement was not renewed, the right to ownership of any building on the land reverted to the landowner. A change of leaseholder required the approval of the landowner under such an arrangement. In New York City, till recently the land on which Rockefeller Center is built was owned by Columbia University and leased to the Corporation that owned the buildings; it has since been purchased by the Corporation. In London, some 300 acres of prime West End land (including Belgravia) is owned by the Grosvenor Trust in behalf of the Duke of Westminster, making him one of the wealthiest people in the world. When a hospital situated there was unable to reach an agreement with the Trust on a new ground rent, it was forced to vacate, leaving the buildings to the landlord. Despite these examples, much of the land in Britain has been released for freehold during recent decades, often because the old land-owning families needed the cash and could not charge the amounts needed to keep up their estates, often to pay death taxes. Freeholds may themselves be held in *fee simple*, allowing the owner to dispose of the poperty as he pleases, or in *fee tail*, carrying certain restrictions regarding its disposition to specified heirs.

fructose / galactose / glucose / sucrose

Carbohydrates are classified into four basic categories, *monosaccharides, disaccharides. oligosaccharides*, and *polysaccharides*. Among these, the monosaccharides, or simple sugars, include *glucose* (also called *dextrose*), which is present in grapes and corn, *fructose* (also called *levulose* or *fruit sugar*), which occurs in green plants, fruits, and honey, and *galactose*, all of which share the same chemical formula but have different structures, hence are called isomers. *Sucrose*, ordinary table sugar, is a disaccharide, or double sugar, formed by the linking of one molecule each of glucose and fructose; it occurs naturally in sugar beets and sugar cane. *Lactose (milk sugar)*, which occurs only in milk, and *maltose*, which is present in beer and malt whisky, are also in this group. The polysaccharides, which are large molecules composed of linked molecules of monosaccharides, include starch and cellulose, the principal component in the structure of plants.

fruit / vegetable

Vegetable is the name given to a large category of herbaceous plants various parts of which—flower, leaf, or root—are used for food. *Fruit* is the name given to those plants the ovary of which are used for food. The attempt to classify plants botanically as fruits or vegetables is a lost cause: there are too many contradictions, and the criteria for distinguishing them are not sufficiently clearcut. In usage, however, plants have come to be called vegetables if they are eaten (usually cooked) during the course of a meal and fruits if they are sweet (or sweetish, with the exception of citrus fruits) and eaten (usually raw) at the end of a meal or between meals.

fuse / fuze

In the U.S., a spelling distinction is maintained between *fuse* a 'device for breaking and electric circuit that is overloaded' or, as a verb, to 'melt together,' and *fuze* a 'device for setting off an explosive charge.' In Britain, both are spelled *fuse.*

gaff rig / Marconi rig / gunter rig / lateen rig / Bermudian rig

These are the names for the most common ways of fore-and-aft rigged sailing vessels. The *gaffsail* is a quadrilateral sail the top of which is fixed to a spar, called a *gaff,* whence the name is derived; the spar has a yoke or similar fitting at one end that allows it to slide up the mast when the sail is hoisted; after hoisting, tension is increased on the leech (the after edge) of the sail by tightening the gaff halyards. A *Marconi rig* is a triangular sail with the luff (forward edge) fitted with bails or slides that allow it to be hoisted up the mast; most such sails are fitted with booms to which the foot is attached, but some are loose-footed; its name comes from the old Marconi radio transmitting and receiving towers which the masts with their standing rigging resembled. The name *Bermudian,* sometimes called *Bermudan, rig* is a Marconi rig that has proportionately a very tall luff in comparison with the length of its foot—what is called by yacht designers a *high aspect ratio.* A *gunter rig* consists of a triangular sail with its leech fastened to a spar which is hoisted aloft on the mast so that the spar is parallel to the mast and, when fully hoisted, resembles the Marconi. The gunter, which is usually seen on dinghies and other smaller craft, is named for a device (invented by a man named Gunter) like the parallel rules used by navigators but having a fitting that slides in a slot in a manner similar to the way the spar of a gunter rig slides along the mast. A *lateen rig*, typically used in the Mediterranean and Near and Middle East, resembles the gunter except that when the triangular sail is hoisted, the long spar attached to one edge, which is hoisted from a point just above its middle, is allowed to swing freely from its halyard at an angle of about 45°, under control of the sheets attached to the boom; its name is from *Latina* 'Latin'—that is, it is a centuries-old rig used by the Romans.

game / sport

Although there are certain diversions that would in all instances be classified as *games*—chess and board games in general, card games, dice, etc.—and others that are always classified as *sports*—swimming, skiing, etc.—there seem to be no criteria for either category that would enable a useful distinction to be established: baseball, football, basketball, cricket, tennis, golf, bowls, and so forth may be referred to as games slightly more often than as sports, but the statistics for such frequency comparisons are lacking or unconvincing. Although it may be true that those activities that require physical exertion of some sort are, properly. sports, it would be foolish to eliminate baseball, etc., from the category of games. All one could say is that all sports are games but that not all games are sports, an observation of doubtful utility. And to confuse the issue still further, horseracing, in which the only physical exertion is expended by the horses and the jockeys, is still referred to as "the sport of kings."

Gestapo / SS

In Nazi Germany, the *Gestapo* (an acronym for *Ge*(*heime*) *Sta*(*ats*) *Po*(*lizei*)) were the state secret police, the *SS* (an abbreviation for *Schutzstaffel* 'protection staff') an elite unit of the Nazi party, a special police force that served as Hitler's personal bodyguard. Both were known for their brutality.

gibe / jibe

Gibe, sometimes spelled *jibe*, means to 'taunt, jeer, mock,' and its noun sense is 'taunt, jeer.' As a nautical term, *jibe*, spelled *gybe* in Britain, means to 'allow the wind to catch the wrong side of a sail' or (of a sail) to 'be caught on the wrong side by the wind'; the noun describes the situation in which that occurs. There is another *jibe* which means to 'agree, be in harmony with': *Our ideas jibed completely. My plan for the campaign jibed with hers.* There is a common British English word, *jib*, which means to 'balk, stop short,' which is not encountered in American usage: *The horse jibbed at the fence and threw its rider.* To make the confusion complete, the noun *jib* is the name for a foresail of a sailing vessel. And if that were not sufficient chaos, some people pronounce *jibe* 'jive,' apparently in the mistaken impression that the jazz term *jive* (unrelated to *gyve* 'fetter') belongs in this potpourri: *Our plans just don't jive.* This quaint illiteracy lends rhythm to the speaker's utterances. The only way of sorting out all these words and their variants is to check them in a dictionary.

good / well

More and more frequently one hears, in response to the innocuous question, "How are you?," the reply "Good!," which to some seems noxious, occasioning in them the rejoinder, "I was enquiring after your health and physical and mental well-being—how you are feeling—not the state of your morals." In other words, *good* is more often than not taken to refer to proper behavior and morality, opposed to *naughty* or *evil; well* means 'in satisfactory health or spirits.' At least some of the difficulty with *good* and *well* arises because (aside from its noun sense, a 'hole in the ground') *well* can serve either as an adjective or as an adverb:

well, *adjective*, healthy; hale: *Is he ill? No he's well.*

adverb, in a proper, successful, good, etc. manner:
How did she do on the exam?
She did very well.

Although this may seem quite straightforward, it is complicated by the fact that the comparatives and superlatives of *well* (the adverb) are the same as those of *good:*

He is a good student; she is a better student; they are the best students in the class.

She did well; he did better; they did the best of all the students.

It is unlikely that anything can be done to resolve the problem—if problem it be—for there is little evidence of a confusion of meaning: those who say "I'm good" in response to "How are you?" mean "I'm in satisfactory health or spirits"; aside from the grammatical problem, they, at least, are not confused about what they intend to convey. This rather neat arrangement is somewhat sullied by the expression *well and good,* which denotes approbation; but consolation might be found in that idiomatic expressions do not always yield readily to formal analysis.

Goth / Ostrogoth / Visigoth

The *Goths* were a Teutonic people having a reputation of being fierce fighters with little culture; they migrated southward from northern Europe between A.D. 200 and 400, invading lands that were part of the Roman Empire. Not a great deal is known about them; they formed into two divisions: the eastern, called the *Ostrogoths,* established a monarchy in Italy a hundred years after the sack of Rome by the *Vandals,* another Germanic people, who had earlier conquered Gaul and the Iberian peninsula and later settled in Africa. (They were followed into Gaul about 500 by the Salian Franks, another Germanic tribe, who, under Clovis I, established an extensive empire and ultimately gave their name to France. It was Charlemagne who later became king of the Franks.) The western division of the Goths, called the *Visigoths,* formed a monarchy in southern France, early in the 5th century, which lasted for about a hundred years (till driven out by the Franks) and in Spain till 711, when they were conquered by the Moors.

gourmet / gourmand

In French, *gourmet* almost invariably means a 'connoisseur of fine food, epicure.' *Gourmand* in French can also mean that but, less often, it means a 'glutton': there is an international association of restaurants whose owners consider themselves purveyors of the best food; they call their association *Relais de Campagne* and their motto is *Route des Gourmands.* English speakers who encounter this name proudly displayed on roadside plaques and in advertising are sometimes a little perplexed, for, in English, the sense 'epicure' for *gourmand* has faded, and that of 'glutton' has taken over: it is beyond imagination why a restaurant that caters to (English-speaking) *gour-*

mets would advertise that it is a haven for gluttons. One day, if the present trend of *gourmand* toward 'glutton' results in a complete changeover of meaning, the association will have to change its motto.

grammar / syntax

To the average person, *grammar* means a 'collection of the rules governing the way language is to be used.' To a grammarian or linguist, it would be difficult to imagine a greater distortion: despite beliefs (bordering on convictions) to the contrary, there are no scholars chained to desks in ivory towers making decisions and issuing pronouncements or proclamations about how language is to be used. Grammarians are linguists who specialize in the descriptions of how languages function, and their work is to examine a language and record, in grammars, their observations. The grammarian—at least, the modern grammarian—is not the one who then takes those observations, draws up a set of "laws" based on them, and then imposes them on others, suggesting that disobedience will result in dire punishment: that function was long ago assumed by teachers and others who strive to acquaint students with the way language is used by the more eloquent among us. For many decades, educators avoided selecting contemporary writers as models, preferring those who were well established. As a consequence, the grammar and style that were taught and held up as the ideals to be emulated almost always harked back at least two or three generations and were slightly old-fashioned. In the 17th century, when the scholars and intelligentsia wrote about and discussed scientific subjects in Latin, a classical education was essential (for those who were educated at all), and the influence of Latin was strong enough to make many believe that English grammar and syntax should be modeled on it; indeed, the lexicon of English, with its heritage from French after the Norman Conquest, was riddled with Romance words, so adding Latinisms seemed both natural and logical. It was in this period that "rules" like "Never end a sentence with a preposition" and "Do not split infinitives" sprang up, not based on any observations of English but on the precepts of Latin (in which only by its position can the object of a preposition be determined and an infinitive, which is one word, cannot, physically be "split"). These relics remain to this day and have no more relevancy to English now than they did then. *Grammar* and *syntax,* which are often used interchangeably, are different, and their distinction is useful: where *grammar* consists of a description all of the elements in a language—its sounds, words, meaningful elements, and utterances—*syntax* focuses on the utterances, particularly on the relationships between the words that determine their order in sentences and other units of speech. Thus, *grammar* refers to the entire study, *syntax* to one part of it only.

grand larceny / petty larceny

Whether a crime is classified as *grand larceny* or *petty* (also, *petit*) *larceny* depends on a monetary dividing line established by a given legal authority: grand larceny describes thefts of items of greater value than those absconded with in petty larceny.

grand mal / petit mal

These may seem to be quaint relics of early medicine, encountered in old novels, but they are quite serious designations for pathological conditions associated with epileptic seizures. A *grand mal seizure* is one in which the person undergoes usually sudden muscular contraction, a stoppage of breathing, and a subsequent series of spasms in which the teeth are tightly clenched and the tongue might be bitten. After the passage of this phase, deep sleep for an hour or more may follow; upon awakening, the person is totally unaware that a seizure has taken place. In a *petit mal seizure*, the person suddenly loses consciousness for a moment, then reawakens, unaware that the seizure has occurred. Sometimes, the interruption may take place in the middle of a conversation and, when it is over, the person continues talking as if nothing had happened. Petit mal seizures afflict children and adolescents most often, especially at the time of puberty. There are several other kinds of seizures—*focal*, or *Jacksonian*, *psychomotor*, etc.—and all are thought attributable to any one or a combination of innate or acquired conditions like cerebral trauma, brain tumor, vascular malfunction, chemical imbalance. They are all grouped together under the general term *epilepsy*, which is described generally as a 'nervous disorder involving periods of loss of consciousness accompanied by spasms.' There are a number of drugs available that, taken as prophylaxis, prevent the attacks associated with the disorder.

grand opera / opera buffa / opera seria

As applied to a dramatic presentation in which all the parts are sung, the first syllable of *opera* is pronounced to rhyme with *mop*. (See also **opera / opus.**) For the most part, *opera* and *grand opera* are synonymous. From Italian, English has borrowed *opera buffa* and *opera seria;* both refer to a form of the opera, developed in 18th-century Italy, the former farcical in nature, the latter dramatic and usually based on a theme taken from a classical source, heroic or legendary; both employ recitative, *opera seria* also marked by the greater use of aria. From the 19th-century French style, English has borrowed *opéra bouffe,* essentially the same as *opera buffa* but not circumscribed by the 18th-century Italian style requirements and generally lighter and satirical. French *opéra comique* and English *comic opera* refer to the same thing, a light opera that contains spoken dialogue and is characterized by a happy ending, as *Il Barbieri di Seviglia,* by Rossini, and *Carmen,* by Bizet. (See also **aria / recitative, opera / oratorio / opera-oratorio / operetta.**)

gravitation / gravity

Gravitation is defined as the mutual force by which all bodies attract one another and is a function of the masses of the bodies, the distance between them, and a constant, called the *gravitational constant* or the *constant of gravitation,* expressed in SI units as 6.664×10^{-11} N m^2kg^{-2}. *Gravity* is the force of gravity on earth or, when specified, on a particular planet, moon, or other celestial object; its technical name today is *acceleration of free fall,* represented by the symbol g and expressed in SI units as 9.80665 m s^{-2} for bodies on the surface of the earth.

gravy / sauce / dressing

In ordinary usage in the U.S., *gravy* is the ordinary word for an ordinary thick or thin, souplike addition to meats, usually made from the drippings of the meat when it is cooked, often spiced and otherwise modified before serving. *Sauce* is also used, though it is often construed as being something that has been prepared separately, not necessarily making use of drippings. *Dressing* is generally reserved for the sauce used on salads and, in a special application, for stuffing. In Britain, *dressing* is not used for stuffing; *gravy* is sometimes regarded as a gluey concoction, not (or barely) fit for human consumption; and the preferred term is *sauce.* In a recent access of pretentiousness, many restaurant operators in the U.S. have adopted the French phrase *au jus* 'with the (meat's) natural cooking juices'; unfortunately, they seem to have been given to understand that the entire phrase means simply 'natural gravy' (instead of '*with* natural gravy'), and, as a consequence, many menus carry the meaningless phrase "served with *au jus.*"

green paper / white paper

In Britain, a *green paper,* or *Green Paper,* is a document, theoretically prepared at royal command, that sets forth proposals of policy for discussion, especially by Parliament. A *white paper,* or *White Paper,* is a document that sets forth the policy of the government on a particular matter before Parliament or to be presented to Parliament. A *command paper* is any document presented to Parliament, theoretically by royal command. Of these, only *white paper* is used outside of Great Britain to any great extent and then chiefly in Commonwealth countries.

Greenwich Mean Time / Standard Time / Daylight Saving Time / British Summer Time

At the time of the invention of the chronometer, a highly accurate clock that enabled seafarers to determine their longitudinal position by ascertaining, from solar and astronomical sightings, their distance from an arbitrary point of reference, it was essential that a standard point of reference be selected. Because Great Britain was, at the time, the most influential of seafaring nations, there was established at Greenwich, just east of London, an observatory, and the line of zero longitude was fixed as passing through that point. Thereafter, all positions were designated as being west or east of Greenwich, and the longitudinal line was named the *Greenwich Meridian.* All (longitudinal) navigational reckoning relied on knowing the current time at the Greenwich Meridian: if one could determine that and the current time at the point where he was situated, he could easily calculate how far from Greenwich he was, for each hour's difference is equivalent to 15° of longitude (approximately 1000 miles at the equator). (In other words, if the earth completes one revolution in 24 hours and the circumference of the earth at the equator is about 25,000 miles, then approximately 1000 miles of its surface passes beneath the zenith—the point directly overhead—every hour; also, if all 360° of the earth's surface pass the zenith in each 24-hour period, then $1/24$th of the surface, or 15°, passes the zenith each hour.) It was essential to fix on a single longitudinal reference time, and the name *Greenwich Mean Time* was the designation given to it. In the United States, the term *standard time* is used to refer to what might otherwise be called "sun time": for any particular locality, standard time of noon is determined by the moment at which the sun's apparent position is at its highest point in the sky between sunrise and sunset. Of course, that point differs with each meridian of longitude around the earth, so, for convenience, time zones approximately 15° in width were established by local legislation. One hundred years ago, the extent of the territorial possessions of Great Britain were so vast throughout the world that it was accurately said, "The sun never sets on the British Empire"; today, however, those territories have become independent nations, and the British Isles are not extensive enough to accommodate more than one time zone. In the continental United States, there are four time zones: Eastern, Central, Mountain, and Pacific; there is an hour's difference in crossing from one to the other—it becomes "earlier" as one moves westward—and a difference of three hours between the time in New York, in the Eastern Time Zone, and Los Angeles, in the Pacific Time Zone: at noon in New York, it is 9:00 a.m. in Los Angeles. As the earth orbits the sun, requiring a year to complete its circuit, it passes through two points, called the winter and summer solstices. (See **equinox / solstice.**) In the northern hemisphere, the time of the summer solstice marks the longest period of exposure to sunlight. Man's habits being what they are, much of that exposure comes at an inconvenient time—quite early in the morning. So the idea was devised to extend the evening hours of sunshine merely by setting all the clocks forward by an hour; by doing so, the effective hours of sunshine before noon were decreased by one hour, those after noon were increased by one hour; as a result, the sun is at its highest point at 1:00 p.m. when this clock change is in effect. The time during this period is called *Daylight Saving Time* in the U.S. and *British Summer Time* in Britain; it is usually put into effect in the northern hemisphere during the month of April; *Standard,* or *Greenwich Mean Time* is reinstituted during the month of October. On occasion, governments have seen fit to set clocks back two hours instead of only one, creating what is called *Double* (*British*) *Summer Time;* on rare occasions, Daylight Saving Time has been extended throughout the winter months. (See also **latitude / longitude.**)

gray matter / white matter

Gray matter is the term used to describe the brownish to reddish-gray masses of tissue that constitute the central nervous system, especially in the brain and spinal cord of vertebrates. *White matter,* a term seldom encountered in informal contexts, describes the whitish myelin sheathing that surrounds and protects and insulates the nerve fibers of the central nervous system of vertebrates.

gros point / petit point

Gros point (pronounced "GROW point") and *petit point* (pronounced "PET-ty point") are the two common stitches used in making embroidery on a backing of canvas, linen, or other material, as used for upholstering chair seats, cushions, etc. They are also called *canvaswork* or, sometimes, *needlepoint,* though *needlepoint* is properly used only of lace. The backing is usually a plain weave (a simple crisscross of warp and weft); in gros point, also called the *Gobelin stitch,* the yarn is stitched so as to pass over two warp and two weft threads; in petit point, also called the *tent stitch,* it is passed over one warp and one weft thread, creating a tighter, smaller pattern to create a finer, more detailed piece of work. In petit point, the interstices between the threads of the backing are much smaller—up to 40 per square inch. The earliest surviving piece of English petit point is the Calthorpe purse, which has about 1250 silk stitches per square inch. Because the interstices in the backing for gros point are proportionately larger, heavier yarn is used, creating a somewhat coarser, less detailed piece of work. (See also **warp / weft, canvaswork / needlepoint / tapestry.**)

guarantee / guaranty / warrantee / warranty

Historically, *guaranty* appeared first, then *guarantee,* followed by *warranty* and *warrantee.* In form, they are all cognates, *warranty* being described by the *OED* as a dialectal variant (in Old French) of OF *guarantie.* Of the older legal applications, only *warrant* survives in the common language as a 'legal document authorizing an officer to search or attach property or, especially, to arrest a person'. There are other senses in contemporary English, but they are largely technical. All these terms are most commonly encountered when a product is purchased and the manufacturer sets forth in an accompanying document certain representations regarding its quality and performance, often with restrictions and usually for a specified time limit. Such a document is properly called a *warranty*, the person to whom it is issued (often an anonymous purchaser who may or may not be required to register his purchase with the manufacturer but is usually required to possess a receipt or some other record to show him as the original buyer) is the *warrantee*, and the issuer the *warrantor*. As far as can be determined, a *warranty* is identical to a *guarantee*, but the picture is considerably muddied by usage. *Guarantee* is, in practice, not only the same as a *warranty* but is also used for the issuer of the assurance and, sometimes, the recipient of the assurance. To make matters worse, *guarantee* and *guaranty* are merely different ways of spelling the same thing, and *guarantor* can mean either the issuer of a *guarantee/guaranty* or the recipient of it. As verbs, *guarantee* and *guaranty* are variants of one another. It would be very neat if the situation with *warranty* could be guaranteed to remain straight, but the contamination of such forms, once the rot sets in, characteristically metastasizes throughout the system. The ultimate neatness could be achieved if *warranty* and *guaranty* could be restricted to the noun sense (plurals, *warranties, guaranties*), the forms *warrantee* and *guarantee* could be restricted to the document or the person receiving it, leaving *warrantor* and *guarantor* with the sense of 'issuer of a warranty or guaranty.' Alas, logical, formal consistency is not guaranteed (or warranteed, or . .) in language. At least consolation can be found in the fact that *guarantee* has not (yet) encroached on a common meaning of *unwarranted*: 'uncalled-for; unjustified.'

gudgeon / pintle

These are the names of the fittings used for attaching a (usually removable) rudder to a boat. The *gudgeon* is one or more sockets fixed at the stern of a boat; the *pintle* is one or more bolts or pins, fixed to the forward edge of a rudder, that fit into the gudgeon and hold the rudder in place. These terms are not, necessarily, confined to nautical applications and are used occasionally in reference to the hardware of door hinges.

gun / rifle

A *rifle* is a firearm in which the inside of the barrel has had a pattern of fine, shallow, spiraling grooves (called *rifling*) cut into it. These impart a spin to the projectile, giving it greater accuracy; hence rifles are used when accuracy is important, as in hunting and, in warfare, for some of the weaponry used aboard cruisers, battleships, and other vessels. A *gun* is a firearm without rifling; guns are used for small arms, like pistols, and for mortars, howitzers, cannons, and other weapons in which accuracy is not the prime consideration. Typical guns, besides those mentioned, are the shotgun, elephant gun, and machine gun. Typical rifles include the Enfield, M-1, Kentucky long rifle, and the recoilless rifle.

harbor / port

A *port* is a haven for vessels that is equipped for loading and unloading ships; a *harbor* is also haven for vessels but it does not, by definition, necessarily include any onshore facilities for storing, loading, or unloading cargo.

hard sell / soft sell

These commercial terms refer to the methods and approaches used in marketing products. In general, as the words suggest, *hard sell* implies an aggressive, forward approach taken to persuade a potential buyer to commit himself to a purchase; *soft sell* implies a more subtle, suggestive approach. The techniques involved may differ, but the purpose remains the same: to convince a buyer to part with his money in return for a product or service. *Hard sell* methods are often felt to be questionable because those who practise them frequently resort to dishonest descriptions of the product or service offered and, sometimes, to techniques that are considered fraudulent, like *bait and switch*, a practice in which a desirable product is offered at a bargain price but, as the sale is about to be concluded, an inferior one is substituted or the customer is urged to buy a more expensive item instead. While *hard sell* is focused entirely on the product, *soft sell*, the aims of which are, of course, identical—to sell the product— approaches the consumer in an unaggressive manner, frequently emphasizing the desirability of doing business with the company, for example, rather than merely buying a product. So-called *institutional advertising, public relations* (as contrasted with "crass" *product publicity*), and other techniques may be employed. Although any method of attracting purchasers for any product or service could be termed "selling," some methods are less offensive (and, possibly, less persuasive, hence less effective) than others. The ends to which companies go in engaging in more or less aggressive approaches are determined to a large extent by the amount of competition encountered in the marketplace. Hence, sellers of highly competitive products like specific brands of beer, cars, appliances, soft drinks, shampoos, laundry soaps, etc., which are bought by consumers to the exclusion of other brands, are more likely to be sold using hard sell techniques; they are marketed differently from products like novels, motion pictures, videotapes, musical records, etc., which consumers may own nonexclusively and which, consequently, are usually subject to soft-sell techniques.

hardware / software / (wetware)

In its simplest application to computer technology, *hardware* refers to the physical equipment itself—the computer with its circuits, storage devices, etc., visual display unit, printer, and so forth. *Software* refers to the programs needed to process the data by computer. *Firmware* is the term used to describe a program that is resident in the read-only memory (ROM) of a computer; this is usually a program, the utility of which has proved sufficiently important in the day-to-day operation of the computer to warrant making it resident in the device. *Wetware* is a facetious coinage used to describe the brain and the brainwork needed to write the computer programs and operate the equipment.

hare / rabbit

The two chief differences between *hares* and *rabbits* is that the former live in the open and bear young that have fur at birth, while the latter live in burrows and bear young that are naked at birth. *Jackrabbits*, despite their name, belong to the hares, cottontails to the rabbits.

harvest moon / hunter's moon

In the northern hemisphere, the *harvest moon* is the first full moon after the autumnal equinox (about September 21st), the *hunter's moon* the next full moon after the harvest moon. In both cases, these are the only full moons during the year to rise close upon the setting of the sun.

hate / despise

Hate means to 'dislike intensely; loathe'; *despise* means to 'look down on contemptuously.' The difference lies in that the second word carries in it the sense of 'looking down' which the former, concerned with indiscriminate contempt, does not.

healthy / healthful

Healthy means 'in good health'; *healthful* means 'yielding or promoting good health.' Thus, people are healthy (if they are fortunate), foods, spas, climates, etc., can be healthful.

heart attack / stroke / heart failure

Stroke was formerly more commonly called *apoplexy,* which is almost the same as the Greek word for 'stroke.' Notwithstanding its status among doctors as a name for an affliction, *apoplexy* is today generally regarded as an old-fashioned word vaguely related to an *apoplectic fit,* the onset of which is brought on by over-excitement and which is associated with stuffy, elderly, overweight gentlemen who become very red in the face particularly after an intake of too much port wine: it evokes images of the kind of illness or distress experienced by Victorian ladies who suffered with *the vapors.* Technically, however, *stroke,* or *apoplexy,* is the name given to a circulatory problem affecting the brain; it may be owing to an embolus or thrombus (which blocks the blood supply) or to hemorrhage (rupture of a blood vessel). In either event, it deprives the brain (or a part of it) of needed oxygen and may lead to paralysis of one or more parts of the body or death. A *heart attack* is the same as a *stroke,* except that it affects the heart, not the brain. The term *coronary* is often used in referring to a heart attack, but it is a shortening of *coronary thrombosis,* which, technically, can arise only from a thrombus; the term *infarct* describes a "heart attack" resulting from either a thrombus or an embolus. *Heart failure* occurs when the heart is unable to pump sufficient blood throughout the body to maintain life; it is occasioned by weakness of the heart muscle, by physical exertion which increases the demand for blood, or by other factors. (See also **embolus / thrombus / thromboembolism.**)

heath / moor

Although a *heath* is generally said to have sandy soil and *moor* peaty soil, there is otherwise little to distinguish between these in terms of precise designation: both are relatively barren tracts covered with bracken, heather, and other characteristic shrubs.

heir apparent / heir presumptive

An *heir apparent* is one who has an unassailable right to inherit. An *heir presumptive* is one whose right to inherit may be interfered with by the birth of a child closer in lineage. Thus, for example, if a queen has no offspring (who would, according to law, inherit the throne on the queen's death or abdication) but she has a younger brother (who would be next in line), the brother would be the *heir presumptive,* and, if no offspring were born to the queen, would inherit. On the other hand, if a child is born to the queen, the child becomes the *heir apparent,* whereupon the brother's former status is lost.

herb / spice

Herbs are, technically, annual or perennial plants whose aerial parts die at the end of each growing season; many of them are used for seasoning foods. A *spice* is any substance used for seasoning foods; among spices from plants there may be herbs as well as other such things as ginger, which comes from a root, nutmeg, ground from the seeds of a tree, cinnamon, made from the bark of a tree, pepper, made from the dried fruit of a plant, and so forth. Although many herbs are used as spices, all are not, and it is confusing to refer to all herbs willy-nilly as spices. Also, spices—*seasonings* might be a more accurate term—come from plants that are not herbs, so it is likewise confusing to refer to all spices as herbs.

high comedy / low comedy

High comedy is the name given to comedies of manners, of drawing-room style involving sophisticated characters, in which the humor depends largely on witty dialogue. *Low comedy* involves ordinary characters, as depicted in television "situation-comedies" ("sitcoms"), old-time burlesque, farce, etc.

High German / Low German

The unfortunate names of these language groups in English belie their origin: *High German* is a translation of German *Hochdeutsch*, in reference to the fact that they were the languages spoken in the inland, somewhat more mountainous parts where German was spoken; *Low German* is a translation of German *Plattdeutsch*, which identified the German spoken in the northern, lowland areas where German was spoken. The terms, in their origins, thus have nothing at all to do with whether one dialect is "better" or "worse" or of "higher" or "lower" class than the other. Because *Hochdeutsch* was for generations the prestige dialect of Berlin, it acquired social connotations of learnedness and sophistication which no amount of linguistic scientific argument has been able to remove. In any event, on a formal, linguistic level, the High German group includes dialects like Modern German, Yiddish, Bavarian, and most of the others spoken in central Germany; Low German gave rise to English, Flemish, Dutch, and other Lowland dialects of the north. (See also **Yiddish / Hebrew.**)

highboy / lowboy

Both terms are applied to chests of drawers, originally designed mainly in the 18th century. The *highboy* is a chest set on relatively tall legs, with an over-all height of about six feet; the *lowboy*, usually with fewer drawers, is set on shorter legs, and has an over-all height of about 30 to 36 inches. Variant names for the highboy are *highdaddy* and *tallboy*.

higher criticism / lower criticism

Higher criticism describes the study of the Bible in which the identification and date of authorship, historical relevancy, interpretation, and details of composition are the object; *lower criticism* describes the

Bible study in which the object is the reconstruction of the original texts.

Highlands / Lowlands

In Scotland, these terms refer to the more northern, mountainous regions, north of the Grampians (*the Highlands*) and the more level southern, central, and eastern regions (*the Lowlands*).

High Mass / Low Mass

In the Roman Catholic Church and the Anglican Communion, the celebrant of a *High Mass* is usually attended by other clergy and assistants and the liturgy is sung rather than said; it usually includes music, a choir, incense, and more elaborate ceremony. A *Low Mass*, celebrated by a priest attended only by an acolyte and, sometimes, another cleric, is simpler, one in which the liturgy is said rather than sung.

Hinayana Buddhism / Mahayana Buddhism / Theravada Buddhism

These are the names of the major branches of Buddhism. The *Hinayana*, the oldest, is active in Sri Lanka, and southeast Asia; its emphasis is on the Pali scriptures and on individual efforts to attain salvation. The *Mahayana*, which predominates in China, Japan, Nepal, and Tibet, emphasizes the ecclesiastical laws set forth in Sanskrit and the tenet that salvation is attainable through faith. Hinayana aims at *arhatship*, that is, the condition of a Buddhist who has attained *nirvana*, freedom from endless reincarnations, while Mahayana aims at *bodhisattva*, that is, the postponement of nirvana to help others towards enlightenment. *Hinayana* derives from the Sanskrit compound meaning 'lesser vehicle' and is sometimes itself called the *Little Vehicle*; *Mahayana* comes from the Sanskrit meaning 'greater vehicle' and is sometimes called *Greater Vehicle*; *arhat* comes from Sanskrit meaning 'worthy of respect'; and *bodhisattva* is a Sanskrit compound of *bodhi* 'illumination' + *sattva* 'existence.' A later development was *Theravada*, extant as the *Sarvastivada* school, which is characterized chiefly by its materialism. (See also **Buddhism / Hinduism.**)

histamine / antihistamine

Considering the wide use of *antihistamines* in numerous pharmaceutical remedies for colds and allergies, *histamine* would appear to be receiving a bad press. It is, however, a completely normal product of the body's reaction against inflammation and intrusive microorganisms to which the body is allergic. The release of histamine produces an increase in the secretion of gastric juices, contraction of the smooth muscles of the uterus, and dilatation of the capillaries and, consequently, a decrease in blood pressure. Antihistamines do not inhibit the release of histamine, they serve to block its effects. To this end, antihistamines come in two basic varieties: those that act as preventives against the symptoms of hay fever, hives, insect bites, etc., are called H_1 *blockers* and include piperazines, ethylenediamines, ethanolamines, and alkylamines; and those, like cimetidine, called H_2 *blockers*, that control gastric secretions and are used in treating duodenal ulcers. The side effects of the former may include nausea, constipation, sleepiness, and a feeling of dryness in the respiratory tract.

homicide / murder / manslaughter

The general term for the killing of a person by another is *homicide.* According to the criminal code prevailing, *murder* is either the intentional killing of another or the malicious killing of another during the commission of a crime, whether intentional or not. *Manslaughter* is the unintentional, accidental killing of another human being—that is, without malice—as in self-defense. In the United States, *involuntary manslaughter* is a category that includes unpremeditated, nonmalicious killing of another through carelessness in the course of a lawful act which might cause another's death, as when driving a car, called *vehicular homicide; voluntary manslaughter* is the killing of another in a state of passion, as in a fight. *Criminal homicide* is characterized as *murder* when recklessness or indifference are determined (as in committing or attempting to commit rape, robbery, arson, burglary, kidnapping, felonious escape, or other felonious crimes) or when the crime is committed with full knowledge and intent. In most states of the United States, two degrees of murder are recognized: *murder in the first degree* (called "murder one" in many of the police dramas made for television) includes murder that is premeditated (as in poisoning, lying in ambush, etc.) or that is committed in the course of perpetrating or attempting to perpetrate the crimes of arson, burglary, rape, or robbery, though this latter condition has been mitigated in a variety of different ways in different states; *murder in the second degree* ("murder two") covers all other instances of criminal homicide.

homograph / homonym / homophone

A *homograph* is a word that is spelled exactly like another but comes from an entirely different source and almost invariably has a different meaning. Examples of homographs are:

stake—a stick.	**stalk**—stem of a plant.
stake—a wager.	**stalk**—to pursue stealthily.
stall—a compartment.	**staple**—a U-shaped piece of wire.
stall—to delay.	**staple**—a raw material.

A *homophone* is a word that sounds exactly like another but differs in meaning; it might be spelled the same way (as are *homographs*), but not necessarily. The following are homophones:

to, too, two	**beat, beet**
choir, quire	**stake, steak**
dear, deer	**wrung, rung, rung**
right, rite, write	**flea, flee**
meet, meat, mete	**bear, bear**

Not all words that are spelled identically are pronounced identically; thus they may be homographs without being homophones, as in the following examples:

subject—noun	**tower**—'something that tows'
subject—verb	**tower**—'tall structure'
lead—'metal'	**read**—present tense of verb
lead—'go in front'	**read**—past tense of verb

The term *homonym* is often used ambiguously for *homograph* and *homophone*. In the event, it is better avoided.

hotel / inn / motel / boatel / hostelry / caravanserai

The generic word for a business offering overnight accommodation in a number of rooms and, often, a wide variety of other facilities, is *hotel. Inn* is a somewhat more colorful, less neutral word that usually carries—or once carried—the connotation of rural quaintness, though that sense has been considerably diluted by the naming of major hotels and large motel chains using the word *inn.* In the 1930s, with the increased use of cars in the United States, so-called *motor hotels* came into being. These were found along roadsides in rural areas and consisted mainly of a number of unconnected small houses, each big enough for a bedroom and lavatory. They were quite inexpensive compared with the (usually) more luxurious hotels; because of their layout they offered the opportunity for illicit rendezvous: to come and go from a room one did not have to pass through a lobby and come under the scrutiny of any staff; in fact, few motor hotels had any staff besides the owner and a chambermaid. The stigma attached to motor hotels as venues for naughty liaisons and dirty weekends inspired owners to adopt the acronym *motel.* Although *motel* survives, beginning in the 1960s there was a revival of *motor hotel,* which had lived down its suggestive reputation and, curiously, was seen by hoteliers as a more staid and formal name than *motel.* Yet, both survive today, even though the often luxurious, high-priced accommodations offered by many throughout the world—some in the heart of a large city—bear little resemblance to the modest overnight places of the 1930s. *Boatel,* which is a motel situated at or near a marina, is, of course, a punning model of a 'motel for boaters.' *Hostelry* is a neutral word for *hotel,* but, depending on its context, can be used disparagingly. *Caravanserai,* or *caravansary,* is the name for a hotel in the Middle East, originally one that offered overnight accommodation for caravans (of the Middle Eastern type); the word is composed of two elements from Persian, *caravan* 'caravan' and *sarai* 'hotel.' Referring to a (Western) hotel as a *caravanserai* in English is not exactly disparaging but connotes indefinable characteristics of quaint foreignness, possibly with some intrigue mixed in.

hot metal / cold type

In typesetting, the traditional methods of casting characters, either individually or a line at a time, involved the pouring of molten type metal into molds, or dies, and were called *hot-metal* systems; in recent years techniques have been developed for the creation of characters by photographic means and, most recently, by the creation of type images by computer. These latter methods are called *cold type* because no molten metal is involved.

house / home

In the title of her novel *A House Is Not a Home*, ex-madam Polly Adler was pointing up the distinction between *home* as a place with all the pleasant connotations of warm, loving family life and *house*, which in her case was used in the oblique sense of 'whorehouse, house of ill repute.' Although that is not the first meaning that is brought to mind by *house*, the word certainly has much the cooler, detached associations of 'building' than does the cosier *home*. Fully aware of the distinctions, those in the business of building and selling houses usually refer to them as *homes*.

House of Commons / House of Lords

These are the names of the two main chambers of the Parliament of Great Britain. The *House of Commons*, which represents all adults excepting members of the *House of Lords*, consists of more than 600 elected members, designated as *Members of Parliament*, who, before the Reform Act of 1832 (and subsequent legislation), represented not the people but the communities of England, Scotland, and Northern Ireland. The Reform Act served to reorganize the system by extending the franchise to all adult males, later to females, as well. The *House of Lords*, for which more than 1000 peers are qualified by hereditary right or by the creation of the sovereign, consists of law lords (who have held high judicial office or have been appointed), spiritual peers (bishops and archbishops of the Church of England), Scottish representatives, and, formerly, Irish peers. The spiritual peers are designated as *Lords Spiritual*, the others as *Lords Temporal*. The main difference between the Houses is that Commons controls all legislation dealing with money, from which consideration Lords is enjoined. One of the main function of the House of Lords is the detailed analysis of bills, for time in Commons may be insufficient. The Law Lords serve as the court of highest appeal in the country. (See also **lower house / upper house.**)

House of Representatives / Senate

The *House of Representatives,* often just called 'the House,' and the *Senate* form the two chambers of the Congress of the United States. Members of the former are called *Representatives* or *Congressmen,* of the latter, *Senators.* Representatives are elected from a specific district of their state, the district being determined by the population: a census is taken every ten years and the number of Representatives is reapportioned accordingly; there may be changes in number, in the constituencies represented, or both. Representatives serve for two years. The Senate is composed of two Senators from each state, each elected at large for a six-year term, with one third of the Senate coming up for election every two years. As there are 50 states, there are 100 Senators. The Congress serves as the Legislative branch of the government, the other two branches being the Executive, as represented by the President, and the Judicial, as represented by the Supreme Court. (See also **lower house / upper house.**)

humidity / temperature

Humidity is the amount of water vapor in the atmosphere; the *relative humidity,* which is usually referred to in reporting weather conditions, is the proportion of water vapor in the air in comparison to the maximum possible amount at the same atmospheric pressure and temperature and is expressed as a percentage. *Temperature* is the measure of the warmth (or lack thereof) in the air. Although comfort is a matter of personal preference, most people are comfortable at a temperature between 70° and 78°F. (21°-26°C) and a humidity of between 30 and 60 percent. The warmer the air, the more moisture it will hold; an increase of 20°F. (11°C) doubles the capacity of the air to hold water vapor. The lower the relative humidity, the easier it is for perspiration to evaporate; as this evaporation is inhibited by increased humidity, the more humid it is, the less comfortable it is. For that reason, a relatively high temperature above 90°F. (35°C) may be comfortable if the relative humidity is low and extremely uncomfortable if the relative humidity is more than 60 percent. The *dew point* is the temperature at which the atmosphere is thoroughly saturated; a drop in temperature below the dew point causes water vapor to condense as water droplets. Early in the morning, when the sun has not yet risen to warm the air and the earth has cooled so that the air is no longer warmed by radiation, this temperature is often reached, resulting in the deposit of water droplets, or dew.

hung / hanged

Pictures are *hung;* people, alas, are *hanged.* The reason for the distinction lies in the history of *hang,* the modern word being a coalescence of two Old English words of different origin. Careful users distinguish between the two, but the difference appears only in the past and the participle:

FORM	PICTURES, ETC.	PEOPLE
hang (infinitive)	*Hang the Picasso here.*	*Let's hang him today!*
hanging (present progressive)	*We were hanging about.*	*They're hanging Danny Deever in the morning.*
hung (past)	*We hung the pictures.*	N /A
hanged (past)	N /A	*They hanged him at dawn.*
hung (past participle)	*The stockings were hung by the chimney with care.*	N /A
hanged (past particple)	N /A	*You are to be hanged by the neck until dead.*

hydrofoil / hovercraft

A *hydrofoil* is a motor vessel equipped with horizontal vanes at the ends of struts that project below the hull in such a way that when the vessel gains sufficient forward speed, the vanes, acting as planing surfaces (like water-skis) lift the hull clear of the surface of the water allowing the craft to skim along, eliminating the drag of the water on the hull. A *hovercraft* (originally a trade name) is a vehicle with a flattish bottom surrounded by a deep skirt, usually of reinforced rubber, and a number of motor-driven, high-powered fans that blow air downwards, at tremendous pressure, towards the surface below the craft. The pressure raises the craft clear of the ground or water below it, and it rides along on a cushion of air, forward motion being imparted by aircraftlike propellers set vertically, usually at the top of the craft for safety. Hovercraft can traverse any relatively horizontal terrain; as they can be land-based, they are used as ferries. Hydrofoils, also used as ferries, require the same mooring facilities as boats, operate in generally calmer waters (like bays), and are more economical to operate.

iamb / trochee / spondee / dactyl / anapaest

These are the names of the most common metrical patterns used in Western poetry. In Classical Greek and Latin, poetic meter was determined by long and short syllables—that is, by their duration when pronounced. In Modern English, metrical rhythm is established by whether a syllable is stressed or unstressed, and a syllable may be part of a word or a word by itself. The following table shows the major meters used in English; each is called a *foot*.

NAME	NO. OF SYLLS.	DESCRIPTION	EXAMPLE
iamb	2	1st unstressed, 2nd stressed	*The stag at eve had drunk his fill.*
trochee	2	1st stressed, 2nd unstressed	*Water, water, everywhere.*
dactyl	3	1st stressed, 2nd and 3rd unstressed	*Forward the Light Brigade. Was there a man dismayed?*
anapaest	3	1st and 2nd unstressed, 3rd stressed	*'Twas the night before Christmas, And all through the house . . .*
spondee	2	both stressed	(Used as an occasional variant.)

The number of metrical feet in a line, or verse, of a poem forms part of its description:

NUMBER OF FEET IN VERSE	NAME
2	DIMETER
3	TRIMETER
4	TETRAMETER
5	PENTAMETER
6	HEXAMETER
7	HEPTAMETER

Thus, a poem may be written in what would be termed *iambic pentameter,* in *dactylic hexameter,* etc.

-ic / -ous

These terms are used to distinguish between two valence states of an element in compounding: in *ferric* chloride, for example, $FeCl_3$, the iron is trivalent, and in *ferrous* chloride, $FeCl_2$, the iron is divalent; in *sulfuric* acid, H_2SO_4, the sulfur is trivalent, and in *sulfurous* acid, H_2SO_3, the sulfur is tetravalent; in *nitric* oxide, NO, the nitrogen is divalent, and in *nitrous* oxide, N_2O, it is monovalent. (See also **-ate / -ite.**)

ice cream / sherbet / sorbet / ice milk / frozen custard

There are so many varieties of frozen desserts of this type and they vary so widely in their content that it is virtually impossible to distinguish them with any measure of precision. *Ice cream* is a flavored mixture of cream; commercial ice cream usually contains less cream and more milk as well as thickeners and other additives, like preservatives. Ice cream made from ideal ingredients is likely to be quite expensive, reducing the total market considerably, so manufacturers substitute lighter liquids for the heavy cream and add emulsifiers, cheaper fats, and other substances to simulate good ice cream. *Ice milk* uses skimmed milk as a substitute for cream. *Sherbet* is made with fruit juice and skimmed or whole milk or cream (though less than used in ice cream), with egg white or gelatin; it is colder and less creamy than ice cream and contains a higher proportion of ice. *Sorbet,* a word borrowed from French, is the same as sherbet: both are borrowings from Arabic (ultimately from Turkish) words meaning a 'drink.' There is nothing special to be said about *frozen custard:* it is what its name describes it to be. But in all of these categories, the quality varies in direct proportion to the ingredients, which vary enormously. For generations, Americans were persuaded that "French" ice cream was the best, though, more recently, native concoctions, especially those made in the northeastern United States, have gained high reputations; in Great Britain, where sherbets (there called "sorbets") are generally of good quality, ice cream is generally of poor quality, even that which is offered as "New England" ice cream, to which it bears little resemblance. Ice cream or *ices*, a term that includes everything from sherbet to shaved ice served in a paper cup with some flavoring poured over it, may be frozen on a stick, a form sold by street and other vendors that has proved popular, especially with children, for decades.

icing sugar / granulated sugar / candy sugar

Icing sugar is the name given in Great Britain to what is called *confectioner's sugar* in the United States; a British variant is *caster sugar* (because it is usually served in a *caster*, a container with perforations at the top for sprinkling caster sugar on food; the more common word for *caster* in the U.S. is *muffineer*). Icing sugar is finely powdered, a consistency that allows it to melt and blend faster than more coarsely ground varieties, and a small amount of cornflour is added to prevent caking. *Granulated sugar* is of somewhat coarser grind, slightly coarser still in Britain than in the U.S.; it is the sugar usually served for use in tea and coffee and for other table uses. *Superfine* or *berry sugar*, somewhere between granulated and icing sugar in fineness, is used for sprinkling on fresh fruits and is suitable for meringues. *Demerara sugar* and *candy* (or *candied*) *sugar* are both varieties of crystallized sugar, the former a golden color with a gravelly look, the latter a dark golden brown and consisting of crystals up to about one eighth of an inch in size; both are manufactured by boiling raw sugar and then allowing it to crystallize. Candy sugar and demerara sugar are usually served for putting in tea or, especially, coffee. In the U.S., *turbinado* is known, mainly in the South, for uses similar to those of demerara, which it resembles; it is a raw sugar that has been washed to remove some of the molasses. American and Canadian *rock candy* is a confection consisting of large crystals of plain sugar and is called *rock sugar* in Britain; it is not the same as *rock*, which is the British term for a stick of peppermint-flavored sugar typically having a colored pattern throughout its length and sold at holiday resorts.

idealism / naturalism / realism

In the context of the fine arts, *idealism* cleaves to the theory that art should depict things as they are idealized in the imagination. Idealism is in contradistinction to *naturalism*, which holds that representation of things should be in form and color as they appear in nature, and to *realism*, which is similar to naturalism but focuses on detailed works that are an accurate imitation of reality, especially emphasizing some of the more sordid aspects of life. The last has given rise to *hard-edge realism*, in which the artist attempts to create a photographic reproduction of a scene. Thus, the paintings of Constable would be said to reflect idealism, those of Reginald Marsh naturalism, and those of Wayne Thiebaud (hard-edge) realism.

ideomotor / sensorimotor

Ideomotor activity is that caused by thought, or an idea; *sensorimotor* is that caused by the senses. Some people, for example, are able to control their blood pressure or pulse at will, a feat that would be classed as ideomotor. An instance of sensorimotor activity would be the contraction of the pupil of the eye as a response to the stimulus of light.

illegal / illicit / illegitimate

Although *illegal* and *illicit* are virtual synonyms, their distribution and use in the language differ to some extent. Both mean 'unlawful; forbidden by law,' but *illegal* is more likely to be the word encountered in contexts of law, while *illicit* has greater frequency when the issue is morality (whether within or outside of the law). One might say *It is illegal to park here;* on the other hand, according to custom, religion, or some other code of behavior, it might be *illicit to marry one's first cousin,* but, because there is no specific statute against the act, it might not be *illegal.* It might be worth noting, too, that while there is a word *licit,* meaning 'legal,' it is quite rare, though *legal* is a very common word, and *illegal* can be said to mean 'not legal' in all the senses of *legal. Illegitimate* is usually the term used to describe a child

born out of wedlock; it cannot be said to mean 'not legitimate' in all
the sense of *legitimate*, which has taken on specialized meanings relating, for instance, to the theater: *legitimate theater* means 'stage plays
produced in major theaters' and is contrasted with radio theater, television theater, vaudeville, and (in the U.S.) off-Broadway and off-off-
Broadway theater. But *illegitimate* could be said to mean 'not having
the stamp of *legitimacy*'; this may appear to be dwelling on a nuance
that is specious, but it must be noted that the proper use of many
words in any language depends on extensive experience with their
connotative and suggested senses, which are not always easy to
describe except by example.   One would, for example, distinguish
between an *illegal use*, an *illicit use*, and an *illegitimate use* of something, say, a trade name: an *illegal use* would be one that is contrary
to law and, presumably, punishable under law; an *illicit use* could be
one that is not condonable and might be clandestine, secret—possibly
"slightly" illegal or shady; an *illegitimate use* would be one that is not
authorized and could be illegal.

imply / infer

One *infers* something said or written by another, who may or may
not have intended that the *inference* be drawn. When a speaker or
writer hints at something and does not express it in a direct, outright
fashion, he is *implying* it by indirection: he is making an *implication*.
Thus, someone who says, "I hope you won't be late" is less likely to be
expressing a genuine hope than hinting that the person addressed
should be on time. If the person addressed has been late on other
occasions, he might infer that the speaker is scolding him for his earlier tardiness.

incandescent / fluorescent

Devices for producing artificial light are of these two basic types. The
incandescent lamp, or *bulb*, is essentially a filament made of a substance (like tungsten) that glows brightly when electricity passes
through it. It was developed by Thomas Alva Edison (1847–1931), who
experimented with hundreds of substances before finding tungsten to
be suitable; today, a variety of materials and configurations is in use,
and lamps, which are at least partially evacuated of air (in order to
avoid burning up the filament), may contain any of a number of dif-

ferent gases for different effects. The *fluorescent lamp,* or *tube,* is a glass tube the inside of which is coated with phosphors that glow when excited by an electrical discharge. The *mercury vapor lamp* contains vaporized mercury which emits a brilliant bluish light when excited by an electric arc produced between electrodes when electricity is supplied to them. A *sodium vapor lamp,* which operates on the same principle, emits a glareless yellow light and is much favored for use in illuminating roads. Powerful searchlights and spotlights used in sports arenas and theaters are often carbon *arc lamps,* in which the electrodes are carbon rods. Such lamps, which are directional, usually have a parabolic mirror and lenses for focusing the beam of light.

incisor / canine / premolar / molar

These are the names for the various kinds of teeth in the human mouth. At the very front, there are eight *incisors,* four each in the top and bottom jaws; on the sides of these, moving towards the back, are the *canines,* also four in number; the eight *premolars* flank these; and finally, on each side, top and bottom, there are three *molars*—twelve in all. The normal human mouth has 32 permanent teeth.

incredible / incredulous

Incredible means 'unbelievable'; *incredulous* means 'unbelieving.' A shop may offer *incredibly low prices,* which the public may regard *with incredulity*—in other words, they do not believe it. If someone remarks, "You're incredible!" what is meant is that it is hard for him to believe that your behavior or way of thinking is truly being experienced on earth; saying that you, yourself, are incredulous would simply mean you are not a believer in what you are experiencing. Thus it would be odd to refer to another person as "incredulous" and to yourself as "incredible."

index / indices

Indexes is a suitable plural for *index* in all contexts. *Indices* is used as a plural in technical and scientific applications. Thus, one might use the latter in referring to more than one *price index,* more than one *index of refraction,* or, in mathematics, to more than superior or inferior number used as an index; but in speaking of a book in which there is, say, a word index and a topic index, the two together would be called *indexes.*

indicative / subjunctive / imperative

These grammatical terms refer to the *moods* of verbs. The *indicative mood* is that used for ordinary, declarative statements (or questions), as that of *singing* in *She is singing an aria from Verdi.* The *subjunctive mood* is that used for conditional or contrary-to-fact statements and for certain subordinate constructions, as that of *were* in *If I were king* (present) or *had known* in *Had I only known . .* (past), and *should go* in *Should he go, she would follow* (future); *stay* in *The teacher asked that he stay after school,* or *be* in *It is important that you be present.* There are many words, once subjunctive forms, that have become auxiliaries in Modern English, *must, should,* and *would,* for example: *We must go. I should leave soon. Would you remove your hat?* Those who think that these forms can easily be replaced by *ought to* are quite correct, but they should bear in mind that *ought* is the past (and subjunctive) form of *owe:* the Modern English *We ought to go* replaces the older form, *We should owe to go.* The subjunctive is used in wishes: *May God have mercy on your soul. Thy kingdom come. Damn you!* (all present); *I should be happy to attend. She would love to go* (both past). *I should have been happy to have attended. She would love to have gone* (both past perfect). Certain words introduce clauses that require the subjunctive:

> **lest:** *Hurry, lest you be late.*
> **so that:** *He left so that she could stay.*
> **in order that:** *She left in order that he might stay.*
> **for fear that:** *I wrote the number down for fear that I might forget it.*

Those who deplore the "disappearance of the subjunctive" usually focus on the replacement of it by the indicative in utterances like, *If I was there, it never would have happened* (in place of *If I had been . .* or *If I were . . ,* for example), generally unaware that proper analysis of scores of modern clichés, idioms, and ordinary language would yield its persistent presence in everyday speech and writing. Although it is impossible to treat as complex a subject as the English subjunctive in a brief compass, examples occur in all of the following common constructions:

You *shall* go, whether you want to or not.
Years passed before I *came to* realize my mistake.
She *should* be taken to the hospital.
Had he only *told* me I could have done something!
It *may* snow tomorrow.
His morals are not what they *might* be.

The *imperative mood* is used to express a command:

Give me that gun!	*Don't* bother me!
Get out of here!	Never *say* 'die'!
Drop dead!	*Let's* not [do it] and say we did.
Kiss me quick!	You *had* better go, now.
Go to hell!	They *shall* not pass!

Such common expressions as those found on street signs are imperatives:

No Parking; No Standing; Walk; Don't Walk; Don't foul the footway; Stop; Slow; Don't Litter.
Also: *Down in front! Viva Zapata! Hats off to the goalkeeper! All aboard! Pass the salt! Danger! Wet Paint! All rise!*

There are a large number of technical names (e.g., optative subjunctive, volitive subjunctive, etc.) to describe each of the myriad applications of that mood. The indicative and imperative moods are not difficult to identify in Modern English; the subjunctive appears in more subtle contexts and, as its forms are not as readily distinguishable in English as they might be in, say, Latin, it must be identified syntactically, which is not always easy to do if one is not an expert grammarian. In any event, notwithstanding the despair of many purists, the subjunctive is far from defunct in English: but one must know where to look for it and how to identify it. Those who believe that it is alive and well in British English may be disappointed: in *The Sunday Times* [18 October 1987, p. 5], the Executive Editor, Brian MacArthur wrote: "NI [News International] is insisting that each tenderer offers a seven-day service." Because *insist* is one of those verbs which, when followed by a clause beginning "that . . ," almost always requires a subjunctive, the form should have been *offer.*

inertial guidance / command guidance

Inertial guidance is a navigation system for airplanes, missiles, and other vehicles that operates independently of external points of reference, using only the calculations of an onboard computer to determine position at any moment. The system is based on an arrangement of three gyroscopes, which maintain their orientation relative to the earth regardless of the movement of the craft; a computer continuously calculates changes of three coordinates from the point of takeoff, displaying them by means of electronic devices. The first practical inertial guidance systems were used to control the V-2 rockets launched against Britain by Germany during WWII. Today they are used by submarines and other craft that may have to operate without the benefit of external observations, as of landmarks, radio, celestial navigation, etc. *Command guidance* employs a system in which a vehicle or missile is controlled externally by radio, radar, laser, or even a direct wire. Various kinds of command guidance systems are in use, among them, *preset guidance,* in which a missile is controlled by commands that are programmed into its control mechanism before launching; *beam-riding guidance,* in which the missile is directed along a radio, radar, or other beam which has been fixed on a target, as an enemy aircraft, by its launching crew; and *homing guidance,* in which a missile is directed by the reflection of radar signals from the target, in the case of heat-seeking devices, by the heat emitted by the engine of a target aircraft or missile, or by other energy radiating from the target.

inferior conjunction / superior conjunction

Inferior conjunction occurs when a celestial body in an orbit between two other bodies moves into a position between them such that all three are in alignment, as when Mercury passes between the earth and the sun. *Superior conjunction* occurs when such alignment takes place with the intermediate body on the far side of one of the two, as when the orbit of Mercury carries it to the side of the sun opposite to that of the earth. The terms are usually applied to planets or moons in the solar system in relation to the sun.

inflammable / nonflammable

The word *inflammable* means 'able to burn'; *nonflammable* means 'unable (or unlikely) to burn.' Because the prefix *in-* (which becomes *im-* before certain sounds) means 'not' in many common English words (for example, *inhospitable, inhuman, insensible, indecent, inade-quate), inflammable* was taken by many people to mean its exact oppo-site, that is 'not flammable,' and serious injuries resulted in the misunderstanding. As a consequence, many English-speaking countries passed laws requiring manufacturers of materials and substances that burned easily to use the word *flammable,* which is felt to be unambig-uous, in place of *inflammable. Inflammable* comes from *inflame,* of course, and not from *in-* 'not' + *flammable* 'combustible.'

informal / slang / taboo

Just as it is impossible when examining a solar spectrum to see a clearcut dividing line between, say, greenish yellow and yellowish green, in viewing levels of language one must recognize that the same sort of continuum prevails: the ability to distinguish among the levels depends on how many levels are established and their criteria. Not-withstanding, even if only two levels existed, "acceptable in polite soci-ety" and "unacceptable," the criteria change all the time, not only because there are many "societies" within any given culture but because those societies change continuously: in the 1930s and '40s, *hell* and *damn* were banned from use on American radio; in 1939, Clark Gable's line, "Frankly, my dear, I don't give a damn!," in *Gone with the Wind,* came as a real shock to many filmgoers; on (late-night) televi-sion in the 1980s one hears the occasional four-letter words, depend-ing on where the program is being broadcast. The prevailing attitudes toward what is and is not acceptable are largely a function of the age of those who make the decisions: the older they are, the more conser-vative they are likely to be. Thus, while the categories *informal, slang,* and *taboo* can be defined, listing words and senses within those cate-gories is quite another matter. Perhaps *taboo* might seem to be the easiest category to deal with: *taboo* describes certain words that deal with sexual acts, sex organs, and bodily functions. But it is important to note that it is not the *meanings* that govern the inhibitions, merely the *words,* the collection of sounds (or, in writing, of letters): it is all right, in an appropriate context on radio or television or in the other popular media to discuss *sexual intercourse, vagina,* and *moving the bowels;* it is not all right to say *fuck, cunt,* and *shit.* Upon reflection, this can be seen to be rather a curious state of affairs, particularly in light of Judeo-Christian culture which, supposedly, destroyed iconism in Biblical times. Language historians may be right in arguing that modern word fetishism is a relic of 17th-century English Puritanism. Whatever its source, it must be reckoned with today by every speaker of the language. In the circumstances, we are left with what we must recognize as criteria of appropriateness in given situations. Thus, in those situations where the use and usage of language is the least important, say, a prison, word choice becomes irrelevant, and words that might otherwise be condemned for any of a variety of reasons are in free circulation. At the other extreme, say, an address delivered before the House of Lords, propriety demands a certain mode of expression; whether that mode be artistic or not is immaterial: it must conform to what is generally regarded as *formal,* which characterizes not only the choice of words but the rhetoric employed in stringing them together. In short, *formal* language usually implies utterances that have been prepared in advance with some care and are often read aloud. (Since all writing is "prepared in advance," it can, depending on its character, also be formal; the writing in a popular newspaper would probably not be classified as formal, but that in scholarly journals would.) *Informal* language is the normal, everyday means of expression: in speech, it describes the impromptu language that all speakers use for normal communication, that people on radio and television use when they are not using materials that were prepared in advance, as in interviews and discussions; in writing, which tends to be slightly more formal in all contexts, it is the language of newspapers and of popular periodicals. The identification of *slang* is extremely difficult. Many people think they know how to label language as slang when they encounter it, but they would be sore put to define it. To be sure, there is nothing wrong in that: the ability to articulate sensibilities is not a requirement for having them and putting them to good use (except, perhaps, among lexicographers). The test is the consistency with which different observers label the same words and that with which an individual observer labels those words after the passage of time: the individual may well feel different about his label for a word on Monday morning from the way he felt on Friday afternoon. *Slang* is defined in many different ways: according to one major dictionary, the criteria of slang include its being "more metaphorical, playful, elliptical, vivid, and ephemeral than ordinary language" (*Random House Dictionary, Unabridged Edition, I & II*); according to another, it is "characterized primarily by connotations of extreme informality and [usually] a currency not limited to a particular region and composed typically of coinages or arbitrarily changed words, clipped or shortened forms, extravagant, forced, or facetious figures of speech, or verbal novelties [usually] experiencing quick popularity and relatively rapid decline into disuse" (*Merriam-Webster Third New International*); in the *OED* it is described as "language of a highly colloquial type, considered as below the level of standard educated speech, and consisting either of new words or of current words employed in some special sense." The last was written almost a hundred years ago and cannot be expected to reflect up-to-date notions about slang. *Slang* remains a vague concept, notwithstanding the use of the word in the titles of dictionaries (some of which fail to define the word in their front matter) and as a frequently encountered word in the current idiom. (See also **colloquial / informal, standard / nonstandard.**)

ingenious / ingenuous

Although these words came from the same source originally, their meanings have diverged to the point where they bear little resemblance to one another today. *Ingenious* means 'resourceful; inventive; characterized by originality'; *ingenuous* means 'naive; innocent.' One possible way of remembering which is which is by recalling that an *ingenue* (or *ingénue*) is, in theater parlance, a young(ish) girl who is innocent, naive, virginal, and generally not characterized by sophistication. *Disingenuous* means 'not as ingenuous, or innocent, as might first appear.'

initiative / referendum / recall

In many countries, but not including Great Britain, the principle of *initiative* has become a statutory right. Providing for the introduction of laws directly by a stipulated number of the people in situations where their representatives do not act swiftly enough or in accordance with their wishes, initiative is rarely employed because it is cumbersome and costly. *Referendum* provides a means by which a proposed law can be voted on directly by the people at the next general election or in a special election. There are various kinds of referendums, as a *constitutional referendum*, in which proposed amendments to a constitution are voted on, a *statutory referendum*, in which laws passed by a legislature or the result of initiative are voted on by the people, etc. Although Great Britain has no explicit provision for referendum, its principles are inherent in the election system. *Recall,* which enables the people to vote officials out of office, is a statutory right under the law of many cities and states of the United States.

innocent / not guilty

In courts in Britain and the United States, people accused of crime plead *not guilty* or *guilty;* they do not "plead innocent."

input / output / throughput

These fairly new terms became current in the language during the 1950s, originally to fill the needs of computer technologists. In computer terminology, *input,* as a noun, refers to the data (whether text or programs) fed into a computer; as a verb, it means to 'feed such data into a computer,' whether it is done by keyboarding, via tape, disk, or modem, by direct connection with another computer, by scanning printed text on a special device, by means of a light pen or "mouse," or by any other medium. *Output,* as a noun, refers to the information, text, or other material generated by a computer, whether it is printed, displayed on a monitor, sent to another computer via any means, etc. *Throughput* refers to the amount of work done by a computer in processing data. *Throughput* appears only occasionally in other contexts (as in reference to the production of a machine); but both *input* and *output* have established themselves firmly in the language and are today used in a wide variety of metaphoric applications of the dominating computer technology sense, which has taken over from earlier senses of the words.

intaglio / engraving / lithography / silk screen

There are many different processes for transferring an image to paper or some other surface to produce multiple copies, some of them developed thousands of years ago. Some processes are suitable for the reproduction of large numbers of copies, as of books and periodicals on presses, others for limited numbers, as of office papers, booklets, etc., by copying machines. Those described here are the methods used for the reproduction of large numbers. (See also **Mimeograph / hectograph / xerography / Photostat.**) The oldest known principle, *letterpress*, or *relief printing*, involves cutting out (by tools or chemicals) on the surface of a wood or metal block or plate the areas that are not to be printed, leaving the image that is to be reproduced—whether one or more alphabetic or numeric characters or a drawing—as a raised surface. This surface is then coated with ink and pressed on paper to transfer the image (reversed, of course) onto the paper. The most commonly seen printing block or plate using this method is the ordinary rubber stamp. A printing block may be made of almost any material hard enough to withstand repeated use but not porous, lest it absorb the ink rather than transfer it to the surface to be printed. Traditionally, printing blocks have been made of wood, bamboo, and a wide variety of metal alloys. Formerly, type (an individual piece of metal containing the raised image of a character) was set by hand; mechanical typesetters have been in use for more than a hundred years, but matter is rarely printed from the type they create: rather, it is printed from plates cast from this type or from impressions taken of this type. Another printing method, called *intaglio*, requires that the image to be printed be cut into the surface of the block, leaving raised the areas that are not to be printed; this cutting may be done by tools or chemicals. The technique calls for the entire block, including the crevices with the image, to be inked; the ink is then scraped off the surface but remains in the crevices. The plate is pressed against the paper, and the ink is transferred onto it. This method is used in *engraving*, in which slightly dampened paper is forced into the design, creating a slightly raised image. In some applications, it is desirable to produce a raised, textured image on the paper; if no ink is used, this method is called *blind embossing*, and the design is usually cut deeper than usual. Engraving is still widely used for invitations, announcements, personal and business notepapers, and so forth, but its expense and the quality of the paper required to make it look good prohibit its general application. A third method of printing is called *lithography*. As the name suggests—it comes from Greek *lithos* 'stone' + *-graphy* 'writing'—the technique originally involved the tracing of an image on a block of stone using a greasy pencil to cover those areas that were not to be printed. A watery ink, which would not adhere to the greased surfaces, was used to transfer the image to paper. This method is still used by artists. In modern commercial applications, however, the image is transferred to a thin metal photosensitized plate and the areas not to be printed are etched with acid. Although the same oily principle and water-based ink are used, the plate is not pressed directly to the paper (or other surface, which may be a packaging material of metal, plastic, or glass) but onto a firm rubber blanket from which the image is then transferred to the final surface. This method is called *offset lithography*, and it is the technique most widely used today in the printing of books, magazines, and many newspapers on high-speed rotary presses. Notwithstanding, many of the finer books published today are printed using letterpress, the quality of which some designers insist cannot be duplicated by offset printing. Textiles and certain large pieces, like posters and works of fine art, are often printed by the *silk screen* process, a direct inking method in which an image is created on a fabric (originally silk) stretched in a frame. Those areas that are not to be printed are coated with wax, which prevents the ink from penetrating the fabric, allowing it to pass through onto the material below only in areas where the image is to appear.

integer / whole number / digit / fraction / natural number

A *whole number* is a number, negative or positive, like *1, 2, 3, 4, 47, –23, 189, –937*; it is the same as an *integer*, but different from a *fraction*, which is a way of writing a mathematical proportion or ratio, a *simple fraction* being one with a whole number for a numerator and a whole number as a denominator, as $^1/_2$, $^5/_8$, $^{1247}/_{2359}$, a *complex fraction* being one with a fraction as the numerator, the denominator, or both. (See also **proper fraction / improper fraction.**) *Figure* is another word for *digit*, which is one of the ten Arabic numerals, 0 through 9. Any of the preceding can be positive or negative, but a *natural number* is a positive integer only.

internal combustion / external combustion

Internal combustion engines include gasoline engines and diesel engines in which the fuel is burnt inside the engine; *external combustion* engines are those, like the steam engine and the steam turbine, in which the fuel is burnt outside the engine to heat water into steam which is used to drive the engine.

interplanetary / interstellar

Interplanetary space refers to the space within the solar system that lies outside the atmospheres of the planets or their moons; it consists mainly of gases, emitted from the sun and transmitted as *solar wind*, and dust. *Interstellar space* is the space between the stars and galaxies that consists mainly of hydrogen with a small amount of dust.

inverse proportion / direct proportion

Two values are said to be in *direct proportion* when an increase (or decrease) in one results in or is related to an increase (or decrease) in the other; for example, the capacity of the atmosphere to hold moisture is in direct proportion to its temperature: as the temperature increases, so does the capacity to hold water vapor. In another example, if the rate of interest on a bank deposit remains constant, then the amount of money one earns in interest will be in direct proportion to the amount one has in the bank. Two values are said to be in *inverse proportion* when an increase (or decrease) in one results in or is related to a decrease (or increase) in the other; for example, the more water one pours into an empty gallon container, the less can be added before the container is full; the greater the elevation above sea level, the lower the atmospheric pressure; the greater the likelihood of security of an investment, the lower the amount of return (conversely, the greater the return, the greater the risk); and, the greater the distance of a surface from a point source of light, the less light will fall on it. (The last of these is an illustration of the *inverse square law,* so called because the illumination on a surface decreases in proportion to the square of its distance from the light source.)

in vitro / in vivo

In vitro, which means, literally, 'in glass' and which suggests 'in a test-tube,' describes the investigation or examination of life processes in the laboratory or in artificially created surroundings. *In vivo,* which means 'in life,' describes the investigation or examination of life processes while they are taking place, in nature.

iotacism / lambdacism / rhotacism / sigmatism

These terms are rather specialized within the realm of phonetics and speech pathology. *Iotacism* refers to the excessive use of the sound "EE" (Greek *iota*) and especially to its substitution in Greek for the sounds of other vowels. Where it is substituted specifically for Greek *eta*, it is called *itacism*. *Lambdacism* refers to the misarticulation of the normal sound of *l* (Greek *lambda*), to its substitution for another sound, as *r*, in *flied lice* for *fried rice*, or to the substitution of another sound for it, as *r* in *Ret it rie* for *Let it lie*. *Rhotacism* (after Greek *rho*) refers to the misarticulation of the normal sound of *r*, to the substitution for it by another sound, as *w*, in *Wight wongs* for *Right wrongs*, and, especially, for the change of *z* to *r* that occurred (between vowels) in the development of many words in Latin: compare *genesis / generis*. *Sigmatism* refers to any misarticulation of the sound *s*, as in lisping, in which unvoiced *th* is substituted for it, in whistling articulations, and so forth.

iron / steel

Iron is a metallic element that is found, in various states of impurity, in nature. It is processed to produce *cast iron, wrought iron* (*q.v.*), and a variety of kinds of *steel*. *Steel* is iron to which carbon and other ingredients have been added to modify it according to the characteristics desired—greater or lesser ductility, malleability, resistance to oxidation (rust), elasticity, etc.

iron / wood

These are the two kinds of clubs used in golf, named for the materials the heads are made of. The head of a *wood* is usually made of wood with a brass sole and face plate. Woods are used for longer shots, as from the tee, for which a *driver* is used, or from some point along the fairway, depending on the terrain, for which a *brassie* (number-two wood) may be used for long, low drives, or a *spoon* (number-three wood), for long, high shots, the faces of the clubs being angled accordingly. The *cleek* (number-four wood," was formerly used for short drives but has been largely replaced by one of the *irons*. The head of an *iron* is made of that metal or some alloy of it. Irons are used for various shots when approaching the green, depending on the lie of the ball and the distance to the cup, and they have faces that are angled accordingly; they have the following numbers and names, with faces progressively more sharply angled from the vertical: 1, *driving iron* (with an almost vertical face); 2, *midiron;* 3, *mid-mashie;* 4, *mashie iron;* 5, *mashie;* 6, *mashie niblick;* 7, *pitcher;* 8, *pitching niblick;* and 9, *niblick* (with a face at an angle of about 45°. The higher the number, the more loft is imparted to the ball and the shorter the distance it will travel. In addition to these is the *putting iron,* or *putter,* used once the ball is on the green; it has a shorter handle than the others and a vertical face so that the ball will roll along the ground.

irons / stays

The nautical expressions *in irons* and *in stays,* which pertain to sailing vessels, are frequently confused. A sailing vessel is said to be *in irons* when she is lying with her head in the wind and with no forward motion or steerageway (which would allow her to be maneuvered). The situation can be extremely perilous, especially in rough weather, for the vessel may begin to move backwards, in which event control is difficult at best, and she may broach to the wind (that is, turn so that her beam, or side, is to the wind). In such tense moments, the only remedy is to put the tiller over all the way in either direction so that the bow is brought off the wind quickly, whereupon the rudder must be brought amidships at once to avoid presenting the beam to the action of the wind and waves. As soon as the vessel has way on (that is, can move forward), she can again be brought under control. When the destination of a fore-and-aft rigged vessel lies in the direction from which the wind is blowing, as she cannot sail directly into the wind, she must tack back and forth (that is, sail a zigzag course) at as close an angle to the wind as possible. As the vessel passes from one tack to the other, with the wind alternately on one side or the other of the sails, during the changeover she moves through a point when the wind is directly ahead, setting the sails to luffing till the wind catches them on the other side, when they again fill. At that moment when the wind is dead ahead and the sails are shaking the vessel is said to be *in stays.* If for any reason—lack of steerageway, a sudden drop or change in the wind, improper helmsmanship—the vessel loses forward motion when in stays, she may find herself in irons.

irony / satire

Satire is the ridicule of an individual, institution, or other subject of criticism, a satire being a piece of writing or art serving as a lightly sarcastic spoof or takeoff, a lampoon. It is usually light-hearted, but not necessarily so: *Gulliver's Travels* (1726), by Jonathan Swift (1667–1745), for example, is a social and political satire, as are *The Rape of the Lock* (1712), by Alexander Pope (1688–1744), and many of the novels of Evelyn Waugh (1903–66). *Irony* is a device, which may be employed in satire, in which a statement made about something or somebody is couched in language that denotes the opposite, or nearly the opposite, of what is intended, as when someone might say, while a storm is raging, "Isn't it just lovely out today!" *Dramatic irony* is a literary device of an entirely different nature: it describes a situation in which the reader (or audience) is made aware of information that one or more characters are ignorant of. (See also **sarcastic/ sardonic.**)

irregardless / regardless

By virtue of the suffix *-less, regardless* is already a negative, meaning 'without regard to; despite': *I must go, regardless of the consequences. She must stay, regardless.* In using *irregardless,* people are creating a redundant negative: since the suffix already makes the word a negative, the negative prefix, *ir-,* is totally unnecessary, making the form "irregardless" a mark of poor style and nonstandard usage.

-ise / -ize

One of several changes urged by Noah Webster in his attempts to reform American spelling was to spell words having a z-sound with a -z- rather than an -s-, which was the British practice. With some consistency in the United States, all such words are spelled *-ize, -ized, -izing, -ization,* etc. Till relatively recently, British spelling continued in its tradition of seeming to prefer the -s- spellings of such words, but, in the past forty years or so, the -z- forms have prevailed. The *OED* describes *-ise* as a variant of *-ize;* other dictionary editors have found various rationales for the use of one spelling in preference to the other, and some anomalies do occur. For instance, the universal practice in the U.S. is to spell *advertise* and *advertisement* as shown; in Britain, one often encounters *advertize* and *advertizement.* British *analyse* and American *analyze* stubbornly retain their respective forms.

isometric / perspective

As these terms apply to mechanical drawings, an *isometric drawing* is one showing all three dimensions to scale with the third dimension drawn at a fixed angle from the plan or elevation view, often at 30°; a *perspective drawing* is one in which the third dimension is drawn so as to simulate the view seen by the human eye, with a suitable *vanishing point* selected. Because perspective drawings distort the dimensions, they cannot be drawn to scale and are usually used to convey some idea of what the completed building or object will look like. (See also **elevation / plan / section.**)

italic / roman

Italic originally referred to the sloping characters of the style of handwriting developed by scribes in Italy before the development of printing, the script referred to in the cliché *fine Italic hand,* which is often rendered as *fine Italian hand.* It was later adopted by typographers who cut what has become known as *italic type* (not usually written with a capital letter and standardly pronounced "i-TAL-ik," not "eye-TALik") and used it to set off words, phrases, or passages that merited special emphasis. *Roman* refers to the vertical style of alphabetical characters adapted from those appearing in inscriptions on ancient Roman monuments. The Romans used only capital letters (called *majuscules*): small letters (*minuscules*—not "miniscules") were not developed till much later. The serifs characteristic of much modern roman type are imitative of the ancient Roman style where they were introduced to finish the ends of letter strokes in an attempt to make them appear more uniform and cut in straighter lines, especially for characters cut into stone. By the time printing from movable type was invented by Johannes Gutenberg (?1400–68), roman type (not usually written with a capital letter) had become the standard established by medieval scribes for ordinary text. Typographically, italic type differs from *oblique* type, which is merely roman type sloped at an angle to the right: differences can be seen in the absence of serifs, in the design of the lower-case *a,* and in other essentials. Most of the so-called italic type styles produced by computer printers are oblique, not italic. Each modern roman typeface has its compatible italic face; in the typestyle of this book, the following first two alphabets (capitals and lower-case) are in roman, the last two are in italic:

ABCDEFGHIJKLMNOPQRSTUVWXYZ

abcdefghijklmnopqrstuvwxyz

ABCDEFGHIJKLMNOPQRSTUVWXYZ

abcdefghijklmnopqrstuvwxyz

(See also **serif** / **sans serif**.)

its / *it's*

Its is the possessive form of *it* and is parallel to the other possessive forms of pronouns, like *his* and *her: The dogs wagged its tail; The sun is doing its best to shine.* *It's* is a contraction for *it is* (*It's a nice day. It's raining*) or for *it has* (*It's been wonderful seeing you again*).

jam / *preserve* / *conserve* / *marmalade* / *jelly*

The distinctions among these terms are not clearcut: *jam* and *preserve* and *conserve* are all names for fruit boiled with sugar till enough of the juices have boiled off to allow the pectin to set. *Conserve* is usually the name reserved for the version that contains whole pieces of fruit and, sometimes, nuts or raisins; in *jam* or *preserve,* the fruits are usually a bit mashed up. *Jelly* does not enter this preserve because it is made from strained fruit and juices, not from the whole fruit. *Marmalade* is jam (or preserve) containing more or less of the rind of the citrus fruit from which it is made, in the same manner as jam, by boiling.

judo / *jujitsu* / *karate* / *kung fu*

These terms refer to oriental "arts?" of self-defense that depend largely on employing an opponent's weight, strength, and balance to his disadvantage. The first three are Japanese in origin; in none of the three are weapons used. *Jujitsu,* also spelled *jujutsu, jiujitsu,* or *jiujutsu,* is a pattern of holds and thrusts intended to throw an adversary or disable him; *judo* is a somewhat refined version of jujitsu developed for sporting events. *Karate,* now practised for sport, is similar to jujitsu but also involves sharp, quick blows to sensitive parts of an adversary's body with the hands, feet, elbows, etc. In *kung fu,* a Chinese version of the foregoing, weapons are sometimes used. (See also **black belt / blue belt / brown belt / green belt / white belt.**)

Julian calendar / Gregorian calendar

The *Gregorian calendar,* in use today, was developed by Pope Gregory XIII (1502–85) and introduced in 1582, though it was not adopted till 1752. It represents a slight revision of the *Julian calendar,* named for Julius Caesar (?100–44 B.C.), who instituted it in 46 B.C. The Julian calendar, ingenious as it was, had made no provision for the precession of the equinoxes: the vernal and autumnal equinoxes (about March 21 and September 22, respectively), when night and day are of equal length, occur when the apparent path of the sun intersects with the plane of the orbit of the earth; owing to various gravitational influences of the sun, moon, and planets, these intersections occur at a slightly later time each year, a "slippage" called the precession of the equinoxes; because no provision for the precession had been made in the Julian calendar, by 1752 the equinoxes were taking place 11 days later than in Caesar's time. (Were the Julian calendar to have remained in effect, the seasons would have been totally reversed in 13,000 years, and the full cycle would have been completed in 26,000 years, called a *Platonic,* or *great year.*) The Gregorian calendar system allowed for this by eliminating leap years (which had been provided for every four years in the Julian calendar) in those years exactly divisible by 400 and by moving the date forward 11 days. For many years there was considerable opposition to the changeover from the Julian to the Gregorian system because the people felt that they were being robbed of those 11 days—in effect that their lives were being shortened by that much time. When adjustments were made, the Julian calendar dates came to be referred to as *Old Style,* the Gregorian as *New Style.*

kakemono / makimono

These are both terms for Japanese scrolls, usually of silk fixed to a firm but pliable backing, containing text, painting, or an illustrated story. A *kakemono* is intended for use as a vertical wall hanging to be rolled up when not in use; a *makimono* is unrolled and viewed horizontally.

katana / wakizashi / kozuka / ko-katana / kogai

These are the names of various weapons and ceremonial gear of the Japanese samurai. The *katana* is the very sharp, curved fighting sword; the *wakizashi* the short dagger used for fighting or for hara-kiri, ceremonial suicide. A ceremonial, ornamented dagger with a detachable blade, worn with the wakizashi, is called a *kozuka*, also called a *ko-katana*. An ornamental bodkin, fitted into a sheath on the scabbard of the katana or wakizashi, is called a *kogai.*

kinetic energy / potential energy

In physics, the *kinetic energy* of a body is its energy in motion that is effectively realized when (or as) the body is brought to rest; the *potential energy* of a body is the energy stored within it as a result of its position, shape, or state. A bullet fired from a pistol, for example, has kinetic energy which is expended when it strikes something; a compressed spring has potential energy which is expended when the compressing force is removed.

kosher / pareve / terefah

Kosher, which has been borrowed by English-speakers to mean 'proper, legitimate, authentic, genuine,' is from Hebrew (via Yiddish) meaning 'fitting, correct.' In Judaic religion it refers to anything that has been approved for consumption or use according to dietary or other law. *Pareve,* or *parve,* (from Yiddish) is the designation given to food that contains no milk or meat in any form and therefore meets the laws of Judaism for dishes that may be served with meat and dairy meals. *Terefah,* or *trefah,* or *tref,* (from Hebrew) designates those things considered unfit for use or foods unfit for consumption under Judaic dietary laws.

krater / kylix / kelebe

The *krater,* or *crater,* a general name for any bowl used for mixing (usually wine and water) by the ancient Greeks, is typically footed with a wide mouth and two handles set horizontally below a flaring neck. The *kelebe* is a special shape of krater, ovoid in shape, with a somewhat narrower mouth and a pair of handles attached vertically from the edge of the mouth to the body. A *kylix* is a shallow, slender-footed drinking cup with a pair of horizontal handles.

Kufic / Neskhi

These describe two forms of script used in writing Arabic. *Kufic* (also spelled *Cufic*) was named after the city of Al Kufa, in Mesopotamia (modern Iraq), where it was developed by scribes making costly copies of the *Koran*. It is rectangular or squarish and, to Western eyes, resembles a stylized geometric design. *Neskhi* (also spelled *Neski*, *Naskhi*), also called *Muhaqqaq*, is the name given to the ordinary cursive script used for Arabic.

lake / pond / lagoon

A *lake* is a relatively large body of inland water surrounded by land; a *pond*, a relatively smaller body of water surrounded by land. There are some bodies of water, properly lakes, that are traditionally called *seas;* the largest of these are the Caspian Sea (169,000 square miles) and the Aral Sea (26,828 square miles). The Dead Sea (370 square miles) falls to the 52nd spot on the list, Great Salt Lake, in Utah, which shares similar characteristics, being six times as large (2300 square miles). The largest lake in the world that is called a lake is Lake Superior, the largest of the Great Lakes in the U.S.; it is 31,820 square miles in area. *Pond* is the designation sometimes used for a small body of water created by damming a stream or river, but Lake Mead, in Arizona / Nevada, formed by Hoover Dam (formerly, Boulder Dam), has an area of 227 square miles. By contrast, the largest lake in Great Britain, Lake Windermere, is less than 60 square miles in extent. A *lagoon* is a body of water similar to a lake or pond save that it connects to the sea and, as at Venice, may be an inlet of the sea; it is the name given to the roughly circular bodies of water enclosed by atolls, in the Pacific Ocean. In some parts of coastal New England, a lagoon is called a pond.

lares / penates

Both *lares* and *penates* were household gods of the Romans, and it is quite difficult to distinguish between them: both were worshiped by libations and offerings of food; both existed as gods of individual households as well as of towns and cities; both were represented as manifestations of any of the major gods (like Jupiter, Minerva, etc.). If there is one difference, it appears to be that the penates were Roman gods in their own right, while the lares were adopted by the Romans from the Etruscans.

large intestine / small intestine

The *large intestine* is the portion of the *lower digestive tract* that includes the *cecum* (or *caecum*), a pouchlike prominence, the *vermiform appendix*, the *ascending, transverse,* and *descending colons* (so called because of the directions in which they pass digested matter), and the *rectum,* which is about 12 cm [5 inches] long and ends in the *anal canal.* At the upper opening of the large intestine is the *ileocecal valve,* which allows digested matter to pass in only one direction. The *small intestine,* which is about 7 meters [23 feet] long, is the portion of the digestive tract that includes the *duodenum,* the *jejunum,* and the *ileum,* which connects with the cecum.

latitude / longitude

The earth is roughly spherical, and it has proved convenient to divide it into segments, like a (peeled) orange, by a pattern of imaginary lines that pass through the poles. These are called *meridians of longitude.* In order to fix positions on the surface of the earth, horizontal concentric rings, at right angles to the meridians, were imagined, the one around the widest point being called the *equator,* the others, parallel to it and resembling slices rather than segments, called *parallels of latitude.* As there are 360° in a circle, there are 360° of longitude. Latitude, however, is measured as being between 0° (the latitude at the equator) and 90°: 90° north latitude is at the North Pole; 90° south latitude is at the South Pole. It became necessary to establish one meridian at 0° longitude, and, because of the worldwide influences of Great Britain at the time, the meridian passing through Greenwich was arbitrarily selected. (See **Greenwich Mean Time / Standard Time / Daylight Saving Time.**) In movement east and west, one passes through degrees of longitude; in movement north and south, through degrees of latitude. Originally, and till recently, all navigational calculations were done by determining position in terms of the distance, east or west, of the Greenwich Meridian, coordinated with the position, north or south, of the equator. Longitude was determined by means of a chronometer, an accurate clock set to Greenwich Mean Time (GMT); by determining the local time (from celestial sightings) and noting the difference between that and GMT, the distance east or west of Greenwich could be calculated. Latitude was determined by sighting a readily identifiable celestial object, like the North Star, regarded as "fixed" in relation to the earth, or a planet, the moon, or the sun, the movements of which relative to the earth were known and recorded in a set of tables called an *ephemeris*. Recent scientific and technological developments, however, have enabled travelers to fix their position by means of radio signals, the fixed positions of artificial satellites, and inertial guidance systems. (See also **inertial guidance / command guidance.**)

laurence / mirage / scintillation

These terms refer to various common optical phenomena. *Laurence* is the name given to the black shimmering, resembling the reflection from a body of water, seen when looking down a level paved road on a sunny day; it is caused by irregularities in the refractive index of the reflected light as it is affected by rising convection currents from the heated surface. A *mirage*, typically associated with the desert, is the projection of far distant objects, frequently inverted and raised above ground level, brought about by the air nearer the ground being denser than that farther up. *Scintillation* is the apparent twinkling of stars and other distant heavenly objects and of other, closer objects (on earth) caused by irregularities in the refractive index of the atmosphere created by its impurities, temperature differences and inversions, layering, and other conditions.

leave / let

Should one say *Leave me alone* or *Let me alone?* That depends on what is meant. *Leave* carries with it the sense of 'depart, depart from,' so *Leave me alone* means 'Go away and allow me to be by myself.' *Let me alone* usually means 'Stop irritating me'; an alternative way of saying the same thing is *Let me be*. It is, of course, more polite to say, *Please leave* (or *let*) *me alone*.

lee / weather

In nautical terminology, the *lee* is the side of a vessel, sail, or part of a vessel situated away from the direction from which the wind is blowing; *weather* designates the side towards which the wind is blowing. Thus, if the wind is blowing from the north, then the north side of the vessel and everything aboard her on that side is said to be on the *weather,* or *windward* side or is said to be *to weather, aweather,* or *to windward.* Similarly, another vessel or anything situated or sighted in the direction from which the wind is blowing would be said to be *aweather* or *to windward.* A distinction is made between these terms in descriptions of the motion of the vessel itself, which would always be *windward* or *to windward,* never "to weather" or "aweather." If the wind is blowing from the north, then the south side is the *lee* and anything spoken of as being *downwind* would be described as being *alee.* In a properly trimmed sailing vessel keeping on a straight course, the *helm,* that is, the tiller or wheel, would be slightly to weather—that is, the upwind side—of amidships, having the effect of putting the rudder slightly alee of amidships. A vessel trimmed so as to sail with the helm on the lee (downwind side) is said to be sailing *by the lee,* which in rough weather can cause the helmsman to lose control over the steering. In order to sail towards the direction from which the wind is blowing, because it is impossible to sail directly into the wind, a sailing vessel must tack back and forth, that is, must sail a zigzag course as close as possible to the wind direction, alternating direction by 90° every so often in order to "make good" the net intended forward motion. If the wind is pressing on the starboard side of the sail of a fore-and-aft rigged vessel it is said to be on a *starboard tack,* if on the port side, then on a *port tack.* In accordance with the rules of the road at sea, in most instances in which sailing vessels meet, the vessel on a starboard tack has right of way over one on a port tack. As the tacks are changed, the sails, booms, and their lines are swept across the deck of the vessel; usually, sheets and any running stays must be adjusted by the crew as the vessel *comes about* ("changes tacks"). It is therefore important to alert the crew of the impending change, both to avoid injury and to ready them for the adjustments to sheets and stays; the helmsman's warning cry is "Ready, about!" followed by a pause to allow the crew to get ready, then "Helm's alee!" to indicate that the tiller or wheel has been thrown over to the lee side, bringing the rudder to weather, and causing the vessel to head up into the wind preparatory to steering her off on the opposite tack. The more quickly this is done the better, lest the vessel be put *in irons* (*q.v.*).

letterpress / offset / intaglio

There are three basic methods for the reproduction of printed images in large quantities, mainly on paper: *letterpress*, in which the image to be printed remains raised by cutting away the background, the surface of the image area is inked, and the ink is transferred to paper or some other surface by means of a press; *offset*, in which an image, regardless of how it was produced, is inked and then 'printed' onto another surface (usually a rubber roller called a *blanket*), from which it is transferred onto the paper or other surface to be printed; and *intaglio*, in which an image, cut into the surface of a plate of wood, metal, or other suitable material, by a tool, acid, or some other means, is inked, the ink on the surface is scraped off, and the ink remaining in the image crevices is transferred onto the paper or other surface to be printed. There are a number of variations of these methods, using a wide variety of materials and of means for transferring the images, but these are the three elementary techniques employed. Mimeograph, hectograph, xerograph, and other methods of reproducing images are generally suitable for smaller quantities than the foregoing, by which many thousands of copies can be printed. Also, laser, dot-matrix, ink-jet, and other kinds of printers that are commonly driven by computers are suitable only for small numbers of copies. (See also **intaglio / engraving / lithography / silk screen.**)

lexicography / lexicology / etymology

Lexicography concerns itself with the preparation of dictionaries of all kinds—monolingual, bilingual, even multilingual, both general and specialized. It requires a curious combination of art, technique, and scholarship, involving a sensitivity to the nuances of language, a mind that is capable of considerable organizational skills, and, as properly practised, a thorough grounding in general and comparative linguistics, philology, phonology and phonetics, and other applicable areas of knowledge. The term *lexicology*, formerly interpreted as synonymous with *lexicography*, has become specialized since the 1940s to mean the 'study of the theory of lexicography,' an expanding though still small subdivision of linguistics. Thus, a *lexicographer* might be anyone who compiles a dictionary, while a *lexicologist* would be a scholar who treats one or more of the many disciplines involved in lexicography but might never have prepared a dictionary. *Etymology*, which is occasionally introduced into terminological discussions by laymen, concerns itself solely with the descriptions of the origins and early histories of words (and phrases); it is a discipline within lexicology and lexicography, and is parallel to phonetics (which deals with the pronunciation of words) and semantics (which deals with their meanings). (See also **phonetics / phonemics, linguistics / philology, dictionary / glossary / lexicon / thesaurus.**)

libel / slander

Both of these terms refer to defamatory statements made about a person. In *libel*, the statements appear in writing, print, pictures, or some other graphic medium; in *slander*, the statements are oral. Although most suits for libel (and all for slander) are civil in nature, there is a provision in some jurisdictions for what is called *criminal libel*, a misdemeanor, in which the four requirements are the durability of the medium, the fact of publication, and the determination of defamation and of malice. In all instances, the maligned party must show that he has been held up to ridicule, shame, or disgrace, that his reputation has been damaged, that his respectability, credibility, and the opinion of him in the minds of right-thinking people have been diminished and impaired.

license / licence / practise / practice

In British spelling, *license* and *practise* are verbs, *licence* and *practice* are nouns: *He has a licence to practise medicine. He has a successful law practice. They should not license poor drivers.* In the United States, *license* is used for both noun and verb: *Every dog has to have a license. Licensing dogs is the job of the dog warden.* Usage varies in the U.S. in the matter of *practice /practise:* some people follow the British practice, others practise the American approach.

lie / fib / falsehood / prevarication / untruth / distortion

Some of these words have developed as euphemisms for the basic word, *lie,* which is a 'statement that is contrary to the truth.' Because *lie* is such a baldly frank and often vicious word, one that admits of no hedging or mitigation, it is often replaced by the Latinate *prevarication* (verb: *prevaricate*), which somehow sounds more clinical and takes the sting out of the impact of *lie.* Also, we speak of *white lies,* which are told for diplomatic reasons, often in order to spare another's feelings or, at least, to do no one any harm; they are further diminished in virulence and importance by calling them "little white lies." And we speak of *black lies,* which are the real thing, deliberate misrepresentations of what is known to be the truth. Other terms for lies are *fabrication, fib,* and *falsehood;* though all of these characterize statements that are not true, they are polite, not fighting words. An *untruth* is slightly different, being a misstatement that may be based on ignorance of the truth or on misunderstanding. *Misstatement* itself, as well as *distortion, warping,* and so forth are all words aimed less at calling a lie a lie than at sparing the feelings of the speaker of falsehoods. A learned word for the act of lying is *mendacity,* but, again, its impact is reduced by its relative low frequency and by its clinical, Latinate sound. *Lie* remains a powerful word in English, one not to be used lightly; calling someone a *liar* can lead to bloodshed, and it often has.

lie / lay

The confusion caused by these words is so common that they might be expected at some time in the future to fall (or lie) together. The problem is caused by three different words which, because they have some forms in common, can be easily mixed up.

WORD & MEANING	PRESENT	PAST / PAST PART.	EXAMPLE
lie 'tell an untruth'	lie, lying, lies	lied / lied	*He lies all the time.* *You are lying to me.* *She has lied to me.*

WORD & MEANING	PRESENT	PAST / PAST PART.	EXAMPLE
lie 'be on a horizontal surface'	lie, lying, lies	lay / lain	*Lie on the floor.* *I am lying down.* *She lay down for a nap.* *The book has lain there for days.*
lay 'put or place (something) on a horizontal surface'	lay, laying, lays	laid / laid	*Now I lay me down to sleep.* *Hens lay eggs.* *The hen laid an egg.* *I laid the book down.*

There seems to be little difficulty with the first word, meaning to 'prevaricate, fabricate.' From the table, one can see why the other two cause trouble: the present of *lay* 'put down' is identical to the past of *lie* 'be recumbent.' Unfortunately, there is no simple mnemonic device that can be called upon to help in remembering the differences: they must be memorized. The confusion is extended to the noun forms: properly, the expression should be *the lie of the land,* but one hears (and reads) *the lay of the land* equally often. Similarly, *lay low* is wrong for *lie low* but is correct for 'lay (someone) out; beat (someone) up.' It might help to bear in mind that the second verb, *lie,* is not used with an object, while the third, *lay,* must have an object. Yet, when one considers that the forms themselves are indistinguishable in some of their most frequent usages, little help can be offered.

like / as

In most cases where two words are confused with one another, word B is substituted for word A and only very rarely vice versa. That is the case with *imply* and *infer,* *uninterested* and *disinterested,* *apprise* and *appraise,* *persuade* and *convince,* and many other pairs where the latter is far more frequently substituted for the former than the other way round. The same holds true for *as* and *like,* which exhibit a similar pattern: instances of substitution of *as* for *like* are impossible to find; people simply do not say, "He is as me in many respects." On the other hand, *like* is often substituted for *as* where the latter serves as a conjunction, as in, *Do as I say, not as I do; like* also replaces *as if* in sentences like *It looks as if she is going to win.* All of these substitutions of *like* for *as* or *as if* are frowned on by those who are concerned about the way other people use the language, so those who worry about such matters should take heed. For those who know enough (traditional) grammar to tell the difference between a preposition and a conjunction, the information that *as* is a conjunction in such constructions, that *like* never serves as a conjunction in standard English, and that, therefore, *like* should not be substituted for *as* when the latter is used as a conjunction would be sufficient to ensure that they would never again commit this linguistic faux pas. But most people either never learned the parts of speech and how to parse a sentence and, if they did, do not remember; in any event, even those who have that knowledge firmly embedded cannot be expected to stop, while they are speaking, to analyze the functions of the words they are uttering. Unfortunately, there is no shortcut, no mnemonic known that will enable a speaker to make the proper choice. For writers, the situation is different: given more time, and alerted to the fact that there is a *like*-for-*as* problem, a writer can look the matter up in a book (like this one) for guidance.

linguistics / philology

In the United States, *linguistics* is the generally accepted, over-all name for 'the study of language'; it has a number of subdivisions, notably *general linguistics* and *comparative linguistics*, the former usually taken to be the study of principles common to all languages, the latter the study of the features shared among languages that have a common origin. *Philology* is the name given to the study of language used in literature. There is no common term "general philology," and *comparative philology* is used as another term for *comparative linguistics.* In Great Britain, *philology* is used as a synonym for *linguistics. Philology* is the older term, more common in writings antedating the 1930s, and a philologist in both Britain and the United States is a scholar who studies the language used in literature. The specialist in linguistics is called a *philologist* (in Great Britain) or a *linguist* (in the United States). The designation is an unfortunate one, for, to the public at large, *linguist* means 'someone who knows or speaks a number of languages,' and linguists have for years tried to solve the problem by insisting that the proper word for a person who speaks many languages is *polyglot,* a word that has proved neither attractive or catchy. So, language specialists who call themselves philologists have only to explain what a philologist does; those who refer to themselves as linguists usually have to offer an immediate explanation of their calling lest they be thought of as polyglots.

literally / figuratively

Literally means 'letter for letter, word for word, in the strictest sense'; it contrasts with *figuratively,* which means 'so to speak, that is to say' and is used to alert the reader or listener to the fact that one is using a word, expression, or idea as a figure of speech, or metaphorically. Because all language is replete with figures of speech—so much so that even linguists sometimes have difficulty in discriminating between literal and figurative use—it is seldom necessary to label what one is saying by announcing, " . . figuratively speaking, of course." In practice, one is more likely to hear " . . literally speaking." For example, if a person says, "I have to run over to Paris for a few days," any hearer who seriously questioned how such a distance might be covered by running, especially with the bodies of water between, would very likely be regarded as mentally deficient. Sometimes, figurative expressions are taken literally as a (very) mild form of humor, and sometimes they form the basis for puns (in which the literal meaning is "played against" the figurative', but only in rare cases do those things occur in natural language. A chestnut like, "I just flew in from Rome and my arms are very tired," illustrates this as does "George Bernard Shaw made a play for Ellen Terry"; to understand the latter, one needs to be aware both that Shaw's correspondence with Terry, a famous actress, suggests an amour and that he wrote *Captain Brassbound's Confession* for her in 1899. Because the language is filled with so many figures of speech, the situations in which people find themselves that are describable in figurative terms may also occur literally. For that reason, people often emphasize the actuality of an event that is described by a figurative expression by adding "literally" or "I mean—literally" to their description. In describing a gas explosion at a furrier's, for example, an observer might report, "You should have seen the fur fly—literally!" This has led to the overuse of *literally* in contexts where it does not belong, contexts where the language is figurative but the speaker, seeking an intensifying word to emphasize the action of an event, uses *literally* in place of some other mode of expression. The results are often ludicrous: *She literally flew off the handle when I told her I was leaving. He literally took it lying down when they told him he was dismissed. His jealousy was literally eating him up. She is literally a snake in the grass. He liter-ally left with his tail between his legs.* It would be redundant to insert *figuratively* for *literally* in such contexts, since no normal person would construe them literally.

littoral / sublittoral / profundal / neritic / oceanic / bathyal

These are all terms that pertain to regions of a body of water—lake or sea. *Littoral* refers to the shoreline of a lake or sea, especially, in reference to the sea, to the region lying between the high- and low-water tidal marks. *Sublittoral* describes the zone of shallow water of a sea between the low-water mark and the edge of the continental shelf, an area where photosynthesis can still occur and where rooted plants can survive, to a maximum of 100 to 200 meters [300-600 feet]. At the lakeside, *sublittoral* designates a zone near the shore not exceeding 6 to 10 meters [18-30 feet]. The deeper parts of lakes and seas are called the *profundal zone*. At the ocean, the deeper parts, more than 200 meters, are the *profundal zone*, but extensive depths, as in the Marianas Trench, are referred to as *bathyal*. The scientific term *neritic* is used to refer to the waters that are directly above the sublittoral zone of the sea. The term *pelagic* designates flora and fau-na that inhabit portions of the oceans near the surface and far off-shore. In technical parlance, *oceanic* refers to the regions of the sea below the pelagic and above the bathyal. The zone below the oceanic is called the *abyssal zone,* and that which lies at the bottom of them all is called the *hadal zone.*

loathe / loath

Loath is an adjective meaning 'reluctant, unwilling' and is more often pronounced with the *-th* unvoiced, as in *both, lath,* and *math. Loathe* is a verb meaning 'despise, abhor, hate' and is almost universally pro-nounced with the *-th-* voiced, as in *lathe, bathe,* and *clothe.* But "more often" and "less often" can be deceiving in language: the statistics are either lacking or poor, and most comments on frequency that are offered by scholars are based on personal impressions; while the per-sonal impressions and observations of an experienced linguist who lis-tens for such things are not without value, they cannot be accepted as accurately representative of what is going on in the language. For instance, *loath* is often pronounced the same way as *loathe;* not only that, it is also spelled *loth* or *loathe: I would be loath* (or *loth,* or *loathe*) *to tell him what I think of him.* The other words in this set are *loathing* 'hatred, contempt, disgust' and *loathsome* 'disgusting, repulsive, revolting,' which, though it is formed on the adjective *loath,* is more often pronounced with the *-th-* of *bathe* than with that of *bath.* The only good reason that can be adduced for keeping the pronunciations of *loath* and *loathe* separate is that in an example like *I am loath to tell her,* if the *loathe* pronunciation is used, it might, in rapid speech, sound like *loathed,* which could be understood to mean "I am (making myself) hateful (if I were) to tell her."

locate / situate

Locate and *situate* are sometimes used interchangeably in the sense of to 'place': *It would be a good idea to locate the shop near the railway station.* Some prefer to keep this use for *situate,* reserving *locate* for the sense to 'find': *The police haven't been able to locate her husband.* But the 'place' meaning for *locate* is so well established in the language that any attempt to dislodge it would be futile. Yet, the converse—*situate* with the meaning 'find'—is not standard. It may be observed that the noun, *location,* is standard for *site* or *situation* in the sense of 'position'; *situation* is often encountered in the metaphorical sense of 'circumstances, state of affairs, condition,' which *location* does not share.

long wave / medium wave / short wave

These terms refer to wavelengths of radio waves generated in transmission. *Long waves* are those with wavelengths greater than 1000 meters; *medium waves* are those with wavelengths of between 100 and 1000 meters; and *short waves* are those with wavelengths of between 10 and 100 meters. In order to broadcast over greater distances, long-wave transmitters must have considerably greater power, hence cost more initially and while operating. For that reason, short-wave broadcasts are generally done over the greatest distances; medium- and long-wave broadcasts are usually for receivers situated closer to the transmitter. (See also **AM / FM.**)

lover / leman / POSSLQ / tally

In the attempt to name a person of the opposite sex with whom one lives out of wedlock, a number of suggestions, some of them facetious, have been put forth. Some object to the old-fashioned term *lover* because it implies sexual intercourse but not the (essential) additional information that the couple are sharing the same living quarters, or because "love" has no place in the relationship, or because it is old-fashioned. The same objections have been raised about *leman,* which is so old-fashioned as to be obsolete or archaic. The term *POSSLQ,* an acronym for "Person of Opposite Sex who Shares Living Quarters" and pronounced by those who use it as 'POSS-l-kew', has gained little momentum except as a curiosity in writing that deals with the "problem"; it is said to have been invented by U.S. census-takers in 1980. *Mistress* is unacceptable because it cannot be applied to a man and implies financial support (which may not be in keeping with the situation). *Boyfriend* and *girlfriend* are unacceptable because they are old-fashioned, sexist, and already have a well-established meaning in the language. Among some, just *friend* had brief popularity, shortlived because people were left without a word for what they formerly called a friend—one with whom they were not living. All three—*boyfriend, girlfriend,* and *friend*—continue to be used by those who give them a peculiar emphasis, not quite as obvious as a grimacing wink or a nudge with the elbow, but more a matter of intonation; but such signals serve little purpose in writing, especially in writing home to mother, to whom reference to a "friend," of either the same or opposite sex, is likely to speak volumes. The insistent *"just* a friend" is often the occasion for the worst kinds of misunderstandings. There is, however, an older word in English, fallen into disuse it is true but apparently ripe for revival. It is *tally* and, as a noun, was long established in the language with the exact meaning needed: 'an unmarried person who lives with a member of the opposite sex as man and wife.' There appears to be no (extant) stigma attached to the word—at least none has been found. It also occurred as an adverb and was used in contexts like *to live tally* (with another). Its etymological origin can be traced to the common (and older) meaning of *tally,* which has to do with the keeping of (financial) records. But that is not entirely a bad thing, either. If it is adopted, the inevitable chestnuts will be uttered about *Tallyho!,* and there are doubtless atrocious associated puns on "dear-hunting" that may darken the horizon. Such peccadilloes are to be expected in English

words, and, merely because two people have entered into a relationship without legal sanction there is no reason why they should lose
their sense of humor. It should be made clear that, at least traditionally, *tally* refers to people of the opposite sex.

Low Church / High Church / Broad Church

These are the names of factions in the Anglican Communion. In
broad terms, *Low Church* (a back formation from *Low Churchman*)
refers to stressing the importance of evangelicalism and *High Church*
to stressing the importance of episcopal church government, liturgy,
ceremony, and traditional forms of worship. Both were manifest in
the 16th century, during the reign of Elizabeth I, and were revived
during the late 19th century, under the influence of the Oxford Movement. The *Broad Church* movement, which came towards the end of
the 19th century, emphasized inclusiveness and was based on liberal
interpretations of doctrine.

lower house / upper house

In bicameral governmental structures, *lower house*, or *lower chamber*,
is the name given to the larger, usually more popular and representative body, *upper house*, or *upper chamber*, to the branch of more limited membership. In Great Britain, the lower and upper houses are,
respectively, the House of Commons and the House of Lords (*q.v.*),
which together constitute Parliament; in the United States, they are
the House of Representatives and the Senate (*q.v.*), which together
constitute the Congress.

lunar eclipse / solar eclipse

In a *lunar eclipse*, the earth passes between the sun and the moon so
that the moon is in the earth's shadow; in a *solar eclipse*, the moon
passes between the sun and the earth, so that the moon's shadow falls
on the earth. Because the earth is larger than the moon, the latter
may be completely obscured from sunlight in a lunar eclipse; the
moon, however, being smaller than the earth, casts a shadow on only
a small portion of the earth's surface, and to the observer within that
shadow, in a solar eclipse the disk of the sun may be totally obscured
from view, with only the corona visible. In a *total eclipse*, the sun is

completely obscured; in an *annular eclipse,* a narrow ring of the sun remains visible when the center of the moon passes over the center of the sun; in a *partial eclipse,* in which the penumbra of the shadow falls on the observer, only part of the sun is obscured. The time taken for a total or annular eclipse varies, but it may last for about three hours, that is, about one and a half hours from "first bite," when the moon just begins to obscure a part of the sun's disk, to total coverage.

luxurious / luxuriant

These words are not synonyms: *luxurious* means 'characterized by luxury, self-indulgence, and the trappings of sumptuous living'; *luxuriant* means 'characterized by abundance and lushness of vegetation.'

macrometeorology / mesometeorology / micrometeorology

These are the names of different aspects of meteorology, the study of weather. *Macrometeorology* is the study of major weather systems and major trends in weather on a global, hemispheric, or continental scale. *Mesometeorology* deals with smaller weather systems, as the weather for a particular area, localized storms and patterns, temperature inversions, and with detailed study of parts of the larger systems examined in macrometeorology. *Micrometeorology* is the study of details within a local weather system, often dealing with such matters as the characteristics of surface boundary layers.

magnum / jereboam / methuselah / nebuchadnezzar

These are the names for larger-than-ordinary bottles of wine, especially champagne. The *magnum* holds 52 fluidounces, the equivalent of about two "ordinary" bottles; the *jereboam,* 104 fluidounces, or four bottles; the *methuselah,* 208 fluidounces, or eight bottles; and the *nebuchadnezzar,* 520 fluidounces, or twenty bottles. All are approximate, but it should be emphasized that the *fluidounce* unit is the same in the Imperial and in the United States systems: it is the pint, quart, and gallon measures that differ. The *Imperial pint* contains 20 fluidounces, the U.S., 16; as there are (in both systems) 2 pints to a quart, the *Imperial quart* contains 40 fluidounces, the U.S., 32; and as 4 quarts make a gallon in both systems, the *Imperial gallon* contains 80 fluidounces, the U.S., 64. Thus, too, in buying gasoline, the Imperial gallon, equivalent to 4.546 liters (0.22 gallon = 1 liter), is equivalent to 1.25 U.S. gallons (1 U.S. gallon = 0.80 Imperial gallon). Consequently, if one compares the gallon prices of gasoline in the U.K. with those in the U.S., allowances must be made. Still, late in 1987, the comparable prices of gasoline in the northeastern U.S. and in southeastern England were such that a U.S. gallon cost $1.00 (about 75p in late 1987) in the U.S.; the same amount (0.80 Imperial gallon) cost £1.36 in England. Contrariwise, an Imperial gallon cost £1.70 ($2.98) in England; the same amount (1.25 U.S. gallons) cost, at U.S. prices, $1.25 in the U.S. In short, the unit price of gasoline in southeastern England is almost 2½ (2.38 to be exact) times as expensive as in the northeastern United States.

main clause / subordinate clause

These terms are useful in identifying various functioning parts of compound, complex, and compound-complex sentences. It is easiest to describe them in the context of examples:

She wanted to kiss me when I went over to her.

A *main clause* of a sentence is one that fulfills the criterion that it can stand alone as a sentence. In this example, *She wanted to kiss me* is the main clause; *when I went over to her* cannot stand alone as a sentence and is called a *subordinate*, or *dependent clause*. Subordinate clauses take any number of forms; they are often introduced by a relative pronoun (like *who, which, that*), a conjunction (like *because, for, but*), or a conjunctive adverb (like *nevertheless, however*). Subordinate clauses are often named for their type, as *relative clause, adverbial clause*, etc.:

His father, who is a composer, wants him to study music.

The main clause is *His father . . . wants him to study music;* the subordinate, or relative clause is *who is a composer.*

When he entered, everyone stood up.

The main clause is *everyone stood up;* the adverbial clause is *When he entered.*

Decorate your house however you like.

The main clause is *Decorate your house;* the adverbial clause is *however you like.*

I went to the party because she invited me.

I went to the party is the main clause; *because she invited me* the subordinate clause. (See also **simple sentence / compound sentence / complex sentence; descriptive modifier / restrictive modifier.**)

malapropism / spoonerism / Irish bull / Tom Swifty

These are all terms that refer to categories of playfulness in language. A *malapropism*, named for the character, Mrs. Malaprop, in Richard Brinsley Sheridan's play, *The Rivals* (1775), who indulged in them, are of the sort that might be described as "fractured idioms," common expressions in which a word or sound has been changed sufficiently to abort the original and to give the entire expression a somewhat twisted, ludicrous interpretation. The name, Mrs. *Malaprop*, comes from the word *malapropos* 'not apropos, inappropriate'; examples are:

You could have knocked me over with a fender.

Lead the way and we'll precede.

We saw an allegory on the banks of the Nile.

Spoonerisms, named for the Reverend W. A. Spooner (1844–1930), who was said to indulge in them (inadvertently or deliberately—the debate has never been quite settled), are expressions in which the sounds have been transposed to create a ludicrous result; examples are:

Our queer old dean . . (for "Our dear old Queen . . ")

. . tons of soil . . (for " . . sons of toil . . ")

Leave no tern unstoned . . ("Leave no stone unturned . . ")

An *Irish bull* is an expression that contains a ludicrous self-contradiction. Just why these were named Irish bulls is not documented, but it probably stems from the typical British derogation of all things Irish; examples are:

May you never live to see your wife a widow!

He lay at death's door and the doctor pulled him through.

I'd give my last dollar to be a millionaire.

The *Tom Swiftie* (or *Swifty*), of more recent (American) vintage, is a statement in the form of a direct quotation, attributed to Tom Swift and constructed in such a way that an adverb, tacked on at the end, describes the statement in a "literal" manner. Tom Swift was the central character in a series of extremely popular American adventure novels written for boys in the 1920s and '30s; why his name was chosen to be so honored is not known. Examples are:

"I know who blew out the candle," said Tom darkly.

"I think I've injured my foot," said Tom archly.

"I would prefer pancakes," said Tom flatly.

mandible / maxilla

The *mandible* is the lower jawbone of vertebrates, the *maxilla*, the pair of bones, side by side, that form the upper jaw. The adjectival forms are *mandibular* and *maxillary.*

Markov process / stochastic process

These terms refer to the likelihood of an event in statistics: in a *Markov process*, named for a Russian mathematician, A. A. Markov (1856–1922), the future values of a random variable are statistically determined by the present state of the system and depend only on the event immediately preceding rather than on the series of positions; in a *stochastic process*, the events are entirely random, without any interdependence on past, current, or future states or events.

marriage / matrimony / wedlock / nuptials

These first three terms all refer to the same thing, the state of a man and woman living as husband and wife, but their distributions in the language are different. The everyday word is *marriage*, which may refer to the ceremony as well as the state: *Clarissa's and Richard's marriage has been a love affair for ten years. Their marriage took place ten years ago next week. Matrimony*, which is used to refer to the state or condition alone, is a more formal term: contrast *wed* with *get married* with *enter into a state of matrimony.* On the other hand, the frequent adjective, *matrimonial*, which has no counterpart with any form of the word *marriage*, is the formal, somewhat awkward alternative to *wedded: wedded bliss; matrimonial bliss. Matrimonial* is more often encountered in legal contexts. *Wedding* refers to the ceremony itself, as does *nuptials*, also a formal word. In its adjective form, *nuptial* is at about the same level as *matrimonial.* And it should be noted that the word is "NUP-chul," not, as so often heard, "NUP-choo-ul." *Wedlock* is a slightly old-fashioned term but persists in many locutions in which *marriage* or *matrimony* seem to be idiomatically out of place, as in *born out of wedlock.*

mass / weight

On a nontechnical, informal level, *mass* and *weight* may be interchangeable words, but in physics, they are quite different. In ordinary terms, *weight* is what one weighs as read off the dial of a scale, *mass* is an agglomeration of matter. To a physicist, *mass* is regarded as a property of all matter, yielding a measure of its resistance to acceleration. Within a gravitational field, mass is measured in units of weight (e.g., kilograms), but weight is considered a force, which is measured in newtons. (A newton is the amount of force required to accelerate a mass of one kilogram by 1 meter per second per second; the standard used for the gravitational force of the earth is 9.80665 newtons.)

material / materiel

Material is the word for any substances of which something is made; it may refer to raw substances, such as sand, water, gravel, and cement for the making of concrete, or to manufactured ingredients, such as steel. It was felt that another word was needed to cover the sense of 'all of the parts and equipment required in any undertaking, as a business, warfare, etc.,' and the French word *matériel* (now usually spelled *materiel*) was adopted for the purpose. It is simply the French word for 'material', but is used in English in a special sense, especially in contrast to *personnel,* which covers the people needed in an enterprise. It came into prominence during WWII in reference to arms and other military equipment.

matter / antimatter

Physicists theorize the existence of an "anti-universe," one in which all atomic charges of the *matter* that are positive or negative in the observable universe are, conversely, negative or positive in *antimatter,* which is made up of *antiparticles.* In antimatter, the positively charged proton of matter is an antiproton of negative charge, equal to that of the electron, and atoms are composed of antiprotons with orbiting positrons instead of positrons with orbiting electrons. When the particles of matter and antimatter collide, both are annihilated. While the theory of antimatter may have validity, no evidence of its existence has been found.

may / might

To express possibility in the present tense, *may* is understood to be somewhat "milder" than *might*, that is, *may* suggests a stronger possibility while *might* makes the possibility less likely. Because *may* also carries the meaning 'is allowed, have permission,' *might* is sometimes preferred in order to avoid ambiguity, chiefly in sentences like *He may go if he can get a ticket*, which could be interpreted either as a possibility or as permission. In the past tense, however, *might*, which is the past of *may,* is generally preferred: *We may go, despite the rain. We might go, despite the rain. We might have gone, despite the rain.* Although *We may have gone* is not frowned on and occurs with great frequency, *We might have gone* is preferred in formal English.

mean deviation / standard deviation

These statistical terms refer to the measurement of the extent to which individual values differ from all of the values observed. The *deviation* of an individual value is the difference between the value of one element in an observed set of values and the value represented by the average, or *mean* of all the values, usually called the *true value.* For example, if in a study of body weights of a certain group it is found that the mean is 130 pounds but that a given individual's weight is 120 pounds, the *deviation* of that unit of data is 10, and the figure representing the average of all such deviations is called the *mean deviation.* (It is neither necessary nor, in some cases, even likely that any individual value will be exactly equal to the mean or that the deviation will be equal to the mean deviation.) The *standard deviation,* a measure of the scattering, or dispersal of the data, is a value calculated by taking the square root of the average of the squares of the individual deviations.

measles / German measles

The technical medical name for the disease *German measles* is *rubella,* that for *measles, rubeola.* Both are contagious viral diseases, usually contracted in childhood; in each case, a single attack confers lifelong immunity, and neither is life-threatening in developed countries. Of the two, measles is the worse, resulting in high temperatures (104° being not unusual), an itchy rash, and complications that may include pneumonia, otitis media (inflammation or infection of the middle ear), laryngitis, and other afflictions. But German measles, while less severe an illness, can result in fetal anomalies if contracted during the first trimester of pregnancy, and all women of childbearing age who are likely to risk exposure and are not immune should be vaccinated.

Merovingian / Carolingian

Both names apply to Frankish dynasties that reigned in western Europe during the Middle Ages. The *Merovingian* was the dynasty established by Clovis I (465–511), who was king of the Franks 481–511; the name *Merovingian* comes from *Merewig,* the name of Clovis's grandfather. The *Carolingian,* or *Carlovingian* dynasty is named for Charlemagne (742–814), though it was founded by his father, Pepin, in 751 and lasted till 911 in Germany and 987 in France.

metaphor / simile

These are among the most important terms used in describing figures of speech and rhetorical devices. Although they are learned terms, they describe elements of everyday language usage—indeed, were it not for *metaphor,* every language would use each word in its lexicon in a very specific application only, and the number of words required would be many times that documented. Broadly, *metaphor* is the use of a word or expression for something to which it does not specifically refer. The word *atom,* for example, denotes in physics and chemistry a particle of matter so small that it cannot be seen; it is used metaphorically in the sentence, *There isn't an atom of truth in that story*—that is, *atom* is not used *literally,* in its scientific sense, but figuratively, in a transferred sense of 'something infinitesimally small.' Indeed, its etymology, from Greek *atomos* 'unable to be cut,' exhibits a use of metaphor. Similarly, *iota* (literally, the 'smallest letter of the Greek alphabet'), *germ* (literally, a 'microbe, invisible to the naked eye'), *scintilla* (literally, a 'spark'), or almost any other word with the same *connotation* of tininess could have been used. Most words combine in their (literal) meanings a number of different characteristics; that is to say, the words *atom, iota, germ,* and *scintilla* have different *denotative* meanings, and the only thing they share in common is the characteristic of diminutiveness. It is this one characteristic that has been fastened on in the above examples, and such applications are profuse in every language, at all levels. In slang, for instance, the expression *snowed under* means 'inundated, as by a huge amount of snow'; another expression, *snow job,* is unlikely to be used literally, but it is a common metaphor, probably created by an ordinary speaker of English and not by a poet or other literary personage. Good writing is, of course, filled with metaphors: in *Othello,* Shakespeare refers to jealousy as "the green-eyed monster"; in the Bible, *Psalms* (18,31) has: "And who is a rock, except our God?" A *simile* is something like a metaphor, but the comparison is expressed by the use of a word like *like:* instead of writing that jealousy *is* "the green-eyed monster," in using a simile Shakespeare would have written that it is "like a green-eyed monster," the quotation from *Psalms* would be "And who is like a rock, except our God?" Many metaphors that have become clichés in the language started life as metaphors: a minor irritation was probably once described as being "like a pain in the neck," but today we say that it (or someone) *is* "a pain in the neck." Similes, because they invariably employ a preposition (*like, similar to,* etc.), which cannot precede the active form of a verb in English, must be nouns or a verb converted to its gerundial (noun) form: for example, *like getting blood from a stone; like building castles in Spain.* Metaphors, on the other hand, can be verbs: *My patience soaps out after hearing an hour of rock and roll* (that is, 'My patience, like a cake of soap, which diminishes with each use till nothing is left, is wearing away to nothing'); *Let us shelve the idea for the time being* (that is, 'Let us treat the idea as if we were putting it away on a shelf till later on'). Both metaphors and similes stir the imagination, and the ability to understand the literal references to which they point depends to a large extent on our fund of knowledge, which can be broadened only by education and experience.

meteorite / meteoroid / micrometeorite

Meteoroids are masses of metal and stone, thought to be the remnants of planets or comets, that travel through space and sometimes pass close enough to the earth to enter its atmosphere, in which event they become luminous. When part of a meteoroid survives its fiery descent, it is called a *meteorite*. A *micrometeorite* is a meteorite less than a micron (one millionth of a meter) in diameter. (See also **comet / meteor.**)

militate / mitigate

In certain contexts, these words can have meanings that are almost opposite, so one should not be substituted for the other. *Militate* means to 'have effect or carry weight' either in favor of or against something: *Her bad record militated against her getting the appointment. His ability to act militated for his winning the award. Mitigate* means to 'reduce in effect, violence, force, intensity, severity; soften; mollify': *The 'losing' of his daughter was mitigated by the gaining of a son-in-law. The tranquillizers mitigated her anxieties over the missing child.*

modern / old style

In typography, *modern* refers to those type designs in which the bottoms of the numerals are set even with the base line of the type on which all the alphabetic characters align (except *g, p, q,* and *y*); in *old style* type, the bottoms of some of the numerals extend below the base line, especially those of the *3, 6,* and *9.*

monetary / fiscal

Monetary means 'pertaining or relating to money or currency'; *fiscal* means 'pertaining or relating to finance and financial matters, especially governmental finances, tax revenues, etc.' A monetary unit is the unit of currency of a country, as the pound sterling of Great Britain, U.S. dollar, French franc, German mark, etc. A monetary policy would concern itself with matters like the exchange rate between international currencies, the units of currencies within a country, etc. The fiscal policies of a country would involve government plans and procedures for the handling of internal and external financial affairs; that would include monetary matters but would not be restricted to them.

monogamy / bigamy / polygamy / digamy / deuterogamy

These terms refer to practices followed in various cultures in the taking of wives or, put differently, in the number of women a man is married to or may be married to. *Monogamy,* the accepted status in Western society, is being married to one woman at a time, but it is also used to describe the practice of marrying only once in a lifetime. *Bigamy* describes the condition, illegal in Western society, of being married to two women at the same time. *Digamy* and *deuterogamy* are the same thing: marriage to a second wife after separation from the first by death or divorce. *Polygamy* is the practice of having more than one wife—usually three or more—simultaneously; it is no longer legal in Western society and was most recently practised in the Church of the Latter-day Saints (Mormons).

monologue / soliloquy

In theatrical terms, a *monologue* is a speech given by an actor usually when he is alone on the stage. It and *soliloquy* are the same thing, but the latter is a rarer, more technical word; it is always used when referring to the speech that begins 'To be or not to be . . ,' in *Hamlet,* and to other speeches like it, that is, to speeches delivered by characters in a play when "thinking aloud" and there is no other character on stage. *Monologue* is the name given to a special kind of theatrical presentation that is not a play, in which an actor, called a *monologist,* or *monologuist,* performs alone on the stage. *Monologue* is also used of any long-winded speech by someone who monopolizes the conversation in a social situation.

monophonic / stereophonic / quadraphonic

In the electronic reproduction of sound, a *monophonic,* or *monaural* system is one that produces a single output signal; there may be more than one input source, and there may be more than one speaker. A *stereophonic,* or *binaural* system produces two output signals from (at least) two input sources; the input signals are transmitted from two or more microphones situated in such a way as to simulate, when speakers are situated similarly in relation to a listener, a so-called two-dimensional effect. A *quadraphonic* system produces four output signals from four or more sources, producing a greatly enhanced stereophonic effect. The word *quadraphonic,* most often encountered with that spelling, is also spelled *quadriphonic.*

monopsony / duopsony / oligopsony

These terms from the theory of economics refer to particular market conditions. In *monopsony,* there is only one purchaser of products for which there may be more than one supplier; an example might be the restricted purchase of domestically manufactured arms by the government of a country. In *duopsony,* two purchasers vie between themselves for the output of one or more suppliers. In *oligopsony,* there are several (but a limited number of) purchasers, each sufficiently powerful to have an effect on the market but no one of them influential enough to dominate it.

motor / engine

Technically, an *engine* is a machine that converts potential energy into kinetic energy to provide motive force in order to do work. A *motor* is either a small engine (as an *outboard motor,* really an engine) or a similar device powered by electricity. The source of propulsion in a car is, willy nilly, referred to as either a motor or an engine; that in an airplane, ship, train, large truck, (space) rocket, etc., is usually called an engine. Perhaps in order to confound matters further, ships with diesel or other internal combustion engines are today termed *motor vessels;* during the days of steam, they were called *steamships. Engine,* the older word by several centuries, is a more general word that was formerly applied to a wide variety of mechanical devices, like *engines of torture, rose engine, engines of war,* and was used metaphorically more often in the past than today.

mousse / soufflé / pudding

A *mousse* is a light, aerated dish made from any of a wide assortment of ingredients beaten with whipped cream and with gelatine or beaten egg whites as a stiffening agent: *fish mousse; chocolate mousse.* A *soufflé* is similar but is not made with cream or gelatine, the setting agent being beaten white of egg. A *pudding* is a dessert made from milk, eggs, and other ingredients and flavorings but is not necessarily beaten. In Britain, *pudding* is also used at an informal level as a generic term for any dessert, a sense not shared in American English. Any of these can be served hot or cold, though most start out by being cooked.

mullion / muntin / glazing-bar

Windows come in two main types, the *casement window,* which is a frame containing one or more panes of glass that is hinged at the side or at the top or bottom, and the (double-hung) *sash window,* which consists of two frames containing one or more panes of glass that fit into grooves at the sides or at the top and bottom and slide past or meet one another. A *mullion* is a semi-structural vertical member between two casement window frames that are set side by side in a wall. *Muntin* is the term used in the U.S. for what is called a *glazing-bar* in Britain, that is, one of the relatively light-weight, vertical or horizontal wood or metal pieces into which the panes of glass are set in a window frame.

nasal / oral

In general language, these terms mean, simply, 'pertaining to the nose' (*nasal*), and 'pertaining to the mouth' (*oral*). In phonetics, *nasal* is used to characterize sounds articulated with the velum (the fleshy flap at the back of the throat) down, allowing the air from the lungs to resonate in the nasal cavities. The nasal sounds in English are represented by the letters *n, ng,* and *m;* in French, for example, one encounters nasalized vowels in words like *an, en, on, fin,* and *un.* In English, all other sounds are *oral,* that is, articulated with the velum closed, preventing the breath stream from resonating in the nasal cavities. In nonprofessional use, *nasal* is also used to describe speech in which all of the sounds are articulated with the velum in relaxed (if not open) position, as a speaker might pronounce them if afflicted with a cold. In some cases, such speech is characteristic of a particular region or community and is called a "nasal twang." (See also **consonant / vowel.**)

nationalization / privatization

In countries where it is legal for the government to own profit-making enterprises, like Great Britain, *nationalization* is the process by which a private enterprise is taken over by and operated under governmental direction, presumably for the benefit of the citizens. The reverse process, in which a government-owned and operated business is returned to private or public ownership, usually by the sale of shares, is called *privatization.*

nauseous / nauseated

Notwithstanding the protestations of those who would guide us along the righteous paths to "good usage," *nauseous,* which was once restricted in meaning to 'sickening, disgusting, revolting,' has slowly but unremittingly moved towards the sense 'sick, affected with nausea'; formerly (and, for purists, to this day), the expression *I feel nauseous* could mean only one thing: "I am nauseating everyone around me." It does not sound awkward to say, *I am nauseated,* but, except to purists, perhaps, that seems to mean "There is something about that is sufficiently revolting to fill me with disgust." In other words, *nauseated* is more often used to express the figurative meaning, *nauseous* to express the literal.

nectar / ambrosia

In classical mythology, *nectar* was the drink of the gods, *ambrosia* the food of the gods.

neologism / nonce word

A *nonce word* is one that has been coined or borrowed for a particular occasion and is unlikely to become a fixture in the language. It was apparently coined by the editors of the *OED,* and the entry for *nonce* in the main dictionary carries a reference to "Vol. I, p. xx" (but the following appears on p. xxx, not xx):

> Words apparently employed only *for the nonce,* are, when inserted in the Dictionary, marked *nonce-wd.*

By the time of publication of the *Supplement,* Volume H-N (1976), enough examples of *nonce-word* (as well as of *nonce-borrowing, -combination, -form, -formation, -meaning*) had been found to create a citation file. Although citations for these *nonce-*compounds do not give examples of nonce words, a diligent search has turned up *rococity* 'the condition of being *rococo,*' *gardenist* 'a specialist engaged in something more than mere gardening,' and *firebrandism* 'the condition of being a firebrand.' *Webster's Third New International* cites "Coleridge coined *mammonolatry* in 1820 as a *nonce word."* It should not be surprising that nonce words go unrecorded in dictionaries generally, for, by their very definition, they are coined to suit the needs of the moment. On the other hand, lexicographers are incapable of predicting the survival of a word, which, as it may turn out, will admirably suit more than the occasion for which it was coined; the editors of the *OED* evidently felt themselves sufficiently qualified to make such predictions and recorded a number of them, though it is not known how many. Some words that started life as nonce words have come to be regarded as *neologisms,* which are "new words in the language." For the past hundred years, in the development of our modern world of technology, the thousands of new devices, drugs, and other artifacts of the 20th century needed to be named, as did the new discoveries of science. At its first appearance in the language, however, not every new word can be considered to have been coined "for the nonce"; also, some neologisms, especially in slang, enjoy a very short life, indeed, because the criterion for certain kinds of slang is that it be fresh and have the element of originality: after a time, slang that has become stale is passed on, as it were, to those speakers of the language who may not normally use slang but who regard some knowledge of it indicative of their knowledgeability and of being *on the qui vive,* at the forefront of fashion. Because what is new to one person may seem old-fashioned or hackneyed to another, what is a neologism to one person may not be so to another. Nonetheless, some words and expressions, especially those that might have first appeared in readily documented sources, like scientific monographs, can justifiably be identified as neologisms. The American physicist, Murray Gell-Mann, coined the word *quork* (in 1964) and applied it as the name of a hypothetical elementary particle. That is surely an example of a neologism. As Gell-Mann explained in a subsequent letter to the editor of the *OED Supplement,* it was not till later that he found *quark* in James Joyce's *Finnegans Wake* and changed the spelling to conform. But whether *quark* is still a neologism, a quarter-century later, depends of the perspective one has of the language.

neuron / axon / dendrite / synapse

These are the main elements associated with a nerve cell. The cell itself is called a *neuron,* or *neurone,* and is made up of the *axon,* which conducts electrical impulses away from the neuron, and the *dendrites,* which are branchlike processes that conduct impulses to the neuron. The *synapse* is the area around the neuron across which a *neurotransmitter,* like acetylcholine or norepinephrine, transmits an electrical signal: when triggered, a neuron transmits an impulse through the axon, causing the release of the neurotransmitter, which carries the charge to another neuron, to a muscle, gland, or other organ which, in turn, either continues the transmission or inhibits it. Synapses have electrical polarity, allowing the impulse to travel in only one direction; they are affected by drugs, fatigue, deficiency of oxygen, and electroshock.

neurosis / psychosis

By itself, *neurosis* denotes a disorder of the central nervous system from any cause; in both informal and professional contexts it has come to be used as a shortened form of *psychoneurosis.* (The adjectival forms, *neurotic* and *psychoneurotic* are similarly used.) *Psychoneurosis* refers to an emotional or physical condition brought about by a mental state, whether it be anxiety, obsession, or some other such disturbance. In Freudian theory it is contrasted with *actual neurosis,* which is manifested by real or imagined physical complaints stemming from actual physical changes that are the result of sexual inhibition. *Psychosis* refers to an emotional disturbance, from any cause, severe enough to impair an individual's ability to function normally in a social environment. Psychotics generally require hospitalization.

New England chowder / Manhattan chowder / Rhode Island chowder

These terms refer to different recipes for the preparation of *chowder,* an American stewlike soup made from seafood—usually clams—with potatoes, onions, and other vegetables and seasonings. They are all basically similar, but *New England clam chowder* is distinguished by the addition of milk or (rarely) cream, *Manhattan clam chowder* by the addition of tomatoes or tomato sauce, and *Rhode Island clam chowder* by the absence of both.

nocturnal / diurnal

For some unaccountable reason, *nocturnal*, meaning 'occurring at, associated with, or active during the night,' is a more frequently used word than *diurnal*, 'occurring during, associated with, or active during the day.' Owls are said to be nocturnal, bears diurnal.

noisome / noisy

Noisome, which means 'noxious, foul, offensive, disgusting, as an odor,' is not, a some people seem to think, a "literary" substitute for *noisy* 'making a lot of noise.' The former comes originally from *annoy* 'irritate' (which is cognate with French *ennui*); the latter comes from *noise* (which is cognate with *nausea*).

nom de plume / nom de guerre / allonym / pseudonym / alias

As people are generally identified by their names, if, for some reason they do not wish to be identified, they simply change their names. All such names, if used as false names, are called *pseudonyms*. Because books written by women were not formerly accorded the same attention, by publishers and public alike, as those written by men, it was not uncommon for female authors to change their names either to men's names or to epicene names. For example, Mme. Lucile Aurore Dupin Dudevant wrote under the name *George Sand*, and Anne, Charlotte, and Emily Brontë wrote under the names, respectively, *Acton, Currer,* and *Ellis Bell*. Such a name is called a *nom de plume*, translated from French into English *pen name*. There are many reasons why an author might choose to be published under a name other than his own, among them simple modesty. The English novelist and critic, Sir Arthur Quiller-Couch, wrote his criticism under the pen name *Q;* the Scottish novelist, H. H. Munro, wrote under the pen name *Saki*. An *allonym* is the name of another writer, usually deceased, adopted as a pen name by someone who wishes not only to remain anonymous but who feels that the allonym chosen lends a certain character to the style or subject under treatment. Thus, the editor of the periodical *American Scholar,* Joseph Epstein, writes editorials under the allonym *Aristides;* G. J. W. Goodman, a figure in the New York financial scene and author of popular books about finance, writes (and broadcasts) under the name *Adam Smith*. The name of *Aristides*, an Athenian statesman nicknamed "the Just," was probably selected because Epstein wishes his commentaries to be so considered; that of *Adam Smith*, an 18th-century Scottish economist, partly because the modern author's subject is financial matters and partly facetiously, because the title of Smith's major work was *The Wealth of Nations*. An *alias* is a name other than one's own by which he is known; because of its habitual use in association with the pseudonyms used by criminals, it has acquired a mildly pejorative taint, so that its application to ordinary people is often facetious. A *nom de guerre* is French for, literally, 'name [used for] war': it was once customary for those entering the French army, especially in chivalric times, to assume a name different from his own, and a knight might be known as "the Knight of the Burning Pestle" after the device on his shield. Today, *nom de guerre* is a variant term for *pseudonym*, used as though one were facetiously referring to life as a "battle" or metaphorically to his writing as a "campaign."

normality / normalcy

The "normal" word in English for the 'state or fact of being normal' is *normality*. In 1920, U.S. President Warren G. Harding delivered a speech in which he said, "America's present need is not heroics but healing; not nostrums but normalcy; not revolution but restoration." The *OED Supplement* contains a citation for 1929: "If . . 'normalcy' is ever to become an accepted word it will presumably be because the late President Harding did not know any better." Citations in the main *OED* for *normalcy* (albeit with a slightly different application) go back to the early 19th century, thus proving that Harding was not the originator of the word. Yet the somewhat old-fashioned controversy still drags on. Although it may be true that the suffix *-cy* is not customarily attached to adjectives ending in *-al* to convert them into abstract nouns, there is no "law" in the language that prohibits such practice, the criterion being clarity. It is interesting to note that the earliest citation listed in the *OED* for *normality* does not antedate that for *normalcy* by a significant number of years; in any event, the appearance of a dated citation in the *OED* indicates merely the first recorded use that was found: it does not suggest that a given word did not exist before that date. It should be obvious that at any time, earlier citations could be discovered for any word in any sense and that by the time the written record of a word is noted it might well have been in use for some time in speech, even for generations. Critics of *normalcy* seem to have overlooked *normalism*, used in very much the same sense: its first record is given as 1891 in the *OED*.

North / East / South / West

The 48 contiguous United States are frequently grouped together by a number of geographic designations that are often rather vague, even to the Americans, and must be quite mystifying to the people of other countries. The following informal lexicon might be helpful, but it must be emphasized that with only a few exceptions they are not delineative, nor are they in all instances mutually exclusive:

New England	the states of the northeastern U.S., specifically, Maine, New Hampshire, Vermont, Massachusetts, Rhode Island, Connecticut.
Northeast	all of the above plus the Middle Atlantic states.
Middle Atlantic states	New York, New Jersey, Pennsylvania, Delaware, Maryland.
Middle West	Missouri, Kansas, Indiana, Illinois, Iowa, Nebraska, Colorado, sometimes Ohio. Also called **Midwest.**
Plains states	North Dakota, South Dakota, Nebraska, Kansas, Oklahoma, sometimes Texas.
Upper Middle West	Wisconsin, Minnesota, North Dakota, South Dakota, Michigan. Also called **Upper Midwest.**
South	Virginia, West Virginia, Kentucky, North Carolina, South Carolina, Tennessee, Georgia, Alabama, Mississippi.
Deep South	Alabama, Georgia, Louisiana, sometimes Texas and Mississippi.
Southeast	South Carolina, Georgia, Alabama, Florida.
Southwest	Texas, Arizona, New Mexico.

West	California, Nevada, Arizona, Utah, sometimes Oregon, Idaho, New Mexico, Wyoming. Also called **Far West.**
Northwest	Washington, Oregon, sometimes Idaho, Montana.
Pacific Northwest	Washington, Oregon.
Sunbelt	Florida, Louisiana, Texas, New Mexico, Arizona, California, sometimes Georgia.
Panhandle	Florida, Texas, Oklahoma.

That leaves Arkansas, which is sometimes thought of as being in the South, sometimes in the Midwest. In the East, **the Coast** refers to the West Coast, almost always California alone; in the West, it refers to the East Coast, almost always New York City, specifically (otherwise, westerners would just say *East*, as in "I have to fly East for a few days," which might mean anywhere between Maine and Washington, D.C.).

novel / novella / short story

These terms describe, though a bit vaguely, works of fiction of different lengths and character. By nature, a *short story* is exactly what its name implies; beyond that, it is characterized by having relatively few central characters and is usually more concerned with plot than with character development. A *novel* is long and, although its plot may be somewhat more intricate, its chief characteristic is generally the development of the personalities of its characters, who are usually more numerous than in a short story. A *novella*, or *novelette*, falls between the two; as its name suggests, it is a small novel, and it shares more characteristics with the novel than with the short story. A *novelette* is a short novel; it may be no longer than a novella but it shares the criteria of a novel. Short stories are usually published in magazines or, as a collection, in books, while novels, novelettes, and novellas are usually published (at least at first) as individual books.

nuclear fission / nuclear fusion

In *nuclear fission*, often called just *fission*, the nucleus of an atom is split under the force of impact by a *fundamental*, or *elementary particle*, releasing in the process an enormous amount of energy. In *nuclear fusion*, often called just *fusion*, two atomic nuclei combine in a *thermonuclear reaction* to form one nucleus, releasing in the process an enormous amount of energy. In nuclear power plants, either a *fission reaction* or a *fusion reaction* is controlled to produce energy; in the sun and in the hydrogen bomb, the fusion reaction is uncontrolled.

nuclear / atomic

An *atom* is the smallest identifiable unit of matter. It consists essentially of a *nucleus*, containing one or more *protons* (positively charged particles), around which orbit one or more *electrons* (negatively charged particles). The number of protons in the nucleus is used to identify which of the 205 *elements* the atom is identified with or a part of. When two or more atoms of different elements bond together chemically they form a *compound*, in which each of the atoms of each of the elements combines with the atoms of the other element (or elements) to form a *molecule*. (See also **atom / molecule**.) If two atoms of different elements are forced to combine in such a way that their nuclei are altered, *nuclear fusion* is said to take place. For example, gold has 79 positive charges in its nucleus; theoretically, atomic fusion of iodine (53) with iron (26) or of copper (29) and tin (50) would produce gold; indeed it would, but the cost of the process would be far greater than the value of the gold produced, hence is not done. Besides, the amount of energy required to accomplish such fusion might be beyond the capacity of available equipment. In the opposite of *nuclear fusion*, *nuclear fission*, the atoms of an element are forced apart; theoretically, subjecting gold (79) to nuclear fission might produce iodine and iron, copper and tin, or, indeed, any other elements in any quantity that would add up to 79 positively charged particles (including 79 atoms of hydrogen, which has just one particle in its nucleus). In practice, the hydrogen atom is used in nuclear fusion: two atoms of hydrogen, with one proton each, fuse to form one atom of helium, which has two protons in its nucleus. Uranium, an unstable element with 92 protons in its nucleus, is often used in nuclear fission, for its nucleus is more easily split than that of other elements. (See also **fission / fusion**.)

number / numeral

As nouns denoting one or more symbols used for a quantity, these words are interchangeable, though their idiomatic distribution may vary. Thus, *number* is used to designate the particular ordering symbol assigned to something (or somebody), as a *social security number, house number, registration number, license number,* and so on. *Numeral* is generally reserved for the name of the number, and one speaks of *Roman* or *Arabic numerals.* In some contexts they are interchangeable: one could buy either new numbers or numerals to fasten to the front of a house. *Numeral* does not appear in any English idioms, while *number* does: *do a number on someone; get* or *have someone's number; do something by the numbers; without number; one's number is up; have someone's number on it; be a back number; a wrong number; in round numbers; safety in numbers; number one; opposite number; number of the beast; number ten,* and so forth. (See also **cardinal / ordinal.**)

numerator / denominator

The *denominator* of a fraction is the part written below the horizontal (or to the right of the diagonal) line (called the *separatrix*); the *numerator* is the part written above (or to the left of) the line. Although no mnemonic for *numerator* is offered, it might serve to recall that *denominator* and *down* both begin with *d-.*

nymphomania / satyromania

Nymphomania is an uncontrollable desire in a woman for sexual intercourse; the corollary desire in a man is called *satyromania, satyriasis,* or *Don Juanism.* Both terms are best reserved for descriptions of psychiatric disorders and ought not be used loosely as synonyms for lustfulness.

obscene / pornographic

The general sense of *obscene* is 'indecent'; in this sense, it is applied to language, *obscene language* being that which contains (in English) four-letter, taboo words, called *obscenities. Obscene* also means 'lewd, lascivious, inciting to sexual excitement or lust'; in this sense, it is sometimes interchanged with *pornographic.* Finally, it is also applied to anything gross, abominable, disgusting, or repugnant, as in *She regards the showing of open-heart surgery on public television as obscene. Pornography* designates material—stories, books, pictures, films, etc.—the purpose of which is to arouse sexual excitement; pornography is usually distinguished from *erotica*, which consists of art, literature, or another medium in which sexual love is treated voluptuously. In the United States, in general legal terms, the characteristic difference between erotic and pornographic matter is that the former may be regarded as a manifest art form while the latter offers no redeeming features beyond its purpose to arouse; in specific legal terms, criteria establishing whether a work is obscene or pornographic rest on the vague assumption of an "average person" with the ability to apply "contemporary community standards"; essentially, this has permitted individual communities in the U.S. to establish their own criteria of obscenity, so that what is allowed in one place may be banned in another. (See also **exotic / erotic.**)

oculist / optometrist / optician / ophthalmologist

There is no ambiguity about the designation *ophthalmologist:* universally, it is a medical practitioner specialized in diseases and disorders of the eye; he does not make or sell eyeglasses or other corrective equipment, as a rule. *Opticians* in the U.S. are in the business of prescribing corrective lenses and selling them and their attendant paraphernalia—frames, contact lens cleaners, etc. In Britain, there are *ophthalmic opticians*, who prescribe corrective lenses and make them and sell them, and *dispensing opticians*, who make and sell corrective lenses but are not allowed to prescribe them. *Optometrist* is a variant name in the U.S. for *optician* and in Britain for *ophthalmic optician*. An *oculist* is, ambiguously, either an ophthalmologist or an optometrist in the U.S.; in Britain, it is a former word for an ophthalmologist.

official / officious

As *official* means 'authorized; done with the approval of some recognized authority' and *officious* means 'interfering; meddlesome; objectionably forward and intrusive,' they should be kept apart. *Official* pertains to authority or position, rarely (as an adjective) to an individual, while *officious* is used of people more often than of things or conditions.

Old Kingdom / Middle Kingdom / New Kingdom

In the history of Egypt, the *Old Kingdom* was the period of just under 500 years between about 2613 and 2181 B.C., including the 4th dynasty (about 2613–2494; eight kings, including Cheops and Chephren), the 5th dynasty (about 2494–2345; nine kings), and ending with the 6th dynasty (about 2345–2181; eight kings, including Pepi II Nefetkare, who reigned for 94 years, the longest reign in recorded history). Preceded by the first three dynasties (about 3100–2613 B.C.; 24 kings, including Menes, the first dynastic king), the 4th dynasty was marked by the building of Zoser's step pyramid, designed by the scribe and architect, Imhotep, who later became a famous doctor and magician, the pyramids and mastabas at Saqqara, and the tombs at Abydos; during the 5th and early 6th dynasties architecture and elaborate design flourished, and the Palermo stone, an important relic, was inscribed with annals going back to the 4th dynasty; toward the end of the period, royal authority began to be eroded, and the decline in the building of public monuments is interpreted as indication of civil strife. The 7th through the 10th dynasties (2181–2040 B.C.) are known as the *First Intermediate Period,* characterized as an interval of dispersal of power and marked by invasion of the Nile delta by Asians and disruption of the social order. During the *Middle Kingdom,* which lasted from about 2133–1603 B.C. and included the 11th through the 14th dynasties, the seat of government was established at Thebes, building again began to flourish, and prosperity was restored, especially under the Pharaohs of the Amenemhet and Sesostris (12th) dynasty, a period regarded as the golden age of art and craftsmanship. At Al Fayyum, whither the capital had been moved, Amenemhet III built a huge, complex mortuary temple; named "the Labyrinth" by Greek writers, it attracted visitors from everywhere. Nubia having been subjugated, the Nubian mines proved a rich source of gold, and Nubian slaves were much in evidence in Egypt; the influence and armies of Egypt extended also into Palestine and Syria. There followed a lacuna of some years during which the Hyksos kings, who, it is thought, might have been of a Semitic people from Asia, established their hegemony over the country from the delta; toward the end of this interval, called the *Second Intermediate Period* (1720–1567 B.C.), the Hyksos were weakened, but scant information is available because the records were either not kept or were destroyed. The 18th dynasty (1567–1320 B.C.), which included such well-known Pharaohs' names as Amenhotep (Amenophis), Thutmose, Queen Hatshepsut, Ikhnaton, and Tutankhamun, marked the beginning of the *New Empire* (1567–525 B.C.), so called because of its wide conquests abroad. The Hyksos power was crushed, and armies under Thutmose I conquered territories as far south as the fourth cataract of the Nile and as far east as the Euphrates. These conquests were later affirmed (partly in putting down a revolt of the Syrians) by Thutmose III, an outstanding strategist, administrator, and artist-designer, considered by some the greatest of all the Pharaohs. His grandson, Amenhotep III (ruled 1375–1357 B.C.), was a religious zealot who devoted himself to the cult of Aton, a sun-god, and to replacing the worship of Amon, an ancient deity well-established since before the founding of the Theban dynasties; he even changed his name, which meant 'Amon is satisfied,' to Akhnaton 'may it please Aton,' and had the name of Amon and any reference to him removed from monuments. He built a new capital, naming it Akhetaton (modern Tell el-Amarna), which was richly decorated and appointed. A memorable personage of his reign was his wife, Queen Nefertiti. Meanwhile, Egyptian power was on the wane in Asia, owing to the neglect of Akhnaton. After an interval, one of his sons-in-law, Tutankhaton, who later changed his name to Tutankhamun, became king; following a reign during which he re-established the temple at Karnak and the worship of Amon, Tutankhamun died, having been Pharaoh for only nine years. He was buried in the famous tomb at Thebes discovered by Howard Carter and Lord Carnarvon in the 1920s. Subsequently, Horemheb, a soldier and supporter of the religion of Amon, acceded to the throne and fully restored Amon to his place of preeminence. The 19th dynasty (1320–1200 B.C.) was marked by the reigns of Ramses I, Seti I, and, especially, of Ramses II (1292–1225 B.C.), under whom, successively, the old monuments were largely rebuilt and restored and new ones, notably Seti's tomb in the Valley of the Tombs of the Kings, the rock temple at Abu Simbel, and the colonnaded temple at Karnak, were completed. The general weakening of Egyptian military strength over the years, brought about partly by complacency, partly by lack of interest among the later rulers of the 18th dynasty and those of the 19th, was met during the 20th dynasty (1200–1085 B.C.) by increased aggression from abroad, both from the conquered peoples of Asia and from raiders, particularly the Libyans. Finally, an invading force was repelled and defeated by Ramses III (1198-1167 B.C.), and the rest of his reign was relatively peaceful. He was succeeded by eight undistinguished kings named Ramses till the end of the dynasty. The 21st dynasty saw the end of the New Empire, and, during the 22nd to the 26th, various kings sat on the throne, including Piankhi of the Cushite (Ethiopian) peoples who had been conquered long before by the Egyptians and, later, Assyrian monarchs. It was not till the 26th dynasty that Psammetichus (663–610 B.C.) was able to take advantage of Assurbanipal's preoccupation with domestic problems and, with the aid of King Gyges of Lydia, establish a prosperous kingdom. His son, Necho, sent an expedition to fight the Babylonians, ruled by King Nabopolassar, who sent his son, Nebuchadnezzar, to engage Necho's forces at Carchemish. The battle (605 B.C.) was an utter rout for the Egyptians; it is listed among the *Fifteen Decisive Battles of the World* by Sir Edward Creasy in his book of that title. By 525 B.C., Egypt fell to the Persians, under the rule of Cambyses. Sporadic records exist for much of the period following: during the reign of Artaxerxes, in 440 B.C., Herodotus visited Egypt, and his account of the later history, which relied partly on the writings of another historian, Hecataeus of Miletus, is the main source of information about the Saite kings. The end finally came in 332, when Alexander the Great reached Alexandria and Ptolemy I was established as the first of the Macedonian kings.

open shop / closed shop / nonunion shop

An *open shop* is any concern in which the choice of belonging or not belonging to a union is up to the employees. A *closed shop* is any concern in which all the employees who do a certain kind of work must belong to a union. A *nonunion shop* is any concern in which none of the employees belongs to a union.

opera / oratorio / opera-oratorio / operetta

An *opera* is a dramatic presentation in which the parts are mostly sung, though some recitative (*q.v.*) may be used. It is performed on a stage, with settings, costumes, and, often, a large cast, including a chorus, all accompanied by an orchestra. Opera evolved as a form in Italy in the late 16th-early 17th centuries, typified by the works of Monteverdi; baroque opera became increasingly popular through the works of Scarlatti and Handel, and the tradition of *opera seria* (*q.v.*), which continues to this day, was established in the late 18th century by Mozart. The 19th century saw a flourishing of opera in the works of Rossini, Meyerbeer, Bellini, Berlioz, Wagner, Mussorgsky, and Verdi; the most popular composer of the 20th century is Puccini, but that is not to suggest that opera is not a contemporary musical expression, with stagings of new operas by Schoenberg, Stravinsky, Britten, Menotti, and Bernstein marking the modern development of the medium since the 1940s. An *oratorio* is a composition, often with a religious theme, performed by soloists, a chorus, and an orchestra without stage settings in a concert hall; early examples of oratorios were performed in the 17th century, in Italy, but the most typical (and most-often heard) is probably Handel's *Messiah* (1742). A composition in which the presentation is staged, as in opera, but the action is static, as in oratorio, is called an *opera-oratorio;* an example is Stravinsky's *Oedipus Rex.* An *operetta* is a light opera with spoken dialogue and dances in addition to arias, recitatives, etc.; typical of the genre are those of the late 19th century by Gilbert and Sullivan. (See also **grand opera / opera buffa / opera seria.**)

opus / opera

An *opus* is a musical composition, usually an instrumental work, by a particular composer. Various publishers and bibliographers have prepared catalogues, some of them specialized to a single composer's works, as Ludwig von Köchel's catalogue of the works of Mozart or Ralph Kirkpatrick's catalogue of the works of Scarlatti. The plural of the Latin word *opus* is *opera* (the first syllable rhymes with *mope*); but the word *opera* (the first syllable rhymes with *mop*) meaning a 'dramatic musical composition with singing' comes from Italian. It is unlikely that the two would be confused in context. (See also **-us, words ending in.**)

-or / -our

In his attempts at simplifying the spelling of American English, the lexicographer Noah Webster (1758–1843) introduced the spellings *honor, humor, color, ardor, odor,* etc., to replace the British spellings with a *-u-, honour,* etc. For the most part, he was successful, but American spelling retains the *-u-*in *glamour,* partly because that word was not of great enough frequency in Webster's time to be mentioned, partly, in all probability, because Americans regard things British as possessed of some cachet. The adjective form, *glamorous,* is so spelled in both places; indeed, the addition of a suffix to British words ending in *-our* miraculously occasions the disappearance of the *-u-*, which is not etymological and should not have been there to begin with: *honorific, honorable, humorous, coloration, odorous, odoriferous*, etc.

oregano / marjoram

It appears that there are two aromatic European herbs widely used as seasonings in cookery. They are *sweet marjoram* and *wild marjoram*. *Wild marjoram* is also known as *oregano* and is so marketed.

organic / inorganic

In the most general terms, *organic* refers to living things (or to things that once lived), *inorganic* to substances like minerals, which exhibit no semblance of life. This leaves in confusion such substances as petrified wood or trees, once organic, now inorganic; but there is no rule that everything must always be explained without exceptions. The term *organic chemistry*, formerly limited to the study comprising compounds found in living organisms, is today used to describe the study of all compounds that contain the element carbon compounded with other elements; *inorganic chemistry* is the study of compounds that contain no carbon.

orient / occident

Orient is another word for 'east'; it comes, via French, from the Latin verb *orire* 'to rise' and refers, of course, to the place where the sun comes up. The *occident* is the west; it comes, also via French, from the Latin verb *occidere* 'to fall or go down.' *Occident* is a somewhat more formal, literary word, seldom met with in ordinary conversation or writing. *Orient*, on the other hand, although it is encountered far more frequently in ordinary English, is yet felt to be more poetic than "the east."

overtone / undertone

Overtones are those that are secondary to the main tones in acoustics or music; used metaphorically, they are suggestions conveyed either by words or by tone of voice, gesture, or other nonverbal communication that are not expressly stated. One might speak of a political candidate's campaign speech that carried overtones of his defeat, or of an optimistic approach to something that had overtones of depression. *Undertones* are also tones secondary to the main tones, but, while *overtones* may have the sense of 'nuances' that are deliberate, *undertones* suggests that the undercurrents are unintentional. These distinctions, however, may be generally regarded as ultrafine, and, for all practical purposes, the two terms are used interchangeably.

oviparous / viviparous / ovoviviparous

These terms describe the three main ways in which animals bear their young. *Oviparous* means 'egg-bearing, egg-producing' and refers to the way birds, most reptiles and fishes, and a few mammals bear their young: the egg is produced, and the young are developed outside the body of the mother. *Viviparous* means 'live-bearing' and refers to the way almost all mammals and a few fishes and reptiles bear their young: the egg is fertilized within the body, the young develop in the mother's body and are brought forth in more or less viable condition. *Ovoviviparous*, a combination of the preceding, describes a procedure in which the young of certain reptiles and fishes (some sharks, for example) are developed in eggs that hatch within the mother's body, where they develop till sufficiently viable, when they are brought forth.

Oxbridge / redbrick

In England, *Oxbridge*, a blend of *Ox(ford)* and *(Cam)bridge* universities, refers to those bastions of higher education and to all the associations their mention engenders: the upper class; (formerly, especially) a liberal arts education; the advantages enjoyed by graduates of those universities in securing employment, especially employment that pays more than graduates of other universities receive, etc.—in short, the advantaged elite. *Redbrick* refers to those universities that were founded relatively recently, during the 20th century, and to their emphasis, real or imagined, on practical subjects, especially applied science and technology; the word has pejorative connotations, especially insofar as it denotes institutions and graduates thereof lacking in the prestige accorded by association with Oxford and Cambridge. In times when the pay of technologists can reach substantial levels and when graduates of redbrick universities can earn enormous amounts of money in finance and associated businesses, income is no longer a criterion of "class" among those who measure such things.

page / *leaf* / *folio*

The general term for each side of one of the several pieces of paper gathered or bound together to make a newspaper, book, or other collection of such pieces written, drawn, or printed on is *page*. It is distinct from a *leaf*, which is the term for the piece of paper (which, of course, has two sides). Thus, a book of 128 pages has 64 leaves. *Folio* is a somewhat more specialized word. In ordinary book printing, it refers to the numbers that are normally assigned to consecutive pages; in times gone by, when such things were less rare, it meant the same as *leaf* when it referred to leaves that were printed on one side only; it also found application in denoting the size of a book, a *folio* being one with pages of the largest size, usually one more than 30cm (11.8in) in height; and in newspaper parlance, it means the page number along with the date and the name of the newspaper—what in book talk would be called the *running head* or *title* or, in some usages, the *keylining*.

Paleolithic / *Mesolithic* / *Neolithic*

These terms are used by anthropologists to mark various stages in the Stone Age in the development of man. The most recent period, the *Neolithic*, was marked by the domestication of animals, the making of earthenware and textiles, the cultivation of the land, with the changes from a hunting to a farming society resulting in the development of settlements, the invention of the wheel, and the use of tools of polished stone, bone, and other materials; it is generally thought to have taken place about 10,000 years ago. The earlier *Mesolithic*, or *Epipaleolithic* period, a transitional period between the *Paleolithic* and the *Neolithic*, is characterized by the earliest domestication of animals, of the dog, in particular, and of the use of the bow and arrow. The *Paleolithic* period is characterized by the use of stone and flint tools and, towards its end, by cave paintings and sculptured stone images. For convenience, the Paleolithic is divided into the *Lower Paleolithic* (500,000–250,000 B.C.), the *Middle Paleolithic* (250,000–60,000 B.C.), and the *Upper Paleolithic* (60,000–10,000 B.C.). The earliest stages of human cultural development are in the *Eolithic,* in which the most primitive stone tools were fashioned. (See also **Stone Age / Bronze Age / Iron Age.**)

Pangaea / Gondwanaland / Laurasia / Arctogaea / Neogaea / Notogaea

Pangaea is the theoretical supercontinent that existed early in the geological formation of the earth; more than 200 million years ago it divided into *Gondwanaland,* a supercontinent in the southern hemisphere that divided to become the continents of Africa, South America, Australia, Antarctica, and India, and *Laurasia,* a supercontinent in the northern hemisphere that divided to become Eurasia and North America. In the scientific study of the distribution of animal species, *Arctogaea* is the name given to the landmasses of North America, Eurasia, and Africa; *Neogaea* that given to Central and South America; and *Notogaea* that given to Australasia.

parameter / perimeter / yardstick

A *parameter* is a quantity that remains constant for a given case but varies depending on the case under consideration. A simple example is the gravitational attraction of the moon: at any given moment it is a constant in relation to a specific point on earth; but as the moon continues in its orbit, the gravitational attraction varies in proportion to the distance of the moon from the earth. The important element of parameters is that they are variable from instance to instance. A *yardstick* is literally a measuring device 3 feet, or 36 inches long; figuratively, it is used to mean 'any device of fixed length against which the size or extent or intensity of something can be measured for comparison.' Thus, using *parameter* in the sense of *yardstick* or *measure* is silly (unless one finds it useful to have a yardstick that measures 34 inches one time it is used, 36½ inches the next, then 35 inches, and so on). *Perimeter* is the 'outside boundary of an enclosed plane area' and has nothing whatsoever to do with *parameter,* notwithstanding the similarity of spelling.

parchment / vellum

Both these are terms for sheepskin, calfskin, goatskin, or the skin of some other suitable animal prepared for use as a writing surface and are today used also to denote paper made in imitation of these. The word *parchment* comes from *Pergamon,* or *Pergamum,* an ancient Greek city of Asia Minor (modern Bergama, in Turkey) where the techniques for its preparation were developed; *vellum* comes from Latin *vitellum* 'calf' and is cognate with the word *veal.* Although they mean the same thing, *vellum* is usually reserved for the genuine article, *parchment* having for some reason become more generalized and more widely used for artificial imitations. *Papyrus,* which yields the word *paper,* is a different kind of writing material altogether: it is made by soaking and then pressing out the pith of a plant of the sedge family that grows along the banks of the Nile. It was in common use by the Egyptians, Greeks, and Romans for almost a thousand years, till about the 5th century A.D. A *palimpsest* is a writing surface prepared in such a way that it can be reused by rubbing out earlier writing; vellum was commonly so treated, and many of the ancient manuscripts that have come down to us are palimpsests.

parentheses / brackets / braces

Usage in the United States and Great Britain differs in the naming of these marks of punctuation:

SYMBOL	GREAT BRITAIN	UNITED STATES
( )	*more common:* brackets *rare:* parentheses	*always:* parentheses
[ ]	square brackets	brackets or square brackets
{ }	braces	braces or curly brackets

These were referred to above as punctuation marks, and the first two are in common use in ordinary text. All, especially the last, which is rarely seen in ordinary text, are used in mathematics and expressions in symbolic logic to distinguish different levels of inclusion, usually from the top downward: (. . [. . { . . } . .] . .). Because of the confusion of names, in the discussion that follows the symbols will be used for clarity. The use of (. .) in text is not entirely straightforward, as there are three common conventions for setting off parenthetical comments and other information in writing English: ellipsis (. .); dashes (— . . —); and commas (, . . ,). Usage varies widely, but it is generally conceded that the use of commas to set off a phrase or clause creates the least degree of separation; dashes are used for the next highest level, especially when a dramatic effect is intended or when the matter between dashes is of an explanatory nature; and ellipses are used for text that is at the lowest level of priority: in other words, nothing that is indispensable should be placed between (. .). It is most important to be consistent within a text; that is, if (. .) are to be used for dispensable information, they should be so used throughout. An astute reader will often be able to determine a writer's style quite quickly, and inconsistencies prove confusing. (Square) brackets are used in special instances, particularly when the author of an article inserts his own comment or other information into matter that is a direct quotation:

(1) To indicate that the beginning of a sentence in the source has been excised and to show that the capital letter shown has been inserted by the author:

"[T]he governments have followed . . . "
(from an original that had:)
"In my opinion, the governments have followed . . . "

(2) To enclose a word that adjusts the grammar of a text to suit the part quoted or, occasionally, to improve the original author's grammar:

"The beaujolais . . . [was] good last year."
(from an original that had:)
"The beaujolais and bordeaux were good last year."

"If only one of the men had sacrificed [his] pride . . . "
(from an original that had:)
"If only one of the men had sacrificed their pride . . . "

(3) To insert a comment of the (present) author's:

"They serve good vittles [*sic*] at the party."

(Square) brackets are sometimes also used for the insertion of other kinds of information, which might otherwise be enclosed in (. .):

The shark was almost 15 meters [49 feet] long.

partly / partially

To the extent that these can be told apart by definition, *partly* means 'not wholly or completely': *He has partly completed the required courses for a degree. Partially* means 'in part; incompletely': *Brass consists partially of copper, partially of zinc.* These meanings are so close as to be almost indistinguishable, for the scintilla of difference between 'not completely' and 'incompletely' is almost indiscernible. Yet, these words have become associated with catch phrases and clichés: people with defective eyesight are said to be *partially* (not *partly*) *sighted*, and in mathematics one speaks of a *partially ordered set* (in contrast to a *totally ordered set* or a *well-ordered set*). And if someone is woolgathering, he might be said to be *partly here* or *there*, not "partially here."

pasteurized / homogenized

In the description of forms in which milk is sold, *pasteurized milk* has been heated to destroy pathogenic bacteria; today, except in rare instances, milk, cream, and most of the products made from them are pasteurized for commercial distribution. *Homogenized milk*, which is also pasteurized, has been processed so that the fat globules have been broken up and distributed evenly throughout; in homogenized milk the cream does not rise to the top as it does in ordinary milk. Homogenized milk, not sold in Britain, is the standard available in the U.S.

pâté / terrine

These words, borrowed from French cookery, are used interchangeably today, but not long ago they were carefully kept apart, and there are some who still insist on maintaining the distinction between them. The French word *pâté* means 'paste' (as in pastry), and a pâté is properly baked in a crust. The French word *terrine* means 'made of earth; earthenware,' and dishes called *terrines* are supposed to be baked in such dishes, without a crust. In current usage, a pâté is usually of a finer consistency than a terrine. The ingredients in both vary widely, but usually consist of some finely minced meat combined with spices, condiments, and other additions that come to the chef's mind (or hand) during preparation.

pedant / pedagogue

These once meant the same thing, 'teacher,' but, while *pedagogue* (also spelled *pedagog* in the U.S.) has retained that sense, *pedant* has become an opprobrious term meaning someone who is entirely concerned with what can be found in books and who places far too much emphasis on niggling details. The adjective *pedantic* means 'exhibiting a boring and unfeeling obsession with the slavish observance of inconsequential rules and minutiae.' *Pedagogical*, or, less often, *pedagogic*, means 'having to do with teaching'; it is usually reserved for rather formal contexts, and it would sound pompous to say of someone who wanted to become a teacher that "He wished to follow a pedagogical career." *Pedantic* suggests *pedantry*, which implies all of the unfavorable associations people may have with school: the stuffiness of some teachers; the excessive showing-off of knowledge and an attempt to put down those who do not possess it; the strict adherence to rules set forth on paper without regard to common sense; the attitude of superiority of many teachers, and so on. Although these words may seem to be related, they are not: *pedagogical* (referring to *pedagogy* or to a *pedagogue*) comes ultimately from the Greek word (via Latin) for a 'boy's tutor'; it is made from the same initial element used in *ped(iatrics)* and *ped(iatrician)*, meaning 'child,' and the same final element appearing in *(dem)agogue*, meaning, in these instances, 'leader.' *Pedantry, pedantic*, by contrast, are traced to the *ped-* of *ped(al)* and *pedi(cure)* meaning 'foot'; the semantic notion is of one who follows in the *footsteps* of others, who engages in (to use an older term) *footling* activities, and whose thinking is, so to speak, *pedestrian*.

peer / equal

The use of *peer* to mean 'equal' in contexts like a *jury of his peers, without peer*, and *peerless*, strikes English speakers as a curious anomaly, because *peer* means 'member of the nobility,' hence, 'someone who is unquestionably superior,' a sense that is reinforced by *peers of the realm*, who constitute the House of Lords to which few speakers of English of any nationality feel equal, and by *peerage*, also referring to nobility. Nonetheless, 'equal' is what it does mean, having its origin in Latin *par*, which appears in English in the same spelling. Thus, peers are truly on a par with the common man (and woman).

penumbra / umbra

An opaque object between a source of light and a surface casts a shadow. If the light source is a point, the shadow is solid black, called an *umbra;* if the source is large, it casts an *umbra* and, around it, an area that is in half shadow, called a *penumbra.*

perfume / cologne / toilet water

All these terms refer to a liquid or, less often, a solid made from a combination of the organic oils present in plants or, sometimes, synthetically manufactured, mixed with alcohol and used to impart a pleasant odor. *Perfume,* also called *scent* in Great Britain, is the most highly concentrated; *cologne,* usually called just *Cologne,* or *eau de Cologne,* named for the city where it was developed early in the 18th century, is a somewhat diluted version of perfume; *toilet water* is a still further diluted version. Although the main popular association with perfume is with its use as a body scent, perfumes are widely used not only in cosmetics but in processed foods, soaps and detergents, plastics, and many other manufactured products.

phonetics / phonemics

Bearing in mind that *phone* is taken to mean a 'speech sound,' the study of *phones* is properly called *phonetics.* On the other hand, *phonemics* is the name for the study of *phonemes,* which require some explanation. As almost all speakers of any language are aware, everyone who speaks the language pronounces it differently. Within a dialect community—especially within a family—the differences may be very slight; but the further apart the speakers, in age or geographically, the more likely it is that they speak with some differences, and in some instances, the differences may become so great as to defy ready understanding between the speech communities. Nonetheless, with the possible exception of the differences between the actual words used rather than how they are pronounced, it is conceded that all are speaking "the same language." In the view of linguists, no one dialect of a language is "better" than another; among those with a less scientific approach to the subject, some dialects may have social or other prestige, and in their eyes, that is enough to make those dialects "better." Everyone who speaks a language speaks a dialect, *dialect* meaning a 'certain way of talking': it has no reference in this context to comedians or actors who speak English with an Italian accent, for example. All speakers of a language have at their disposal a number of speech sounds which, in combination, are used to utter the words and sentences of the language. In English, there are about 40 such sounds, which are called *phonemes.* Each phoneme has a discrete set of characteristics, characteristics that are independent of whether the sound is uttered by someone from Texas, from Melbourne, from Edinburgh, or from East Grinstead. Although there is rarely complete agreement among experts in almost any field, most linguists concur that the characteristics that determine a consonantal phoneme number four: its *place of articulation;* whether it is *voiced* or *unvoiced* (also called *voiceless*); whether it is a *stop* or a *continuant;* and whether it is *nasal* or *non-nasal.* There are, of course, vowel phonemes, as well, but—at least for English—those are all voiced, non-nasal, and continuants, their distinctive characteristics being *place of articulation* (that is, *back, central,* or *front,* and *low, mid* or *high*), relative *tenseness* or *laxness* of the speech organs involved, and whether the lips are *rounded* or *unrounded.* These characteristics of phonemes are called *distinctive features,* and a few examples will illustrate their function. The sounds *p* and *b* differ only in that the former is unvoiced (or voiceless) and the latter is voiced; in respect of the three other distinctive features, they are identical: both are articulated using both lips, both are stops (that is, they cannot be "continued" as can the sounds *s* and *z*); and both are non-nasal (unlike the sounds *m, n,* and *ng,* the only nasal consonants in English). Similarly, *p* and *t* differ only with respect to their place of articulation; in other respects, they share the same distinctive features. Among the vowels, the vowel sounds of *beet* and *boot* differ in several respects: *ee* is what would be called high, front, unrounded and somewhat tense, while *oo* would be characterized as high, back, rounded, and relatively lax. It is the distinctive feature of voice /voicelessness that enables speakers of English to distinguish between *bit* and *pit, pig* and *pick, big* and *pig, dot* and *tot, got* and *cot, zoo* and *Sioux* or *sue, thy* and *thigh,* and between *vat* and *fat;* place of articulation enables the distinction between *pit /bit, tot /dot,* and *cot / got;* stop /continuant enables the distinction between *toe* and *so, do* and *zoo,* and so forth. The distinctive features of the phonemes of languages differ; for example, French has nasal and non-nasal vowels, an irrelevant feature for English. It is essential to note the difference between those features that are distinctive features of phonemes in a language and those that are not. For example, while there is a definite *phonetic* difference (depending on which dialect one speaks) between the pronunciations used by speakers of different dialects of English, there is no *phonemic* difference, for both are speaking the same language and the distinctive features of the phonemes remains the same, even though certain shifts may occur: the New Englander still speaks differently from the Englishman, Scotsman, Australian, or Texan, but the differences are phonetic, not phonemic. (See also **consonant / vowel, nasal / non-nasal.**)

phylum / class / order / family / genus / species

These are terms used in the biological taxonomy (scientific naming) of animals. (For the taxonomy of plants, see **division /class /order / family /genus /species.**) The major categories are those listed above, in descending order. The very lowest level is called a *variety, breed,* or *subspecies.* Thus, we may speak of, say, a cocker spaniel, which is a *breed, subspecies,* or *variety* of dog belonging to the genus *Canis,* belonging to the family *Canidae* (which also includes the coyotes, foxes, hyenas, jackals, and wolves), which are members of the order of *carnivores* (*Carnivora*), which are members of the class of *mammals* (*Mammalia*), which are members of the subphylum of *vertebrates* (*Vertebrata*)—which is large enough to include all animals with spines—which belong to the phylum *Chordata.* It is easier to see the relationship when it is arrayed in this fashion:

PHYLUM: *Chordata* (having a notochord, dorsal tubular nerve cord, and pharyngeal gill slits)

   SUBPHYLUM: *Vertebrata* (having a bony or cartilaginous skeleton)

      CLASS: *Mammalia* (warm-blooded, with mammary glands, a thoracic diaphragm, and a heart with four chambers)

         ORDER: *Carnivora* (having teeth specialized for eating flesh)

            FAMILY: *Canidae* (dog, fox, hyena, etc.)

               GENUS: *Canis* (dog, wolf, etc.)

                  SPECIES: *Canis familiaris* (domestic dog)

                     VARIETY / BREED / SUBSPECIES: *cocker spaniel*

pickle / gherkin

A *pickle* is a cucumber that has been steeped in brine for long enough to impart a flavor to it; it is used as a condiment. A *gherkin* is an immature or small cucumber that has been pickled. There are many different kinds of pickling broths, and pickles may be flavored with dill or other spices and are often steeped in a pickling juice containing vinegar, creating sour pickles. Gherkins are usually pickled in a juice that imparts a sweetish flavor.

pig iron / cast iron / wrought iron

Iron poured out of a blast furnace is cast into ingots, called *pigs* because of their shape, in which form it is stored (as *pig iron*) till it is made into steel, *cast iron*, or *wrought iron*. Cast iron is a molten alloy that is molded by pouring into a mold made of sand or some other refractory material; it is made up of iron, carbon, and other ingredients the addition of which depends on which characteristics of malleability, brittleness, etc., are required. Similarly, *wrought iron* is an alloy containing little carbon the composition of which produces a metal that can be readily worked, that is, 'wrought.'

pitiful / pitiable / piteous

Although these words share the sense 'exciting or evoking pity; worthy of pity,' their applications differ slightly. *Piteous* is not employed in speaking of people: *piteous moan; piteous wail. Pitiable* means 'able to be pitied; lamentable' as well as 'miserable; wretched': *the pitiable poor; We found them in a pitiable state. Pitiful,* on the other hand, though it can be used to describe an action, condition, sight, moan, or cry, e.g., *pitiful poverty)* is more often used in the sense of 'insignificant; trifling; small; mean or wretched; below contempt' (*a pitiful effort*), often in its adverbial form: *a pitifully meager output of work.*

plagiarism / infringement

The general term for trespassing on the rights of others in a number of applications is *infringement:* violation of the rights granted under either patent or copyright law is called *infringement.* When the violation is specifically of copyright, the term for the appropriation of the original work of another and presenting or publishing it as one's own is *plagiarism.*

Plantagenet / Lancaster / York / Tudor / Stuart / Hanover / Saxe-Coburg-Gotha / Windsor

These are the names of the royal families of England after the reigns of William I (1066–87), William II (1087–1100), Henry I (1100–35), and Stephen (1135–54).

Plantagenet kings: Henry II (1154–89), Richard I "the Lionheart" (1189–99), John (1199–1216), Henry III (1216–72), Edward I (1272–1307), Edward II (1307–27), Edward III (1327–77), and Richard II (1377–99).

Lancastrian kings: Henry IV (1399–1413), Henry V (1413–22), and Henry VI (1422–61, 1470–71).

York kings: Edward IV (1461–70, 1471–83), Edward V (1483), and Richard III (1483–85).

Tudor rulers: Henry VII (1485–1509), Henry VIII (1509–47), Edward VI (1547-53), Mary I (1553-58), and Elizabeth I (1558–1603).

Stuart rulers: James I (1603–25), Charles I (1625-49); [the monarchy was abolished in 1649, and there was no monarch till 1660]; Charles II (1660–85), James II (1685–88), William III (1689–1702) together with Mary II (1689–94), and Anne (1702–14).

Hanoverian rulers: George I (1714–27), George II (1727–60), George III (1760–1820), George IV (1820–30), William IV (1830–37), Victoria (1837–1901), and Edward VII (1901–10).

In 1917, the family name, *Saxe-Coburg-Gotha,* which was the name of Victoria's husband, Albert, was changed to *Windsor.* As *Windsor,* the rulers include George V (1910-36), Edward VIII (1936), George VI (1936–52), and Elizabeth II (1952–). (See also **England / Scotland / Wales / Ireland / Britain / United Kingdom / Commonwealth, red rose / white rose.**)

Polynesia / Melanesia / Micronesia

The Greek word *nesos* 'island' is used as a suffix common to all these names. Respectively, their etymological meanings are 'many islands,' 'islands inhabited by black-skinned people,' and 'tiny islands.' All refer to the archipelagos in the south and southwest Pacific Ocean. In application, *Polynesia* consists of the Cook Islands (Lower Cooks and Northern Cooks), Mangareva Island, Marquesas Islands (French, *Îles Marquises*), Samoa Islands (including American Samoa and Western Samoa), Society Islands, Tonga (also called Friendly Islands), Tuamotu Archipelago (also called Low Archipelago or Paumotu Archipelago),

and Tubuai Islands (also called Austral Islands). *Melanesia* consists of
the Bismarck Archipelago (including the Admiralty Islands, Lavongai,
New Britain, and New Ireland islands and part of Papua New Guinea),
Fiji, and the Louisiade, Loyalty, New Caledonia, Santa Cruz, and Solomon islands. *Micronesia* consists of Nauru Island and the Caroline,
Kiribati, Mariana (formerly Ladrone), and Marshall islands; the *Federated States of Micronesia*, a group of islands within the United States
Trust Territory, consists of Kosrae, Ponape, Truk, and Yap islands.
These three groups are part of *Oceania*, which includes all the islands
of the central, south, and southwest Pacific, sometimes Australasia
and the Malay Archipelago, as well.

port / starboard / larboard / posh

It is essential aboard any boat or ship to identify one side from the
other: "left" and "right" would not do, for they depend on the direction one is facing. To avoid any misunderstanding or ambiguity in the
giving of orders, all positions are fixed. Facing forward—that is, toward the bows of a vessel—the *port* side is at the left, the *starboard* at
the right, to one's back is the *stern*. These parts of a ship or boat
remain the same regardless of the direction in which one might be
facing. *Aport* means 'to, toward, at, or on the port side'; *astarboard*
means 'to, toward, at, or on the starboard side'; *aft* means 'to, toward,
at, or on the stern'; *abaft* means 'on, toward, or at the sternward
side', as one might describe a hatch ('deck opening') as being *abaft the
mainmast*. In former times, the steering apparatus of a vessel was situated on her starboard side, hence that side came to be called the
steer(ing)board. In the event, when a vessel tied up at a wharf, the
steering gear being on the starboard, she moored with the port side
to the wharf, whence the designation *port* for that side. *Port* was formerly called *larboard*, which is said to have come from *lade* + *board*
'the side of a ship from which it was loaded'; all this makes good
sense, but there is no corroborative evidence for these etymologies.
Because *larboard* could be misunderstood as *starboard*, especially
when the wind was howling in the rigging, the change to *port* made a
great deal of sense. The term *posh* 'luxurious' is often said to be an
acronym of *port out /starboard home*, supposedly the more luxurious
accommodation on a vessel sailing between England and India, apparently because that side would always be facing land. In a lengthy and
detailed exchange in 1966 and 1971 in *The Mariner's Mirror*, the jour-

nal of the Society for Nautical Research, that fanciful acronymic deri-
vation was finally laid to rest, though none of the alternatives has
proved acceptable, either: any efforts to connect the word with the
"Pacific and Orient Steamship Company," with "plush," "push," "(in the
style of a) pasha," etc., have been to no avail. Yet, the error persists;
in recent years a distillery in the United States offered a new brand
of gin which was named *Posh*, and attendant promotion sought to
perpetuate the acronymic origin. Although the gin passed muster, the
etymology did not.

positive / comparative / superlative

These are the names of the gradations in the comparison of adjectives
in English. The *positive* is the ordinary form of the word, as in *good,
lively,* or *terrifying.* The *comparative* form conveys the sense of greater
intensity of the adjective, as in *better, livelier,* or *more terrifying.* The
superlative form reflects the greatest intensity of the adjective, as in
best, liveliest, or *most terrifying.* It will be seen that a small number of
very common words have different forms for their various parts, that
the majority of words of one and two syllables form their comparatives and superlatives by the changing or addition of the endings *-er*
and *-est,* and that most words of three or more syllables form their
comparatives or superlatives by the prefixing of the word *more* or
most. Adverbs may also be compared in English, and their forms usually employ *more* or *most: violently, more violently, most violently.* Some
adverbs, however, have been formed from adjectives of the kind first
described above; *better* functions as an adverb (*You should try to behave better. I waited for better than an hour. We thought better of going
to Syria for a holiday.*), as does *best* (*Mother knows best. You had best
get ready for school.*).

practical / practicable

The emphasis of *practical* is on the suitability of an idea or theory to
a real application; it is also used of a person in reference to his ideas
or views: *You are not being practical if you think that the computer can
be programmed to write the play. Practicable* means 'workable; able to
be put into practice': *Two ideas that have not yet proved practicable are
a perpetual-motion machine and an antigravity ray.* The implication is
usually that if something is not practical, then it is unlikely that it

ever will be, while if it is not practicable, that may be because existing technology has not yet provided for it.

precipitous / precipitate

Precipitate means 'sudden; rash; headlong'; *precipitous* means 'steep,' and it was formed on the adjective *precipitate*. The former is used in many contexts: *a precipitate decision; a precipitate halt to the proceedings; a precipitate undertaking*. The latter is somewhat more restricted in application, referring mainly to cliffs and other physical features. Both are closely associated with *precipices* which is one of the reasons they are often confused. The noun *precipitate* 'substance that settles out from a solution or mixture' also carries the sense of 'falling (down).'

preface / foreword / introduction

These terms relate to what is, in the publishing business, generally called the *front matter* or, informally, the *prelims* (for *preliminary materials or matter*) of a book. *Preface* and *foreword* are the same thing: the former is the Latinate term, the latter the English. A third term, *prologue*, is sometimes used; it is virtually synonymous with the first two but is of Greek origin and is used occasionally as the title of an opening remark. Some publishers prefer one over the other, but there is no distinction, and books do not have both. The content of a preface or foreword is usually a brief comment about the purpose of the book; it may be written by the author or editor or by another whose name, associated in some way with the book, will be felt to lend it some cachet in the marketplace. If by the author or editor, it may also include acknowledgments to those who aided in the preparation of the work; if by someone other than the author or editor, acknowledgments may appear in another section, called "Acknowledgments." Prefaces, or forewords, are usually brief, seldom more than four pages in length. An *introduction* is often a longer, more formal exposition of the purpose of the book and contains an outline of the subject. Introductions are published in textbooks, reference books, and other works of nonfiction, and they often include explanations of the various kinds of information the book contains. Thus, a dictionary introduction usually describes the style used for pronunciations, etymologies, and the ordering of information of the main text, among other things. The name *prolegomenon*, occasionally given to a rather formal essay which serves as the introduction to a longer work, is encountered chiefly in academic contexts.

prefix / infix / suffix

In the construction of words in a language like English, a *prefix* is a meaningful element that can be attached to the beginning of a word to change its meaning, like *anti-* in *anticoagulant*, which is made up from *anti-*'against, counteracting' + *coagulant* 'something that causes a liquid to clot,' or *ante-* in *antebellum*, from *ante-* 'before' + *bellum* 'war,' meaning 'before the war.' An *infix* is an element inserted into the middle of a word to change its meaning or grammatical function. Infixes are not used productively in Modern English; an example from an older stage of the language might be the *-n-* that marks the present tense of *stood* by changing it to *stand*. A *suffix* is an element that can be added to the end of a word to change its meaning or function, like *-able* in *pardonable*. Both prefixes and suffixes occur in profusion in English. These may be *bound* forms (that is, like *ante-, pre-, -ly, -tion*, etc., they do not normally occur unless attached to a word), or *free* forms (that is, like *under, anti, able, graph*, etc., words in their own right which are used to form compounds). Many words contain strings of prefixes and suffixes attached to the same root. For example, *noninterchangeability* is made up of *non-* + *inter-* + *change* + *-abil-* (a combining form of the suffix *-able*) + *-ity*. The meaning is transparent to any speaker of the language. Although the suffixes that create grammatical modifications in the words to which they are attached are, indeed, suffixes, they are sometimes called by linguists *desinences*, or simply *endings*. These would include the *-s* and *-es* used to distinguish the third person singular of common verbs from the other persons (I, you, we, they *run* or *pass* contrasted with he, she, it *runs* or *passes*). Even *zero* is considered an ending: consider the fact that *run* has no ending (*zero*) when compared with *runs* and *running*.

premise / premiss

Meaning 'assumption,' both forms are found, *premise* more frequently than *premiss*, and they are pronounced identically, as "PREM-iss."

prescribe / proscribe

The *pro-* prefix in *proscribe* means 'situated or occurring before or in advance'; although it is formally from the same Latin preposition, *prō*, it does not here mean 'for, in favor of, in place of.' The noun, *proscription*, goes back to the root form (Latin *proscription-*), which described the Roman practice of issuing in a public notice a list of outlaws who were placed under an edict of prohibition, whose property was confiscated, and whom the populace, presumably, were to have nothing to do with. As this was a list 'written beforehand,' it was a *proscription*. *Proscribe* and *proscription* today have the sense of 'interdict, prohibit' and 'interdiction, prohibition.' *Prescription* and *prescribe*, although they literally have to do with 'writing beforehand,' also refer to a special application of the words in law, in which they refer to prior right or title. This sense was later transferred to the medical practice of ordering a medication for use as a remedy.

presently / soon

At an earlier stage of the language, *presently* meant 'at present'; its meaning later shifted to 'soon, anon.' The current trend is to use the word to mean 'at present' not, of course, in an attempt to revive an older stage of usage but simply because it sounds as if that is what it ought to mean. Those whose knowledge of "tradition" is only decades deep regard this usage with consternation bordering on contemptuous denigration, but theirs appears to be a lost cause.

pressurize / pressure

In Britain, the verb meaning to 'bring pressure to bear on (someone or something)' is more commonly *pressurize*, though *pressure* is sometimes used; in the U.S., the word is invariably *pressure*, *pressurize* being reserved solely for the sense to 'increase the (atmospheric) pressure in a closed container.'

presumptive / presumptuous

Presumptive means 'based on a presumption; presuming, based on grounds of probability': *Even though his aunt had died, it was presumptive of him to transfer the money to his own account.* *Presumptuous* means 'assuming an unwarranted, unauthorized responsibility; boldly arrogating a privilege': *That presumptuous upstart had no right to bor-row my dinner jacket.* (See also **assume /presume.**)

pretence / pretext

In some contexts, these words are used interchangeably, but there is a slight difference between them: *pretense* (spelled PRETENCE in Britain) means 'act of pretending, as in affectation; an instance of make-be-lieve; false or insincere action': *He is a terrible coward, and his ranting is mere pretense.* The associated noun is *pretension* and is often used in the plural: *Their pretensions in trying to make people believe them wealthy are irritating and tiresome.* The adjective is *pretentious: She puts on such pretentious airs that no one can stand her.* Pretext is some-what narrower in scope of meaning, being confined mainly to the sense of 'false excuse, misleading action,' hence has the connotation of being purposefully concealing, possibly for dishonest motives: *He got past the security guards on the pretext of saying he was a plumber.*

preventive / preventative

The common English suffix *-ive,* attached to a verb, creates an adjec-tive with the meaning 'tendency or relation toward, disposition to [the action described by the verb]'. Thus:

> *create + -ive = creative*
> *relate + -ive = relative*
> *probate + -ive = probative*

Not all adjectives ending in *-ive* are formed on verbs; some are formed on nouns. Thus, we have:

> *connotat(ion) + -ive = connotative*
> *denotat(ion) + -ive = denotative*
> *cognit(ion) + -ive = cognitive*

For some reason, the term *preventive,* common these days especially in the phrase *preventive medicine,* has become *preventative,* which, any purist will be quick to point out, does not—cannot—exist. (Lan-guage purists are linguistic fundamentalists: if asked where all the new words come from, they frequently point to the dictionary, which is their Bible.) To be sure, *preventative* cannot have come about solely on analogy with words like *denotative* or *connotative;* as there is no attested form "preventate" or "preventation," it cannot have been compounded from those. The answer probably lies in a combination of circumstances, partly owing to models like *denotative* and partly to the meter of the resulting word: for some speakers, *preventative* rolls more trippingly off the tongue than *preventive;* also, being a syllable longer, it sounds a little more important and learned than a shorter word might. There are many elements that determine the construct of lexical elements in the language, and linguists know too little about them for proper analysis, let alone prediction of the trends that prevail.

principal / principle

Because these words are pronounced identically, they are not confused in speech, only in writing. *Principal* is usually an adjective meaning chief, important, key': *The principal reason I want you to stay is that I don't want to leave the house empty while I am away.* It is often used as a noun to refer to the head of a school or, in Great Britain, to the executive in charge of a section in the civil service; also, in business and in law, it is used of someone who is directly involved in an endeavor, in contrast to his agents or brokers: advertised offerings of real estate, businesses for sale, and so forth may specify *Principals only* if the advertiser does not wish to deal with representatives or other agents. A *principle* is a rule of some sort, often of behavior or moral standards, but it is also used in reference to basic facts: *Lithography is based on the principle that oil and water do not mix. The screw is based on the principle of the inclined plane. She stands by her principles and would never lie.* Someone who is *principled* has high standards of morality and behavior; someone who is *unprincipled* has low standards (or, effectively, no standards) and behaves accordingly: *The guards at the concentration camp were totally unprincipled.*

private school / public school

In the United States, a *private school* is any educational institution below the level of college or university that charges fees to students and operates for the profit of its owners; a *public school* is a similar institution that is operated by a municipality, county, or state and is free to students. In England, *private school* has the same meaning as in the U.S., but *public school* has acquired a set of meanings all its own. A *public school* in England was originally one maintained at public expense. In earlier times, *public* in the sense of 'attended by other pupils' was contrasted with *private* in the sense of 'private tutorship at home'; beginning in the 19th century, *public* has been applied to the old endowed grammar schools that draw their pupils from the well-to-do classes and prepare them for entrance to one of the older, established universities or for the civil service; typically, they are boarding schools, and order is maintained by upper classmen. In 1867, "An Act for the better government and extension of certain Public Schools", was passed affecting what came to be called the "Seven Public Schools," namely, Eton, Winchester, Westminster, Harrow, Rugby, Charterhouse, and Shrewsbury; in more recent times, this number has trebled. From this, various phrases like *public-school boy, public-school training* or *education,* etc. have emerged. (See also **college / university.**)

programming / programing

In the good old days, when the word described a list of events, or performers, or both, life was simpler, and the spelling was *programme* (with *programmed* and *programming*) in Britain and *program* (with *programed* and *programing*) in accordance with the accepted practices in the United States. In the 1950s, the word was applied, first in the U.S., to the sequential pattern of instructions that controls the operation of an electronic computer. Although in its earlier incarnation, the *-ed* and *-ing* forms of the verb had been relatively infrequent, those who were involved with computers—and, of necessity, those who were drawn into the net—found it convenient to talk about *programming a computer, computer programming, having programmed a computer to accomplish certain tasks,* etc., and these forms came to be used daily, eventually by a very large of people. Because experts in computer technology were clearly not experts in American spelling practices, they followed their own rules, among which appears, "Thou shalt double final consonants of verbs when adding *-ed, -ing, -able, -er,* or, for that matter, almost any other suffix or ending." None of this was paid much attention in Britain—after all, the Americans had finally come to their senses and were starting to spell things the "right" way. But after a few years a curious phenomenon occurred: so thoroughly overwhelming was the American influence in the computer business that people in Britain began to distinguish between two spellings: *programme* was retained to refer to a catalogue of events, etc., but *program* became the prevalent form for all of the computer senses; the forms *programmer, programmed, programming,* were used for both. Meanwhile, in the United States, *program* was retained for radio, theater, television, and other such listings as well as for computer instructions, with *programmer, programmed, programming* as the associated oblique forms. The standard American oblique forms for the entertainment lists remained with the single consonant, but, as computer specialists come to outnumber those in the entertainment business who know how to spell American English, it is likely that *programed* and *programing* have had their day.

prone / supine

In its literal sense, *prone* means 'lying face down, prostrate,' and *supine* means 'lying face up.' Figuratively, *prone* means 'likely, inclined' and is followed by *to: She is prone to believe you. I am prone to irritability.* *Supine,* also used figuratively to mean 'lethargic, indifferent,' is largely literary and is not encountered as often as *prone.*

proper fraction / improper fraction

A *proper fraction* is one in which the denominator is larger than the numerator, like $2/3$; in an *improper fraction,* the numerator is larger than the denominator, like $5/2$. Improper fractions are usually kept in that form for ease of calculation, but they are otherwise more commonly rewritten in the form of an integer with a fractional remainder, in which $5/2$ would appear as $2^1/_2$.

prophecy / prophesy

The spelling with the *-s-* is the verb, the one with the *-c-,* the noun; the final syllable of the verb rhymes with "sigh," that of the noun with "see."

proportional / proportionate

Both of these words refer to the express or tacit comparison between or among the magnitudes of two or more things. Except for clichés like *proportional representation* and the observation that, when occurring as the last word in a phrase or clause, *proportionate* seems to be more common, they are largely interchangeable, notwithstanding the attempts of writers of usage books to keep them apart on the flimsiest of detailed rationalizations.

proposal / proposition

Both *proposal* and *proposition* mean (in one of their senses) 'plan or something proposed or offered,' but the former is somewhat less formal in presentation, the latter usually more carefully and elaborately spelled out. Thus, we speak of a *business proposition,* not a 'business proposal.' In at least one application, *proposition* means a 'solicitation for sexual intercourse,' and that sense is not shared by *proposal,* which is an offer of marriage, a distinction worthwhile maintaining.

proved / proven

As past participles of *prove, proved* and *proven* are simple variants. When the form is used as an adjective, *proven* is preferred, possibly because of the rhythm of the sentence and for euphony: *It has been proved* (or *proven*) *that he committed the crime. He is a proven* (not *proved*) *liar.*

provided / providing

These are both conjunctions and have identical meaning: 'on the condition; with the understanding; in the event.' They are sometimes followed by *that: Providing* (that) *she arrives in time, we shall go. She will be elected, provided* (that) *she gets enough votes. Henry Ford offered to supply his Model T car in any color provided it was black.* At one time, stylists insisted on the inclusion of *that,* but informal usage has prevailed, and *that* is more often omitted than not.

psychologist / psychiatrist

As may be logically derived, a *psychologist* practises *psychology,* a *psychiatrist, psychiatry.* Psychiatry is a branch of psychology, a term that encompasses all aspects of the scientific study of human and animal behavior; depending on its application, the term *psychology* is often modified by a descriptive term, as in *behavioral psychology, clinical psychology, social psychology, experimental psychology, educational psy-*

chology, etc. *Psychiatry* is a branch of the practice of medicine that treats mental disorders, and in most countries a medical degree is required of psychiatrists, who, like other doctors, may administer medication. A psychologist or *analyst* (also called *lay analyst*) may or may not be required to have a license, depending on where a practice is carried on. In general, it might be said that psychologists and analysts treat psychoneuroses, while psychoses come under the treatment of psychiatrists. Because it is not a simple matter to distinguish between the severity of such conditions, the situation is often vague. (See also **neurosis / psychosis.**) *Psychoanalysis* is a specific method of treating people who are mentally disturbed, whether neurotic or psychotic, and is focused on the investigation by various techniques of the unconscious and subsconscious minds.

puppet / marionette

A *puppet* is a small figure of a person, animal, etc., usually consisting of a head, arms, and a cloth body open at the bottom to allow a person to insert a hand to make the doll move and gesticulate in various ways in a theatrical performance often behind a proscenium that is raised to conceal the person, called a *puppeteer.* A *marionette* is a jointed figure with strings or wires attached to various parts so that a concealed person can manipulate it from above on a stage in a theatrical performance. Marionettes are sometimes quite large—perhaps three or four feet tall. In southest Asia there grew up a tradition of puppets made of a flat, rigid material that were maneuvered from below by stiff wires to perform before a screen; lighted from behind, the shadows of these figures fall on the screen which is viewed from the other side by an audience. The popular Muppets and other figures are three-dimensional versions of these.

purism / permissiveness

By *purism* and *purist,* linguists mean, respectively, "those principles and the people who support them directed by the notion that there exists a 'correct' way to use a language and that any divergence from that righteous path yields 'bad' and 'wrong' usage." *Permissiveness* is a term of opprobrium leveled at linguists and others who, while they do not deny that there are more and less effective ways to use language, maintain that it is pointless to discuss "right" and "wrong," for, if language is viewed as a system of communication, in the scientific view the criteria of "good" and "bad" language must be determined by whether or not it successfully communicates: in other words, artistic presentation and style are not relevant criteria. Linguists view the field of linguistics as a scientific examination of how language works and what it is; in order to do that, they must first describe it as thoroughly as possible. Like any other investigator in any field, the linguist does not pass judgment on what is being investigated any more than the biologist utters opinions about microbes. Linguists who style themselves as *descriptivists* are described by the purists as *permissivists*, and are consistently condemned for not "doing something about the deplorable state of the language." Clearly, if any proper description of a language is to be complete, it must include comment on whether or not it succeeds as a medium of communication; thus, ambiguity in language, which interferes with its success to communicate, is so categorized by linguists—but without the attachment of any stigma: the failings of ambiguous language merely form a part of the description of language and how it works or does not work. Contrary to the beliefs of the purists, certain (descriptive) linguists do concern themselves with style in language and with a description of its poetic, artistic, evocative, and other aspects. Most purists' notions of language are born of the conviction that the domain of "good" and "proper" language lies somewhere over the horizon of reality: modesty (or cowardice) usually prevents them from suggesting that their own usage is impeccable and immaculate, consistently in keeping with the "perfection" that they know to exist. Invariably they point to some other speaker or writer—often one no longer living—whose use of the language is an unassailable paragon of expression. Even when the most blatant grammatical anomalies in the writing of such paragons is called to their attention, purists remain unconvinced. Purists resist—often deny—the notion that language changes, notwithstanding the burden of evidence available. They acknowledge differences between the Old English of *Beowulf* and the Middle English of *The Canterbury Tales* and the Early Modern English of Shakespeare and the English of the early 19th century and that of today; but those relatively major changes in grammar, form, pronunciation, etc., are conveniently swept aside in pursuit of the "ideal" form (of which, in their opinion, there can be only one). It seems in order, therefore, to offer a list of words which, not very long ago, were described in one way or another as unacceptable. The list is taken from a book of usage published in 1915, the same year in which Fowler's *English Usage*, the bible of the purists, was published. It is expected that most speakers of English in the latter years of the 20th century will be surprised to find that the listed items, which form a part of everyday English that is acceptable today, even to purists, could have been condemned at so recent a time. In the following list the categories are those of the authors of *A Guide to the English Language*, London and Edinburgh, 1915, in a chapter entitled Errors in Vocabulary, as are the comments interspersed here and there. The only one that is still on the list of "condemned" usages is marked with an asterisk. Specifically criticized senses and occasional comments are shown where they are pertinent.

AMERICANISMS:

donate	antagonize	placate
transpire*	interment	can ('preserve')
crowd ('set; coterie')	calculated ('planned')	canned goods
fix ('repair; do up')	squelch	tinned goods
fizz ('as soda')	beau ('boyfriend')	wallow
help ('domestic servant')	just ('simply')	smudge
tough ('difficult')	standpoint "sadly frequent in literature"	
fix up ('organize; arrange')	"lamentably frequent"	

GRATUITOUS FOREIGN WORDS:

coup de grace	ipso facto	malaise
impasse	éclat	de rigueur
à la mode	marquisette	macramé

CONDEMNED NEOLOGISMS:

bemused	forthright	highbrow
greaten	obscurantist	forceful

VULGARISMS:

lots of	quite the . .	didn't use to
kid ('child')	get even	rub in
nicely ('well')	right away	turn up ('arrive')

SLANG:

cad	bounder	get going
square deal	below par	in hot water
by hook or (by) crook	sink or swim	to the hilt
mind one's P's and Q's	laugh in one's sleeve	in the dumps
not see the wood for the trees		

EXAGGERATION AS SLANG:

heavenly   first-rate   awfully

love (e.g., dancing)

MISCELLANEOUS:

start ('begin')   middle / center   in / into

Although most of the foregoing are completely natural in colloquial (if not standard) usage today, they are still sometimes frowned upon in writing (e.g., *love* for *like*, *in hot water*, etc.). But one would be sore put to find fault with *smudge*, *standpoint*, or any of the "GRATUITOUS FOREIGN WORDS."

At the time the book was compiled, "AMERICANISM" was a distinctly uncomplimentary label. While it cannot be denied that the style and eloquence of anyone's language could, with few exceptions, be improved, those qualities are not at issue among purists: they are of the opinion that there is only one "correct" way to use language, that fewer and fewer are aware of it, and that still fewer employ it. For the most part, linguists, lexicographers, and other language specialists become the whipping dogs of the purists on the grounds that they not only fail to engage in combat the forces of evil that would destroy the language, but also merely describe the heinous usages of their contemporaries without even condemning them. It is not, of course, the function of a scholar to condone or condemn the object of his observation but to investigate it, describe it, analyze it, and develop theories about how it works and, if possible, why. Because nonprofessionals rarely read professional journals on linguistics, the main media through which the results of scholarly research on language are revealed to them are dictionaries, books of usage, and the often uninformed commentaries that appear in the popular press. It must be said that lexicographers are not always consistent in their treatment of the language they describe. For instance, is a dictionary to reflect a cool, scholarly detached examination of the lexicon of the language for the professional, or is it to be regarded as a useful tool for the nonprofessional? If it is to cleave assiduously to the former characterization, then it becomes clear that it will not enjoy coveted success among the latter; because dictionaries, which are expensive to prepare and publish, are put out by companies motivated by profit, it is likewise clear that the ideal dictionary would appeal greatly to the general public without any sacrifice of linguistic scholarship. But such scholarship is not always easy to reflect in a work designed to cater to public demand. For example, scholarship demands that all possible words of a given frequency or greater ought to be listed, pronounced, defined, and etymologized in a dictionary, the constraints being its economic size and cost. Yet, because of the pressures of the marketplace, certain four-letter words (and, formerly, all such words) are often omitted from dictionaries for publication in the United States. On the other side, it would seem almost a truism to point out that part of a thorough description of the language would necessarily include accurate information regarding the way its users feel about it—that is, is a particular sense of a word considered by many users (especially educated users) to be vulgar, or slang, or nonstandard, or offensive, or informal, or formal, or dialectal, or belonging to some other category that warrants calling attention to it by means of a label? A certain, well-known publisher whose editors failed to exhibit thoughtful consistency in their treatment of the answers to such questions has found itself the target of obloquy. A case in point regarding consistency: if a given four-letter word is labeled "usually considered vulgar," how can a well-informed speaker of the language reconcile that with what he feels are the facts? How is the naive user of the dictionary to understand "usually" in this context? And how is any user to interpret the absence of any comment regarding, say, the definition of *infer* given as "hint"? The lexicographer's reply to these criticisms may be that the dictionary truly and accurately reflects his findings; on the other hand, people—even other scholars—expect such findings to be interpreted by wise counselors, and in the present case, they were not only disappointed but furious at having been let down. The irony of this situation lies not in the fact that the lexicographers who prepared the dictionary in question were being "permissive," as their critics accused, but, if anything, not sufficiently descriptive, which, in the minds of the precisians, is an equally reprehensible transgression.

put / call

In the parlance of the stock exchange, a *put*, or *put option* is a contract allowing for the sale of a specified quantity of shares at a specified price for a specified period. A *call*, or *call option* is a contract allowing for the purchase of a specified quantity of shares at a specified price for a specified period.

QWERTY keyboard / Dvorak keyboard

People often wonder why the standard English typewriter keyboard, with the letters arrayed, starting from the top left, QWERTY, was so designed. The frequency with which alphabetic characters appear in English words, according to E. Cobham Brewer's *Dictionary of Phrase & Fable,* is the following, in descending order:

E, T, A, I, S, O, N, H, R, D, L, U, C,
M, F, W, Y, P, G, B, V, K, J, Q, X, Z

Those familiar with the keyboard of the Linotype will recognize most of the top row—except for the S, which, in that keyboard comes between N and H—for it is produced by running the fingers across the keyboard and is often inadvertently printed. Thus, there seems to be some reasoning behind the arrangement of letters on the Linotype. Yet, even that arrangement was not as efficient as it might have been, for one would expect the most frequent letters to be on the keys under the index, middle, and fourth fingers, not starting with the little finger. It appears that the developers of the earliest typewriters had a mechanical problem: unlike some of today's typewriters, all such machines originally consisted of type bars arranged in a kind of basket; pressing a key actuated a lever which caused the type bar to rise up and strike the ribbon which transferred the type image to the paper. The early typewriters had the most frequently used letters arranged so that they were actuated by keys at the center of the keyboard, but that meant that the distance the type bar traveled before striking the ribbon was, in all cases, the shortest. The mechanical springs used to return the type bar to its resting position could not work fast enough to avoid jamming against one another in rapid typing; the letters were rearranged in a pattern that would make jamming less likely, and that is the arrangement that became traditional. At least two serious attempts have been made over the years to revise the keyboard layout; one of them, developed by Lillian Malt, even went so far as to reject the notion of any kind of "keyboard" as it is known, employing instead a pair of controls shaped to fit the hands and containing the keys a unique arrangement. This highly efficient ergonomic "keyboard" was demonstrated to provide for much faster, more efficient typing than any other, but efforts to establish it failed in the face of the traditional QWERTY (and flat keyboard) setup. The other major effort to revise the keyboard layout resulted in what is called the *Dvorak* keyboard, for August Dvorak, who developed it in

the 1930s. It is an ordinary keyboard physically, but the pattern of
the keys is unusual:

!	@	#	$	%	^	&	*	(	)	{	+	~
1	2	3	4	5	6	7	8	9	0	[	=	'

•	<	>	P	Y	F	G	C	R	L	?	}
'	,	.	p	y	f	g	c	r	l	/	]

A	O	E	U	I	D	H	T	N	S	—
a	o	e	u	i	d	h	t	n	s	-

:	Q	J	K	X	B	M	W	V	Z
;	q	j	k	x	b	m	w	v	z

In more and more offices (and homes, as well), the word processor is
usurping the place of the typewriter. Because the word processor is
an electronic computer, the keys do not actuate type bars but operate
electrical switches, and the switching pattern can be changed by programming one table of equivalents in place of another—in effect re-
mapping the keyboard. In this environment, interest in the Dvorak
layout is widening, and, as more people experiment with it and find it
to be more efficient, the old-fashioned QWERTY arrangement may
eventually be replaced.

racket / racquet

For some unaccountable reason, certain writers in the United States
have taken to the notion that the word spelled *racket* in the U.S. is
spelled *racquet* in Britain, completely ignoring the fact that *racket* is, if
anything, the more common spelling in Britain today and that Americans, though they may spell the tennis implement *racket*, without exception spell the "other" game *squash racquets*. Both countries have
their *racketeers*, but they do not pursue their careers in the *rackets* at
Wembley Stadium or at Forest Hills.

radius / ulna

Although people may know that these are the names of the bones in
the forearm, they sometimes have trouble remembering which is
which. The *radius* is the outer one, the *ulna* the inner, longer one. A

possibly usable mnemonic might be to remember that *inner* and *ulna* both contain the letter *n*.

railroad / railway

All commentators on the language in Great Britain seem to have been subjected to a brainwashing experiment which has successfully persuaded them that they all say *railway* while all Americans say *railroad*. Although the former may have some validity, the latter has none; in fact, one of the largest freight companies in the U.S. till the 1960s went by the name *Railway Express*, and there were formerly numerous railroad companies, owning rights of way and rolling stock, that had the word *railway* in their titles.

raise / rear

In the sense of 'nurture, bring up one or more children,' *raise* and *rear* are interchangeable, the former being somewhat more frequent and, to some, sounding slightly tinged with the dialectal brush.

rational number / irrational number / transcendental number

A *rational number* is a number that can be expressed exactly as the ratio between two other numbers; for example, 0.5, which can be expressed as $1/2$, or $8^{-1/3}$ (the reciprocal of the cube root of 8), which can be expressed as $1/2$, or 0.666 . . . , which can be expressed as $2/3$. An *irrational number* is one that cannot be expressed exactly as the ratio between two numbers; for example, the ratio between the circumference of a circle and its radius π, or *pi*, which is called a *transcendental number*, or $7^{1/2}$ (the square root of 7), which is called a *surd*, neither of which can be given a specific value.

red rose / white rose

The *white rose* and the *red rose* were symbols, respectively, of the English royal houses of York and of Tudor, heirs of Lancaster; taken from the traditional badges of the two houses, the symbols were not commonly used at the time and were popularized later on by Shakespeare and Scott. The dispute between the families, which Scott dubbed the Wars of the Roses, arose in 1453 as a result of the dissatisfaction with the rule of Henry VI, a member of the Lancastrian family which had occupied the throne since 1399, who was considered incompetent, both administratively and mentally. The Yorkists had a legitimate claim by virtue of descent from the third and fifth sons of Edward III; the Lancastrians were descended from John of Gaunt, the fourth son of Edward III. In 1455, violence broke out at the first battle of St. Albans. After considerable infighting, skirmishes, seesawing occupations of and claims to the throne, Edward IV, son of the Duke of York, assumed the throne in 1461. Except for a brief interval (1470–71) in which the Lancastrians forced him into exile and Henry VI regained the throne, Edward reigned till 1483, when he died, leaving as heir Edward V, who was 13 years of age. Although it is generally accepted that Edward V and his brother Richard ("the princes in the Tower") were killed at the order of Richard of Gloucester, their uncle, who assumed the throne and ruled from 1453 as Richard III, the facts have never been confirmed to the satisfaction of historians and remain moot. The story of Gloucester's assassination of the princes was widely believed at the time, offended many, and caused the disaffection of Yorkist supporters. In 1485 Henry Tudor, the claimant through the Lancastrian line, killed Richard at the battle of Bosworth Field and assumed the throne as Henry VII. And so ended the Wars of the Roses. It is perhaps unnecessary to point out that the red rose adopted as a symbol of the British Labour Party in the 1980s bears no symbolic connection with the royal house of Tudor. (See also **Plantagenet / Lancaster / York / Tudor / Stuart / Hanover / Saxe-Coburg-Gotha / Windsor.**)

referee / umpire

Both of these are terms for judges in sporting contests, arbiters who determine that the sports are being conducted according to the rules. They mean the same thing, but their distribution is different: baseball, boxing, and cricket have *umpires;* basketball has *referees;* American football has both. Usage varies in describing the judges in other contests.

reflecting telescope / refracting telescope

There are many kinds of telescope for viewing the heavens, and not all of them are optical. There are also many kinds of optical telescopes, but the two main categories are the *reflecting* and *refracting* varieties. In all optical devices, the light must be allowed to enter a chamber of some sort. In a reflecting telescope, the light enters an open tube at the back end of which is a parabolic mirror that focuses the light to a point where there is a magnifying lens arrangement for viewing by the observer or the camera, spectrometer, or other instrument. In a refracting telescope, the light enters the tube through a complex of magnifying lenses which allow for the direct viewing of the objects.

refurnish / refurbish / redecorate / renovate

Furbish, a relatively uncommon word, means to 'clean up; brighten,' and *refurbish* means, simply, to do it again. Thus, an interior or exterior (as a neighborhood) might be refurbished. *Refurnish* means to 'provide with new furnishings, as furniture, carpeting, lighting, window treatment, etc.'; one might refurnish a home, office, or other interior space, but not (usually) an outside area (unless it be with trees, garden furniture, etc.) . . *Redecorate* in Britain means to paint or wallpaper an interior again, while in the U.S. it is far more general, referring to the installation of built-in cabinets, wardrobes, etc., as well as the replacement of carpets, furniture, and other items. In the U.S. *decorator* is short for *interior decorator,* a term used for a designer of interiors in both varieties of English; in Britain, a *decorator* is usually a painter or paperhanger, rarely a designer. Similarly, if an American says he is having his home decorated, he means its interior is being designed, while an Englishman means it is being painted, papered, or both. *Renovate*, a Latinate word meaning 'renew,' is used when a place or its furnishings, a painting, or anything else is restored to "as-new" condition—at least, that is what dictionaries say. In practice, however, one speaks of *restoring* a painting, meaning to 'put it into as good a condition as possible,' and restoring a car, building, or monument, meaning to 'make it look as good as new, bring it back as close as possible to its original condition'; on the other hand, *renovating* a home, building, or monument means to 'put it into as good condition as possible (considering what time and use or abuse have done to it), especially by replacing many damaged parts', and one would rarely speak of 'renovating a car.'

regret / remorse

Both of these words have been in the language for centuries; both came into English from Middle French, that is, after the Norman Conquest (1066)—in fact, during the 14th or 15th century; *regret* is probably the more common of the two, *remorse* having a somewhat more formal, learned feeling. Their meanings are not easy to separate: both mean to 'be sorry for something that has occurred.' *Regret* carries no explicit admission that the person doing the regretting is the one responsible for the regrettable incident; a person may regret that the parade or picnic was canceled because of rain. Thus, *regret* is an expression of sympathy, an acknowledgment that the speaker understands how the other person feels and is sorry for him, for the situation in which he has been placed by circumstances, and so forth. *Remorse* implies much more strongly a sense of guilty responsibility and it also reflects a greater feeling of personal pain and anguish than mere sympathy. Also, *remorse* occurs only as a noun and, in *remorseful,* as an adjective, while *regret* occurs both as a noun and a verb and, in *regretful* and *regrettable,* as adjectives (with different meanings). Just because there are more forms of one word than another, that is not a sufficient reason to assume that it is more frequent in the language or behaves with greater versatility: the most frequent word in English, *the,* occurs in one form alone and exhibits very little (if any) semantic versatility.

relation / relative

Dictionaries show one sense of each of these words defined identically: 'a person connected to another by blood or marriage; a kinsman.' While that may be true denotatively—that is, technically—the words are not exactly the same connotatively or stylistically. One may refer to a *poor relation* but "poor relative" in the same sense is rarely encountered. *Relation* seems to be more of a dialectal word, not quite as formal as *relative.*

repellent / repulsive / repugnant

These words are used to describe things that are not only unattractive but that actively create a distaste, dislike, or aversion in the person experiencing them. *Repellent* and *repulsive* are closely related: both are traced back to the Latin verb *repellere* 'to drive back' from *re-*'back; again' + *pellere* 'to make move by beating or striking.' Their meanings are close, but *repellent* carries with it more the sense of driving a person away by causing disgust or aversion, while *repulsive* has the sense of causing disgust or loathing but without such a strong physical implication. In their verbal applications, their difference is less evident: one can either *repel* or *repulse* an attacking force. *Repugnant* means 'disgusting; offensive' without any physical implication of 'driving away.' One might find an idea repugnant, but less likely repellent or repulsive; on the other hand, one might find an odor repellent or repulsive but less likely repugnant. Of the three, *repulsive* is the most frequently used (*repulsive personal habits; repulsive looks*); *repellent* is much less frequently used (*repellent looks; repellent manners*); and *repugnant* is the rarest, being, like *repellent*, a somewhat learned word (*a repugnant notion; a taste in foods that I find repugnant*).

repetitious / repetitive / repeated

The meanings of these three words are so close that the distinctions among them are very fine, and their confusion is common. *Repeated* describes something that occurs again and again; on wallpaper, for example, one would describe the design as one repeated every 30 inches (or whatever), and one would speak of "the repeated design of a floral bouquet" on, say, a printed textile. *Repetitious,* though it means the same as *repeated,* is used in contexts where boredom is the main characteristic: *a repetitious musical theme; repetitious wording in a document;* in other words, situations in which the repetition is unnecessary. *Repetitive,* which means almost the same thing, is used where it is felt that the repetition is characteristic of the thing described, but no criticism (as of being boring) is necessarily attached to it. One might describe a theme as being repetitive, meaning that it occurs again and again, without implying that it is boring. In this sense, *repeated* and *repetitive* are the closest in application, with *repetitious* reserved mainly for those contexts where the cloying dullness of repetition is to be emphasized.

requirement / requisite / perquisite / prerequisite

Little difficulty arises from *requirement,* which is merely 'that which is required, needed, or desired'; one of its other senses, 'something demanded as a condition or obligation' (*Passing the entrance exam is a requirement for admission.*) is not relevant to the question at hand. A *requisite* is something that is a 'necessity; an essential.' Though *requisite, prerequisite,* and *perquisite* resemble one another superficially, it should be noted that *prerequisite* has a *pre-* before it: it means nothing more than a 'requisite required beforehand, an advance condition or necessity.' A *perquisite,* is something else entirely; it is an additional payment of some kind made over and above a worker's wages or salary. Usually shortened to *perk* (sometimes, especially formerly, spelled *perq*), it might be in the form of money (as a bonus, for instance), in the form of being provided with a company car, privileges at a company-owned holiday home, or any of a variety of other emoluments regarded as desirable by the employee. At a time in Britain when wages and salaries were frozen or taxes on incomes beyond a certain level were punitive, the granting of perks to employees was an approved way of offering reward for jobs well done or for inducing certain people to join the staff of a company. Although, in the late 1980s perks—particularly the company-supplied car—continue to be important, because of changes in the economy they are no longer the chief means of compensation, for money has again become fashionable.

restful / restive

These words not only mean different things but are distributed differently in the language: *restful* means 'of a nature, mood, or atmosphere that allows a person to relax and feel at ease'; *restive* means 'nervously active; fidgety.' *Restful* is seldom said of people, but it might be used in reference to their behavior or attitude; *restive,* on the other hand, is used almost entirely of people and animate things: a *restive horse.*

rest home / convalescent home / nursing home / old folks' home / retirement home

In the usage of some, all these terms except the last refer to the same kind of place, a residential facility where elderly people go or, more often, are sent when they can no longer take care of themselves. It seems worthwhile, however, to distinguish among them insofar as is possible. A *convalescent home* is a residential facility, staffed by a nurse (with a doctor on call) where people go to recuperate from an illness, from surgery, or the like. There is nothing inherent about such places that restricts their occupants to the elderly, but such is usually the case; many convalescent homes refuse patients known to be terminally ill. A *nursing home* is a residential facility for the chronically ill, whether the illness be physical or mental. Thus, in practice, though nursing homes may not knowingly admit terminally ill patients, because so many old people with senile dementia or similar afflictions are accepted, they effectively do admit them. *Old folks' home* is an old-fashioned term for any residential facility for the elderly who are not ill but who need looking after because their families, if they exist, are unable to take car of them and they cannot take care of themselves. A *retirement home* can be any place, a private residence or a hotel or similar establishment, where people go to live after they retire from working. It may be a private home in a warmer climate, as in the Sun Belt in the United States, along the south coast in England, in Spain, etc.; but it need not be: some prefer colder climates. It is usually a residence that is smaller than the one previously occupied and simpler and cheaper to maintain, often with nearby (or associated) facilities for sporting and other activities of interest to the individuals involved. Increasingly, such residences have been built in clusters, called *residential* or *senior citizen communities*, to offer facilities accessible to all the residents and thereby reduce their cost to the individual. Because many people remain vigorously active following retirement, such facilities do not necessarily offer medical, nursing, food, or other attended services. But some do, and there appears to be nothing in their designation to distinguish them from those that do not.

revenge / vengeance

These nouns mean the same thing and can be used interchangeably. But it may be worth noting that *revenge* is of much greater frequency and that *vengeance* is, perhaps, a more formal word—at least it is found in more formal contexts, like "Vengeance is mine, . . saith the Lord" (Rom. 12:19). *Vengeance*, which functions only as a noun, is associated with the verb *avenge*; this, too, appears in more formal contexts than the verb *revenge*.

Rh-negative / Rh-positive

These terms refer to the absence or presence, designated, respectively, as *Rh-negative* (Rh–) and *Rh-positive* (Rh +), of the *Rh-factor*, in a human being's blood. Named for the *rhesus* monkey, in the blood of which it was first found, the factor is one of a number of heritable antigens in the red blood cells (erythrocytes) of 85 percent of the people. Although problems once arose as a result of blood transfusions between Rh– and Rh + donors and recipients, the positive or negative Rh factors of all blood types are noted when a laboratory ascertains the blood type of an individual. The chief problem remaining occurs when there is Rh factor incompatibility between a mother and her fetus: because the antigens in the fetal blood are incompatible with the blood of the mother, antibodies are formed in the mother's blood which are transmitted via the placenta to the infant, resulting in a condition called erythroblastosis fetalis, a type of hemolytic anemia which, without intervention, can be fatal. In almost all cases, however, the incompatibility is determined at an early stage and the condition can be prevented by intrauterine transfusion or by exchange transfusion of the infant immediately following birth. Similar reactions may occur as a result of ABO incompatibility, but they are usually less severe.

rite / ritual

Both these words come from the Latin word *ritus* 'religious ceremony,' but they have become specialized to some extent. *Rite*, the earlier borrowing, refers more generally to the entire ceremony: *rites of passage; fertility rites. Ritual* is usually taken to mean the various activities associated with a rite—that is, the specific actions engaged in when partaking of a rite. *Ritual* has also been used for the more general metaphoric extension, in which one speaks of the *flag-raising ritual, wine-serving ritual,* etc.

river / estuary / fjord / stream / brook / creek / rill / rivulet

The general word for a 'moving body of water with banks on each side' is *river;* although rivers may be of any size, the word is usually reserved for those of greater width, depth, and swiftness. The other general term among those listed above is *stream,* but it is difficult to find official names with *stream* as a part of them. *Brook* is a frequently used word for a small, usually local river. *Creek* is used in Great Britain for a narrow inlet, usually from the sea, and elsewhere for any small stream or tributary. *Fjord* (also spelled *fiord*), originally a Norwegian word, designates rather long inlets from the sea that are between tall steep cliffs. *Rill, rivulet, streamlet* are poetic terms. An *estuary* is a place where a river meets the sea, that is, the mouth of the river; at this juncture the river is usually tidal and partly salt, or brackish: the extent to which ocean tides affect an estuary, how far up the river their effect is felt, and where the salt water ends and the fresh begins depend on many factors, among them, the physical configuration at the mouth, the strength of the tide, the volume of water being carried by the river, its speed, etc.

Roman Empire / Holy Roman Empire

The *Roman Empire* was the name given by historians to the extensive lands and peoples, conquered by Rome, who later came under a loosely unified rule. Its period was from about 27 B.C. till A.D. 476 (the fall of Rome) and it encompassed all of Africa north of the Sahara, the western end of the Arabian peninsula (coextensive with modern Israel), Anatolia (modern Turkey), most of Europe west of the Urals and down to the Black Sea (including the Iberian peninsula, modern France, Switzerland, southern Germany, Austria, Hungary, and the Balkans), and the southern part of Britain, as far north as Hadrian's Wall. The *Holy Roman Empire*, which encompassed a much smaller territory, dates from Charlemagne (A.D. 800) or, according to some, from the accession of Otto the Great of Germany (A.D. 962), who styled himself as Roman Emperor, till the renunciation of the title (1806) by Francis II. It included modern East and West Germany, Austria, Switzerland, and northern Italy, and was coextensive with the Western Roman Empire as established in A.D. 395. So called because its spiritual head was the pope, the Holy Roman Empire was described by Voltaire as "neither holy, nor Roman, nor an empire."

Roman numerals / Arabic numerals

Roman numerals, which employ a conventional pattern of letters of the Roman alphabet in a prescribed pattern, are used today, usually as capitals but occasionally as small letters, in limited applications, as for paginating the front matter of books, in inscriptions dating the erection of buildings, in designating the numbers of kings or queens with the same name in a given country as well as the numbers of popes, in copyright notices on films and television programs (usually to help obscure their age by being harder to read), and so forth. They were replaced in all practical applications during the 12th century by the Arabic system of numerical notation. *Arabic numerals*, only ten in number, including the zero, are regarded generally as one of the most important contributions to the science of mathematics—in fact, one without which modern mathematics could not exist. The importance of the Arabic system extends from notation to the calculation of the simplest functions, like multiplication and division, which were extremely cumbersome using Roman numerals. For convenience, here are the most common Roman numerals with their Arabic equivalents:

1 - I	7 - VII	14 - XIV	21 - XXI . .	100 - C
2 - II	8 - VIII	15 - XV	30 - XXX	200 - CC
3 - III	9 - IX	16 - XVI	40 - XL	300 - CCC
4 - IV	10 - X	17 - XVII	50 - L	400 - CCCC
(or IIII)	11 - XI	18 - XVIII	60 - LX	(rarely CD)
5 - V	12 - XII	19 - XIX	70 - LXX	500 - D
6 - VI	13 - XIII	20 - XX	90 - XC	1000 - M

The date 1899 would appear as MDCCCXCIX, 1900 as MDCCCC or MCM, 1919 as MCMXIX, and 1988 as MCMLXXXVIII; the year 2000, eagerly awaited by at least one candy manufacturer, will be MM.

salary / wage

The person who receives regular payment for his work, on a weekly, monthly, or other periodic basis, is earning a *salary;* one who is paid either by the hour (for the hours worked) or for the amount of work done (for each item he has worked on or completed, for the volume of what he has produced, etc.) is being paid a *wage.* Generally, professional and clerical workers are paid salaries, factory, occasional workers, and those in the trades—plumbers, electricians, etc.—are paid wages.

salon / *saloon*

The distribution of the meanings of these words varies between British and American usage. The most common meaning of *saloon* in the U.S. and Canada is a 'public bar.' This sense, however, has acquired so many bad connotations over the years—from the rowdy sort of bar characteristic of the western American frontier to the sleazy speakeasy of the Prohibition era—that in some states (New York, for example) it is illegal for a proprietor to call his place of business a "saloon." Although North Americans are vaguely aware of and can recognize the British use of *saloon* to designate a style of car body, they do not use the word in that sense, preferring *sedan*. Most of the British uses of *salon* are shared with speakers of U.S. and Canadian English, but Americans, especially, use it in the context of *beauty salon*, the place of business of a ladies' hairdresser. The use in North America of *salon* for 'reception or living room in a home' would be unusual; likewise, they would never, as the British do, refer to a *dancing saloon* or *saloon bar*, or use *saloon* for "lounge."

sarcastic / *sardonic*

These words are relatively close in meaning but are not exact synonyms. As for their being interchangeable, that rather depends on the precision with which the language is used. *Sarcastic* means 'derisive, tauntingly contemptuous, ironically sneering,' while *sardonic* means 'bitterly scornful, cynically disdainful.' *Sardonic*, for which the noun is the somewhat awkward *sardonicism*, carries with it overtones of superiority and irony; it is said to be derived from the Greek name of a Sardinian plant the ingestion of which was said to cause laughter ending in death; the medical term, *risus sardonicus*, describes an involuntary spasm of the facial muscles, resembling a ghoulish grin, sometimes seen in cases of tetanus, or lockjaw. *Sarcasm*, the noun from which *sarcastic* derives, goes back to a Greek verb, *sarkazein* 'to tear flesh.' Neither word is friendly or playful, but *sarcastic* is more down-to-earth and vicious, while *sardonic* implies an aloofness, though not much less virulent. (See also **irony** / **satire**.)

scalene / *isosceles* / *equilateral*

A *scalene* triangle is one with unequal angles and sides of unequal length. An *isosceles* triangle is one with two angles equal to each other and the sides opposite them of equal length. An *equilateral* triangle is one in which all three angles are each of 60° and all three sides are of equal length.

Scylla / Charybdis

The literary expression *between Scylla and Charybdis* is identical in meaning to the modern *between a rock and a hard place,* and there may be some justification in proposing that the latter is an "explanatory corruption" of the former. Although many modern sources identify Scylla with a rock between Sicily and Italy and Charybdis with a whirlpool nearby, they were both rocks according to Homer's *Odyssey.* Scylla, nearer to Italy, was named for its occupant, according to some legends a fearful female monster that barked like a dog, had twelve feet, six long necks, and mouths equipped with three rows of teeth; Charybdis was also eponymous for its resident female monster, which three times each day swallowed the waters of the sea and three times threw them up again. It can easily be seen how such two formidable creatures could pose a serious threat to shipping; likewise, the confusion between Charybdis the rock (on which grew an immense fig tree) and Charybdis its inhabitant could have perpetuated the puzzling question of which was the rock, which the whirlpool. The notion that *between a rock and a hard place* might be a paraphrase of the classical metaphor lies in the suggestion that *Scylla* "SILL-a" is relatively easy to pronounce, while the spelling of *Charybdis* "ka-RIB-dis" makes it look like a "hard place (to pronounce)."

seal / sea lion

Seal is the general name for the familiar carnivorous marine mammals; *sea lion* is the name given to any of several species of large, eared seals found in the northern Pacific.

sedition / treason

Treason is the attempt to overthrow the government of one's own country by any means, especially by betrayal to a foreign power; in the United States, allegiance to an enemy of the state and giving the enemy aid and comfort are the essential criteria for treason. *Sedition* is any action against the government to which one owes allegiance; it includes incitement of others to commit treasonable acts, belonging to an organization that advocates the overthrow of the government, publishing or distributing any material that calls for a change in the existing government by illegal means, and, in general, "disturbing the tranquillity of the state."

serenade / aubade

A *serenade* is a musical piece or song, often a love song, performed or sung in the evening. An *aubade* is a musical piece or song performed or sung to greet the dawn or to one's loved one in the morning; it is sometimes called a *matin song*. A *nocturne* is a composition, usually for the piano, played at night and often having a dreamy quality.

serif / sans serif

It will be seen that the type in which the text of this book is set displays tiny lines at the ends of the characters, as the small horizontal bits on the capital I and the little hooklike projections that can be found on all other alphabetic characters except o, O, and Q and on some numbers. These are called *serifs,* and they probably originated, at the time when type molds were cut by hand or, some say, with the techniques used by stonecutters in chiseling letters in order to demarcate the ends of letters and allow them to line up at the tops and bottoms to create the appearance of an even line. Centuries later, when type came to be cast in metal, the serifs were adopted as a design element, which persists till today in what is called Old Style type. Type without serifs, called *sans serif* (or *sanserif*), was designed mainly in the last hundred years. As can be seen in the illustration below, it is sometimes difficult to distinguish characters in certain forms of sans serif type, especially the lower-case l from the capital I and the number 1. For comparison, here are two alphabets:

SERIF

A B C D E F G H I J K L M N O P Q R S T U V W X Y Z
a b c d e f g h i j k l m n o p q r s t u v w x y z
1 2 3 4 5 6 7 8 9 0

SANS SERIF
A B C D E F G H I J K L M N O P Q R S T U V W X Y Z
a b c d e f g h i j k l m n o p q r s t u v w x y z
1 2 3 4 5 6 7 8 9 0

set-in sleeve / raglan sleeve / dolman sleeve

The coats of most men's suits have *set-in sleeves*, that is, sleeves that are made separate from the body of the garment for later attachment to an armhole. With more or less padding, depending on the style prevailing, the set-in sleeve gives the appearance of a square shoulder. Set-in sleeves are also used in shirts, sweaters, overcoats, etc. The *raglan sleeve*, named for Fitzroy James Henry Somerset, 1st Baron Raglan (1788–1855), who commanded the British troops in the Crimean War, is cut so that the cloth from the outer cuff of the sleeve to the collar is in one piece; the seam by which it is attached to the body of the garment runs from the collar, diagonally across the front or back just below the shoulder, down to the armhole. Whether it was named *raglan* to honor Somerset or because he favored it is not reported; it seems unlikely that he was designing clothing when off the battlefield. A *dolman sleeve* is one that is quite wide at the armhole, tapering down to a narrow cuff at the wrist or forearm. Usually cut in a style similar to that of the raglan, the dolman derives from a woman's mantle with capelike flaps for covering the arms, which were not encased in sleeves.

sewn binding / perfect binding / side-wire binding / saddle-wire binding / burst binding

Books and magazines consist of a number of leaves that are fastened together in some fashion; these terms describe the most common ways in which that is done. Most publications are printed on sheets or rolls of paper which are then folded in any of a variety of ways (depending on how large a surface has been printed and on the size of the ultimate book or periodical). For example, if a sheet measuring approximately 26 × 40 inches is folded into quarters (13 × 20 inches) and then folded twice again (creating a packet about 6.5 × 10 inches), it can be seen that if three sides are trimmed (leaving the fourth side for binding), one would be left with 16 leaves—that is, 32 pages—each measuring about 6 × 9 inches. In book manufacture, this is called a *forme, section,* or *signature, forme* being the preferred name in Britain, *signature* the more common in the U.S., and *section* occurring occasionally in both. These signatures are then fastened together to make the book, the quantity depending on how many pages it is to consist of. In *saddle-wire binding*, which is the way many popular magazines are bound, the trimmed sheets are the height of the normal page and twice the width; these are then folded in half and one or more wire staples are driven through the crease to fix the sheets together, forming a booklet. Another method is to gather together several such sets of pages, as one might to produce a set of signatures for a book, and to drive wire staples through the entire folded signature from the side. This is called *side-wire binding*; it is used for publications that contain a larger number of pages and are to be of a more permanent nature, as scholarly journals, which are intended to be kept for some time. In most instances, a separate cover is glued over the outside of the bound signatures, for durability, for design purposes, for appearance, or for all of these reasons. *Sewn binding*, also called *Smyth-sewn* after the manufacturer of the original equipment used, is traditionally considered the best; it is also the most expensive. The signatures are sewn up individually and then sewn together; a tough fabric, like cambric, is then glued over the back of the gathered signatures before the covers, called *boards*, are fastened on, in a process called *casing-in*. This binding method proves the most durable, provided that the materials are of good quality and that the work is done properly. In a modern modification of sewn binding, the signatures are gathered together, then their backs are notched (as with a saw) and glue is forced into the notches, holding the pages firmly. This method, called *burst binding*, is relatively new and has only become practical since the development of the powerful glues required. The cheapest form of book binding is that used for paperbacks, telephone directories, and the like. In it the gathered signatures have their backs cut off flush, then glue is applied to the squared-off back and a piece of cloth or paper is fastened to it; a paper cover is then glued onto the outside and trimmed off so that it is flush to the edges of the trimmed pages on the other three sides. This technique is called *perfect binding*; research has not yielded the background of the name: considering the generally low quality, it could scarcely be descriptive, and it is thought that it might have been the trade name of an early machine devised to do the work. It does not seem to be related in any way to the verb *perfect*, which means to 'print the other side of a sheet already printed'; a *perfecting press* is one that prints both sides of a sheet or roll (*web*) of paper simultaneously.

Shakespearian sonnet / Spenserian sonnet / Petrarchan sonnet

Sonnets are 14-line, self-contained poems, written in iambic pentameter and arranged, depending on the type (and rhyme-scheme), into three quatrains and a couplet (which summarizes and epitomizes the spirit of the poem), or into an octave and a sestet. The *Shakespearian sonnet,* also called the *Elizabethan* or *English sonnet,* consists of three quatrains and a couplet with the rhyme-scheme *abab cdcd efef gg.* The *Spenserian sonnet,* also of three quatrains and a couplet, has an interlocking rhyme-scheme: *abab bcbc cdcd ee.* The *Petrarchan,* or *Italian sonnet* consists of an octave rhyming *abbaabba* and a sestet rhyming either *cdecde* or *cdcdcd.*

shall / will / should / would

The distribution of these forms is frequently a matter of style, for, with some minor exceptions, they cannot be said to be used "incorrectly." To express the simple future tense, some people insist that *shall* must be used with *I* and *we, will* with *you, he, she, it,* and *they.* In common practice, however, *will* is used with all these persons. Some subtle stylists maintain that there is a semantic difference between *shall,* used to express simple futurity in *I shall* and *we shall,* and *will,* used to express determination, desire, etc. Thus, they say, *I shall* means 'I am going to . . ', while *I will* means 'I want to . . , I am determined to . . . ' It is very doubtful that such fine nuances of meaning are made by many writers and, if they are, that they are shared by their readers. A somewhat less subtle difference does arise when *shall* is used with *you, he, she, it,* and *they:* if so used, the construction does often express an imperative idea: *You shall be at school on time hereafter.* If one is to use *shall* with *I* and *we* and *will* with the other persons, then it is appropriate to use *should* and *would* with similar distribution. This observation must be tempered by admonitions. In the English of the 19th century and earlier, *would* was felt more keenly to carry the meaning of 'want, wish, desire': *I would go* was more likely to mean 'I want to go' than as a replacement for *will* as a simple future. *Would* functions as the past and past participle of *will,* in the main: *He would go if he could;* because of the uncertainty of future events, *would / should,* the past tense forms of the subjunctive, are used in conditional statements about future events: *If it should rain, she would stay home.* But it also serves as a polite form for *will: Would you be good enough to get off my foot? Would you mind not shouting?* These are more often statements than questions. *Should* is used in three important ways: it expresses obligation, equivalent to *ought to* (*You should try to be there early.*); it serves as the subjunctive marker for verbs in the infinitive (*Should you go, I think you would enjoy yourself.*); and it functions as a marker of politeness when used with the first person (*I should like to see you tonight. We should prefer meeting you tomorrow.*), though as far as meaning goes, it here serves as the form preferred over *would.* In almost all of their applications, *shall* and *should* reflect a slightly more formal and elegant style when used with the first person, singular and plural, than *will* and *would,* but that is not to say that the latter are to be construed as incorrect.

silica / silicon / silicone

Silica is another name for *silicon oxide* (also called *silicon dioxide*), an abundant compound in the earth's crust occurring in many forms, notably as quartz and ordinary yellow sand (which contains an admixture of iron oxide). Amethysts and opals are gemstone manifestations of quartz. Because of its properties, silica has many applications, as in the making of refractory brick for furnaces, in glass that is shock-resistant and capable of sudden temperature changes, and in the manufacture of silica gel, widely used as a drying agent which turns pink when moisture is absorbed, whereupon its properties can be reactivated by simply heating it to drive off the water. *Silicon* is the name of an element, the second most abundant on earth, which is used in a variety of compounds, as for abrasives, and particularly in the manufacture of *silicon chips,* semiconductors made so that they can perform many different electronic functions with wide application in the integrated circuits used in computers and other electronic devices. *Silicone* is an organic grouping of silicon with oxygen, producing a polymer with a number of industrial applications, among them a rubbery substance used for cosmetic implants.

simple fraction / complex fraction

A *simple fraction* is one having a whole number, or integer, in both the numerator and denominator, like $^1/_2$, $^2/_3$; a *complex fraction,* also called a *compound fraction,* is one having a fraction in either the numerator or denominator or both, like

$$\frac{2/_3}{5}, \frac{2/_3}{4/_5}, \text{ or } \frac{3}{4/_5}.$$

simple fracture / compound fracture / comminuted fracture / greenstick fracture / hairline fracture

There are a number of terms used in medicine to describe the various kinds of fractures that can occur to the bones of the body; those listed here are the most commonly encountered by the layman. A *simple fracture* is, as the name implies, a break across a bone without any unusual complications. A *compound fracture*, also called an *open fracture*, is one in which the jagged pieces of broken bone have protruded through the skin. A *comminuted fracture* is one in which there are several pieces of bone at the place of fracture. In a *greenstick fracture*, which is more like to occur in young people whose bones are less brittle, the bone is partly broken and splintered lengthwise at the outer edge of the arc of the break, as a green stick would appear if an attempt were made to break it. A *hairline fracture* is one, often to a flat bone, as a skull bone, that is a crack without noticeable separation but with enough possible movement of the parts to cause injury to the tissues.

simple sentence / compound sentence / complex sentence

These are—or were at one time—convenient terms for describing the various forms in which sentences are usually constructed, provided that one cleaves to the traditional notion that a sentence is a string of words with a subject, a predicate, and (sometimes) an object. In this scheme, examples of *simple sentences* are *She likes me, He lies, He eats pomegranates,* and *Kiss me* (in which the subject—if not the object— is said to be "understood"). A *compound sentence* is one with two or more independent clauses, each of which could stand alone as a simple sentence; they may be linked by a coordinating conjunction like *and, or, but,* and so forth, or they may merely be placed side by side: *The dog barked and the man ran away. The hurricane struck: not a house remained standing.* A *complex sentence* is one with an independent clause and a dependent clause: *Penelope, who hates almost everyone, likes me. Eustace eats pomegranates, which are good for you. If you get a chance, kiss me. When the dog barked, Ebenezer ran away. After the hurricane struck, not a house remained standing.* There is also a *compound-complex sentence,* which combines the features of the last two described: *While John was eating a pomegranate, Penelope kissed me, and Ebenezer ran away.* There is no restriction on the length of a sentence, which is categorized on the basis of its elements.

sine / cosine / tangent

These are names for the commonest trigonometric functions only one of which, *tangent,* has entered the language in a general sense. In a right triangle, the *sine* of either of the other angles is expressed as the ratio between the length of the side opposite the angle and the length of the hypotenuse (the side opposite the right angle). The *cosine* of either one of the angles is the ratio between the length of the adjacent side and the length of the hypotenuse. And the *tangent* of either angle is the ratio of the length of the side opposite to that of the side adjacent. The more common sense of *tangent,* a 'going-off in an entirely different direction,' comes from the use of the word to designate a line or surface that just touches another line or surface: considered from the point where they touch, the two diverge in different directions, one being said to 'go off at a tangent'; ideas, statements, etc. that diverge from the main topic and are therefore irrelevant to it are said to be *tangential.* As geometric functions, sine, cosine, and tangent are used in other ways sufficiently complex to warrant reference to a textbook.

single cuff / barrel cuff / double cuff / French cuff

Single cuff is the British term for what Americans usually call a *barrel cuff,* that is, a cuff of a long-sleeved shirt that is not folded over itself and is fastened with a button, rarely requiring a cufflink. *French cuff* is the American term for what the British usually call a *double cuff,* a cuff of a long-sleeved shirt that is doubled over on itself and is fastened with a cufflink that passes through the four buttonholes provided.

singular / plural / dual

In contemporary English, the grammar of nouns and verbs is affected by number—whether they are *singular* 'one and only one' or *plural* 'more than one.' Other languages, especially older ones, record also a *dual* 'two and only two'; in such languages, *plural* means 'three or more.' English once had a dual number; it survives in words like *both*, *between*, *betwixt* (archaic) *twain*, and, possibly, in *either* and *neither.* These are the most common examples of number, but *trial* 'three and only three' has been recorded in Polynesian and Melanesian languages and *quadrual* 'four and only four' in some Austronesian languages. In English, no special form of the verb for duals remains: the plural form is used for all subjects numbering two or more. But confusion sometimes arises between the use of a singular or a plural verb form in connection with nouns that may be considered collective in nature, as *company,* *(theatrical) cast, family,* etc. Practice differs, depending on dialect: in Britain, more often than not, such words are treated as plurals, and we find *The company are planning to expand; The cast are ready for rehearsal. The family are going on a picnic.* In the U.S., however, the trend is the reverse, and collectives are generally deemed to be singular: *The company is planning to expand,* etc.

sloop / ketch / yawl / schooner / catboat

All of these terms apply today to rigs of sailing yachts, though in the past they were used of commercial and naval vessels. A *sloop* is a single-masted vessel, with the mast stepped about one third of the way aft (toward the stern) from the bows; it may be further described in terms of the kinds of sails carried, that is, if the mainsail is quadrilateral, it is called a *gaff-rigged sloop*, if triangular, a *Bermudan-* or *Marconi-rigged sloop*, and so forth. It may be further distinguished from a *cutter,* which has a single mast stepped somewhat more amidships to allow for the setting of more than one headsail. *Ketches, yawls,* and *schooners* all have two masts. Schooners have a larger mast amidships and a smaller mast forward. Both ketches and yawls have a larger mast forward and a (much) smaller mast near the stern: although it is sometimes difficult to tell them apart, especially at a distance, the yawl has its aftermast—also called a *mizzenmast* or *jigger—* set aft of the rudderpost, while the ketch has its mizzen set forward of the rudderpost. Just as in the case of the sloop, these other vessels can be described in greater detail by the shape and kinds of sails they carry. *Catboats* have a single, often unstayed mast set in the bows; there is seldom space to set a headsail (unless the boat is equipped with a bowsprit), and the mainsail, which may be gaff- or Marconi-rigged, is usually quite large.

smelt / smolt

Admittedly, these words differ by only a vowel sound, but so do thousands of words in the language—*hat / hut / hit / hoot / height; lick / lack / luck / look / like / lake,* etc.—and yet people often mix up *smelt* and *smolt.* A *smelt* is any of a variety of specific fishes of the order *Osmeridae; smolt* is the name given to the life stage of the salmon (and, sometimes, the sea trout) between the *parr* and the *grilse* stages, when the fish is about two years old, during which it is slender and silvery and migrates to the sea. The *Osmeridae* include fishes that resemble the trout. The name *Osmeridae* contains the root *osm-,* which comes from the Greek word for 'smell'; but the *smelt* has its name from a Norwegian word, *smelta* 'whiting,' and there is no reason to expect these fishes to smell any different from any other fishes.

smooth muscle / striated muscle

These are the names of the two basic kinds of muscles in the human body. *Smooth muscle,* which is short and involuntary, is that in the viscera; it reacts slowly and is not paralyzed if its neural stimuli are interrupted. *Striated muscle,* which is long and voluntary, comprises all of the skeletal muscles, including the myocardium, which does not contract as readily as the others; striated muscle responds quickly to stimuli and is paralyzed by their interruption.

snake / serpent / reptile

Reptile comes from the Greek word meaning 'crawl'; *serpent* comes from the Latin word meaning 'crawl'; and *snake* comes from the Germanic word meaning 'crawl.' Thus, there is little left in doubt about the kinds of animals under discussion, though today we might associate *crawl* more closely with an activity requiring feet and prefer *slither. Reptile* is the general word for the class of cold-blooded animals that includes snakes (as well as turtles, dinosaurs, and other beasts). *Snake* and *serpent* mean exactly the same thing, but like many words that are virtual synonyms, they are not used in the same way. *Serpent* is a word found mainly in poetic and other literary contexts: we may refer to a *snake in the grass,* but it was a *serpent* that entered the Garden of Eden. In poetic contexts, too, *serpent* is often found referring to any kind of *reptile,* from a dragon or a dinosaur to a gila monster.

solid gold / gold-filled / rolled gold / gold plated / gold leaf / gold foil

The first four of these terms are descriptions of the various methods employed by those who deal with gold artifacts. *Solid gold* suggests that the object consists of pure gold all the way through; in fact, pure gold is almost never used because the metal is too soft and malleable to be practical for most purposes, so an alloy consisting of gold and another metal is used. The percentage of pure gold in the alloy is designated in *karats* (spelled *carats* in Britain), 24 karats signifying pure gold; *24-karat* occurs in the language as a metaphor meaning 'pure through and through, unadulterated,' but it is used in derogation as often as in praise: *He's a 24-karat fool.* An 18-karat piece would thus be made of three parts of gold to one of some other metal, usually brass. *Gold-filled* pieces are made of a laminate of some base metal, like brass, to which a layer of gold has been bonded. *Rolled gold* (also called *filled gold* in the U.S.) is the same as *gold-filled* except that the gold must make up at least five percent of the total weight. Items that are *gold plated* consist of a metal with a thin layer of gold deposited on it electrolytically; in some objects, the underlying metal may be silver, but the gold plating may be no more than a few microns thick, just enough to lend color and, in some cases, protection against the corrosion of the baser metal underneath. Gold is so malleable that it can be hammered out into extremely thin sheets; this process, which requires some skill, is called *goldbeating* and is traditionally done between parchmentlike layers of sheepskin. The thinnest product of the goldbeater's skill is called *gold leaf;* if it is slightly thicker, it is called *gold foil.* Gold leaf is used in decorative lettering on glass; gold foil is applied in the arts, in furniture manufacture, in the ornamentation of exterior architectural domes, and the like, where greater durability is a requirement.

South / Deep South

In the United States, the *South* is usually taken to refer to the region that includes states, with the exception of Maryland and Delaware, that are south of the Ohio river and of Mason and Dixon's line (usually called the Mason-Dixon Line). The *Deep South* usually refers to those states that border on the Gulf of Mexico. Like many such terms, these are rather vague, especially the *Deep South,* which is often used in relation to the politics, mores, culture, and ideologies that are typically associated with the people who live in the southeastern United States.

spasmodic / sporadic

These words should be kept apart: *spasmodic* means 'having to do with or characterized by spasms; jerky'; *sporadic* means 'at irregular intervals; occasional.' Thus, one might speak of *sporadic rain, sporadic visitors,* or *sporadic eruptions* (of a volcano), but *spasmodic* does not fit into such contexts. Sudden, unexpected, or jerky movements might be *spasmodic,* which describes convulsive and involuntary muscular contractions and should be used only sparingly as a metaphor. (See also **continual / continuous / constant.**)

species / specie

The most common use of *specie* today is in the sense of 'coin or money' especially as contrasted with bullion or paper money; it is traced to a Latin phrase, *in specie,* meaning 'in kind.' *Species,* which can be either a singular or a plural noun, means 'kind, variety'; it is used in biology to designate a group of organisms that have more identifying characteristics in common than a genus (of which one or more species form a subset). (See also **phylum / class / order / family / genus / species.**)

speed / velocity

At one time, it seemed important to maintain a distinction between *speed* and *velocity,* and physicists were particularly keen on the difference. To ordinary mortals, the terms are interchangeable, both referring to the distance covered divided by any arbitrary unit of time but usually expressed in miles per hour, kilometers per hour, feet per second, meters per second, etc., depending on the object: the speed of a tape through a tape recorder, for example, is measured in inches per second. To physicists, however, the preceding definition obtains only for *speed. Velocity* is a measure of the distance covered *in a specified direction.* Thus, velocity is designated a *vector quantity* (because both the direction and the speed are included); speed is designated a *scalar quantity* (because the measurement can be shown as a scale).

speedometer / mileometer / odometer / tachometer

The distinctions among these devices is useful, and careful speakers maintain them. Fitted to a vehicle (usually a motor vehicle), a *speedometer* is a device that continuously records the speed at which the vehicle is traveling, usually in miles per hour or kilometers per hour. A device called a *mileometer* (or *milometer*) in Great Britain and an *odometer* in the United States and Canada records the distance covered (in miles or kilometers). A *tachometer* is a device that displays or records (properly, a *tachograph*) continuously the number of revolutions that a shaft is turning per unit of time; fitted to a car, a tachometer displays the number per minute of revolutions of the drive shaft. Some engines are also equipped with an *hourmeter*, which counts the number of hours that the engine has operated; such information is essential for engines in boats and airplanes, in which the distance covered is not necessarily directly related to the number of hours the engine has operated.

spurious / specious

Both of these words have as at least one of their meanings 'false,' but *spurious* means 'not real or genuine, fake; counterfeit' and comes from the Latin word *spurius* 'of illegitimate birth,' and *specious* means 'apparently or superficially true or correct, deceptively genuine or pleasing but, at bottom, false, incorrect, without merit, or offensive' and comes from Latin *speciosus* 'plausible.' The latter word is related to Latin *specere* 'to look at' and carries with it the notion of 'outward appearance'; at an earlier stage of the language, the meaning of *specious* was focused on that sense and was used with the meaning 'fair, beautiful.' Thus, both overlap in the meaning 'not genuine,' but a *specious argument* would be one that seems all right but is not, while a *spurious coin* would be one without any pretensions whatsoever.

square knot / granny

Traditional in nautical circles is the inability of a landlubber to consistently tie a *square knot*, achieving a *granny* about half the time. The square knot is a simple knot used to fasten together two ends of string or rope (usually called *line* in nautical contexts) so that they will not come apart. The method is simple and can be used, for example, in tying a package: the end at the left is crossed over the one at the right, then turned round underneath it to form an overhand knot; then the end at the right is crossed over the one at the left and brought round it to pass through the loop so formed; when the ends are pulled tight, the result is a square knot, so called because it looks "square." The granny is formed by starting out the same way, but, at the second stage, instead of bringing the right end over the left as in the square knot, the left is again brought over the right. For lines that are not made of slippery material, like polypropylene, the square knot holds very well, becoming tighter when stress is applied to it, yet possible to untie; on the other hand, the granny knot, also known as *granny's knot* and *granny's bend,* is nothing but a crude slipknot, and it can come apart or, worse, jam to make it hard to untie. The dictionaries that venture an etymology for the granny suggest that the inept knot is so called contemptuously, in reference to what one might expect from a grandmother (aboard a ship, trying to be a sailor). Such instances of bad press for grannies (of the familial persuasion) is uncommon in the language: perhaps "with affectionate tolerance for the amateur" might be a more accurate description.

stalactite / stalagmite

In limestone caves, the continual dripping of water containing calcium carbonate creates deposits of the mineral on the floor and accretions that hang down from the roof. Over a period of thousands of years these build up into cones and other unusual shapes and sometimes join to form columns. Those that project upwards from the floor are called *stalagmites;* those that hang from the roof of the cave are called *stalactites.*

stanch / staunch

Stanch means to 'stop the flow of a liquid, especially blood'; thus one might stanch a wound or the blood from a wound. *Staunch* means 'loyal; steadfast; dependable,' and the two words should not be confused.

standard / nonstandard

Linguists and others who specialize in the description of language sometimes find it convenient to use terms that categorize the various levels at which language is used. Mere examination of the terms listed above should make the reader suspicious of any clearcut distinctions that might be forthcoming: it is easy enough to define the core senses of these words, but their delineating borders are very fuzzy, indeed. Although many people seek an authoritarian approach to language, one that will inform them, once and for all, what is right and wrong, what is acceptable and unacceptable, both in usage and grammar, no matter which authority is chosen sooner or later they encounter something to disagree with. An example might be the ending of the preceding sentence with a preposition (notwithstanding its adverbial nature), which, once they have learned the clichée, "Never end a sentence with a preposition," becomes fixed in the minds of certain people who accept it as a Law of Good English (along with "Never split an infinitive"). Actually, neither of these "laws" has the remotest connection with the English language: they stem from the attempt by 17th-century pedants to impose Latin grammar on the English language. In Latin, the language of the intellectual elite of the time, it is physically impossible to split infinitives, for all of them consist of single words, roots with an infinitive ending (as in modern French, Spanish, Italian, German, etc.); also, notwithstanding that Latin, because the relationships among the words in a sentence depend more on their inflectional endings than on their position, enjoys a freedom of word order, it nonetheless demands that a preposition precede the word it affects. These rules simply do not apply in English. Winston Churchill, who was no mean stylist when it came to the rhetoric of English, is often quoted as having offered, in response to a criticism that he had ended a sentence with a preposition, "That is something up with which I shall not put," which points up the ludicrous ends to which one must sometimes go in order to avoid this silly "rule." It is quite natural and totally unambiguous to say, *That is something I shall not put up with,* thus ending the sentence with two prepositions; granted, it does not make for acceptable Latin, but the language is English, and the grammar and syntax of Latin are entirely inappropriate to it. Of course, one must be careful to avoid the ambiguities that might result from careless word order; but such are the pitfalls of grammar and the fallibility of languages of all kinds that ambiguity can arise anywhere. Within the context of what is right and wrong in language, linguists and, especially, teachers of English many years ago hit upon the terms *standard* and *nonstandard* as being less emotionally evocative that "right" and "wrong." If language is regarded as a natural phenomenon, not an artifact, then it can readily be seen that there is nothing inherently good or bad about anything in language, unless one considers failure to communicate as something evil. Language is a social instrument—perhaps the most important one available—and the ability to express oneself in a manner recognizable as on a par with the best writers in the language clearly has a desirable social, communicative, and artistic effect. Likewise, using language in a certain manner may identify a speaker as one with whom others might not wish to associate because of his lack of education, intellect, taste, or refinement or because of a difference in social class. Deplorable though such prejudices may be, as long as they are a fact of life, it behooves speakers to whom such social contacts are important to remove the stigmata of nonstandard language use from their repertoires. In order to do that, they must be able to identify nonstandard language as such, and the older dictionaries were helpful in labeling certain senses of words as nonstandard; for instance, a definition given under the entry for *infer* might be "to imply," labeled "*Nonstandard*" to alert the user that it is not standard in English to substitute *infer* for *imply.* Most well-educated people today have been exposed to the notions about language that are expressed here, namely, that if a speaker finds it expedient to use language in a certain way he should learn how to do so. Theoretically, modern grammarians, lexicographers, and others who offer comment on language usage are merely "reporting" their findings; that is, if they advise that a particular usage be avoided, their justification comes from "the way the language is used by educated speakers." But it must be remembered that such commentators consider themselves to be among those "educated speakers," and it is not always easy to determine whether their criticisms of certain usages (disguised, as they are, as "findings" among the literati) are genuine or merely the parroting of earlier purists' opinions or expressions of private prejudices. (See also **colloquial / informal, informal / slang / taboo.**)

statute mile / nautical mile / international mile

The word *mile* itself is traced to Latin *milia passuum* 'thousand paces' (5000 feet) and was evidently originally a military designation, though there is no known connection between *mile* and *military.* As an arbitrary measure of distance, the *statute,* or *land mile* became conventionalized to 5280 feet, or 1760 yards, or 1.60934 kilometers. (The kilometer is 3280.8 feet, or about $5/8$ of a mile; for purposes of approximation, one can multiply kilometrage by 0.6 to get mileage and mileage by about 1.6 to get kilometrage.) At an earlier time, the statute mile was equivalent to 1620 English yards (which were then somewhat longer, having since apparently yielded to the pressures of inflation). The *nautical mile* is equivalent to one minute of the circumference of the earth at the equator; because the accuracy with which that dimension has improved over the years, the length of the nautical mile has been accordingly modified, its present length being 6076.11549 feet, or 1.150779 statute miles, or 1.852 kilometers. In other words, if the circumference of the earth is considered as 360°, and one minute is one sixtieth of one degree, then the nautical mile is $1/21,600$th of the circumference of the earth. For the purposes of navigation it is far more sensible to use a measure with a physical rather than an arbitrary basis. The *nautical mile* was also called the *geographical,* or *sea mile;* in its present configuration, it is known as the *international nautical,* or *air mile.* The American term *country mile* is not a unit of measure; it means 'considerable distance,' presumably because miles in the country seem so much longer than those in a city; it is used as a term of exaggeration, usually in contexts referring to the missing of a goal: *The golfer missed the green by a country mile.*

steeple / spire

A *steeple* is a structure built atop a church tower or similar construction in various styles of architecture. A *spire* is a pointed construction that forms the top of the steeple. Steeples and spires may be circular, square, or polygonal in plan. They are largely ornamental but are often used to house bells, as in a church, or a clock, usually one that has a face on each side of the base of the steeple.

strategy / tactics / stratagem

Strategy is the name given to the planning of a war, of a battle, or of some other kind of contest or competition: one talks not only of the strategy of the Battle of Jutland but of the sales strategy needed to persuade more people to buy replacement windows in a given area. In the military sense, strategy is distinguished from *tactics* in that the latter concerns itself with the details of the deployment and movement of forces, while the former is of much broader focus. A *strata-*

gem is any kind of a deception or trick used to gain advantage over an enemy, or someone perceived to be in an adversary position.

stratum / strata

Latin neuter nouns borrowed by English end in *-um*. There is no particularly good reason why their plurals should not conform to normal English plurals and appear as *-ums,* but many do not. In fact, some do—*minimum, minimums; maximum, maximums,* for example—but their Latin plurals lurk in the background, available for pedantic, academic writers who seem to believe that using Latinisms in their otherwise English text lends to it the imprimatur of culture and, perhaps, unassailability. Thus, one does encounter *minima* and *maxima,* though, except in the most technical scientific contexts, they seem affected. In the case of *stratum,* however, the singular form is far less frequent than the plural, *strata,* and the plural has assumed the function of the singular. Therefore, one often hears *She belongs to a different strata of society.* Examples of the use of *strata* in ordinary language as the subject of a singular verb are lacking, perhaps because people who use this somewhat educated term are still too uncomfortable with it to take it that far. (See also **data / datum, -us, words ending in.**)

strike / wildcat strike / sitdown strike / slowdown / work to rule / strike action

A labor *strike* of any kind is a refusal of workers to work owing to a dispute with the ownership or management of their employing company; it usually involves *picketing,* which involves the employees' making their grievances known by marching outside the place of work carrying signs and trying to persuade other workers not to enter; it may also involve *secondary boycott,* illegal in some countries, in which the striking employees attempt to persuade other companies from carrying on business with the employer. A *sit-down strike* is one in which the employees occupy the place of work and prevent other workers from entering to carry on their work. A *wildcat strike* is one called by employees without the supervision of their union and without a vote of the union membership. A *slowdown* is a form of protest by employees in which they work with deliberate slowness, reducing the productivity of the employing company. A *work-to-rule* action is a protest in which the employees' carefully perform their jobs to the precise descriptions laid down in a rulebook. The term *strike action* is usually selected by employees who are legally forbidden from striking in the customary ways, because they are postal or other civil service workers, because they have a valid, unexpired contract with their employer, or for some other reason. There are other kinds of strikes that do not involve refusal to work: in a *rent strike* tenants with grievances against their landlord refuse to pay rent; in a *hunger strike* an individual or a group of people refuse to eat in order to call attention to grievances they have against some authority, etc.

style / grammar

Even the casual observer who compares the way English is used today with the way it was used by Shakespeare notices many differences in style, vocabulary (lexicon), and syntax. The grammar of the language, however, has changed very little, though allowance must be made for Shakespeare's having exercised poetic license, particularly in word order. Comparison between Contemporary English and that of 100 (or even 50 or 75) years ago reveals differences, too, though they may be a little harder to discern because the changes are much more subtle, far less obvious. The most obvious changes can be seen in the words we use: today's English is riddled with technical and scientific terms, which most of us can use and understand. The English of the 19th century makes no mention of *radio, television, transistors, lasers, poliomyelitis, AIDS, organ transplants, microwave cookers,* and the myriad objects and ideas that form an integral part of our everyday lives. But a careful reading of, say, the novels of Jane Austen or Mark Twain, even those of later writers like H. G. Wells or Sinclair Lewis, reveals changes in style: there is something a bit old-fashioned about their writings, though it is not easy to identify exactly what it is. Language changes continuously, but (except for lexicon) so gradually that the briefer the interval between samples, the more difficult it is to discern the relatively minor differences. The differences between Modern English and Shakespearian English are less pronounced than those between the language of Shakespeare and that of Chaucer; likewise, learning to read the Middle English of Chaucer, who wrote in the 14th century, is of little help in understanding the Old English of the *Beowulf* epic, which dates from the 8th century. Those stages in the development of English represent major changes in the grammar of the language; the grammar of English has changed very little between the 16th-century version used by Shakespeare and that in use today. What have changed and what change from generation to generation in ways that are more readily apparent are the vocabulary and style of the language. Some of the differences in style are, to be sure, attributable to changes in vocabulary: the word stock of a contemporary speaker and writer is different from that of his grandfather, even his father. In addition, the level of language has changed from generation to generation: the language of today used in newspapers, magazines, and books and, especially, on radio and television is much less formal than that of our forebears; for one thing, today's English contains many more slang and colloquial words and expressions than yesterday's did. In many ways, those who criticize Modern English usage for being too "permissive," for "allowing" the intrusion of "grammatical errors" are criticizing the style of the language. There may be something to be said about the failures of modern educational systems in teaching the foundations of traditional usage, leading to the almost prevalent inability among many speakers to use "correctly" words like *like* and *as, infer* and *imply, lie* and *lay,* etc. But this leads one to two observations: first, that confusions of that type in the language may spell the doom, in the near future, of any need to maintain their distinctions; and, second, that examination of usage books written a hundred and fifty years ago reveals that critics in those days were upset by exactly the same problems that beset the writers of usage books today. If the majority of English speakers persist in making the same "errors," then it is unlikely that they will remain as errors forever. Even on a contemporary level differences can be noted between usage in England and in the United States: purists insist that we should say *different from:* in Britain it is not considered good usage to say *different to;* but American speakers seem to prefer *different than.* Which of the three will prevail? It is impossible to predict. In deciding whether to follow the recommendations of those who try to "improve" our usage of English, each person must decide what is most appropriate for him: it is probably less important for a bus driver or a carpenter to follow those recommendations than for a teacher or writer. Some teachers and writers employ usage that is condemned by the critics because they feel that such a style will bring them closer to a less well-educated audience. But that is very unlikely, for those who are less well-educated have no difficulty in understanding "good" English and, besides, would probably prefer to be taught by those who write and speak in a more educated way.

successful / successive

Successful is associated with the noun *success,* and it means 'having attained what was being sought.' (Since so much of society today seeks financial independence, *success* is usually equated with 'financial success,' and *successful* with 'wealthy.' But those are modern connotations only: one can be successful in his work without, necessarily, acquiring wealth from it.) *Successive* is associated with the noun *succession,* and it means 'following without an interval or interruption'; it may refer to things or people (*successive waves of attack; successive applicants*). We speak of *succession* in discussing the order in which monarchs gain the throne; speaking of their *success* would involve determining how well they rule. Some of the possible confusion can be traced to the basic verb, *succeed,* from which all these forms derive: it can mean either 'follow one upon another' or 'attain a goal.' But the syntax of the words is different: *One succeeds to the throne* and *George VI succeeded George V* (was king right after him), but *One succeeds in his attempt at overthrowing the king* (perhaps).

symphony / concerto

Although the precise distinctions between these instrumental musical forms become extremely technical, it may be usefully pointed out that a *symphony* is generally in four movements and is performed by an entire orchestra, while a *concerto* is in three movements and is performed by a soloist with the background of an orchestra, the theme of the latter being to emphasize the virtuosity of the soloist.

synonym / antonym

At the simplest level, a *synonym* is a word that has the same meaning as another, an *antonym* one that has the opposite meaning. Estimates of the total number of words in the English language vary, for a number of reasons. In the first place, it is not always easy to decide on a useful definition of *word:* Is a word to be 'any collection of letters with a space on each side'? Are expressions that cannot be semantically analyzed into their components (like *up the creek, come up smiling, down in the mouth, kick the bucket*) to be treated as words? Should combinations that are, effectively, compounds (like *sodium chloride, theory of relativity, differential calculus, inertial guidance*) be treated as words? Are inflected forms (like *be, am, is, are, was, were, been, being;* or *ox, oxen)* different words or the same word? As can be seen, the answer to the basic question "What is a word?" is not readily at hand. One thing is certain: no matter how large the dictionary, no dictionary has ever listed all the words of a language, no matter how *word* might be defined. The largest dictionaries available have listed several hundred thousand "entries." which, in the United States is taken to mean not only all of the words that are defined, but their inflected forms and variants, words that are listed (for spelling) but not defined, and even changes in parts of speech (e.g., *run*, the verb, counts as one entry; as a noun it counts as another; and of idiomatic expressions like *run into, run across, run over,* etc., each counts as well). The average college-size dictionary in the U.S. that advertises "160,000 entries" actually contains a little more than half that number of words with definitions. (Of course, many of the words have more than one definition, but that is a different matter.) Even the largest dictionaries barely scratch the surface of the language: general dictionaries do not contain the words or the definitions widely used in many specialized fields, like law, medicine, chemistry, the many branches of technology, and so on; these dictionaries do not even cover the general language exhaustively. And this is not a criticism that is answerable on the grounds that the language changes too rapidly for any dictionary to keep up with it: even the everyday language is not completely covered. Whether it should be is another question; the point is that it is not, notwithstanding claims to the contrary by the publishers of dictionaries. Ordinary dictionaries are only one way of looking at words: in order to find a word with the meaning they are seeking to express, people resort to dictionaries of synonyms, which may be arranged in any of a variety of ways to enable users to gain access to the kinds of information they want. Many popular general dictionaries include synonymic information about selected words; even though it is usually not very thorough, such information in a general dictionary has the virtue of having the dictionary's definitions handy, so that nuances of meaning, levels of usage, and other useful material can be readily referred to. Dictionaries of synonyms are extremely popular, particularly among writers, who use them as a shortcut to being reminded of the word they need to express a certain idea: such books ought to be employed merely as "promptories," to remind their users of words that are familiar to them; otherwise, the blind selection of an unfamiliar word listed as a synonym may yield a ludicrous or inappropriate result. Of those synonym dictionaries that are in print today, none has definitions; therefore, the user must rely either on his own knowledge of the suggested substitution or look it up in a dictionary. Unfortunately, even the best dictionaries do not provide the kinds of information about words of the general language that would enable a user to make the proper choice. The notion of synonymy is very strong among English speakers, the popular notion being that there is such a thing as a synonym. As those who are sensitive to the language are well aware, there is really no such thing as a synonym if, by *synonym*, we are to understand a 'word substitutable for another in all contexts.' At one level, *table salt*, usually called just *salt*, is synonymous with *sodium chloride;* but the distribution and frequency of the two terms are completely different: except facetiously, no one would ask to "Please pass the sodium chloride" at the dinner table; on the other hand, no chemist would use the language so loosely as to refer to just *salt* (in contrast to *a salt* or, specifically, *sodium chloride* or some other particular *salt*). *Antonyms* are another matter, for the notion of "oppositeness" in language varies considerably. On a literal level, for example, *black* and *white* are certainly opposites (and antonyms) in some contexts; but not in the context of skin color: white people are only very rarely *white*, black people are all different shades of *brown*, and yellow people cannot accurately be called *yellow* at all. Besides, among antonyms, which are only rarely sought after, the same problems of distribution in the language are encountered as among synonyms: the appropriate antonym of *good* is sometimes *naughty*, sometimes *bad*, sometimes *evil*, sometimes *impure*, sometimes *undependable*, and so forth, depending on the context. Dictionaries make the attempt to account for context, to a certain extent; synonym dictionaries pay little heed to context, and the burden is put on the user to select the *mot juste.*

table d'hôte / à la carte / prix fixe

These terms, borrowed from French, are used in restaurants to describe the fare offered; the first two are often combined on the same menu. *À la carte*, literally 'according to the menu,' allows the diner to choose any individual dishes from among those listed separately, as from a selection of hors d'oeuvres, soups, meats or fishes, vegetables, salads, desserts, and beverages. *Table d'hôte*, literally '(according to the) table of the host,' offers a selected combination of dishes at a single price lower than would have been charged had the dishes been selected individually by the diner; it may include an hors d'oeuvre, fruit juice, or soup, together with a main course consisting of meat, fish, or the like with vegetable and potato, a salad, and, sometimes, dessert and a beverage as well. *Prix fixe,* literally 'fixed price,' refers to the same practice as table d'hôte.

table / shelve

In British English, these words mean opposite things: *shelve* means to 'postpone, put aside (temporarily),' *table* means to 'present for action, as a bill to a legislative body.' *Shelve* carries that meaning in American English, but for some inexplicable reason, *table* means to 'shelve.' This curious state of affairs in the United States for what would superficially appear to be a relatively transparent metaphor, in which one might expect that putting something on a table would, logically, mean that it was being presented for consideration, action, or the like, has not been satisfactorily explained.

tartan / plaid

A *tartan* is a rectangular pattern created by crisscrossing lines and bars of color; each pattern is associated with a particular Scottish clan and is regarded as a symbol of the clan. In less rigorous application, a tartan is any fabric bearing a pattern that may be a genuine tartan. In formal usage, a *plaid* (pronounced "PLAD" or "PLAYED" in Britain but only "PLAD" in North America) is a long, shawllike garment in a tartan pattern worn as part of Highland costume. Loosely, plaid is the same as the informal use of tartan.

that / which

In constructing relative clauses, speakers of English are offered a number of options. In short, easily understood contexts, one option is to omit the relative pronoun entirely if the subordinate clause is restrictive; in longer or more involved contexts, the choice is from among *who / whom, that,* and *which.* (For a discussion of the first of these, see **who / whom.**) In formal use, *that* is preferred as the relative pronoun in restrictive clauses, but it is often omitted in less formal language: *The dog (that) I saw is yours. The drug (that was) developed to combat epilepsy has saved countless lives.* Usually—but, in practice, not always—*which* is reserved for nonrestrictive clauses: *The dog, which I saw, was yours. The drug, which was developed to combat epilepsy, has saved countless lives.* In the latter set of example sentences, the clauses embraced by commas are nonrestrictive, that is, they are not essential to the meaning and may be omitted without distorting the sense. In *The dog (that) I saw is yours*, the fact that the subject of *saw* actually saw the particular dog is not only critical to the meaning, it also states that only one dog was seen, that *I* was the one who saw it, and that although "I" might have done other things to it, the important thing worth mentioning is that I *saw* it. Thus, as in giving testimony, were the speaker to stress *I* or *saw*, it would make no difference, the meaning could not change. Similarly, the second sentence emphasizes the fact that "the drug that has saved countless lives is the one that was developed to combat epilepsy," and the implication is very strong that the lives that were saved were those of epileptics. On the other hand, the drug mentioned in the second, "which" example, about which the almost incidental information is given that it was (originally) developed to combat epilepsy, might have saved the lives of people suffering from leprosy, cancer, heart disease, or the Tasmanian pip. Likewise, the dog in the "which" example is emphatically stated to be "yours," but the fact that "I" saw it is so incidental as to seem almost irrelevant. It is of particular note that omission of the relative pronoun unequivocally suggests the omission of *that* (together with a verb, in some instances), except in sentences where the nonrestrictive clause becomes, in effect, an appositive phrase: *The cat, (which was) always prowling about, finally caught the mouse. The canary, (which is) a carnivore, attacked the horse.* It should be noted, too, that these parenthetical words are regarded as optional: in older, traditional grammar, it was tempting to analyze sentences like these and to describe "which was, which is," etc. as "understood," a practice or technique that might have provided a convenient way of looking at them but was not entirely in keeping with a scientific approach: language should be analyzed on the basis of the evidence provided, not on elements that might be present were different kinds of utterances to be examined. (See also **descriptive modifier / restrictive modifier, who / that.**)

thin / thinly

For some unaccountable reason, recent western culture has produced the cliché, "— is the greatest thing since sliced bread." Why or how sliced bread has acquired such cachet is hard to fathom, but where sliced bread is available it is usually offered as, simply, "sliced" and as "thinly sliced." *Thinly* is properly an adverb, modifying the verb *slice;* but there is a difference between *sliced thin,* which means 'sliced so as to be thin,' and *sliced thinly,* for which is hard to imagine a sense: slicing can be done *quickly, slowly, sloppily, neatly, well, badly,* and a great variety of other ways, but it cannot be done "thinly"—the language simply has no provision for such an action. It is not the slicing that is thin, it is the bread; thus, the sensible form would be "thin-sliced" bread, that is, "bread sliced so that it is thin" and not " . . so that it is thinly." It must be said that the number of bread packages bearing the legend "Thinly Sliced' is so overwhelmingly enormous (in comparison with the number of entries like this one, multiplied by the number of usage books published in the English language) that the battle—if it can be called that—is for a lost cause. Now and then a glimmer of hope scintillates in the dark: some bakeries persist, against the rising (yeasty) trend, in printing "Thin-Sliced" on their packages. The foregoing should help bread slicers through *thick* as well as *thin.*

this / that

As pronouns, *this* has a long tradition of referring to 'what is to follow', and *that* of referring to 'what has already been mentioned': *This is what I want to do: to go out to dinner. You suggested going out to dinner, and that is what I want to do.* In recent decades, however, *this* appears to have begun to usurp the position of *that* in such contexts, and one often hears, *You suggested going out to dinner, and this is what I want to do.* To those accustomed to the traditional functions of *this* and *that,* such usage grates on the ear, and only the next generations of speakers will determine whether the displacement will become standard. In the meantime, the substitution is considered nonstandard. In other contexts, physical nearness is usually the criterion: *This is a picture of my last duchess* suggests that the picture is in the immediate vicinity, as on a nearby wall; *That is a picture of my last duchess* suggests that the picture is more remote, usually not closer than across the room. Yet, the usage is often ambiguous; for instance, indicating a picture in a photo album one is holding or on television, either *this* or *that* might be used. Similarly, in querying someone on the telephone, one might say, *Who is this?* or, less often

Who is that? But if someone else has answered the telephone, another person wishing to know who is calling would say, *Who is that?* and the caller would naturally say *This is the bank manager* (or whoever it happened to be). It is possible that *this* and *that* have been affected by their use by non-native speakers in whose native languages the distinction may be lacking: in French, for example, *ce, cet,* and *cette* offer no opportunity to distinguish between the sense of 'this' and 'that,' and one must resort to *ceci, cela* and *celui-ci, celui-la.*

tied house / free house

In Britain, a *tied house* is a public house owned either entirely or in part by a brewery, which requires the pub to feature its own brands of beer. A *free house* is independently owned and sells the beers of any brewery, often those of several.

tiger lily / day lily / calla lily

A *tiger lily,* so called because its flower is orange with black stripes and splotches, has a long single stem and petals that flare out. A *day lily,* so called because its flowers last only for a day, is sometimes confused with the tiger lily because some common varieties of it are also orange. The day lily has stems two to three feet long which rise from a thick cluster of thin, arching leaves. The *calla lily* has a white, funnel-shaped flower with an orange spadix; it is the flower often associated with funerals.

till / until / 'til

The original English word was *till;* for meter, rhythm, euphony, emphasis, or whatever reason, it acquired a variant, *until,* which was later, in less formal contexts, contracted to *'til.* The form *'till* is not attested except as a misspelling of *'til* or *till.* Some speakers mistakenly believe that *till* is a less formal contraction of *until,* but it is *'til* that is the contraction.

timidity / temerity

One who is *timid* is shy and retiring: he exhibits *timidity.* One who is *timorous* is nervously fearful or afraid. One who exhibits *temerity* is rash and bold—*temerarious* is the adjective—just the opposite of the first two.

tolerance / toleration

Having two words that treat different aspects of the same concept is a convenience, and the distinction between them adds to the language. *Tolerance* is the 'attitude of one who tolerates,' *toleration* the 'act of tolerating': the former carries in it the sense of a spirit of liberality, the latter the sense of leniency in permitting something to occur without taking (adverse) action against it. The adjective, *tolerant*, is in reference to either sense.

tortoise / turtle / terrapin

These are all four-legged reptiles with a shell above (called the *carapace*) and below (called the *plastron*) the body. The shell is actually the bony *exoskeleton* (*q.v.*) of the animal. The *tortoise* is terrestrial (lives mainly on land), the *turtle* is marine (lives mainly in the water). According to some sources, *tortoise* comes from *Tartarus*, the Classical Greek name for Hades, and was so named because that was thought to be where the animal originated; the word was influenced by an Old French word, *tortue*, which was, in turn, influenced by Latin *tortus* 'twisted,' applied because the southern European varieties of tortoises have legs that appear to be twisted. *Turtle* comes from French *tortue* 'tortoise'; it was influenced by the English word *turtle*, which is totally unrelated and is seen in *turtledove*, a kind of bird that has nothing to do with tortoises or reptiles. Because of the affection that turtledoves show for their mates, the word *turtle* came to be a common pet name in English long before it was associated with reptiles; that earlier sense of *turtle* has faded out, and even turtledoves seem somewhat archaic today. Despite its superficial appearance and sound, the *terra-* in *terrapin* has no connection with the Latin word for 'earth': *terrapin* is a word of Algonquian origin; it refers to tortoises which, in the New World, were known to the inhabitants as dwellers on land or in lakes and marshes. It is possible, however, that Latin *testudo* 'tortoise' had some influence, and it is interesting to note that the metaphoric extension of this word in Latin referred to a rooflike shelter used by soldiers besieging the walls of a town. It consisted either of a wooden structure wheeled up to the walls or simply of the soldiers' shields interlocked over their heads to ward off missiles thrown from above.

tortuous / torturous

Both these words come from a Latin word that means 'twisting,' but *torturous* is an adjective derived from *torture* and has to do with 'torment; the infliction of pain,' while *tortuous* refers to the form taken by a twisting, winding road or way. Reasoning might be tortuous in that it is convoluted, but, as it is unlikely to cause physical pain, it is unlikely to be torturous.

toupee / wig / fall / transformation

A *toupee*, also called a *hairpiece*, is false hair worn by a man to cover a bald spot. If it is a complete head of false hair for covering an entirely bald head or the natural hair, as in costume, disguise, etc., it may be called a *toupee* or a *wig*, whether worn by a woman or by a man. A *transformation* is a wig or a partial covering of hair, usually for a woman. A *fall*, or *switch*, is a piece of false hair worn long by a woman, usually one that falls straight down; *fall* is sometimes applied to a coiffure in which all or part of the hair is worn so as to hang down.

triumphal / triumphant

If one can cope with the fact that the suffix *-al* means 'of, pertaining, or relating to' and that *-ant* (which comes from Latin) is similar to English *-ing*, it might help to remember that *triumphal* means 'of, pertaining to, or relating to a triumph' while *triumphant* means 'triumphing.' Thus, a person may be triumphant, but a commemorative arch can be only triumphal.

Tropic of Cancer / Tropic of Capricorn

The *Tropic of Cancer* (named after the sign of the zodiac where it touches the celestial sphere, or ecliptic) is an imaginary ring around the earth, parallel to and about 23° north of the equator, that marks the northernmost points where the sun is directly overhead at the summer solstice (about June 21st). The *Tropic of Capricorn* (named after the sign of the zodiac where it touches the celestial sphere) is an imaginary ring around the earth, parallel to and about 23° south of the equator, that marks the southernmost points where the sun is directly overhead at the winter solstice (about December 21st). See also **Arctic Circle / Antarctic Circle.**)

troposphere / stratosphere / ionosphere / exosphere

For convenience in describing their various characteristics, the levels of the earth's atmosphere have been given names, the patterns of which can most easily be related in a table:

NAME	HEIGHT	DESCRIPTION
troposphere	7km at the poles; 28km at the equator	breathable air; temperature diminishes with increased height
stratosphere	up to 50km	air not life-sustaining; temperature relatively constant
ionosphere	up to 1000km	temperature increases; atomic oxygen above 100km; no nitrogen above 150km; ionized gases reflect radio wavelengths except those between 8mm and 20m (used for television)
(Parts of ionosphere)		
D-layer	50 to 90km	reflects radio waves of lower frequencies
E-layer	90 to 150km	(also called the *Heaviside* or *Heaviside-Kennelly layer*); reflects radio waves of medium frequency
F-layer	150 to 1000km	(also called the *Appleton layer*); most effective for radio wave reflection
exosphere	400 to 1000km	the outer reaches, where the density of air molecules is very low

Because the F-layer does not reflect the radio waves used in television and other transmissions, artificial satellites are placed into fixed orbit to serve for the reflection (*passive satellites*) or for the amplification and retransmission of signals (*active satellites*).

true north / geographic north / magnetic north

These are terms in navigation. *True* or *geographic north* refers to the precise point at 90° north latitude where the theoretical North Pole is situated. This is not necessarily (or usually) the site of the *magnetic north pole*, the place pointed to by a fully adjusted compass; the magnetic north pole wanders about and may be as much as 11° or 12° away from true north. Such difference as may exist, called *variation*, is shown on navigation charts and is compensated for in calculating the position of a vessel or aircraft. In the late 1980s, magnetic north was moving toward true north at the rate of nine minutes a year, or more than a full degree in seven years. In 1987 the runways at Heathrow (London) airport, which are given numbers that correspond to their (magnetic) compass headings (dropping the final zero), were redesignated 27 (formerly, 28) and 09 (formerly, 10), reflecting an accumulated change in the position of magnetic north over the preceding 40 years. In addition to the displacement of magnetic north from true north, local conditions (either natural or artificial, as may be occasioned by the amount of metal in the vicinity of the compass) may cause a disparity in compass readings; that difference is called *deviation*. As a result of deviation, a compass reading of "north" may be different from the norm; if it is not corrected for deviation or variation, that reading would be called *compass north*, though the term is not common since a navigator would be unlikely to find an inaccurate compass useful.

turboprop / ramjet / jet / rocket / pulse jet

Till about 45 years ago, all but experimental airplanes were powered by internal combustion engines. Anyone familiar with fireworks is aware that rockets are tubular affairs that contain an explosive which, when ignited, propels the device high into the air (whereupon various colored displays appear). The principle of the rocket has been well known for thousands of years, but in recent years, much of the useful experimental work was done by Robert Hutchings Goddard

(1882–1945), an American physicist. The difference between a rocket
and the other methods for propelling objects, vehicles, etc., is that the
rocket carries within it not only fuel but the oxygen and other chemicals that enable it to function outside the earth's atmosphere. The
principle of the rocket, which enables it to operate in space, is that
the burned fuel and other gases that are ejected from the rear serve
as a mass against which the vehicle pushes; thus, not only can it operate outside the atmosphere, but it operates better, since it is not re-
tarded by the resistance of the air. For this reason, the rocket engine
is called a *reaction engine*. (Rockets like fireworks do not carry their
own oxidants, hence can function only in the atmosphere from which
they can draw oxygen.) The rocket, as well as the *turbojet* and *ramjet*,
are *jet propulsion* engines. Such engines are used in boats and other
vehicles, but mainly in aircraft. Both the *ramjet* and the *turbojet* are
air-breathing. In the *ramjet* engine the air through which it passes is
taken into the front of the engine where it is constricted, increasing
its velocity; fuel is injected into the airstream and ignited, the ejection
of the gases from the rear providing forward motion. The *turbojet*
operates in the same way, except that the entering air is compressed
before entering a combustion chamber where it is ignited to provide
power for driving a turbine which ejects the gases rearward to provide forward motion. A *turbopropeller engine*, or *propjet*, is a turbojet
engine equipped with a propeller which is driven by the turbine, to
add to the thrust provided by the ejected gases; in aircraft, the turboprop, as it is usually called, is used for shorter, intracontinental
flights. In a *pulse-jet engine*, the air intake at the front of the engine is
regulated by a system of louvers which open to let in air and are
then closed by the force of combustion of the fuel, alternately opening and closing rapidly; forward motion is imparted as in other jet
engines. There are various combinations of jet engines that have been
developed and are in use for different applications. The turbopropeller engine, for example, has proved economical only for shorter
flights, while the turbojet is the standard engine used in longer-range
flights.

tweeter / woofer

Among the elements that make up the high-fidelity components of a
sound reproduction system are combinations of loudspeakers that
consist of several speakers made so as to better reproduce sounds of

different frequencies: those for the reproduction of high-frequency sounds are called *tweeters,* those for sounds of low frequency, *woofers.* Formerly, and occasionally today, a combination of the two into one is used, the high-frequency speaker set within the low-frequency element; this is called a *tweeter-woofer.*

type / token

These terms are used in various disciplines, in slightly different applications but with essentially the same senses, *type* referring to a class or set of things of which a *token* is a concrete example. Thus, in grammar, *noun* is a type, and *book, house, nation, computer* are tokens; in zoology, *mammal* is a type, and at one level *Homo sapiens,* the families *Canidae* (all dogs), *Felidae* (all cats), *Cervidae* (all deer) are all tokens; at another level, you and I are tokens of the type *Homo sapiens,* "Rover" a token of the type *Canidae,* "Minou" of the type *Felidae,* "Bambi" of the type *Cervidae.*

typhoid / typhus

Typhoid, usually called *typhoid fever* (sometimes, *enteric fever),* is so named because its symptoms somewhat resemble those of *typhus;* but the two are separate diseases. Typhoid is an acute infectious disease characterized by high fever, delirium, a red rash, cough, (often severe) headache, and, in complications, involves intestinal hemorrhage or perforation. It is caused by a bacillus, *Salmonella typhi,* which is most commonly distributed by food or water contaminated by human feces. Typhus is caused by any of various species of *Rickettsiae,* organisms that resemble both bacilli and viruses. It is transmitted by the bites of fleas, mites, or ticks from infected rodents, mainly rats. It was once thought that the great plagues of the Middle Ages might have been epidemics of typhus, but it is now generally accepted that they were caused by another bacillus, *Yersina pestis,* which is also transmitted by fleabite from infected rats.

upper respiratory tract / lower respiratory tract

The *upper respiratory tract,* which functions to conduct air to and from the lungs, consists of the *trachea* (popularly called the *windpipe),* the *larynx,* the *pharynx,* the *frontal, sphenoidal,* and *maxillary sinuses,* the *ethmoidal air cells* (many mucus-lined cells in the facial bones), and the *nose* and *nasal cavity.* The *lower respiratory tract* includes the *bronchi,* and the *lungs.* It is in the lungs that the exchange between oxygen and carbon dioxide occurs in the respiratory cycle, between the surface of *alveoli* and the tiny capillaries that surround the alveolar wall. The alveoli are connected to *alveolar sacs,* which are connected with *alveolar ducts;* these, in turn, feed into the *bronchioles,* which are small branches of the bronchi.

upstage / downstage / stage left / stage right

In theatrical parlance, *upstage* means 'toward the rear of the stage, further away from the audience', *downstage* just the opposite: 'closer to the curtain, footlights, and audience.' *Upstage* also occurs as a verb, meaning to 'steal the show from someone; predominate in a situation.' The use of *downstage* as a verb is not attested. It may be easy to remember the difference from the verb *upstage:* it refers to an actor's moving toward the rear of the stage, while continuing to face the audience, causing his fellow actor or actors to turn their backs to the audience, thus making their words hard to hear and concealing their actions. Thus, someone who upstages another is stealing his thunder and making his performance ineffectual. Because stage directions are given from the point of view of the audience (which invariably faces the stage) and not from that of the actors (who might be facing in any direction), *stage left* and *stage right* refer to the left and right parts of the stage as the audience views it. Similarly, directions like *enter left* and *exeunt right* designate left and right of the audience.

-us, words ending in

There are many nouns in English ending in *-us* that were borrowed from Latin. (These do not include the English adjectives that came from Latin adjectives ending in *-us,* all of which are conventionally spelled with an *-ous* ending in English.) Although many such words form their plurals by changing the *-us* to *-i* (usually pronounced "eye" in English), not all of them do, and there is no way of knowing which is which. The reason for their different behavior is that some come from the second declension in Latin, which has a plural ending in *-i,* and some come from the fourth declension, which in the plural changed the *-us* ending to *-ūs* (that is, from a *u*-sound like that in *book* to one like that in *boot*). Words in the first group include mainly technical borrowings, like *coccus / cocci, thalamus / thalami, embolus / emboli, thrombus / thrombi,* etc., and a few common words, like *alumnus / alumni, stimulus / stimuli, nucleus / nuclei,* etc. Words in the second group, like *thesaurus* and *prospectus,* which are from the fourth declension, form their English plurals by adding *-es: thesauruses, prospectuses,* not "thesauri, prospecti." Some are particularly troublesome, partly because they originated in Greek with the ending *-os* (for which the plural is usually *-oi*) but were borrowed into Latin and given the common *-us / -i* ending because they were placed into the second declension. *Hippopotamus* is such a word: as a Greek loanword in Latin, its English plural should be *hippopotamuses;* but if one regards *hippopotamus* as borrowed from Latin, then *hippopotami* is correct; as matters stand in the language at present, either is acceptable. *Octopus* is a special case because the Greek ending is not *-us* but *-pous,* meaning 'foot', the compound word *octopus* meaning 'eight-footed one'; the plural of *octopus* might properly be *octopoda* on the Greek model, but such forms would get short shrift in English, and *octopuses* remains the preferred choice of the nonpedantic. Similar treatment is accorded words like *chorus / choruses,* etc. Unfortunately for the cause of consistency (and notwithstanding the belief of many that it is a "systematic, logical" language), Latin also has some neuter nouns ending in *-us,* notably *onus* and *opus.* The dictionaries unanimously give *onuses* as the plural of *onus,* which is just as well, for its formal Latin plural is *onera,* which reveals the word's root, *oner-,* which appears in the adjective form, *onerous.* The Latin plural of *opus* is *opera,* which leads to a problem of the distribution of these words in English. By convention, *opus,* with the plural *opuses* or *opera,* has become a term used mainly in music bibliography to refer to a single work by a composer, though it also occurs in ordinary language referring to a creation by any artist, especially an important masterwork, or *magnum opus. Opera* in the sense of a 'theatrical drama which is largely sung' was borrowed from Italian, not directly from Latin, and, with the *opera* plural of *opus* in English forms what is called a doublet. As can be seen, there are no hard and fast rules or even loose guidelines that can be given in the matter of forming plurals of words ending in *-us* in English—except one: all English nouns that end in *-a, -o, -um,* or *-us* are susceptible to having peculiar plurals and, if one is in doubt about their formation, they should be checked in an up-to-date dictionary.

use / usage

Use is taken to mean 'application, the act of employing,' as in *the uses of history, The can opener will be put to good use. We have no use for another TV. Usage* means 'the manner in which something is custom-arily or habitually applied, employed, or used,' as in *good English us-age, Rough usage has damaged the desks.*

utopia / dystopia / subtopia / subutopia

In 1516, Sir Thomas More (1478–1535) published a book called *Utopia*, in which he described an imaginary, idyllic isle enjoying ideal law and politics. He had invented the word *utopia* from Greek *ou* 'not' + *topos* 'place' (and not, as some may think, from *eu-* 'good' + *topos*). The name came to be used metaphorically for 'any ideally perfect place.' Early in the 18th century, Jeremy Bentham coined the term *cacotopia*, meaning a 'place where everything is bad,' made up from Greek *caco-* 'bad' + *topos*, apparently in the mistaken belief that the *U-* in *Utopia* came from Greek *eu-* 'good.' A half century later, according to the earliest citations in the *OED*, John Stuart Mill coined *dystopia*, based on Greek *dys-* 'bad' + *topos*, meaning a 'wretched, miserable place where everything goes wrong.' More recently, *subtopia*, or *subutopia*, which plays on *sub-* both in its sense of 'beneath' and in its connota-tive connection with *suburb*, was coined in Great Britain to describe a suburban area that has been developed enough to destroy the beaut-ies and advantages of open, country living but not to the point where the benefits of a sense of community and identity was felt by its residents.

vaccinate / inoculate

To be etymologically precise, one can be *vaccinated* only with cowpox vaccine (for *vaccine* comes from Latin *vacca* 'cow'). In practice, howev-er, vaccination is the same as *inoculation:* in both, modified microorga-nisms from an animal with the same or a similar disease to the one to be prevented are injected into a healthy person; the person's system reacts by acquiring a mild form of the disease to which his body re-sponds by producing antibodies; these antibodies remain in the per-son's system for a period of time (how long depends on the disease, the vaccine, and other factors) and prevent his getting the disease. Inoculation may be done by injection or by scratching the surface of the skin and introducing the substance (called an *inoculum*) by rubbing it in. (It may be worthwhile to point out that *inoculate*, etc., are spelled with one *n* near the beginning.)

Vandal / Hun

Although the documentation of the history of the civilized peoples of Europe before about 1000 A.D. is sufficient to allow modern investigators to reconstruct many of the events that took place in classical Greece, Rome, and Byzantium, the information concerning the millions of people of Europe and western Asia who did not belong to those cultures or were not at war with them is very sparse. With few exceptions, there are virtually no extant written records, nor, indeed, is it known whether they had a writing system. Much of what is known is gleaned from information contained in references to the people when they came into contact with the Romans (after 100 B.C.) and particularly from the writings of Julius Caesar. In the circumstances, it seems likely that modern views have been colored by contemporary prejudice. Because many of those cultures were probably tribal and undoubtedly lacking in culture compared with the Greeks and Romans, they were not looked upon with much curious affection by their contemporary historians and chroniclers. Yet, they were consistently characterized as "warlike," even though their raids and incursions took place in a relatively short interval (from the point of view of history). There is evidence, for example, of the existence of the *Huns*, a nomadic Asiatic people that dominated much of Asia and eastern Europe, from before 300 B.C.; their entire reputation for being "warlike" appears to have been acquired as a result of their invasions of the Roman Empire during the 4th and 5th centuries A.D. It would seem that they behaved themselves for at least 1000 years, carrying on without recorded incident, which is more than can be said about the nations and peoples of western Europe during the past 1000 years. Toward the end of the 4th century, they conquered the Ostrogoths. They came into prominence under the leadership of Attila (?406–53), whose name means 'little father' and who acquired his sobriquet, "Scourge of God," by means other than benign and benevolent; in 447, the Huns invaded Scythia (a region north and east of the Caspian and Black seas), Media (roughly contiguous with modern northwestern Iran), and Persia (a large area extending from near Egypt to the border of India). They then turned their attention to eastern Europe, taking Thermopylae, Gallipoli, and, by mere threat, exaction of tribute from Constantinople. Their invasion of Europe, across the Rhine, was not terminated till 451, possibly near Châlons-sur-Marne, in France, by the combined forces of the Romans and the Visigoths. After a campaign in Italy, Attila returned to Pannonia (approximately equivalent to modern Hungary and Yugoslavia), where he died two years later. Within a few short years, the vast empire he had collected but failed to consolidate fell apart. The *Vandals* were a Germanic people who came from the north and extended their territories greatly, chiefly as the result of migration; in 406–07, they invaded Gaul, Spain, and western Africa. Rome had fallen victim to their incursions during the 3rd and 4th centuries A.D., and the Visigoths soon invaded Italy and captured Rome. In Gaul, they were ultimately defeated by the Franks, and they migrated across the Pyrenees into Spain, one of their tribes, called the Asdingian Vandals, occupying Galicia, another, the Silingian Vandals, Andalusia. These latter were virtually destroyed in the following decades, and the Asdingians took possession of Andalusia. In about 428, the entire populace—some 80,000 men, women, and children in all—set sail for Africa, and by 430, under the leadership of Gaiseric, Hippo, Cirta, and Carthage were the only three African cities belonging to Rome that had not been taken by the Vandals. In 439, Carthage, the third most important city of the Roman empire, fell. The Vandal occupation lasted almost a century, during which the city became a port from which piratical forays were launched against all shipping with such success that the Vandals became the greatest maritime power in the Mediterranean. In 455, came Gaiseric's attack on Rome, which succumbed, marking what is generally taken as the terminal date of the Roman empire. Many commentators have pointed out that as the sack of Rome was an orderly affair in which everything of value was taken from the city in a fortnight, there is no known justification for identifying the Vandals with *vandalism*. Ultimately, after the succession of a weak king as ruler of the Vandals, the Byzantine emperor Justinian in 533 sent an expedition under Belisarius, who retook Carthage, soundly defeating the Vandals and, finally, spelling their doom. After the quelling of a subsequent uprising, in 536, the Vandals disappeared from the pages of history.

venal / venial

Venal, which goes back to Latin *venum* 'sale,' is related to *vend* 'sell,' which originated in the Latin phrase *venum dāre* 'to offer for sale.' It retains the semantic notion of 'sell' in its modern meaning, 'available for bribery; mercenary; susceptible to corruption; capable of being bought.' Venial has a different origin, going back to Latin *venia* 'forgiveness,' which is ultimately traceable to *venus* 'love.' It means 'easily forgiven' (which may be taken as having something to do with love) and occurs most frequently in contexts that refer to *venial sins*. Venal, on the other hand, is (unfortunately) applied to public officials.

violin / viola / cello / double bass

These are the names of the members of the *violin* family, a class of stringed instruments, without frets, that are played by plucking (for which the musical direction is *pizzicato*) or by drawing a bow across the strings (for which the musical direction is *arco*). The family evolved from the *viols, fiddles,* and *rebecs.* The *viol* family, which remained in use till it was replaced by the violins in the 17th century, had frets and six strings. It consisted of the *double-bass viol,* also called *violone,* the lowest string of which was tuned to the D two octaves below middle C with each of the other strings tuned to a fourth or third above (D, G, C, E, A, and D); the *bass viol,* also called *viola da gamba* 'leg viola,' was tuned an octave above the double-bass viol; the lowest string of the *tenor viol* was tuned to the A below middle C (the other strings, successively, to D, G, B, E, and A); and the *treble viol,* the lowest string of which was tuned to the D below middle C (with the other strings tuned to G, C, E, A, and D). The *lyra viol,* or *viola bastarda,* a five-stringed, unfretted addition, was tuned to a range intermediate between those of the tenor and bass viols. Another bass member of the violin family is the *cello,* or *violoncello,* which has four strings, the lowest tuned to C two octaves below middle C, and is played with a bow; it has a range of more than four octaves and has been used for accompaniment (as a *continuo,* or *thorough bass*), as a solo instrument, and in the string quartet. The *fiddle,* which appeared in a large number of variations and in many cultures with one or more strings, may be viewed as the direct precursor of the violin in the sense that it was unfretted and played with a bow. Related to it was the *rebec,* a medieval instrument resembling the fiddle in having three or four strings but with a pear-shaped body; it was made in three sizes, tuned to bass, tenor, and soprano. There was also a small, pocket version of the rebec, called a *kit,* having a longish fingerboard attached to a tiny body, used by dancing masters till the 18th century.

Virgin Birth / Immaculate Conception

Immaculate Conception refers to the Roman Catholic dogma that the Virgin Mary was conceived in the womb of her mother, Anne, without the stain of original sin, in anticipation of the birth of Christ. The *Virgin Birth* refers to the birth of Christ by Mary without impairment of her virginity.

wait for / await

There is no difference in meaning between *wait for* and *await* in *We were awaiting her* and *We were waiting for her,* though it would be more likely to hear (or read) *We were awaiting her arrival; We were waiting for her arrival* would not be idiomatic English, and *We were waiting for her to arrive* would be more natural. Any difference between the idiomatic uses of these variants must be laid at the door of English style: *await* seems more literary, but that does not in any way detract from the standard status of *wait for.* (See also **wait for / wait on.**)

wait for / wait on

When used to mean 'wait for' or 'await,' as in *The crowd waited on him for three hours in the rain, wait on* is dialectal; it is common in many dialects of American English, but is not often heard in Britain. The usual sense of *wait on* in both language communities is 'attend,' whether in the general sense of 'act as a servant or attendant to' or in the specific sense of 'serve at table.' (See also **wait / await.**)

warp / weft

In a textile loom, the *warp* is the set of threads or yarn stretched lengthwise, between which the yarn is woven, from side to side (selvage to selvage), to form the *weft. Woof* is another word for *weft.*

washing soda / baking soda / caustic soda / soda

In the United States and Canada, *soda*, used by itself and in appropriate context, usually means any carbonated beverage, often flavored, what is called in Britain a *fizzy drink*. If it is unflavored, it is called *soda water* in the U.S.; if flavored, it is also called *soda pop* or, sometimes, just *pop*; it is also used attributively, as in *pop bottle*. In other uses, *soda* refers to inorganic compounds (salts) of sodium, particularly *washing soda*, or *sal soda*, (sodium carbonate in its decahydrated form), used as a cleansing agent; *baking soda* (sodium bicarbonate, bicarbonate of sodium, or sodium acid carbonate), used in fire extinguishers, in laboratories as a reagent, in baking as a substitute for yeast, and in medicine as an antacid; and *caustic soda* (sodium hydroxide), which is used chiefly in industrial applications. It is sometimes used to mean sodium monoxide, which reacts with water to form sodium hydroxide and is a poison used in some commercial compounds for cleaning drains. (See also **baking powder / baking soda.**)

wasp / bee

Essentially, among the insects that are somewhat similar in certain respects, the *bees* and the *wasps* are the ones that occur in varieties that might be confused. Both occur in a number of forms, mainly categorized as *social*, like the *honeybee*, and *solitary*, like the *carpenter bee*. Among the wasps, the *paper wasp* is social and the *digger wasp*, so called not because it comes from Australia but because it digs holes in the ground, decayed wood, or a hollow twig where it stores live insects for its larvae to eat, is solitary. Wasps are distinguished by a longish body with a very narrow waist, hence the term *wasp-waisted* for the women's fashion of the turn of the century characterized by a nipped-in waist, or, occasionally, as a descriptive term for women so constructed. Bees, on the other hand, have rather chubby bodies and belong to a different family of insects. There are many varieties of bees and wasps, and most people who live in the temperate zones are familiar not only with those already mentioned but particularly with the *bumblebee*, which is rather large and hairy. The *hornets* are any of several varieties of *paper wasps*, that is, social wasps that build a papery nest usually attached to a tree or to the eaves under the projecting roof of a house. *Yellowjackets* are wasps that have body parts colored in yellow and black. Both the bee and the wasp are capable of stinging by means of a specially modified ovipositor, situated at the rear of the abdomen, by which venom is injected through the skin; the bee has a barbed sting which, once injected, cannot be withdrawn, and the insect dies; the wasp has a smooth sting, which can be used again. Bees and wasps are said to *sting,* while mosquitoes and other insects are said to *bite,* for a good reason: bees and wasps have stingers; other insects use their mouthparts (which vary considerably in configuration) to do their worst. Ants, for example, bite by means of a pair of mandibles; mosquitoes insert a proboscis into the skin for drawing off blood, leaving behind an irritant poison.

waterproof / water-repellent / water-resistant

At one time, the wrist watches that could be worn (without damage) when swimming or diving were called *waterproof,* as were outer garments that were designed to keep people dry in the rain. Governmental agencies took over and *waterproof* as a designation went down the drain, on the premise that nothing, in the long run, is literally *waterproof.* In its stead, manufacturers were to use *water-repellent* to describe garments that shed water, are resistant to the absorption of water, and, generally, keep the wearer dry; if the wearer got slightly damp because of the penetration of some water through the fabric, it was to be designated *water-resistant.* The term *water-resistant,* however, was also to be used for watches that are warranted to continue functioning after immersion in the sea at various depths or fastened to the propellers of ships. The entire picture is muddied by the fact that these are now the private currency of trade law and no longer the legal tender of ordinary speakers of English. It is possible, to be sure, to make garments of materials (like plastics) that are virtually impervious to water, though they are likely to allow too little evaporation of perspiration to be wearable with any comfort; likewise, it is possible to manufacture a watch that would be literally waterproof. In practice, however, such namings are forbidden by law, and people are sufficiently aware of the interdictions to say, when one mentions he is wearing a waterproof watch, "You mean 'water-resistant.'"

whisky / whiskey

In Great Britain, the word is spelled *whisky;* therefore, Scotch whisky appears in that form on labels. In Ireland and the United States, the word is spelled *whiskey.* Both the Irish and the Scots feel that they have a vested interest in the word because its origin is traced to Gaelic *usquebaugh* 'water of life,' the Irish claiming that the source of this water is Irish Gaelic *uisce beathadh* and the Scots that it is Scots Gaelic *uisge beatha*. Most people, including the Irish and the Scots, are sensibly more concerned about its destination than its origin.

white belt / green belt / blue belt / brown belt / black belt

These belts or sashes denote the graded levels of training or achievement attained by someone in the martial arts of judo or karate. The *white belt* marks the novice trainee, in the first year; the *brown belt*, the fourth year of training. The *black belt* is worn by the person who has reached a prescribed level of competence as is the *blue belt*. All are worn with the traditional costume. Although usage may vary, a person describing the level he has reached usually says, "I am a black [or other] belt," not "I have a black [. .] belt."

who / whom

The choice between *who* and *whom* is, theoretically, a straightforward one, for *who* is the form used when the word is the subject of a verb, *whom* when it is the object of a verb or preposition. Yet, examples abound that are inconsistent with these apparently simple observations. The most common occurs when the preposition becomes separated: although some people may have difficulty with, *To whom do I owe the money?*, most would not; the proportion changes markedly for a sentence in the form, *Whom do I owe the money to?* This is not altogether difficult to understand, for there are strong forces in the word order of English that cause the subjective form, *who*, to gravitate toward the beginning of an utterance, among them that the first noun or pronoun is usually the subject of the sentence and that in questions and other instances where pronouns are used that can serve either as relatives and interrogatives, the *who* form is expected as normal. Besides, more so in speech than in writing, which affords the leisure of being able to return to the scene of the crime to rearrange the evidence, people simply do not expend whatever effort may be required to anticipate the effect of what they have not yet said on what has already been uttered. (English word order being, more or less, sequential, that is not surprising; other languages function differently: in German, for example, the verb frequently appears at the end of the sentence, which speakers of that language have to keep in mind.) There are other forces at work, as well: the title of Hemingway's book, *For Whom the Bell Tolls,* probably better known than the Donne poem from which the quotation was borrowed, has become such a cliché that one is unlikely to hear . . *for who the bell tolls* . . or, indeed, *who* used in parallel constructions. But *Who the bell tolls for (is none of my business)* is another matter. Word order sometimes wreaks havoc on grammar, as in instances in which speakers (or, in this case, writers, too) have trouble in identifying the difference between the object of one verb and the subject of another: *The poor, who they said were on the increase, are sleeping rough.* This should be *who,* not *whom,* for it is the subject of *were,* not the object of *said.* But when the word is the subject of an infinitive, the objective case prevails: *I don't know whom they thought to be guilty.* For years *The New Yorker,* under the title, "The Omnipotent *Whom,*" has published as squibs quotations of *whom* used for *who.* Examples can be found everywhere, even in Dickens ("Instinctively apprehensive of her father, whom she supposed it was, she stopped in the dark") and Shakespeare ("Arthur, whom they say is kill'd tonight On your suggestion"). (See also **whoever / whomever.**)

who / that

As relative pronouns, *who* is generally used in referring to people, *that* in referring to ideas, objects, people, and animals. But "generally" is not "always," as the following common examples show: *The man that I saw in the shop is not the one who took my handbag.* Here the use of *that* for people competes with its use in a restrictive clause. (See also **that / which.**) Some awkwardness is felt by speakers when they encounter a choice between *whose* and *of which: The book, whose cover is torn, has been returned* is more likely to be heard or read, particularly in all but the most formal contexts, than *The book, the cover of which is torn, has been returned,* which sounds stilted. Similarly: *the dog whose leash was missing; the house whose roof had been blown away.* Historically, *whose* is the older form, *of which* a relative parvenu. *Whose* cannot, however, be used in all contexts: *St. Peter's, a reproduction of which stands in Montreal* . . does not allow the substitution of *whose.* (See also **who / whom.**)

whoever / whomever

Like other pronouns in the language, the *whoever* form is used when it is the subject of a verb or preposition, the *whomever* form when it is the object. The problem arises because the words occur in contexts that can be confusing for those who are not careful. In *Please give the book to whomever you choose, whomever* is the object of the preposition *to;* in *Please give the book to whoever wants it, whoever* is the subject of *wants,* and the way English works, that grammatical status takes precedent over the preceding *to.* The usual additional explanation is that *whoever wants it* is a clause that forms the object of *to;* but that is not especially helpful to those who might well be justified in viewing *whomever you choose* also as a clause that is the object of *to.* The more formal *whosoever* and *whomsoever* function in a parallel fashion. Dictionaries also record *whosesoever* as the possessive of *whosoever: Whosesoever book it might be should take it away;* the form does not fall trippingly off the tongue, is awkward at best, and could well be avoided in favor of the normal *whosever.* (See also **who / whom.**)

wool / linen / cotton / silk

Wool is a textile made by spinning the fibers of the coat of a sheep, goat, yak, vicuña, or other, similar animal. The coats of some animals are called 'wool,' those of others, 'hair,' and there does not seem to be any ready way to distinguish between them. Thus, we speak of *camel's hair,* though camels are ruminants (like vicuñas and yaks). Evidently, when the hair of the animal is somewhat curly, it is referred to as wool, when rather straight, as hair. *Silk* comes from silkworms, which are larvae that spin a cocoon of very fine thread; in commercial production of silk, these cocoons are unwound and the threads twisted together to form silk yarn, which is then woven into fabric. Both *cotton* and *linen* come from plants, the former from the soft, downy-white boll of a plant cultivated in warm climates, the latter from the stem of the flax plant. These are referred to as *natural fibers* (to distinguish them from *synthetic fibers* like *nylon, polyesters,* etc.) and may be used by themselves or in combination with a synthetic to improve crease resistance, water resistance, and other required characteristics.

wreak / wreck / wrack / rack

Wreak is not a common word in English except in the idioms *wreak havoc* and *wreak vengeance,* in which it means 'inflict.' *Wreck* is a common enough word meaning 'destroy.' *Wrack* is a rare word meaning 'destruction' and occurs almost exclusively in the phrase *wrack and ruin.* All three of these words are probably etymologically connected, but their precise relationship is not known. *Rack* is a variant of *wrack* and sometimes appears in its place in *wrack and ruin;* it seems also to be related to *rack* 'broken or drifting clouds,' which is cognate with Swedish *vrak* 'wreckage,' but it has nothing to do, etymologically, with *rack* 'instrument of torture.'

X chromosome / Y chromosome

The sex chromosome that carries the genes that determine femaleness in humans and in many other species is the *X chromosome.* It is larger than the *Y chromosome,* which carries the genes that determine maleness. If there are two X chromosomes, a female is produced; one X and one Y produce a male.

Yiddish / Hebrew

Yiddish and *Hebrew* are two entirely different, unrelated languages—which is not to say that they have nothing to do with one another, only that their association is similar to that between English, which is a Germanic language, and French, which is a Romance language: in each case, the former has borrowed many words from the latter. Yiddish, once the lingua franca of Jews almost everywhere, is today spoken by only a few million people, virtually none of them using it as their only means of communication. It is the official language of only one nation, Birobizhan, officially the Jewish Autonomous Region of the U.S.S.R. Yiddish belongs to the High German group of languages, along with Modern German, Bavarian, and other dialects. Although it contains many borrowings from Slavic and from Hebrew and is written in Hebrew characters, it is a Germanic language in structure and origin. It was spoken by Jews mostly in eastern Europe prior to WWII, dying out to a great extent as those people were slaughtered during the Holocaust. It survived mainly among emigrants from eastern Europe, chiefly to the United States during the latter part of the 19th and first third of the 20th centuries. Before and after WWII,

many of those Jews who could emigrated to Palestine, later Israel, but
when the state of Israel was established (1948) Hebrew was adopted
as its official language; Yiddish was regarded somewhat scornfully,
and the language brought by the immigrants suffered the same fate
at the hands of their children and grandchildren as it suffered elsewhere in the world: they have failed to perpetuate it as a living language, and the number of its speakers has diminished considerably. In
the latter 1980s, a revival of interest in Yiddish seems to bode well for
its survival, but there is no telling for how long. *Hebrew* (along with
Arabic) belongs to the Semitic branch of the Afro-Asiatic family of
languages, which is not connected in any known way with the Indo-
European family (any more than with the Sino-Tibetan, Japanese,
Malayo-Polynesian, Iroquoian, or any other unrelated family). After
the Roman siege at Masada and the mass suicide of the remnants of
organized Jewish civilization (73 A.D.), except for its use in scripture
and liturgy, Hebrew remained virtually a dead language from that
time till its revival by Israel.

zenith / nadir

These are originally technical terms applied to points on the celestial
sphere, the *zenith* being the point directly above the observer, the *nadir* the point directly below. They are used metaphorically to refer,
respectively, to the 'highest thing or goal obtainable, acme' (*Her career
reached its zenith in the 1960s*) and to the 'lowest depths reachable,
absolute bottom' (*My fortunes have reached their nadir, so I have no
place to go but up*).

zero / absolute zero

Absolute zero is the name given to the temperature (–273.15° Celsius
or –459.67° Fahrenheit) at which all motion of atoms and molecules
theoretically ceases. It is 0°Kelvin. *Zero* on the Celsius scale is the
temperature at which water freezes (equivalent to 32° Fahrenheit);
zero on the Fahrenheit scale has no particular meaning. (See also **Celsius scale / Fahrenheit scale / Kelvin scale / Réaumur scale.**)

Index

A Note on the INDEX

1. Entries in the Index appear in several forms, which ought to be distinguished:

   (a) Entries in *italics* (e.g., *burglary, burro*) are references to definitions, comments, and other information about the term itself.

   (b) Entries in roman (e.g., burglary, Caesar) are used in the text as words or illustrations but are not, necessarily, commented on. Thus, *burglary* refers the the entry **burglary /** where "*burglary*" is defined and discussed. But "burglary" is also mentioned in the entry for **homicide /** though it is not discussed there.

   (c) Entries in quotation marks in the index follow the style in the text.

2. (a) Most of the entries in the text have unique headings (e.g., **European plan / American plan, prefix / infix / suffix.** To save space, these have been shortened to include only the first term, up to and including the virgule, and thus appear in the Index as **European plan /, prefix /.**

   (b) In a few cases, however, the same term may appear as the first element in the heading of more than one entry; to avoid ambiguity, references to such entries have been extended to include the second term. Thus, there are three entries that contain "*acute*" as the first element; these are shown at the left, below, with the form in which they appear in the Index at the right:

acute / chronic	**acute / chronic**
acute / grave / circumflex / umlaut / tilde / cedilla	**acute / grave**
acute / obtuse	**acute / obtuse**

Index

advertize (Brit.)   *-ise* /
advertizement   *-ise* /
advertizement (Brit.)   *-ise* /
Aeolia   **Acadia** /
aerobic   **aerobic** /
aestivate   **estivate** /
affect   **affect** /
affectation   **affect** /
affected   **affect** /
affection   **affect** /
affective   **affect** /
Africa   **Goth** /
African wild ass   **ass** /
Afro-Asiatic family   **Yiddish** /
aft   **port** /
agave   **circadian** /
agèd   **acute** / **grave** /
agglutinating languages   **adjective** /
aggravate   **aggravate** /
agitato   **adagio** /
agnostic   **agnostic** /
agnosticism   **agnostic** /
agranulocyte   **erythrocyte** /
A horizon   **A horizon** /
AIDS   **bacteria** /
air mile   **statute mile** /
airspeed   **airspeed** /
Akhetaton   **Old Kingdom** /
Akhnaton   **Old Kingdom** /
Alabama   **North** /
à la carte   **acute** / **grave** /; **table d'hôte** /
alastrim   **chickenpox** /
Albanian   **centum** /
albeit   **all right** /
alcohol thermometer   **barometer** /
ale   **ale** /
alee   **lee** /
Alembert, d', Jean Le Rond (?1717–83)   **encyclopedia**
Alexander the Great (356–323B.C.)   **Old Kingdom** /
Alexandria   **Old Kingdom** /

Al Fayyum   **Old Kingdom** /
alias   **nom de plume** /
alif   **acute** / **grave** /
alimentary canal   **alimentary canal** /
Al Kufa   **Kufic** /
alkylamine   **histamine** /
allargando   **adagio** /
allegretto   **adagio** /
allegro   **adagio** /
allele   **dominant** /
allergy, remedy for   **histamine** /
alligator   **alligator** /
all one   **all right** /
allonym   **nom de plume** /
allopathy   **allopathy** /
alloy   **element** /
all right   **all right** /
all together   **altogether** /
allude   **allusion** /
allusion   **allusion** /
almost   **all right** /
alone   **all right** /
alpha wave or rhythm   **alpha wave** /
already   **all right** /
alright   **all right** /
alternate   **alternate** /
alternating current   **AC** /
alternative   **alternate** /
alternator   **alternator** /
-al, the suffix   **normality** /; **triumphal** /
although   **all right** /
alto   **bass** /
altogether   **altogether** /
alto-rilievo   **alto-rilievo** /
altruism, altruist   **altruism** /
alumna, alumnae   **alumnus** /
alumnus / *alumni*   **-us, words ending in**
alveolar ducts   **upper respiratory tract** /

alveolar sacs **upper respiratory tract** /
alveoli **upper respiratory tract** /
always **all right** /
AM **AM (VHF)** /
amaze **amaze** /
ambiguity **purism** /
ambrosia **nectar** /
amend **amend** /
amendment **amend** /
Amenemhet **Old Kingdom** /
Amenemhet III **Old Kingdom** /
Amenhotep **Old Kingdom** /
Amenhotep III **Old Kingdom** /
Amenophis **Old Kingdom** /
American bison **buffalo** /
American Civil War **Confederate States of America** /
AMERICANISMS **purism** /
American plan **European plan** /
American Samoa **Polynesia** /
amethyst **silica** /
amiable **amiable** /
amicable **amiable** /
amid **amid** /
amidst **amid** /
Amon **Old Kingdom** /
among **amid** /; **among** /
amongst **among** /
amongst **amid** /
amoral **amoral** /
amorphous **amoral** /
amplitude modulation **AM (VHF)** /
amuse **amuse** /
an **a** /
an-, the prefix **amoral** /
anadromous **anadromous** /
anaerobic **aerobic** /
anal canal **large intestine** /
analog, analogue **analog** /
analog computer **analog** /
analogous **analogous** /
analyse **-ise** /

analyse (Brit.) **-ise** /
analysis **analysis** /
analyst **psychologist** /
analytical **analysis** /
analyze **-ise** /
analyze, analyse **analysis** /
anapest **iamb** /
Anatolian **centum** /
Andalusia, occupied by Vandals **Vandal** /
andante **adagio** /
andantino **adagio** /
androgen **androgen** /
-androus, the suffix **diandrous** /
anechoic **amoral** /
aneroid barometer **barometer** /
anger or irascibility, seat of **black bile** /
angles **acute / obtuse**
Anglican Communion **High Mass** /; **Low Church** /
anhydrous **amoral** /
animal **animal** /
Anne, mother of Virgin Mary **Virgin Birth** /
Anne (r.1702–14) **Plantagenet** /
annoy **noisome** /
'annoy' **aggravate** /
annual **circadian** /
annual plant **herb** /
annular eclipse **lunar eclipse** /
anode **cathode** /
anomaly **amoral** /
anorexia **anorexia** /
anorexia nervosa **anorexia** /
-ant, the suffix **triumphal** /
Antarctic Circle **Arctic Circle** /
ante-, the bound form **prefix** /
ante-, the prefix **antipasto** /; **prefix** /
anterior **anterior** /
anthrax **bacteria** /
anthropology **exact science** /

anti, the free form   **prefix** /
anti-, the prefix   **prefix** /
anti-, variant of *ante-* prefix
   antipasto /
Antigua and Barbuda   **England** /
antihistamine   **histamine** /
antimatter   **matter** /
antiparticles   **matter** /
antipasto   **antipasto** /
antiperspirant   **deodorant** /
antiproton   **matter** /
antique   **antiques** /
"anti-universe"   **matter** /
antonym   **synonym** /
antonyms in dictionaries
   dictionary / **glossary** /
anvil   **anvil** /
anxious   **anxious** /
apéritif   **claret** /
apéritifs   **antipasto** /
aphasia   **amoral** /
apogee   **apogee** /
apologetics   **apologetics** /
apoplectic fit   **heart attack** /
apoplexy   **heart attack** /
aport   **port** /
apothecaries' weight (table)
   avoirdupois weight /
apothecary   **druggist** /
appetizer   **antipasto** /
apple   **abstract noun** /
Appleton layer   **troposphere** /
applied science   **exact science** /
appraise   **appraise** /; **like** /
appreciate   **deprecate** /
apprise   **like** /
apprise, apprize   **appraise** /
appropriate English   **style** /
Arabic numerals   **Roman numerals** /
Arabic script   **Kufic** /
Arachnidae   **bug** /
arachnoid   **arachnoid membrane** /
Aral Sea   **lake** /

arbiters   **referee** /
Arcadia   **Acadia** /
archaic   **archaic** /
archipelago   **Polynesia** /
architectural support   **atlas** /
arc lamp   **incandescent** /
arco   **violin** /
Arctic Circle   **Arctic Circle** /
Arctogaea   **Pangaea** /
arc welding   **braze** /
ardor, ardour   **-or** /
area rug   **carpet** /
argentum   **archaic** /
arhat   **Hinayana Buddhism** /
arhatship   **Hinayana Buddhism** /
aria   **aria** /
Aristides   **nom de plume** /
arithmetic progression
   arithmetically /
arithmetic series   **arithmetically** /
Arizona   **North** /
Arkansas   **North** /
Armenian   **centum** /
arraignment   **arraignment** /
arras   **canvaswork** /
arson   **homicide** /
Artaxerxes   **Old Kingdom** /
Art Deco   **antiques** /
Art Deco   **atlas** /
Artemis   **dryad** /
arteries, hardening of
   arteriosclerosis /
arterioles   **artery** /
arteriosclerosis   **arteriosclerosis** /
artery   **artery** /
arthropod   **bug** /
arthropod   **centipede** /
Arthropoda   **bug** /
artichoke   **artichoke** /
artificial satellites   **latitude** /
artistic language   **purism** /
Art Nouveau   **antiques** /
as   **like** /

Ascanians of Phrygia   **Ashkenazi** /
ascender   **ascender** /
ascending colon   **large intestine** /
Asdingian Vandals   **Vandal** /
A shares   **common stock** /
Ashkenaz   **Ashkenazi** /
Ashkenazi   **Ashkenazi** /
Asians invade Nile delta   **Old
  Kingdom** /
Asiatic wild ass   **ass** /
as if   **like** /
assemblage   **assemblage** /
associative law   **associative law** /
assume   **assume** /
assumption   **assume** /
Assurbanipal   **Old Kingdom** /
Assyrian conquerors of Egypt   **Old
  Kingdom** /
astarboard   **port** /
asterisk   **dagger** /
asterism   **dagger** /
asthenic   **ectomorph** /
asthenic build   **ectomorph** /
Asti spumante   **champagne** /
astronomy   **exact science** /
asymmetry   **amoral** /
-ate   **-ate** /
atheism   **agnostic** /
atheist   **agnostic** /
atherosclerosis   **arteriosclerosis** /
athletic   **ectomorph** /
atlas   **atlas** /
atman   **Buddhism** /
atoll   **atoll** /
atom   **atom** /; **nuclear** /
atom bomb   **atom bomb** /
atomic bomb   **atom bomb** /
Aton   **Old Kingdom** /
atrium of the heart   **artery** /
Attila   **Vandal** /
attributive adjectives in English
  adjective /

attributive nouns in English
  adjective /
aubade   **serenade** /
aubusson   **canvaswork** /
auction bridge   **contract bridge** /
auditory nerve   **anvil** /
au jus   **gravy** /
aurora australis   **austral** /
aurora borealis   **austral** /
Austen, Jane (1775–1817)   **style** /
austral   **austral** /
Australasia   **Polynesia** /
Australia)   **austral** /
Australia   **England** /
Austral Islands   **Polynesia** /
authoritarian   **authoritarian** /
authoritative   **authoritarian** /
authority   **authoritarian** /
autogiro, autogyro   **autogiro** /
Autumnal Equinox   **equinox** /
autumnal equinox   **Arctic Circle** /
auxesis   **auxesis** /
auxiliaries   **indicative** /
auxiliaries, use of, in English
  adjective /
ave.   **abbreviation** /
avenge   **revenge** /
averse   **adverse** /
avoirdupois weight (table)
  avoirdupois weight /
await   **wait for** / **await**
aweather   **lee** /
axon   **neuron** /

B

Babylonians   **Old Kingdom** /
bacilli   **bacteria** /
backwardation   **backwardation** /
bacteria   **bacteria** /
bacterial enzyme   **DNA** /
bacterium   **bug** /
bad   **bad** /
badly   **bad** /

baguio **cyclone** /
Bahamas, the **England** /
bait and switch **hard sell** /
baking powder **baking powder** /
baking soda **baking powder** /;
   washing soda /
balance control by the brain
   cerebrum /
balcony **balcony** /
Baltic **centum** /
band **band** /
band theory **conductor** /
Bangladesh **England** /
baptized Jews and Moors
   Ashkenazi /
Barbados **England** /
Barbieri di Seviglia, Il **grand opera** /
baritone **bass** /
bar mitzvah **bar mitzvah** /
barnacle **bug** /
Barocci, Federigo **baroque** /
barometer **barometer** /
baroque **baroque** /
baroque music **baroque** /
baroque opera **opera** /
barrel cuff **single cuff** /
barrister **barrister** /; **council** /
base **DNA** /
baseball **game** /
base metal **base metal** /
basketball **game** /
bas mitzvah **bar mitzvah** /
basophil **erythrocyte** /
bas relief **alto-rilievo** /
bass **ale** /; **bass** /
basso cantante **bass** /
basso profondo **bass** /
basso-rilievo **alto-rilievo** /
bass viol **violin** /
bathyal zone **littoral** /
bat mitzvah **bar mitzvah** /
battery (terminals) **cathode** /
baud **bit** /

Baudot, J.M.E. (1845–1903) **bit** /
Bavarian **High German** /
bay **cape** /
beam **beam** /
beam-riding guidance **inertial**
   guidance /
bear **bull** /
bearish **bull** /
bear market **bull** /
beat for *beaten* **bad** /
Beaufort Scale **breeze** /; **cyclone** /
Beaufort, Sir Francis (1774–1857)
   breeze /
Beaujolais **claret** /
Beaujolais nouveau **claret** /
beauty **abstract noun** /
beauty salon **salon** /
bee **wasp** /
beer **ale** /
beer **fructose** /
behavioral psychology **psychologist** /
Belgian endive **chicory** /
Belgravia **freehold** /
Belize **England** /
Bell, Acton **nom de plume** /
Bell, Currer **nom de plume** /
Bell, Ellis **nom de plume** /
Bellini, Vincenzo (1801–35) **opera** /
belovèd **acute** / **grave** /
belvedere **belvedere** /
bemuse **amuse** /
Bentham, Jeremy (1748–1832)
   utopia /
Beowulf **dramatic poetry** /;
   purism /; **style** /
Bergama **parchment** /
bergère **bergère** /
Berlin **enclave** /
Berlioz, Hector (1803–69) **opera** /
Bermudan rig **gaff rig** /
Bermudan-rigged sloop **sloop** /
Bermudian rig **gaff rig** /
Bernstein, Leonard (b.1918) **opera** /

berry sugar **icing sugar** /
beside **beside** /
besides **beside** /
best **good** /
beta wave or rhythm **alpha wave** /
better **best** /; **good** /
better than **better than** /
between **among** /; **singular** /
between a rock and a hard place
  Scylla /
between Scylla and Charybdis
  Scylla /
betwixt **singular** /
B horizon **A horizon** /
bi-, the prefix **bi-** /; **bisect** /
Bible **metaphor** /
bicameral governmental structure
  lower house /
bicarbonate of soda **baking**
  powder /
bicarbonate of sodium **washing**
  soda /
biconvex **concave** /
biennially **bi-** /
bigamy **monogamy** /
big band **band** /
big bang theory **big bang theory** /
Big Dipper **austral** /
billiards **billiards** /
billion **billion** /
bimetallic thermometer **barometer** /
bimonthly **bi-** /
binary notation **bit** /
binaural **monophonic** /
"biological clock" **circadian** /
biology **exact science** /
bionomics **ecology** /
bird migration **circadian** /
Birobizhan **Yiddish** /
bisect **bisect** /
Bismarck Archipelago **Polynesia** /
bit **bit** /
bite **wasp** /

bitter **ale** /
biweekly **bi-** /
Bizet, Georges (1838–75) **grand**
  opera /
black belt **white belt** /
black bile **black bile** /
black-footed ferret **ferret** /
black lies **lie** / **fib** /
Blackshirts **Blackshirts** /
blind embossing **intaglio** /
blood **black bile** /
blood pressure, normal **diastole** /
blood transfusion **donor** /
blood type **Rh-negative** /
blood vessels **artery** /
blue **Blue** /
blue belt **white belt** /
blue-collar workers or *jobs* **blue**
  collar /
board fence **fence** /
board game **game** /
boards **sewn binding** /
boat **boat** /
boatel **hotel** /
boat house **boat** /
boat rudder fittings **gudgeon** /
bodhisattva **Hinayana Buddhism** /
body temperature **cold-blooded** /
body types **ectomorph** /
boiling point of water **Fahrenheit**
  scale /
Bolshevik **Bolshevism** /
Bolshevism **Bolshevism** /
bolt **bolt** /
bond **bond** /
bone china) **china** /
bookbinding **folio** /
book bindings **sewn binding** /
book pages **page** /
book sizes **folio** /
book value **book value** /
Bordeaux **claret** /
boreal **austral** /

borough   *city* /
Boston / Washington, D.C.   *city* /
Bosworth Field, Battle of   *red rose* /
botany   *exact science* /
both   *each* /; *singular* /
Botswana   *England* /
bottles of wine   *magnum* /
botulism   *bacteria* /
Boulder Dam   *lake* /
bound form   *bound form* /
bound forms   *prefix* /
Bourgogne   *claret* /
bowl for mixing   *krater* /
bowls   *game* /
boyfriend   *lover* /
braces   *parentheses* /
brackets   *parentheses* /
bradycardia   *bradycardia* /
brahman   *Buddhism* /
brain   *gray matter* /
brain wave   *alpha wave* /
brandy   *brandy* /
Brass   *brass* /
brass band   *band* /
brassie   *iron* / *wood*
Braze   *braze* /
breed   *phylum* /
breve mark   *acute* / *grave* /
Brewer, E. Cobham (1810–97)
    QWERTY keyboard /
bridge   *contract bridge* /
bring   *bring* /
Britain   *Roman Empire* /
British Commonwealth of Nations
    England /
British Isles   *England* /
British Labour Party   *red rose* /
British Summer Time   *Greenwich*
    Mean Time /
Britten, Benjamin (1913–76)   *opera* /
Broad Church   *Low Church* /
bronchi   *upper respiratory tract* /

bronchioles   *upper respiratory*
    tract /
Bronstein, Lev Davidovich
    Bolshevism /
Brontë, Anne (1820–49)   *nom de*
    plume /
Brontë, Charlotte (1816–55)   *nom*
    de plume /
Brontë, Emily (1818–48)   *nom de*
    plume /
Bronx, (the)   *city* /
bronze   *brass* /
brook   *river* /
Brooklyn   *city* /
brown belt   *white belt* /
Browning, Robert (1812–89)
    dramatic poetry /
Brownshirts   *Blackshirts* /
Buddhism   *Buddhism* /
Buddhism   *Hinayana Buddhism* /
budgerigar   *budgerigar* /
budgie   *budgerigar* /
buffalo   *buffalo* /
bug   *bug* /
bulimia   *anorexia* /
bulimia nervosa   *anorexia* /
bulimorexia   *anorexia* /
bulkheading   *dock* /
bull   *bull* /
bull boat   *boat* /
bulldog edition   *edition* /
bullion   *species* /
bullish   *bull* /
bull market   *bull* /
bumblebee   *wasp* /
bumboat   *boat* /
burgh   *city* /
-*burgh*, names ending in   *city* /
burglar   *burglary* /
burglary   *burglary* /
burglary   *homicide* /
burgundy   *claret* /
burlesque   *high comedy* /

burro **ass** /
burst binding **sewn binding** /
Bush **bush** /
business enterprise **corporation** /
business proposition **proposal** /
butterfly **butterfly** /
byte **bit** /
by the lee **lee** /

C

cabaña **acute** / **grave** /
cacotopia **utopia** /
caecum **large intestine** /
Caesar, Julius (?100–44 B.C.) **Julian**
    calendar /; **Vandal** /
caiman **alligator** /
calfskin **parchment** /
California **North** /
call **put** /
calla lily **tiger lily** /
call option **put** /
calm **breeze** /
Calorie **calorie** /
Calthorpe purse **gros point** /
caltrop **dock** /
Cambridge University **Oxbridge** /
Cambyses **Old Kingdom** /
camel's hair **wool** /
Canada **England** /
canapé **antipasto** /
can buoy **can buoy** /
candy (or candied) sugar **icing**
    sugar /
Canidae as family **phylum** /
canine **incisor** /
Canis as genus **phylum** /
cannons **gun** /
cantata **aria** /
Canterbury Tales, The **purism** /
cantò **acute** / **grave** /
canvaswork **canvaswork** /; **gros**
    point /
cape **cape** /

Cape buffalo **buffalo** /
capillary **artery** /
capital letter **ascender** /
Captain Brassbound's Confession
    literally /
carapace **tortoise** /
carat **carat** /
caravanserai **hotel** /
caravel **carvel-built** /
carbohydrates **fructose** /
carburetor **diesel engine** /
Carchemish, battle of **Old**
    Kingdom /
card game **game** /
cardigan **cardigan** /
cardinal **cardinal** /
caret **carat** /
Carlovingian **Merovingian** /
Carmen **grand opera** /
Carnarvon, Lord **Old Kingdom** /
carnivore **carnivore** /
carnivores (Carnivora) as order
    phylum /
Caroline Islands **Polynesia** /
Carolingian **Merovingian** /
carom billiards **billiards** /
carpenter bee **wasp** /
carpet **carpet** /
carpet knight **carpet** /
Carter, Howard (1873–1939) **Old**
    Kingdom /
Carthage **Vandal** /
carvel **carvel-built** /
carvel-built **carvel-built** /
caryatid **atlas** /
case law **civil law** /
casement window **mullion** /
casing-in **sewn binding** /
Caspian Sea **lake** /
caster **icing sugar** /
caster sugar **icing sugar** /
casting **casting** /
cast iron **iron** / **steel; pig iron** /

catadromous **anadromous** /
catboat **sloop** /
cathode **cathode** /
cathode-ray tube **cathode** /
caustic soda **washing soda** /
cave paintings **Paleolithic** /
cease and desist **flotsam** /
cecum **large intestine** /
cedilla **acute** / **grave** /
celestial sphere **Tropic of Cancer** /; **zenith** /
cello **violin** /
cellulose **fructose** /
Celsius **zero** /
Celsius-Fahrenheit conversion formula **constant** /; **Fahrenheit scale** /
Celsius scale **Fahrenheit scale** /
Celtic **centum** /
centerboard trunk **centerboard** /
centigrade scale **Fahrenheit scale** /
centipede **bug** /; **centipede** /
Central Time Zone **Greenwich Mean Time** /
centrifugal force **centrifugal force** /
centripetal force **centrifugal force** /
centum languages **centum** /
century plant **circadian** /
ceramic ware **china** /
cerebellum **cerebrum** /
cerebral hemispheres **cerebrum** /
cerebrum **cerebrum** /
ceremony **Low Church** /
chain printer **dot-matrix printer** /
Châlons-sur-Marne **Vandal** /
chamber orchestra **band** /
Champagne **champagne** /
characteristic **characteristic** /
Charlemagne (742–814) **Goth** /; **Merovingian** /; **Roman Empire** /
Charles I (r.1625-49) **Plantagenet** /
Charles II (r.1660–85) **Plantagenet** /
Charterhouse **private school** /

Charybdis **Scylla** /
Chaucer, Geoffrey (?1340–1400) **style** /
Chelsea **city** /
chemical bond **element** /
chemist **druggist** /
chemistry **exact science** /
chemist's (shop) **druggist** /
Cheops **Old Kingdom** /
Chephren **Old Kingdom** /
chest of drawers **highboy** /
chianti **claret** /
chickenpox **chickenpox** /
chicory **chicory** /
china **china** /
China **Hinayana Buddhism** /
chlorate **-ate** /
chloric **-ate** /
chlorite **-ate** /
chlorous **-ate** /
cholesterol **arteriosclerosis** /
Chordata as phylum **phylum** /
C horizon **A horizon** /
chorus / *choruses* **-us, words ending in**
chowder **New England chowder** /
Christ, birth of **Virgin Birth** /
Christian church, relationships of **apologetics** /
Christian errors, refutation of **apologetics** /
Christian faith, defense of **apologetics** /
Christian unity, securing of **apologetics** /
chromosomes **DNA** /
chronic **acute** / **chronic**
chronometer **Greenwich Mean Time** /; **latitude** /
Church Latin **classic** /
Church of the Latter-day Saints **monogamy** /
cimarrón **acute** / **grave** /

cimetidine *histamine /*
cinnamon *herb /*
circadian *circadian /*
circumflex accent *acute / grave /*
circumflex, inverted *acute / grave /*
Cirta *Vandal /*
citations in dictionaries *dictionary /*
   glossary /
citations in the *OED* *normality /*
città *acute / grave /*
City of London *city /*
civil law *civil law /*
claret *claret /*
classic *classic /*
Classical *classic /*
Classical Arabic *classic /*
classical art *classic /*
classical education *classic /*
Classical Greek *classic /*
Classical Latin *classic /*
classical music *classic /*
classic example *classic /*
classics, the *classic /*
clean bomb *atom bomb /*
cleek *iron / wood*
clichés *metaphor /*
climatology *exact science /*
clinical psychology *psychologist /*
clinker-built, clincher-built *carvel-built /*
close company *corporation /*
close corporation *corporation /*
closed corporation *corporation /*
closed shop *open shop /*
closely held corporation
   corporation /
Clovis I (465–511) *Goth /;*
   Merovingian /
club soda *club soda /*
clubs used in golf *iron / wood*
coastline, features of *cape /*
Coast, the *North /*
cocci *bacteria /*

coccus / cocci **-us, words ending in**
cochlea *anvil /*
cocker spaniel as breed *phylum /*
C.O.D. *abbreviation /*
Cognac *brandy /*
cognate *doublet /*
cold-blooded *cold-blooded /*
cold front *cold front /*
cold, remedy for *histamine /*
cold type typesetting *hot metal /*
Coleridge, Samuel Taylor (1772–1834)
   dramatic poetry /; either .. or /
coliseum *coliseum /*
colisseum *coliseum /*
collage *assemblage /*
collectible, collectable *antiques /*
collective nouns *singular /*
college *college /*
colloid *element /*
colloidal solution *element /*
colloquial *colloquial /*
colloquy *colloquial /*
cologne *perfume /*
colon *large intestine /*
colophon *colophon /*
Colorado *North /*
coloration *-or /*
coloratura soprano *bass /*
color, colour *-or /*
colt *colt /*
Columbia University *freehold /*
column *beam /*
combination *band /*
combo *band /*
come about *lee /*
comedy of manners *high comedy /*
comet *comet /*
comic opera *grand opera /*
command guidance *inertial*
   guidance /
command paper *green paper /*
commas *parentheses /*

comminuted fracture **simple fracture** /
common **common** /
common law **civil law** /
common share **common stock** /
Commons, House of **House of Commons** /
common stock **common stock** /
Commonwealth of Nations **England** /
communication **purism** /
communism **Bolshevism** /
commutative law **associative law** /
company **corporation** /
comparative **positive** /
comparative linguistics **linguistics** /
comparative of adjectives in English **adjective** /
comparative philology **linguistics** /
compare **compare** /
comparison **compare** /
comparison of adjectives **conjugation** /
comparison of adjectives **positive** /
compass north **true north** /
compass reading **true north** /
compensatory damages **compensatory damages** /
complement **compliment** /
complex **complex** /
complex fraction **integer** /; **simple fraction** /
complex sentence **simple sentence** /
complex sentence **main clause** /
complicate **complex** /
complicated **complex** /
complication **complex** /
compliment **compliment** /
compose **compose** /
composed of **compose** /
compound **element** /; **nuclear** /
compound **atom** /
compound-complex sentence **simple sentence** /

compound-complex sentence **main clause** /
compound fraction **simple fraction** /
compound fracture **simple fracture** /
compound preposition **due to** /
compound sentence **simple sentence** /
compound sentence **main clause** /
compounds with carbon **organic** /
compounds without carbon **organic** /
comprise **compose** /
comprised of **compose** /
computer equipment **hardware** /
computer programs **hardware** /
concave **concave** /
concavo-concave **concave** /
concavo-convex **concave** /
concertina **accordion** /
concertmaster **concertmaster** /
concerto **symphony** /
concrete noun **abstract noun** /
CONDEMNED NEOLOGISMS **purism** /
conditional statements **indicative** /
condominium **cooperative** /
conduction band **conductor** /
conductor, extrinsic **conductor** /
conductor, n-type **conductor** /
conductor, p-type **conductor** /
conductor (electrical) **conductor** /
conductor (musical) **concertmaster** /
confectioner's sugar **icing sugar** /
Confederacy, the **Confederate States of America** /
Confederate army **Blue** /
Confederate States of America **Confederate States of America** /
Congress **lower house** /
Congressmen **House of Representatives** /

Congress of the United States
   House of Representatives /
conjugation of verbs **conjugation** /
conjunction **main clause** /
conjunctive adverb **main clause** /
Connecticut **North** /
connotation **connotation** /;
   metaphor /
conserve **jam** /
consistent with **due to** /
consonant **consonant** /
consonant **diphthong** /; **phonetics** /
Constable, John (1776–1837)
   idealism /
constant **constant** /; **continuous** /
Constantinople, tribute exacted by
   Huns **Vandal** /
constant of gravitation **gravitation** /
constitutional law **civil law** /
constitutional referendum **initiative** /
consul **embassy** /
consulate **embassy** /
contact flight **contact landing** /
contact landing **contact landing** /
contagious magic **contagious**
   magic /
contango **backwardation** /
contempt **contemptible** /
contemptible **contemptible** /
contemptuous **contemptible** /
continual **continuous** /
continuant **consonant** /; **phonetics** /
continuo **violin** /
continuous **continuous** /
contract bridge **contract bridge** /
contraction of heart muscles
   diastole /
contralto **bass** /
contrary-to-fact statements
   indicative /
contrast **compare** /
conurbation **city** /
convalescent home **rest home** /

convergent evolution **convergent**
   evolution /
convergent series **convergent**
   series /
conversational language **colloquial** /
conversion of Celsius to Fahrenheit
   Fahrenheit scale /
conversion of Fahrenheit to Celsius
   Fahrenheit scale /
convex **concave** /
convexo-concave **concave** /
convexo-convex **concave** /
conviction **convince** /
convince **convince** /; **like** /
Cook Islands **Polynesia** /
coöperate **acute** / **grave** /
cooperative **cooperative** /
copyright **copyright** /
coral reef **atoll** /
cordonazo **cyclone** /
coronary **heart attack** /
coronary arteries **artery** /
coronary thrombosis **heart attack** /
corporation **common stock** /;
   corporation /
corpus callosum **cerebrum** /
corpus luteum **endocrine** /
Corvidae **crow** /
Corvus **crow** /
cosine **sine** /
costa **acute** / **grave** /
côte **acute** / **grave** /
cotton **wool** /
cottontail **hare** /
council **council** /
councillor **council** /
councilor **council** /
counsel **council** /
counsellor **council** /
counselor-at-law **council** /
count noun **count noun** /
count noun **fewer** /
country mile **statute mile** /

county **city** /
couplet **Shakespearian sonnet** /
cove **cape** /
cowpox **chickenpox** /
coy / quiet **doublet** /
crab **bug** /
cranial nerves **cranial nerves**
cranial nerves, mnemonics for
names **cranial nerves**
crash boat **boat** /
crater **krater** /
crawdaddy **crayfish** /
crawfish **crayfish** /
crayfish **crayfish** /
cream of tartar **baking powder** /
cream sherry **claret** /
Creasy, Sir Edward (1812–78) **Old
Kingdom** /
creek **river** /
crepuscular **butterfly** /
cricket **game** /
Crimean War **set-in sleeve** /
criminal homicide **homicide** /
criminal law **civil law** /
criminal libel **libel** /
critic **criticism** /
criticism **criticism** /
criticize **criticism** /
critique **criticism** /
crocodile **alligator** /
Crocodilia **alligator** /
crocodilians **alligator** /
cromlech **cromlech** /
crow **crow** /
crustacean **bug** /
crustacean **crayfish** /
crystal **crystal** /
crystal ball **crystal** /
crystal-gazing **crystal** /
crystallized quartz **crystal** /
cuckold **cuckold** /
Cufic **Kufic** /
cultivation of land **Paleolithic** /

cultural development, earliest human
Paleolithic /
cum dividend **cum dividend** /
cum laude **cum laude** /
cunt **informal** /
curly brackets **parentheses** /
currency **monetary** /
cursèd **acute / grave** /
Cushite peoples in Egypt **Old
Kingdom** /
cut a rug **carpet** /
cutter **sloop** /
-cy, the suffix **normality** /
cyclone **cyclone** /
cyclonic activity **cyclone** /
cyclopedia, cyclopaedia
encyclopedia /
Cynic **Cynic** /
cynical **Cynic** /
Cyprus **England** /
cytoplasm **DNA** /
cytosine **DNA** /
Częstochowa) **acute / grave** /

D

dactyl **iamb** /
dactylic hexameter **iamb** /
dado **dado** /
dagger **dagger** /
daggerboard **centerboard** /
dais / dish / disk **doublet** /
daisy-wheel printer **dot-matrix
printer** /
damn **informal** /
dance band **band** /
dancing saloon **salon** /
Daphnis **Acadia** /
Daphnis and Chloe, Longos **Acadia** /
Darwin, Charles (1809–82)
convergent evolution /
dashes **parentheses** /
data **data** /
data processing **data** /

datum **data** /
Daylight Saving Time **Greenwich Mean Time** /
day lily **tiger lily** /
DC **AC** /
Dead Sea **lake** /
debenture **bond** /
decapod **bug** /
decapod **crayfish** /
Decapoda **bug** /
deciduous **deciduous** /
deciduous teeth **deciduous** /
decigram **avoirdupois weight** /
deck **balcony** /
declarative statements (or questions) **indicative** /
declension **conjugation** /
decorator **refurnish** /
decry **decry** /
Deep South **North** /
defamatory statements **libel** /
definiendum **definiens** /
definiens **definiens** /
definition **definiens** /
definitions in dictionaries **dictionary** / **glossary** /
Delaware **North** /
delta wave or rhythm **alpha wave** /
Demerara sugar **icing sugar** /
demi- **demi-** /
demibastion **demi-** /
-demic, the suffix **endemic** /
demicannon **demi-** /
demiculverin **demi-** /
demilune **demi-** /
demimonde **demi-** /
dendrite **neuron** /
denominator **numerator** /
denotation **connotation** /
denotative **metaphor** /
deodorant **deodorant** /
deoxyribonucleic acid **DNA** /
deoxyribose **DNA** /

dependent clause **main clause** /
depository, depositary **depository** /
deprecate **deprecate** /
depreciate **deprecate** /
depth of focus **focal-plane shutter** /
descender **ascender** /
descending colon **large intestine** /
descriptive modifier **descriptive modifier** /
descriptivist **purism** /
descry **decry** /
design patent **copyright** /
desinence **prefix** /
desoxyribonucleic acid **DNA** /
despise **hate** /
destroço **acute** / **grave** /
determinative modifier **descriptive modifier** /
deuterogamy **monogamy** /
deviation **mean deviation** /; **true north** /
dew point **humidity** /
dextrose **fructose** /
di-, the prefix **bisect** /
dia-, the prefix **bisect** /
diacritical marks **acute** / **grave** /
diadromous **anadromous** /
diaeresis **acute** / **grave** /
diagnose **diagnosis** /
diagnosis **diagnosis** /
dialect **phonetics** /
dialectal **dialectal** /
dialectic **dialectal** /
dialectical **dialectal** /
Diana **Acadia** /
diandrous **diandrous** /
diastole **diastole** /
dice **game** /
Dickens, Charles (1812–70) **common** /; **who** / **whom**
diclinous **dioecious** /

dictatorship of the proletariat
  Bolshevism /
dictionaries **abridged** /
dictionaries, preparation of
  lexicography /
dictionary **dictionary** /
  encyclopedia; dictionary /
  glossary /
Dictionary of Phrase & Fable
  QWERTY keyboard /
Diderot, Denis (1713–84)
  encyclopedia /
dieresis **acute** / **grave** /
diesel-electric engine **diesel engine** /
diesel engine **diesel engine** /
diesel engine **internal**
  combustion /
die stamping **casting** /
different from **different from** /;
  style /
different than **different from** /;
  style /
different to **different from** /; **style** /
digamy **monogamy** /
digestive tube **alimentary canal** /
digger wasp **wasp** /
digit **integer** /
digital **analog** /
digital computer **analog** /
digraph **diphthong** /
dilatation **dilatation** /
dilate **dilatation** /
dilation **dilatation** /
dimeter **iamb** /
diode **conductor** /
dioecious **dioecious** /
diphthong **diphthong** /
direct current **AC** /
direct mail **direct mail** /
direct proportion **inverse**
  proportion /
direct quotation **parentheses** /
dis-, the prefix **bisect** /; **distrust** /

disaccharide **fructose** /
discover **discover** /
discreet **discreet** /
discrete **discreet** /
discreteness **discreet** /
discretion **discreet** /
disingenuous **ingenious** /
disinterested **disinterested** /; **like** /
dispensing optician **oculist** /
dispersal of data **mean deviation** /
dissect **bisect** /
distaff side **distaff side** /
distinctive feature **consonant** /
distinctive features **phonetics** /
distortion **lie** / **fib** /
distrait, distraite **distraught** /
distraught **distraught** /
distributive law **associative law** /
distrust **distrust** /
diurnal **butterfly** /; **circadian** /;
  nocturnal /
divergent evolution **convergent**
  evolution /
divergent series **convergent series** /
dividend **bond** /
dividend payment **cum dividend** /
D-layer **troposphere** /
DNA **DNA** /
DNA, mitochondrial **convergent**
  evolution /
DNA, nuclear **convergent**
  evolution /
dog, domestication of **Paleolithic** /
dolman sleeve **set-in sleeve** /
dolmen **cromlech** /
domestication of animals
  Paleolithic /
dominant **dominant** /
Dominica **England** /
Don Juanism **nymphomania** /
donkey **ass** /
Donne, John (1573–1631) **who** /
  whom

donor **donor** /
doping **conductor** /
Doria **Acadia** /
dorsal **anterior** /
dot-matrix printer **dot-matrix
   printer** /
double-bass viol **violin** /
Double (British) Summer Time
   Greenwich Mean Time /
double cuff **single cuff** /
double-dagger **dagger** /
"double helix" **DNA** /
double sugar **fructose** /
doublet **doublet** /
doublet **-us, words ending in**
doublet, example of **-us, words
   ending in**
downbeat **downbeat** /
downstage **upstage** /
downtown **city** /
downwind **lee** /
dramatic irony **irony** /
dramatic poetry **dramatic poetry** /
dramatic soprano **bass** /
drawing **casting** /
dreamboat **boat** /
dressing **gravy** /
drinking cup **krater** /
drink of the gods **nectar** /
driver **iron** / **wood**
driving iron **iron** / **wood**
drop forging **casting** /
druggist **druggist** /
drugstore **druggist** /
dryad **dryad** /
dry cell (terminals) **cathode** /
dry recitative **aria** /
D.S.O. **abbreviation** /
dual **singular** /
ductless gland **endocrine** /
Dudevant, Lucile Aurore Dupin
   (1804–76) **nom de plume** /
due to **due to** /

du nord **austral** /
duodecimo **folio** /
duodenum **large intestine** /
duopsony **monopsony** /
duplicate bridge **contract bridge** /
dura mater **arachnoid membrane** /
dura mater encephali **arachnoid
   membrane** /
dura mater spinalis **arachnoid
   membrane** /
Dutch **High German** /
Dvorak, August (1894–d.?)
   QWERTY keyboard /
Dvorak keyboard **QWERTY
   keyboard** /
dwarf **dwarf** /
dynamism **dynamism** /
dynamo **alternator** /
dysphemism **euphemism** /
dystopia **utopia** /
Dzhugashvili, Iosif V. **Bolshevism** /

E

each **each** /
eager **anxious** /
ear **anvil** /
eardrum **anvil** /
Early Modern English **purism** /
earthenware **china** /
earthenware and textiles,
   development of **Paleolithic** /
earth science **exact science** /
East **North** /; **orient** /
East Coast **North** /
Eastern Time Zone **Greenwich
   Mean Time** /
East Germany **East Germany** /
East Germany **enclave** /
eating disorders **anorexia** /
eau de Cologne **perfume** /
ebb tide **ebb tide** /
eclipse **lunar eclipse** /
ecliptic **Tropic of Cancer** /

ecology **ecology** /
economic **economic** /
economical **economic** /
economic rent **economic** /
economic zone **economic** /
ectoderm **ectoderm** /;
   endothelium /
ectoderm **ectomorph** /
ectomorph **ectomorph** /
Edison, Thomas Alva (1847–1931)
   incandescent /
edition **edition** /
educationalist **educator** /
educational psychology
   psychologist /
educationist **educator** /
educator **educator** /
Edward I (r.1272–1307)
   Plantagenet /
Edward II (r.1307–27) **Plantagenet** /
Edward III, (r.1327–77)
   Plantagenet /; **red rose** /
Edward IV (r.1461–70, 1471–83)
   Plantagenet /; **red rose** /
Edward V (r.1483) **Plantagenet** /;
   red rose /
Edward VI (r.1547–53)
   Plantagenet /
Edward VII (r.1901–10)
   Plantagenet /
Edward VIII (r.1936) **Plantagenet** /
eel spawning **anadromous** /
effect **affect** /
effective **affect** /; **effective** /
effectual **effective** /
effeminate **effeminate** /
effete **effeminate** /
efficacious **effective** /
efficient **effective** /
ego **egoist** /
egoism, egoist **altruism** /; **egoist** /
egotism, egotist **egoist** /
Egypt **Old Kingdom** /

Egyptian motifs **atlas** /
eightmo **folio** /
eirenics **apologetics** /
either **each** /; **either .. or** /;
   singular /
either .. or **either .. or** /
élan vital **dynamism** /
E-layer **troposphere** /
electric **electric** /
electrical **electric** /
electrode **cathode** /
electrolytic cell (terminals)
   cathode /
electron **nuclear** /
electronic **electric** /
electronics **electric** /
element **element** /; **nuclear** /
element **atom** /
elementary particle **nuclear fission** /
elephant gun **gun** /
elevation **elevation** /
Elizabeth I (r.1558–1603)
   Plantagenet /
Elizabeth II (r.1952–) **Plantagenet** /
Elizabethan sonnet **Shakespearian**
   sonnet /
ellipsis **parentheses** /
embassy **embassy** /
embolism **embolus** /
embolus **embolus** /; **heart attack** /;
   -us, words ending in
embryonic cell layers **ectoderm** /
emend **amend** /
emendation **amend** /
emigrant **emigrate** /
emigrate **emigrate** /
emigré **emigrate** /
emotion **cerebrum** /
emotions and passion, seat of
   black bile /
empty state **conductor** /
enclave **enclave** /

encyclopedia **dictionary** /
  encyclopedia
encyclopedia, encyclopaedia
  encyclopedia /
Encyclopédie **encyclopedia** /
endemic **endemic** /
ending **prefix** /
endings of nouns, adjectives, verbs
  adjective /
endive **chicory** /
endocarditis **bacteria** /
endocrine gland **endocrine** /
endoderm **ectoderm** /;
  endothelium /
endoderm **ectomorph** /
endogenous **endogenous** /
endomorph **ectomorph** /
endoskeleton **endoskeleton** /
endothelium **endothelium** /
energy **kinetic energy** /
enervate **enervate** /
Enfield rifle **gun** /
Engels, Friedrich (1820–95)
  Bolshevism /
engine **motor** /
engineering **exact science** /
engine of torture **motor** /
engine of war **motor** /
England **England** /
English **High German** /
English and Latin compared
  adjective /
English royal families **Plantagenet** /
English sonnet **Shakespearian
  sonnet** /
English Usage **purism** /
English usage **style** /
English yard **statute mile** /
ennui **noisome** /
ensemble **band** /
enteric fever **typhoid** /
enter into a state of matrimony
  marriage /

enter left **upstage** /
entoderm **ectoderm** /;
  endothelium /
entoderm **ectomorph** /
environment **ecology** /
environmental studies **exact
  science** /
Eolithic **Paleolithic** /
eosinophil **erythrocyte** /
ephemeris **latitude** /
epic poetry **dramatic poetry** /
epidemic **endemic** /
epilepsy **grand mal** /
epileptic seizure **grand mal** /
epinephrine **endocrine** /
Epipaleolithic **Paleolithic** /
epiphytotic **endemic** /
episcopal church government **Low
  Church** /
epithelium **endothelium** /
epizootic **endemic** /
Epstein, Joseph (b.1937) **nom de
  plume** /
equable **equable** /
equator **latitude** /
equilateral triangle **scalene** /
equinox **equinox** /
equinoxes, precession of the **Julian
  calendar** /
equitable **equable** /
equity law **civil law** /
Erechtheum **atlas** /
erotic **exotic** /
erotica **obscene** /
erythroblastosis **Rh-negative** /
erythrocyte **erythrocyte** /
escarole **chicory** /
esophagus **alimentary canal** /
esters **-ate** /
estivate **estivate** /
estradiol **androgen** /
estrogen **androgen** /; **endocrine** /
estrus **circadian** /

estuary **river** /
ETAION SHRDLU **QWERTY keyboard** /
ETAISONHRDLU **QWERTY keyboard** /
etc. **abbreviation** /
ethanolamine **histamine** /
Ethiopian peoples in Egypt **Old Kingdom** /
ethmoidal air cells **upper respiratory tract** /
ethylenediamine **histamine** /
Etna **atoll** /
Eton **private school** /
être **acute** / **grave** /
etymologies in dictionaries **dictionary** / **glossary** /
etymology **lexicography** /
euphemism **euphemism** /
euphemisms **lie** / **fib** /
Euphues **euphemism** /
Euphues and His England **euphemism** /
Euphues, the Anatomy of Wit **euphemism** /
euphuism **euphemism** /
European plan **European plan** /
Europe, invasion of by Huns **Vandal** /
evangelicalism **Low Church** /
Evangeline, Henry Wadsworth Longfellow **Acadia** /
evergreen **deciduous** /
evil **abstract noun** /; **good** /
exact science **exact science** /
EXAGGERATION AS SLANG **purism** /
'exasperate' **aggravate** /
excessive use of sounds **iotacism** /
exchange rate **monetary** /
exclave **enclave** /
exclusive economic zone **economic** /
ex dividend **cum dividend** /

Executive branch **House of Representatives** /
exemplary damages **compensatory damages** /
exeunt right **upstage** /
exocrine gland **endocrine** /
exogenous **endogenous** /
exoskeleton **endoskeleton** /; **tortoise** /
exosphere **troposphere** /
exotic **exotic** /
exotic dancer **exotic** /
experimental psychology **psychologist** /
explode **explode** /
explosive **explode** /
exponential progression **arithmetically** /
exponential series **arithmetically** /
expression, mode of **informal** /
extemporaneous **extemporaneous** /
external combustion **internal combustion** /
extravert **extrovert** /
extrinsic semiconductor **conductor** /
extrovert **extrovert** /
extrusion molding **casting** /

F

fabrication **lie** / **fib** /
face value **book value** /
facial nerve **cranial nerves**
Fahrenheit **zero** /
Fahrenheit-Celsius conversion formula **constant** /; **Fahrenheit scale** /
Fahrenheit scale **Fahrenheit scale** /
fall **toupee** /
false hair **toupee** /
falsehood **lie** / **fib** /
falsetto **bass** /
farce **high comedy** /
farming society **Paleolithic** /

farther **farther** /
Far West **North** /
fascists **Blackshirts** /
fauteuil **bergère** /
faze **faze** /
fear **abstract noun** /
Federal Republic of Germany **East Germany** /
Federal Republic of Germany **enclave** /
Federal Union **Confederate States of America** /
Federated States of Micronesia **Polynesia** /
fee simple **freehold** /
fee tail **freehold** /
feeze **faze** /
female **feminine** /
femaleness **X chromosome** /
female side of a family **distaff side** /
feminine **effeminate** /; **feminine** /
feminine rhyme **feminine rhyme** /
feminism, feminist **feminine** /
fence **fence** /
fenestra ovalis **anvil** /
fenestra vestibuli **anvil** /
ferric **-ic** /
ferrous **-ic** /
fertility rites **rite** /
fetch **bring** /
fewer, comparative of *few* **fewer** /
fewest, superlative of *few* **fewer** /
few, positive of *fewer, fewest* **fewer** /
fib **lie** / **fib** /
fibula **fibula** /
fiction, works of **novel** /
fiddle **violin** /
FIFO **FIFO** /
Fifteen Decisive Battles of the World **Old Kingdom** /
fighting words **lie** / **fib** /

figuratively **literally** /; **metaphor** /
figure **integer** /
figures of speech **metaphor** /
Fiji **England** /; **Polynesia** /
filariasis **endemic**
filet **filet** /
filet mignon **filet** /
filled gold **solid gold** /
fillet **filet** /
filly **colt** /
finance and financial matters **monetary** /
finches, fourteen species of **convergent evolution** /
fine Italian hand **italic** /
fine Italic hand **italic** /
Finnegans Wake **neologism** /
fiord **river** /
firearm **gun** /
firebrandism **neologism** /
fireworks **turboprop** /
firm **corporation** /
firmware **hardware** /
first **first** /
first degree murder **homicide** /
first-in, first-out **FIFO** /
First Intermediate Period **Old Kingdom** /
first mortgage **first mortgage** /
first violinist **concertmaster** /
firth **cape** /
fiscal **monetary** /
fiscal policies **monetary** /
fish or *fishes* **fish** /
fission **nuclear fission** /
fission bomb **atom bomb** /
fission reaction **nuclear fission** /
fizzy drink. **washing soda** /
fjord **river** /
flammable **inflammable** /
flatware **flatware** /
flaunt **flaunt** /
flax **wool** /

F-layer *troposphere* /
Flemish *High German* /
Flemish drapery *canvaswork* /
floating dock *dock* /
floating pier *dock* /
floating wharf *dock* /
flood tide *ebb tide* /
Florida *North* /
flotsam and jetsam *flotsam* /
flout *flaunt* /
flowering *circadian* /
fluid *fluid* /
fluidics *fluid* /
fluidounce *magnum*
fluorescent lamp *incandescent* /
fluorescent tube *incandescent* /
flying carpet *carpet* /
FM *AM (VHF)* /
foal *colt* /
focal-plane shutter *focal-plane shutter* /
focal seizure *grand mal* /
folio *folio* /; *page* /
folio edition *folio* /
food of the gods *nectar* /
foot *iamb* /
football *game* /
forbidden band *conductor* /
fore-and-aft rigged sailing vessels *gaff rig* /
forearm bones *radius* /
forego *forgo* /
foregone conclusion *forgo* /
foreign words in English *acute* / *grave* /
foreword *preface* /
for fear that *indicative* /
forging *casting* /
forgo *forgo* /
formal *informal* /
formal language *style* /
forme *sewn binding* /
former *former* /

forming *casting* /
fortified wine *claret* /
forty-eightmo *folio* /
For Whom the Bell Tolls *who* / *whom*
foumart *ferret* /
four-letter words *informal* /; *obscene* /
four-o'clock *circadian* /
Fowler, Henry W. (1858–1933) *purism* /
fraction *numerator* /
français *acute* / *grave* /
France *Goth* /
Francis II (r.1792–1806) *Roman Empire* /
Frankish dynasties *Merovingian* /
Franks *Goth* /; *Vandal* /
frascati *claret* /
fraternal twins *fraternal twin* /
fraud *hard sell* /
free form *bound form* /; *prefix* /
freehold *freehold* /
free house *tied house* /
freezing point of water *Fahrenheit scale* /
French cuff *single cuff* /
French disease *chickenpox* /
French Empire *atlas* /
French pox *chickenpox* /
frequency modulation *AM (VHF)* /
frère *acute* / *grave* /
fresh breeze *breeze* /
fresh gale *breeze* /
friend *lover* /
Friendly Islands *Polynesia* /
frith *cape* /
frontal sinuses *upper respiratory tract* /
front matter *preface* /
frozen custard *ice cream* /
frozen desserts *ice cream* /
fruit *fruit* /

f/stop *focal-plane shutter* /
fuck *informal* /
fuel injection *diesel engine* /
Führer *acute* / *grave* /
full moon *harvest moon* /
full-wave rectifier *conductor* /
fundamental constant *constant* /
fundamental particle *nuclear
   fission* /
furbish *refurnish* /
further *farther* /
furthermore *farther* /
fuse *fuse* /
fusion *nuclear fission* /
fusion bomb *atom bomb* /
fusion reaction *nuclear fission* /
fuze *fuse* /

G

gaff *gaff rig* /
gaff-rigged sloop *sloop* /
gaffsail *gaff rig* /
Gaiseric *Vandal* /
galant style *baroque* /
Galàpagos Islands *convergent
   evolution* /
Galicia, Spain, occupied by Vandals
   Vandal /
Gallipoli, taken by Huns *Vandal* /
gallon, Imperial and U.S. *magnum* /
Gambia, The *England* /
game *game* /
gangrene *bacteria* /
garçon *acute* / *grave* /
gardenist *neologism* /
Garonne wine *claret* /
gas *fluid* /
gasoline engine *diesel engine* /
gasoline engine *internal
   combustion* /
gastric mucosa *endocrine* /
Gaul *Goth* /
Gaul, invasion by Vandals *Vandal* /

Gautama, Siddhartha (c566–480 B.C.)
   Buddhism /
gavial *alligator* /
gazebo *belvedere* /
Gb *abbreviation* /
Gdańsk) *acute* / *grave* /
Ge(heime) Sta(ats) Po(lizei) *Gestapo* /
gelding *colt* /
Gell-Mann, Murray (b.1929)
   neologism /
gender and sex *feminine* /
gender terms *feminine* /
gene *X chromosome* /
general damages *compensatory
   damages* /
general linguistics *linguistics* /
generator *alternator* /
genetic characteristics *bacteria* /
genetic engineering *DNA* /
gentle breeze *breeze* /
geographical mile *statute mile* /
geographic north *true north* /
geology *exact science* /
geometric progression
   arithmetically /
geometric series *arithmetically* /
George I (r.1714–27) *Plantagenet* /
George II (r.1727–60) *Plantagenet* /
George III (r.1760–1820)
   Plantagenet /
George IV (r.1820–30) *Plantagenet* /
George V (r.1910–36) *Plantagenet* /
George VI (r.1936–52) *Plantagenet* /
George Sand *nom de plume* /
Georgia *North* /
germ *bacteria* /; *metaphor* /
German *High German* /
German Democratic Republic *East
   Germany* /
German Democratic Republic
   enclave /
Germanic *centum* /
Germanic people *Goth* /

German measles   **measles** /
Germany   **East Germany** /
Gestapo   **Gestapo** /
get married   **marriage** /
Ghana   **England** /
gherkin   **pickle** /
gibe   **gibe** /
Gilbert Is. (former name of Kiribati)
   Polynesia /
Gilbert, Sir William S. (1836–1911)
   opera /
ginger   **herb** /
girder   **beam** /
girlfriend   **lover** /
glamorous   **-or** /
glamour   **-or** /
glass   **crystal** /
glass   **fluid /; silica** /
glazing-bar   **mullion** /
globe artichoke   **artichoke** /
gloominess, seat of   **black bile** /
glossary   **dictionary / glossary** /
glossopharyngeal nerve   **cranial
   nerves**
glucose   **fructose** /
glutton   **gourmet** /
GMT   **latitude** /
goatskin   **parchment** /
goat, wool from   **wool** /
gobelin   **canvaswork** /
gobelin stitch   **gros point** /
go boating   **boat** /
Goddard, Robert Hutchings
   (1882–1945)   **turboprop** /
gold   **solid gold** /
goldbeating   **solid gold** /
gold-filled   **solid gold** /
gold foil   **solid gold** /
gold leaf   **solid gold** /
gold plated   **solid gold** /
golf   **game** /
golf clubs   **iron / wood**
Gondwanaland   **Pangaea** /

Gone with the Wind   **informal** /
good   **good** /
"good" and "bad" language   **purism** /
Goodman, G. J. W. (b.1930)   **nom de
   plume** /
goodness   **abstract noun** /
Goths   **Goth** /
Götterdämmerung   **acute / grave** /
gourmand   **gourmet** /
gourmet   **gourmet** /
government-owned and operated
   business   **nationalization** /
Graafian follicle   **endocrine** /
grain (weight)   **avoirdupois weight** /
gram   **avoirdupois weight** /
gram calorie   **calorie** /
grammar   **grammar** /
grammar   **style** /
grammarians   **grammar** /
grammar of some languages
   adjective /
grammatical gender and natural sex
   feminine /
grand larceny   **grand larceny** /
grand mal seizure   **grand mal** /
grand opera   **grand opera** /
granny   **square knot** /
granny's bend   **square knot** /
granny's knot   **square knot** /
granulated sugar   **icing sugar** /
granulocyte   **erythrocyte** /
graph, the free form   **prefix** /
GRATUITOUS FOREIGN WORDS   **purism** /
grave accent   **acute / grave** /
gravitation   **gravitation** /
gravitational constant   **gravitation** /
gravitational constant   **constant** /
gravity   **gravitation** /
gravy   **gravy** /
gray   **Blue** /
gray matter   **gray matter** /
Great Britain   **England** /

Great Britain, Parliament of *House
  of Commons* /
great calorie *calorie* /
Greater London *city* /
Greater Vehicle *Hinayana
  Buddhism* /
Great Lakes *lake* /
great pox *chickenpox* /
Great Salt Lake *lake* /
great year *Julian calendar* /
green paper *green paper* /
greenstick fracture *simple
  fracture* /
Greenwich, England *Greenwich
  Mean Time* /
Greenwich Mean Time *Greenwich
  Mean Time* /
Greenwich Mean Time *latitude* /
Greenwich Meridian *Greenwich
  Mean Time* /
Greenwich Meridian *latitude* /
Greenwich Village *city* /
Gregorian calendar *Julian
  calendar* /
Gregory XIII (1502–85), Pope *Julian
  calendar* /
Grenada *England* /
Grenadines, the *England* /
grilse *smelt* /
gros point *gros point* /
Grosvenor Trust *freehold* /
ground rent *freehold* /
groundspeed *airspeed* /
guanine *DNA* /
guarantee *guarantee* /
guarantie *guarantee* /
guaranty *guarantee* /
gudgeon *gudgeon* /
Guide to the English Language, A
  purism /
guilty *innocent* /
gulf *cape* /
Gulliver's Travels *irony* /

gun *gun* /
gunter rig *gaff rig* /
Guyana *England* /
guyot *atoll* /
gybe *gibe* /
Gyges, King of Lydia *Old
  Kingdom* /
gyve *gibe* /

H

h, pronunciation of *acute / grave* /
h-, a or an before *a* /
H_1 blocker *histamine* /
H_2 blocker *histamine* /
hàček *acute / grave* /
hadal zone *littoral* /
had best *best* /
had better *best* /
Hadrian's Wall *England /; Roman
  Empire* /
ha-ha *fence* /
Hahnemann, Dr. Samuel (1755–1843)
  allopathy /
hair *wool* /
hairline fracture *simple fracture* /
hairpiece *toupee* /
half-wave rectifier *conductor* /
Halley's comet *comet* /
hamadryad *dryad* /
hamlet *city* /
hammer *anvil* /
hamza *acute / grave* /
hamzah *acute / grave* /
Handel, George Frederick
  (1685–1759) *opera* /
hang *hung* /
hanged *hung* /
Hanoverian rulers *Plantagenet* /
Hansen's disease *bacteria* /
hara-kiri *katana* /
harbor *harbor* /
hard-edge realism *idealism* /

Harding, Warren G. (1865–1923)
  normality /
hard sell   *hard sell* /
hardware   *hardware* /
hare   *hare* /
harmonic progression
  arithmetically /
harmonic series   *arithmetically* /
Harrow   *private school* /
harvest moon   *harvest moon* /
hate   *hate* /
Hatshepsut, Queen   *Old Kingdom* /
haven   *harbor* /
Hawaii   *atoll* /
headland   *cape* /
health   *abstract noun* /
health and temperament, control of
  black bile /
healthful   *healthy* /
healthy   *healthy* /
heart attack   *heart attack* /
heart failure   *heart attack* /
heart, muscles of   *diastole* /
heath   *heath* /
Heathrow Airport (London)   *true
  north* /
Heaviside-Kennelly layer
  troposphere /
heavy build   *ectomorph* /
Hebrew   Yiddish /
Hecataeus of Miletus (d.476B.C.)   *Old
  Kingdom* /
hectogram   *avoirdupois weight* /
hectograph   *letterpress* /
heir apparent   *heir apparent* /
heir presumptive   *heir apparent* /
helicopter   *autogiro* /
hell   *informal* /
Hellenic   *centum* /
helm   *lee* /
"Helm's alee!"   *lee* /
hemi-   *demi-* /
hemianopsia   *demi-* /

hemicrania   demi- /
hemidemisemiquaver   demi- /
Hemingway, Ernest (1899–1961)
  who / whom
hemiplagia   demi- /
Hemiptera   bug /
hemisphere   demi- /
hemizygote   demi- /
hemoglobin   *erythrocyte* /
hemolytic anemia   *Rh-negative* /
hemorrhage   *heart attack* /
Henry I (r.1100–35)   *Plantagenet* /
Henry II (r.1154–89)   *Plantagenet* /
Henry III (r.1216–72)   *Plantagenet* /
Henry IV (r.1399–1413)
  Plantagenet /
Henry V (r.1413–22)   *Plantagenet* /
Henry VI (r.1422–61, 1470–71)
  Plantagenet /; red rose /
Henry VII (r.1485–1509)
  Plantagenet /
Henry VIII (r.1509–47)   *Plantagenet* /
hepatitis   *bacteria* /
heptameter   *iamb* /
herb   *herb* /
herb   *oregano* /
herbaceous   *a* /
herbaceous plants   *fruit* /
herb, a or an before   *a* /
herbivore   *carnivore* /
Herculaneum   *atoll* /
hereditary characteristics   *DNA* /
Herodotus (?484–?425B.C.)   *either ..
  or /; Old Kingdom* /
herpes   *bacteria* /
herpesvirus   *chickenpox* /
hexameter   *iamb* /
hibernate   *estivate* /
hibernation   *circadian* /
hi-fi components   *tweeter* /
high aspect ratio   *gaff rig* /
highboy   *highboy* /
High Church   *Low Church* /

high comedy **high comedy** /
highdaddy **highboy** /
higher criticism **higher criticism** /
high-fidelity components **tweeter** /
high-frequency sounds **tweeter** /
High German **High German** /
High German **Yiddish** /
Highland costume **tartan** /
Highlands **Highlands** /
highly inflecting languages
    adjective /
High Mass **High Mass** /
high relief **alto-rilievo** /
high tide **ebb tide** /
Hinayana Buddhism **Hinayana
    Buddhism** /
Hinduism **Buddhism** /
hinny **ass** /
Hippo **Vandal** /
hippopotamus, plural of **-us, words
    ending in**
"hisher" **feminine** /
histamine **histamine** /
historical, a or an before **a** /
history **exact science** /
history, a or an before **a** /
Hitler's personal bodyguard
    Gestapo /
Hochdeutsch **High German** /
hock **claret** /
hole **conductor** /
hollowware **flatware** /
Holy Roman Empire **Roman
    Empire** /
homeopathic magic **contagious
    magic** /
homeopathy **allopathy** /
homeothermal **cold-blooded** /
Homer **dramatic poetry** /; Scylla /
homicide **homicide** /
homing guidance **inertial guidance** /
homogenized milk **pasteurized** /
homograph **homograph** /

homoiothermal **cold-blooded** /
homoiothermic **cold-blooded** /
homoiothermous **cold-blooded** /
homologous **analogous** /
homonym **homograph** /
homophone **homograph** /
homothermal **cold-blooded** /
honest, a or an before **a** /
honeybee **wasp** /
honeymoon bridge **contract
    bridge** /
honorable **-or** /
honor, honour **-or** /
honorific **-or** /
hooklike symbol **acute** / **grave** /
Hoover Dam **lake** /
Horemheb **Old Kingdom** /
hornet **wasp** /
hors d'oeuvre **antipasto** /
horse **ass** /
horseracing **game** /
horseshoe crab **bug** /
hostelry **hotel** /
hotel **hotel** /
hotel, a or an before **a** /
hot-metal typesetting **hot metal** /
hour, a or an before **a** /
household gods of the Romans
    lares /
House of Commons **House of
    Commons** /
House of Commons **lower house** /
House of Lords **House of
    Commons** /
House of Lords **lower house** /
House of Representatives **House of
    Representatives** /
House of Representatives **lower
    house** /
"House, the" **House of
    Representatives** /
hovercraft **hydrofoil** /
howitzers **gun** /

hulls of wooden vessels *carvel-built* /
human body types *ectomorph* /
human cultural development, earliest *Paleolithic* /
human relationships *exact science* /
humidity *humidity* /
humor *black bile* /
humor *high comedy* /
humor, humour *-or* /
hundredweight *avoirdupois weight* /
hung *hung* /
hunger strike *strike* /
Hun *Vandal* /
hunter's moon *harvest moon* /
hunting society *Paleolithic* /
hurricane *cyclone* /
hurricane *breeze* /
husband and wife, state of *marriage* /
hybrid computer *analog* /
hydrofoil *hydrofoil* /
hydrogen bomb *atom bomb* /
hydrogen bomb *nuclear fission* /
Hyksos kings *Old Kingdom* /
hypoglossal nerve *cranial nerves*
hypothetical form, symbol for *dagger* /
hysterical, a or an before *a* /

I

-i, plurals formed using *-us, words ending in*
-i plurals of -us words *-us, words ending in*
iamb *iamb* /
iambic pentameter *iamb* /
Iberian peninsula *Goth* /
-ic *-ate* /
-ic, as a chemical suffix *-ic* /
ice cream *ice cream* /
ice milk *ice cream* /

ices *ice cream* /
icing sugar *icing sugar* /
Idaho *North* /
idealism *idealism* /
identical twins *fraternal twin* /
ideomotor *ideomotor* /
IGFET *abbreviation* /
Ikhnaton *Old Kingdom* /
ileocecal valve *large intestine* /
Îles Marquises *Polynesia* /
ileum *large intestine* /
Iliad *dramatic poetry* /
illegal *illegal* /
illegitimate *illegal* /
illicit *illegal* /
Illinois *North* /
illogical *amoral* /
illude *allusion* /
illusion *allusion* /
"illusionist" *allusion* /
illustrations, contextual in dictionaries *dictionary* / *glossary* /
illustrations, pictorial in dictionaries *dictionary* / *glossary* /
im-, the prefix *inflammable* /
Imhotep *Old Kingdom* /
imitative magic *contagious magic* /
Immaculate Conception *Virgin Birth* /
immigrant *emigrate* /
immigrate *emigrate* /
immoral *amoral* /
imperative *shall* /
imperative mood *indicative* /
imperfect flower *dioecious* /
Imperial gallon *magnum* /
Imperial pint *magnum* /
Imperial System *avoirdupois weight* /; *magnum* /
implication *imply* /
implode *explode* /
imply *imply* /; *like* /

impossible **amoral** /
impression **edition** /
impromptu **extemporaneous** /
improper fraction **proper fraction** /
in-, the prefix **amoral** /
inc. **common stock** /
incandescent bulb **incandescent** /
incandescent lamp **incandescent** /
incisor **incisor** /
in common **common** /
incorporated **common stock** /
incredible **incredible** /
incredibly **incredible** /
incredulity **incredible** /
incredulous **incredible** /
incus **anvil** /
indexes, plural of *index* **index** /
India **England** /
Indiana **North** /
Indic **centum** /
indicative mood **indicative** /
indices, plural of *index* **index** /
indictment **arraignment** /
indiscretion **discreet** /
Indo-European family **Yiddish** /
Indo-European languages,
   classification **centum** /
induce **convince** /
inducement **convince** /
inertial guidance **inertial guidance** /
inertial guidance **latitude** /
infarct **heart attack** /
infer **imply** /; **like** /
infer and *imply* **style** /
inference **imply** /
inferior conjunction **inferior**
   conjunction /
infinitive, splitting an **grammar** /;
   standard /
infix **prefix** /
inflame **inflammable** /
inflammable **inflammable** /
inflecting languages **adjective** /

inflection **conjugation** /
inflection **accent** /
inflections **adjective** /
influenza **endemic**
informal **colloquial** /; **informal** /
information **data** /
information, basic unit of **bit** /
information, transmission speed
   bit /
information inserted in quotations
   parentheses /
infringement **plagiarism** /
-*ing,* the suffix **triumphal** /
-*ing* as meaningful element **bound**
   form /
ingenious **ingenious** /
ingenue **ingenious** /
ingenuous **ingenious** /
inhibition in language **informal** /
in irons **irons** /
initiative **initiative** /
injection molding **casting** /
ink-jet printer **dot-matrix printer** /
inn **hotel** /
inner ear **anvil** /
innervate **enervate** /
inoculate **vaccinate** /
inoculation **vaccinate** /
inoculum **vaccinate** /
in order that **indicative** /
inorganic **organic** /
inorganic chemistry **organic** /
input **input** /
insect **bug** /
Insecta **bug** /; **butterfly** /
insectivore **carnivore** /
insects **wasp** /
insertion of information in
   quotations **parentheses** /
in stays **irons** /
institutional advertising **hard sell** /
instrument landing **contact**
   landing /

insulator **conductor** /
intaglio **intaglio** /; **letterpress** /
integer **integer** /
intellectual functions of the brain
   cerebrum /
interior decorator **refurnish** /
internal combustion **internal**
   combustion /
internal combustion engine **diesel**
   engine /
internal combustion engines in
   airplanes **turboprop** /
international law **civil law** /
international nautical mile **statute**
   mile /
interplanetary space **interplanetary** /
interstellar space **interplanetary** /
intestinal mucosa **endocrine** /
in-, the prefix **inflammable** /
in the same boat **boat** /
intonation **accent** /
intrinsic semiconductor **conductor** /
introduction **preface** /
introvert **extrovert** /
invent **discover** /
inventory control **FIFO** /
inverse proportion **inverse**
   proportion /
inverse square law **inverse**
   proportion /
invertebrates **bug** /
inverted circumflex **acute** / **grave** /
investor **corporation** /
in vitro **in vitro** /
in vivo **in vitro** /
involuntary manslaughter **homicide** /
involuntary muscles **smooth**
   muscle /
Ionia **Acadia** /
ionic compound **atom** /
ionosphere **troposphere** /
iota **metaphor** /
iotacism **iotacism** /

Iowa **North** /
ir-, the prefix **irregardless** /
Iranian **centum** /
irascibility or anger, seat of **black**
   bile /
Ireland **England** /
irenics **apologetics** /
Irish bull **malapropism** /
Irish Free State **England** /
iron **iron** / **steel; iron** / **wood**
irons (in irons) **irons** /
ironstone **china** /
irony **irony** /
irrational number **rational**
   number /
irregardless **irregardless** /
irreplaceable **amoral** /
irrespective of **due to** /
'irritate' **aggravate** /
-ise, the suffix **-ise** /
-ish as meaningful element **bound**
   form /
island **atoll** /
islands (or islets) of Langerhans
   endocrine /
isolating languages **adjective** /
isomer **fructose** /
isometric drawing **isometric** /
isosceles triangle **scalene** /
Israel **Yiddish** /
issue **edition** /
isthmus **cape** /
itacism **iotacism** /
Italian sonnet **Shakespearian**
   sonnet /
Italic **italic** /
Italic **centum** /
italic type **italic** /
-ite **-ate** /
its **its** /
it's, contraction for it has **its** /
it's, contraction for it is **its** /
-ive, the suffix **preventive** /

-ize, the suffix *-ise* /

J

jackdaws **crow** /
jack-in-the-pulpit **animal** /
jackrabbit **hare** /
Jacksonian seizure **grand mal** /
jam **jam** /
Jamaica **England** /
James I (r.1603–25) **Plantagenet** /
James II (r.1685–88) **Plantagenet** /
Japan **Hinayana Buddhism** /
Japanese scrolls **kakemono** /
jazz band **band** /
jejunum **large intestine** /
jelly **jam** /
Jenner, Edward (1749–1823)
  chickenpox /
jereboam **magnum** /
Jerez **claret** /
Jerusalem artichoke **artichoke** /
jet propulsion **turboprop** /
jetsam **flotsam** /
jetty **dock** /
Jewish Autonomous Region of the
  U.S.S.R. **Yiddish** /
Jews, lingua franca of **Yiddish** /
Jews of Europe **Ashkenazi** /
Jews of Spain and Portugal
  Ashkenazi /
jib **gibe** /
jibe **gibe** /
jigger **sloop** /
jiujitsu **judo** /
jiujutsu **judo** /
jive **gibe** /
John of Gaunt (1340–99) **red rose** /
John (r.1199–1216) **Plantagenet** /
joist **beam** /
joule **calorie** /
Joyce, James (1882–1941)
  neologism /
Judaic dietary laws **kosher** /

Judaic religion **kosher** /
judges in sporting contests
  referee /
Judicial branch **House of
  Representatives** /
judo **judo** /
judo **white belt** /
Jugenstil **antiques** /
jujitsu **judo** /
jujutsu **judo** /
Julian calendar **Julian calendar** /
jump ship **boat** /
jury of his peers **peer** /
Justinian I (483–565; r.527–565)
  Vandal /

K

kakemono **kakemono** /
Kansas **North** /
karat **carat** /
karat, carat **avoirdupois weight** /
karate **judo** /
karate **white belt** /
Karnak **Old Kingdom** /
katana **katana** /
Keats, John (1795–1821) **dramatic
  poetry** /
keels of boats **centerboard** /
kelebe **krater** /
Kelvin **zero** /
Kelvin scale **Fahrenheit scale** /
Kentucky **North** /
Kentucky long rifle **gun** /
Kenya **England** /
ketch **sloop** /
keylining **page** /
kilocalorie **calorie** /
kilogram **avoirdupois weight** /
kilometer **statute mile** /
kinetic energy **kinetic energy** /
Kings **city** /
Kiribati **England** /

Kiribati (formerly Gilbert Islands)
  Polynesia /
Kirkpatrick's catalogue of Scarlatti
  opus /
kit **violin** /
knot **breeze** /
knotmeter **airspeed** /
Köchel's catalogue of Mozart **opus** /
kogai **katana** /
ko-katana **katana** /
Koran **Kufic** /
kosher **kosher** /
Kosrae Island **Polynesia** /
kozuka **katana** /
krater **krater** /
krill **crayfish** /
kung fu **judo** /
kylix **krater** /

L

labels in dictionaries **dictionary** /
  glossary /
Labyrinth **Old Kingdom** /
lace **canvaswork** /
lactose **fructose** /
lagan **flotsam** /
lager **ale** /
lagoon **lake** /
lagoon **atoll** /
laid **lie / lay** /
lain **lie / lay** /
lake **lake** /
lake, largest in Great Britain **lake** /
lake, largest in world **lake** /
Lake Mead **lake** /
Lake Superior **lake** /
Lake Windermere **lake** /
lambdacism **iotacism** /
Lambeth **city** /
lampoon **irony** /
Lancastrian kings **Plantagenet** /
landlord **freehold** /
land mile **statute mile** /

langouste **crayfish** /
langoustine **crayfish** /
language **standard** /
language change **purism /; style** /
language levels **standard** /
language purists **preventive** /
lapstrake **carvel-built** /
larboard **port** /
lares **lares** /
largamente **adagio** /
large calorie **calorie** /
large intestine **large intestine** /
larghetto **adagio** /
largo **adagio** /
larynx **upper respiratory tract** /
laser printer **dot-matrix printer** /
last **former** /
last-in, first-out **FIFO** /
lateen rig **gaff rig** /
Latin and English compared
  adjective /
Latin influence on English grammar
  grammar /
Latinisms in English **grammar** /
latitude **latitude** /
latter **former** /
Laurasia **Pangaea** /
laurence **laurence** /
Lavongai Island **Polynesia** /
Law Lords **House of Commons** /
lawyer **council** /
laxness **phonetics** /
lay **lie / lay** /
lay analyst **psychologist** /
laying **lie / lay** /
lay low **lie / lay** /
lay of the land **lie / lay** /
lays **lie / lay** /
lead crystal **crystal** /
leader **concertmaster** /
leaf **page** /
leaf shutter **focal-plane shutter** /
leap year **Julian calendar** /

leasehold **freehold** /
least, superlative of little **fewer** /
leave **leave** /
lee **lee** /
leeboard **centerboard** /
legal **illegal** /
leg, bones of the **fibula** /
Legislative branch **House of
Representatives** /
legitimacy **illegal** /
legitimate **illegal** /
legitimate theater **illegal** /
leman **lover** /
Leninism **Bolshevism** /
Lenin, Nikolai (1870–1924)
Bolshevism /
Lepidoptera **butterfly** /
lepidopterist **butterfly** /
leprosy **bacteria** /
leptosome **ectomorph** /
Lesotho **England** /
less, comparative of little **fewer** /
-less, the suffix **irregardless** /
'lesser vehicle' **Hinayana
Buddhism** /
lest **indicative** /
let **leave** /
letterpress **intaglio /; letterpress** /
leucocyte **erythrocyte** /
leukocyte **erythrocyte** /
levels of language **informal** /
levulose **fructose** /
Lewis, Sinclair (1885–1951) **style** /
lexicographer **lexicography** /
lexicography **lexicography** /
lexicography, theory of
lexicography /
lexicologist **lexicography** /
lexicology **lexicography** /
lexicon **dictionary / glossary** /
lexicon **style** /
liar **lie / fib** /
libel **libel** /

Libyan raiders in Egypt **Old
Kingdom** /
licence **license** /
license **license** /
licit **illegal** /
lie **lie / fib** /
lie **lie / lay**
lie and lay **style** /
liebfraumilch **claret** /
lied **lie / lay**
lie low **lie / lay**
lie of the land **lie / lay**
lies **lie / lay**
lifeboat **boat** /
LIFO **FIFO** /
ligan **flotsam** /
ligature **acute / grave** /
light airs **breeze** /
like **metaphor** /
like **like** /
like and as **style** /
like-for-as problem **like** /
lily **tiger lily** /
limited **common stock** /
limited company **common stock** /
limited company **corporation** /
linen **wool** /
linguist **linguistics** /
linguistic fundamentalists
preventive /
linguistics **linguistics** /
linguistics **purism** /
linguists **grammar /; purism** /
Linotype **QWERTY keyboard** /
liquid **fluid** /
liquidated damages **compensatory
damages** /
literally **literally** /
literally **metaphor** /
lithography **intaglio** /
little, positive of less, least **fewer** /
Little Vehicle **Hinayana Buddhism** /
"little white lies" **lie / fib** /

littoral zone **littoral** /
liturgy **Low Church** /
live tally **lover** /
loanwords **acute** / **grave** /
loath **loathe** /
loathe **loathe** /
loathing **loathe** /
loathsome **loathe** /
lobster **bug** /; **crayfish** /
localized weather systems
   macrometeorology /
locate **locate** /
location **locate** /
logarithms **characteristic** /
logo **colophon** /
logotype **colophon** /
London, City of **city** /
London Stock Exchange
   backwardation /
Longfellow, Henry Wadsworth
   Acadia /
longitude **latitude** /
longitude **Greenwich Mean Time** /
long mark **acute** / **grave** /
Longos **Acadia** /
long ton **avoirdupois weight** /
long wave **long wave** /
Lords, House of **House of**
   Commons /
Lords Spiritual **House of**
   Commons /
Lords Temporal **House of**
   Commons /
loth **loathe** /
loudness **accent** /
loudspeakers **tweeter** /
Louisiade Island **Polynesia** /
Louisiana **North** /
love **abstract noun** /
love boat **boat** /
lover **lover** /
Low Archipelago **Polynesia** /
lowboy **highboy** /

Low Church **Low Church** /
Low Churchman) **Low Church** /
low comedy **high comedy** /
lower-case letter **ascender** /
lower chamber **lower house** /
Lower Cooks **Polynesia** /
lower criticism **higher criticism** /
lower digestive tract **large**
   intestine /
lower house **lower house** /
lower jawbone **mandible** /
Lower Paleolithic **Paleolithic** /
lower respiratory tract **upper**
   respiratory tract /
low frequency sounds **tweeter** /
Low German **High German** /
Lowlands **Highlands** /
Low Mass **High Mass** /
low relief **alto-rilievo** /
low tide **ebb tide** /
Loyalty Island **Polynesia** /
ltd. **common stock** /
lunar day **ebb tide** /
lunar eclipse **lunar eclipse** /
lungs **upper respiratory tract** /
luxuriant **luxurious** /
luxurious **luxurious** /
Lydia, king of **Old Kingdom** /
lying **lie** / **lay**
Lyly, John (?1554–1606)
   euphemism /
lymphatic system **endocrine** /
lymphocyte **erythrocyte** /
lyra viol **violin** /
lyric poetry **dramatic poetry** /
lyric soprano **bass** /
-ly, the bound form **prefix** /

M

Macedonian kings of Egypt **Old**
   Kingdom /
machine gun **gun** /

macrometeorology
   macrometeorology /
macromolecular compound   **atom** /
macron   **acute** / **grave** /
magna cum laude   **cum laude** /
magnetic north pole   **true north** /
magnum   **magnum** /
magnum opus   **-us, words ending in**
Mahayana   **Hinayana Buddhism** /
Mahayana Buddhism   **Hinayana Buddhism** /
mail order   **direct mail** /
main clause   **main clause** /
Maine   **North** /
maître   **acute** / **grave** /
major weather systems
   macrometeorology /
majuscule   **italic** /
make a snooker   **billiards** /
makimono   **kakemono** /
maladie Anglaise   **chickenpox** /
malapropism   **malapropism** /
Malaprop, Mrs.   **malapropism** /
malapropos   **malapropism** /
Malawi   **England** /
Malay Archipelago   **Polynesia** /
Malaysia   **England** /
Maldives   **England** /
male   **feminine** /
maleness   **X chromosome** /
male side of a family   **distaff side** /
malleus   **anvil** /
Malta   **England** /
Malt, Lillian   **QWERTY keyboard** /
maltose   **fructose** /
malt whisky   **fructose** /
mammals (Mammalia) as class
   phylum /
mammonolatry   **neologism** /
mañana   **acute** / **grave** /
mandible   **mandible** /
mandibular   **mandible** /

Mangareva Island   **Polynesia** /
Manhattan   **city** /
Manhattan clam chowder   **New England chowder** /
manslaughter   **homicide** /
mantissa   **characteristic** /
Marconi rig   **gaff rig** /
Marconi-rigged sloop   **sloop** /
mare   **colt** /
Mariana Islands (formerly Ladrone Is.)   **Polynesia** /
Mariner's Mirror, The   **port** /
marionette   **puppet** /
Maritime Provinces, Canada   **Acadia** /
marketing terms   **hard sell** /
market value   **book value** /
Markov, A. A. (1856–1922)   **Markov process** /
Markov process   **Markov process** /
marmalade   **jam** /
Marquesas Islands   **Polynesia** /
Marranos   **Ashkenazi** /
marriage   **marriage** /
marriage   **monogamy** /
Marshall Islands   **Polynesia** /
marten   **ferret** /
Marx, Karl (1818–83)   **Bolshevism** /
Mary I (r.1553-58)   **Plantagenet** /
Mary II (r.1689–94)   **Plantagenet** /
Maryland   **North** /
Masada, Roman siege at   **Yiddish** /
masculine   **effeminate** /; **feminine** /
masculine rhyme   **feminine rhyme** /
mashie   **iron** / **wood**
mashie iron   **iron** / **wood**
mashie niblick   **iron** / **wood**
Mason-Dixon Line   **South** /
mass   **mass** /
Massachusetts   **North** /
mass noun   **count noun** /
mass noun   **fewer** /
material   **material** /

materialism **dynamism** /
matériel **material** /
mathematics **exact science** /
matin song **serenade** /
matrimonial **marriage** /
matrimony **marriage** /
matter **matter** /
matter, smallest unit of **atom** /
Mauritius **England** /
maxilla **mandible** /
maxillary **mandible** /
maxillary sinuses **upper**
 respiratory tract /
may **may** /
mdse. **abbreviation** /
Mead, Lake **lake** /
mean **mean deviation** /
mean deviation **mean deviation** /
measles **endemic** /; **measles** /
measure **parameter** /
mechanical drawing **isometric** /
mechanism **dynamism** /
méchant **acute** / **grave** /
Media, invasion of by Huns
 Vandal /
medicine **exact science** /
medium wave **long wave** /
megalopolis **city** /
Melanesia **Polynesia** /
Melville, Herman (1819–91)
 edition /
Member of Parliament **House of**
 Commons /
memorabilia **antiques** /
memory **cerebrum** /
mendacity **lie** / **fib** /
Menes **Old Kingdom** /
menhir **cromlech** /
meninges **arachnoid membrane** /
meniscus **concave** /
Menotti, Gian Carlo (b.1911) **opera** /
Menshevik **Bolshevism** /
Menshevism **Bolshevism** /

menstrual **circadian** /
mental disorders **psychologist** /
menu **table d'hôte** /
mercury barometer. **barometer** /
mercury thermometer **barometer** /
mercury vapor lamp **incandescent** /
Merewig **Merovingian** /
meridians of longitude **latitude** /
merisis **auxesis** /
Merovingian **Merovingian** /
mesoderm **ectoderm** /;
 endothelium /
mesoderm **ectomorph** /
Mesolithic **Paleolithic** /
mesometeorology
 macrometeorology /
mesomorph **ectomorph** /
mesothelium **endothelium** /
messenger RNA **DNA** /
Messiah **opera** /
metaphor **metaphor** /
meteor **comet** /
meteorite **meteorite** /
meteoroid **meteorite** /
meteorology **exact science** /;
 macrometeorology /
methuselah **magnum** /
metrical rhythm **iamb** /
metric ton **avoirdupois weight** /
metric weight (table) **avoirdupois**
 weight /
Meyerbeer, Giacomo (1791–1864)
 opera /
mezzo-rilievo **alto-rilievo** /
mezzo-soprano **bass** /
Michigan **North** /
microbe **bacteria** /
micrometeorite **meteorite** /
micrometeorology
 macrometeorology /
Micronesia **Polynesia** /
Micronesia, Federated States of
 Polynesia /

microorganism *bacteria /; bug /*
Middle Atlantic states *North /*
middle ear *anvil /*
Middle English *purism /; style /*
Middle French *regret /*
Middle Kingdom of Egypt *Old Kingdom /*
Middle Paleolithic *Paleolithic /*
middle relief *alto-rilievo /*
Middle West *North /*
midget *dwarf /*
midiron *iron / wood*
mid-mashie *iron / wood*
Midsummer *equinox /*
midtown *city /*
Midwest *North /*
might *may /*
migration of birds *circadian /*
mile *statute mile /*
mileometer *speedometer /*
military band *band /*
militate *militate /*
milk *pasteurized /*
milk sherry *claret /*
milk sugar *fructose /*
milliard *billion /*
milligram *avoirdupois weight /*
millipede *bug /; centipede /*
Mill, John Stuart (1806–73) *utopia /*
milometer *speedometer /*
Mimeograph *letterpress /*
mineral *animal /*
mineralogy *exact science /*
mining *exact science /*
"miniscules" *italic /*
Minnesota *North /*
minuscule *italic /*
mirage *laurence /*
mis-, the prefix *distrust /*
misarticulation *iotacism /*
misère *acute / grave /*
Mississippi *North /*
Missouri *North /*

misstatement *lie / fib /*
miss the boat *boat /*
mistress *lover /*
mistrust *distrust /*
mite *bug /*
mitigate *militate /*
mitochondrial DNA *DNA /*
mitochondrial DNA molecule *convergent evolution /*
mixing bowl *krater /*
mixture *element /*
mizzenmast *sloop /*
Moby Dick, Herman Melville *edition /*
mode of expression *informal /*
moderate breeze *breeze /*
moderate gale *breeze /*
modern *modern /*
Modern German *High German /*
moisture in the atmosphere *humidity /*
molar *incisor /*
mole *dock /*
molecule *atom /*
monandrous *diandrous /*
monaural *monophonic /*
monetary *monetary /*
monetary policy *monetary /*
monetary unit *monetary /*
monoclinous *dioecious /*
monocyte *erythrocyte /*
monoecious *dioecious /*
monogamy *monogamy /*
monologist *monologue /*
monologue *monologue /*
monologuist *monologue /*
monophonic *monophonic /*
monophthong *diphthong /*
monopsony *monopsony /*
monosaccharide *fructose /*
Montana *North /*
Montemayor *Acadia /*

Monteverdi, Claudio (1567–1643)
  opera /
monthly *circadian* /
moods of verbs *indicative* /
moon *abstract noun* /
moor *heath* /
Moors *Ashkenazi* /; *Goth* /
more in comparison of adjectives
  positive /
More, Sir Thomas (1478–1535)
  utopia /
more than *better than* /
Mormons *monogamy* /
morning glory *circadian* /
morphemes *adjective* /
mortars *gun* /
mortgage *first mortgage* /
mortgagee *first mortgage* /
mortgagor *first mortgage* /
most in comparison of adjectives
  positive /
motel *hotel* /
moth *butterfly* /
mot juste *synonym* /
motor *motor* /
motor functions of the brain
  cerebrum /
motor hotel *hotel* /
motor vessel *motor* /
Mountain Time Zone *Greenwich
  Mean Time* /
mousse *mousse* /
mouth of a river *river* /
moving the bowels *informal* /
Mozart, Wolfgang Amadeus
  (1756–91) *opera* /
M-1 rifle *gun* /
mRNA *DNA* /
mucus *black bile* /
muffineer *icing sugar* /
Muhaqqaq *Kufic* /
mule *ass* /
mullion *mullion* /

municipality *city* /
municipal law *civil law* /
Munro, H. H. (1870–1916) *nom de
  plume* /
muntin *mullion* /
Muppets *puppet* /
murder *homicide* /
murder, degrees of *homicide* /
murder in the first degree
  homicide /
murder in the second degree
  homicide /
"murder one" *homicide* /
"murder two" *homicide* /
muscle, kinds of *smooth muscle* /
muscles, involuntary *smooth
  muscle* /
muscle, smooth *smooth muscle* /
muscles of the heart *diastole* /
muscle, striated *smooth muscle* /
muscles, voluntary *smooth
  muscle* /
muscular build *ectomorph* /
muscular control by the brain
  cerebrum /
Mussorgsky, Modest (1839–81)
  opera /
mutation *DNA* /
mutual *common* /
mutual friend *common* /
myelin sheathing *gray matter* /
"My Last Duchess" *dramatic
  poetry* /
myocardium *smooth muscle* /
myriapod *bug* /
Myriapoda *bug* /; *centipede* /

N

-n-, the infix *prefix* /
Nabopolassar *Old Kingdom* /
nadir *zenith* /
naïve *acute* / *grave* /
naming chemical compounds *-ate* /

nasal   **nasal** */; phonetics* /
nasal   **consonant** /
nasal cavity   **upper respiratory**
   tract /
Naskhi   **Kufic** /
nationalization   **nationalization** /
natural fibers   **wool** /
naturalism   **idealism** /
natural number   **integer** /
natural science   **exact science** /
natural sex and grammatical gender
   feminine /
naughty   **good** /
Nauru   **England** /
Nauru Island   **Polynesia** /
nausea   **noisome** /
nauseated   **nauseous** /
nauseous   **nauseous** /
nautical mile   **statute mile** /
nautical mile   **breeze** /
nautical mile per hour   **breeze** /
navigation   *latitude* /
Nazi Germany   **Gestapo** /
Nazi party   **Gestapo** /
neap tide   **ebb tide** /
Nebraska   **North** /
nebuchadnezzar   **magnum** /
Nebuchadnezzar   **Old Kingdom** /
Necho   **Old Kingdom** /
neck   **cape** /
nectar   **nectar** /
needlepoint   **canvaswork** */; gros*
   point /
Nefertiti, Queen   **Old Kingdom** /
negative prefix   **irregardless** /
negative terminal   **cathode** /
neither   **each** */; either .. or /;*
   singular /
neither .. nor   **either .. or** /
Neogaea   **Pangaea** /
Neolithic   **Paleolithic** /
neologism   **neologism** /
Nepal   **Hinayana Buddhism** /

nereid   **dryad** /
Nereus   **dryad** /
neritic zone   **littoral** /
nerve cell   **neuron** /
Nesbit, E. (*Edith Nesbit Bland*
   1858–1924)   **dryad** /
Neskhi   **Kufic** /
Neski   **Kufic** /
ness   **cape** /
net capital value   **book value** /
neuron   **neuron** /
neurone   **neuron** /
neurosis   **neurosis** /
neurotic   **neurosis** /
neurotransmitter   **neuron** /
neutron bomb   **atom bomb** /
neutrophil   **erythrocyte** /
Nevada   **North** /
New Britain Island   **Polynesia** /
New Caledonia Island   **Polynesia** /
New Empire of Egypt   **Old**
   Kingdom /
New England   **North** /
New England clam chowder   **New**
   England chowder /
New Hampshire   **North** /
New Ireland Island   **Polynesia** /
New Jersey   **North** /
New Mexico   **North** /
New Style   **Julian calendar** /
Newton's law of gravitation
   constant /
New York   **city** */; North* /
New York City   **North** /
New Yorker, The   **who** */ whom*
New Zealand   **England** /
niacin   **abbreviation** /
niblick   **iron** */ wood*
Nigeria   **England** /
(night) depository   **depository** /
nirvana   **Buddhism** */; Hinayana*
   Buddhism /
nitrate   **-ate** /

nitric   *-ate /; -ic /*
nitrite   *-ate /*
nitrous   *-ate /; -ic /*
noble metal   **base metal /**
nocturnal   **butterfly /; circadian /; nocturnal /**
nocturne   **serenade /**
noise   **noisome /**
noisome   **noisome /**
noisy   **noisome /**
nom de guerre   **nom de plume /**
nom de plume   **nom de plume /**
nominal damages   **compensatory damages /**
nonce word   **neologism /**
nonflammable   **inflammable /**
non-nasal   **phonetics /**
non-nasal   **consonant /**
nonrestrictive clause   **that /**
nonrestrictive modifier   **descriptive modifier /**
nonstandard   **standard /**
nonunion shop   **open shop**
nor   **either .. or /**
norepinephrine   **endocrine /**
norepinephrine   **neuron /**
normal   **abnormal /**
normalcy   **normality /**
normalism   **normality /**
normality   **normality /**
North, the   **Confederate States of America /**
North Carolina   **North /**
North Dakota   **North /**
Northeast   **North /**
'northern'   **austral /**
Northern Cooks   **Polynesia /**
Northern Ireland   **England /**
north frigid zone   **Arctic Circle /**
North Pole   **true north /**
Northwest   **North /**
nose   **upper respiratory tract /**

not guilty   **innocent /**
Notogaea   **Pangaea /**
noun, forms of the   **conjugation /**
nouns, grammatical gender of   **feminine /**
nouns, sex of   **feminine /**
nouns, subclasses of   **feminine /**
noun endings   **adjective /**
Nova Scotia   **Acadia /**
novel   **novel /**
novelette   **novel /**
novella   **novel /**
n-type conductor   **conductor /**
Nubia   **Old Kingdom /**
nuclear DNA   **DNA /**
nuclear DNA   **convergent evolution /**
nuclear fission   **nuclear /; nuclear fission /**
nuclear fusion   **nuclear /; nuclear fission /**
nuclear power plants   **nuclear fission /**
nucleic acid   **bacteria /**
nucleotide   **DNA /**
nucleus   **nuclear /**
nucleus / nuclei   **-us, words ending in**
number   **integer /; number /**
number-four wood   **iron / wood**
number-three wood   **iron / wood**
number-two wood   **iron / wood**
numeral   **number /**
numerator   **numerator /**
nun buoy   **can buoy /**
nuptial   **marriage /**
nuptials   **marriage /**
nursing home   **rest home /**
nutmeg   **herb /**
nylon   **wool /**
nymphomania   **nymphomania /**
nymphs   **dryad /**

O

-o, plurals of words ending in *-us,*
 words ending in
obelisk **dagger** /
oblique type **italic** /
obscene **obscene** /
obscene language **obscene** /
obscenities **obscene** /
obsolete **archaic** /
obtuse **acute** / **obtuse**
occident **orient** /
occluded front **cold front** /
Oceania **Polynesia** /
oceanic zone **littoral** /
octave **Shakespearian sonnet** /
octavo **folio** /
octopus, meaning of **-us, words
 ending in**
octopus, plural of **-us, words
 ending in**
oculist **oculist** /
oculomotor nerve **cranial nerves**
odometer **speedometer** /
odoriferous **-or** /
odor, odour **-or** /
odorous **-or** /
Odyssey **dramatic poetry** /**; Scylla** /
Oedipus Rex **opera** /
oestradiol **androgen** /
oestrogen **androgen** /
Offa's Dyke **England** /
off-Broadway theater **illegal** /
official **official** /
officious **official** /
off-off-Broadway theater **illegal** /
offset **letterpress** /
offset lithography **intaglio** /
of which **who** / **that**
ogonek **acute** / **grave** /
Ohio **North** /
-oi, Greek plurals ending in **-us,
 words ending in**

Oklahoma **North** /
Old English **purism** /**; style** /
old folks' home **rest home** /
Old Kingdom of Egypt **Old
 Kingdom** /
old style **Julian calendar** /**;
 modern** /
Old Style type **serif** /
olfactory nerve **cranial nerves**
oligopsony **monopsony** /
oligosaccharide **fructose** /
"*Omnipotent Whom, The*" **who** /
 whom
omnivore **carnivore** /
on a slow boat to China **boat** /
oner-, Latin root of *onus* **-us,
 words ending in**
onerous **-us, words ending in**
on the carpet **carpet** /
onus **-us, words ending in**
onus, plural of **-us, words ending
 in**
opal **silica** /
open fracture **simple fracture** /
open shop **open shop** /
opera **grand opera** /**; opera** /**; -us,
 words ending in**
opera **aria** /
opera, as plural of *opus* **-us, words
 ending in**
opéra bouffe **grand opera** /
opera buffa **grand opera** /
opéra comique **grand opera** /
opera-oratorio **opera** /
opera seria **grand opera** /**; opera** /
operetta **opera** /
ophthalmic optician **oculist** /
ophthalmologist **oculist** /
Oporto **claret** /
optative subjunctive **indicative** /
optical phenomena **laurence** /
optician **oculist** /
optic nerve **cranial nerves**

optometrist **oculist** /
opus **opus** /; **-us, words ending in**
opuses, as plural of *opus* **-us,**
  words ending in
opus, plural of **-us, words ending**
  in
or **either .. or** /
oral **nasal** /
oratorio **opera** /
oratorio **aria** /
orbit, points in earth's **apogee** /
orchestra **band** /
ordinal **cardinal** /
ordinary share **common stock** /
ordinate **abscissa** /
oread **dryad** /
oregano **oregano** /
Oregon **North** /
organic **organic** /
organic chemistry **organic** /
organicism **dynamism** /
organ transplant **donor** /
orient **orient** /
oriental "arts?" of self-defense
  judo /
original sin **Virgin Birth** /
orvieto **claret** /
-os, Greek words ending in **-us,**
  words ending in
osmosis **absorption** /
ossicle **anvil** /
osteomyelitis **bacteria** /
Ostrogoths **Goth** /
Othello **metaphor** /
Otto the Great (912–73; r.962–73)
  Roman Empire /
ounce **avoirdupois weight** /
Our Mutual Friend **common** /
-ous, as a chemical suffix **-ic** /
-ous, names ending in **-ate** /
-ous, the ending **-us, words ending**
  in
-ous **-us, words ending in**

outboard motor **motor** /
outer ear **anvil** /
output **input** /
ovarian function control
  endocrine /
over for *more than* **better than** /
overthrow of all noncommunist
  states **Bolshevism** /
overtone **overtone** /
oviparous **oviparous** /
ovoviviparous **oviparous** /
ovulation **circadian** /
owing to **due to** /
Oxbridge **Oxbridge** /
Oxford Movement **Low Church** /
Oxford University **Oxbridge** /

P

Pacific Northwest **North** /
Pacific Time Zone **Greenwich**
  Mean Time /
page **page** /
Paleolithic **Paleolithic** /
Palermo stone **Old Kingdom** /
Palestine, influence of Egypt on
  Old Kingdom /
palimpsest **parchment** /
Pali scriptures **Hinayana**
  Buddhism /
pandemic **endemic**
paneling **dado** /
Pangaea **Pangaea** /
Panhandle **North** /
panic **abstract noun** /
Pannonia **Vandal** /
pão **acute / grave** /
paper **parchment** /
paper **parchment** /
paper money **species** /
paper wasp **wasp** /
Papua New Guinea **England** /;
  Polynesia /
papyrus **parchment** /

parakeet **budgerigar** /
parallels of latitude **latitude** /
parameter **parameter** /
paranasal sinuses **adenoid** /
parathyroid glands **endocrine** /
parchment **parchment** /
parentheses **parentheses** /
pareve **kosher** /
Parliament **lower house** /
Parliament of Great Britain **House of Commons** /
parr **smelt** /
parrakeet **budgerigar** /
parrot **budgerigar** /
part and parcel **flotsam** /
partial eclipse **lunar eclipse** /
partially **partly** /
partially ordered set **partly** /
partially sighted **partly** /
partly **partly** /
partly here **partly** /
partly inflecting languages **adjective** /
partly there **partly** /
partnership **corporation** /
parts of speech in dictionaries **dictionary** / **glossary** /
par value **book value** /
parve **kosher** /
passion and emotions, seat of **black bile** /
passive satellites **troposphere** /
pasteurized milk **pasteurized** /
pasto **antipasto** /
pastoral romances, setting of **Acadia** /
pâté **acute** / **grave** /; **pâté** /
patent **copyright** /
patio **balcony** /
Paumotu Archipelago **Polynesia** /
payable **account receivable** /
pd. **abbreviation** /
peach brandy **brandy** /

ped. **abbreviation** /
pedagog **pedant** /
pedagogical **pedant** /
pedagogue **pedant** /
pedant **pedant** /
pedantic **pedant** /
pedantry **pedant** /
pedestrian **pedant** /
peer **peer** /
peerage **peer** /
peerless **peer** /
peer of the realm **peer** /
pelagic zone **littoral** /
penal code **civil law** /
penates **lares** /
peninsula **cape** /
pen name **nom de plume** /
Pennsylvania **North** /
pennyweight **avoirdupois weight** /
pentameter **iamb** /
penumbra **penumbra** /
Pepi II Nefetkare **Old Kingdom** /
Pepin (?–768) **Merovingian** /
pepper **herb** /
perennial plant **herb** /
perfect binding **sewn binding** /
perfect flower **dioecious** /
perfecting press **sewn binding** /
"perfection" in language **purism** /
perfume **perfume** /
Pergamum **parchment** /
Pergamon **parchment** /
perigee **apogee** /
perimeter **parameter** /
periodical cicada **circadian** /
periods, use of in abbreviations **abbreviation** /
perk **requirement** /
permanent teeth **deciduous** /
permanent teeth **incisor** /
"permissive" **style** /
permissiveness **purism** /
permissivist **purism** /

perq **requirement** /
perquisite **requirement** /
Persia, invasion of by Huns
   Vandal /
Persians **Old Kingdom** /
personality and body type
   ectomorph /
personnel **material** /
perspective drawing **isometric** /
persuade **convince** /; **like** /
petit larceny **grand larceny** /
petit mal seizure **grand mal** /
petit point **gros point** /
Petrarchan sonnet **Shakespearian**
   sonnet /
petty larceny **grand larceny** /
pharmacist **druggist** /
pharyngeal tonsils **adenoid** /
pharynx **alimentary canal** /; **upper**
   respiratory tract /
phase **faze** /
philology **linguistics** /
phlegm **black bile** /
phlogiston **archaic** /
phone **phonetics** /
phoneme **phonetics** /
phonemes **consonant** /
phonemics **phonetics** /
phonetics **phonetics** /
phonetics **lexicography** /
phonological classification **centum** /
physical science **exact science** /
physics **exact science** /
pi **rational number** /
pia mater **arachnoid membrane** /
Piankhi **Old Kingdom** /
picketing **strike** /
pickle **pickle** /
pier **dock** /
pig iron **pig iron** /
pineal gland **endocrine** /
pintle **gudgeon** /
piperazine **histamine** /

"Pippa Passes" **dramatic poetry** /
pistil **dioecious** /
pistillate **dioecious** /
pistols **gun** /
pitch **accent** /
pitcher **iron** / **wood**
pitching niblick **iron** / **wood**
piteous **pitiful** /
pitiable **pitiful** /
pitiful **pitiful** /
pitifully **pitiful** /
Pittsburgh **city** /
pituitary gland **endocrine** /
pizzicato **violin** /
place of articulation **consonant** /;
   phonetics /
plagiarism **plagiarism** /
plague **typhoid** /
plaid **tartan** /
Plains states **North** /
plan **elevation** /
plano-concave **concave** /
plano-convex **concave** /
Plantagenet kings **Plantagenet** /
plastron **tortoise** /
Platonic year **Julian calendar** /
Plattdeutsch **High German** /
plc **common stock** /
"plead innocent" **innocent** /
plonk **claret** /
plural **singular** /
plutonium **atom bomb** /
pneumonia **bacteria** /
pocket billiards **billiards** /
poetic language **purism** /
poetic license **style** /
poetic meter **iamb** /
poetry, forms of **dramatic poetry** /
poikilothermal **cold-blooded** /
poikilothermal **circadian** /
polecat **ferret** /
polemics **apologetics** /
poliomyelitis **bacteria** /

polyandrous **diandrous** /
polyesters **wool** /
polygamy **monogamy** /
polyglot **linguistics** /
Polynesia **Polynesia** /
polysaccharide **fructose** /
Pompeii **atoll** /
Ponape Island **Polynesia** /
pond **lake** /
pony **colt** /
pool **billiards** /
pop **washing soda** /
Pope, Alexander (1688–1744)
   irony /
porcelain **china** /
porch **balcony** /
pornographic **obscene** /
pornography **obscene** /
port **claret** /; **harbor** /
portal veins **artery** /
porter **ale** /
portico **balcony** /
port out / *starboard home* **port** /
port side **port** /
port tack **lee** /
posh **port** /
positive **positive** /
positive terminal **cathode** /
POSSLQ **lover** /
post **beam** /
posterior **anterior** /
potential energy **kinetic energy** /
pound **avoirdupois weight** /
pox, pocks **chickenpox** /
practicable **practical** /
practical **practical** /
practice **license** /
practise **license** /
pre-, the bound form **prefix** /
pre- as meaningful element **bound form** /
precession of the equinoxes **Julian calendar** /

precipice **precipitous** /
precipitate **precipitous** /
precipitous **precipitous** /
precisians **purism** /
predicate adjectives in English
   adjective /
preface **preface** /
preference shares **common stock** /
preferred stock **common stock** /
prefix **prefix** /
prelims **preface** /
premeditated murder **homicide** /
premise **premise** /
premiss **premise** /
premolar **incisor** /
preposition, compound **due to** /
preposition, ending a sentence with
   a **grammar** /; **standard** /
prerequisite **requirement** /
prescribe **prescribe** /
prescription **prescribe** /
presently **presently** /
preserve **jam** /
preset guidance **inertial guidance** /
pressure **pressurize** /
pressurize **pressurize** /
presume **assume** /
presumption **assume** /
presumptive **presumptive** /
presumptuous **presumptive** /
pretence **pretence** /
pretense **pretence** /
pretension **pretence** /
pretentious **pretence** /
pretext **pretence** /
prevaricate **lie** / **fib** /
prevarication **lie** / **fib** /
preventative **preventive** /
preventive **preventive** /
preventive medicine **preventive** /
primary cell layers **ectoderm** /
"princes in the Tower" **red rose** /
principal **principal** /

principle **principal** /
principled **principal** /
printing **edition** /
private company **common stock** /
private enterprise **nationalization** /
private school **private school** /
privatives **amoral** /
privatization **nationalization** /
prix fixe **table d'hôte** /
pro-, the prefix **prescribe** /
product publicity **hard sell** /
profundal zone **littoral** /
prognosis **diagnosis** /
prognosticate **diagnosis** /
programme, programmed,
   programming **programming** /
program, programed, programing
   programming /
programs, computer **hardware** /
prolegomenon **preface** /
prologue **preface** /
promontory **cape** /
prone **prone** /
pronoun **whoever** /
pronoun, forms of the
   conjugation /
pronouns of reference **feminine** /
pronunciation **accent** /; **acute** /
   grave /
pronunciations in dictionaries
   dictionary / **glossary** /
proper fraction **proper fraction** /
prophecy **prophecy** /
prophesy **prophecy** /
propjet **turboprop** /
proportional **proportional** /
proportional representation
   proportional /
proportionate **proportional** /
proposal **proposal** /
proposition **proposal** /
proprietorship **corporation** /
propriety **informal** /

proscribe **prescribe** /
proscription **prescribe** /
prospectus, plural of **-us, words**
   ending in
protein **bacteria** /; **DNA** /
proton **nuclear** /
proton **element** /
prove **proved** /
proved **proved** /
proven **proved** /
provided (that) **provided** /
providing (that) **provided** /
przecinek **acute** / **grave** /
psammead **dryad** /
Psammetichus **Old Kingdom** /
pseudonym **nom de plume** /
psychiatrist **psychologist** /
psychiatry **psychologist** /
psychoanalysis **psychologist** /
psychologist **psychologist** /
psychology **psychologist** /
psychology **exact science** /
psychomotor seizure **grand mal** /
psychoneurosis **neurosis** /
psychoneurosis **psychologist** /
psychoneurotic **neurosis** /
psychosis **neurosis** /
psychosis **psychologist** /
Ptolemy I **Old Kingdom** /
p-type conductor **conductor** /
public company **common stock** /
public corporation **common stock** /
public limited company **common**
   stock /
public relations **hard sell** /
public school **private school** /
Puccini, Giacomo (1858–1924)
   opera /
pudding **mousse** /
pullover **cardigan** /
pull the rug out from under someone
   carpet /
pulmonary veins **artery** /

pulse-jet engine **turboprop** /
punctuation marks **parentheses** /
punitive damages **compensatory
damages** /
puppet **puppet** /
puppeteer **puppet** /
pure science **exact science** /
purine **DNA** /
purism **purism** /
purist **purism** /
Puritanism **informal** /
put **put** /
put option **put** /
putter **iron** / **wood**
putting iron **iron** / **wood**
pyknic **ectomorph** /
pyrimidine **DNA** /

Q

Q **nom de plume** /
quadraphonic **monophonic** /
quadriphonic **monophonic** /
quadrual **singular** /
quark **neologism** /
quarto **folio** /
quartz **crystal** /; **silica** /
quatrain **Shakespearian sonnet** /
quay **dock** /
Queens **city** /
Quiller-Couch, Sir Arthur
   (1863–1944) **nom de plume** /
quintal **avoirdupois weight** /
quork **neologism** /
quotations, information inserted in
   parentheses /
QWERTY **QWERTY keyboard** /

R

rabbit **hare** /
rack **wreak** /
racket **racket** /
racketeer **racket** /
racquet **racket** /

radar **abbreviation** /
radio tube **conductor** /
radio waves **long wave** /
radius **radius** /
rafter **beam** /
raglan sleeve **set-in sleeve** /
Raglan, 1st Baron (1788–1855) **set-
in sleeve** /
railroad **railroad** /
railway **railroad** /
Railway Express **railroad** /
raise **raise** /
ramjet **turboprop** /
Ramses I **Old Kingdom** /
Ramses II **Old Kingdom** /
Ramses III **Old Kingdom** /
random variable, values of **Markov
process** /
Rankine scale **Fahrenheit scale** /
rape **homicide** /
Rape of the Lock, The **irony** /
ratbite fever **bacteria** /
rational number **rational number** /
rat leaving a sinking ship **boat** /
raven **crow** /
reaction engine **turboprop** /
read-only memory **hardware** /
"Ready, about!" **lee** /
real for *really* **bad** /
rear **raise** /
Réaumur scale **Fahrenheit scale** /
rebec **violin** /
recall **initiative** /
receivable **account receivable** /
recessive **dominant** /
recipient **donor** /
recitative **aria** /
recitative **opera** /
recitativo accompagnato **aria** /
recitativo secco **aria** /
recitativo stromentato **aria** /
recoilless rifle **gun** /
recombinant DNA **DNA** /

rectifier, full-wave *conductor* /
rectifier, half-wave *conductor* /
rectum *large intestine* /
reçu *acute / grave* /
red blood cell *erythrocyte* /
redbrick *Oxbridge* /
red carpet *carpet* /
red corpuscle *erythrocyte* /
redecorate *refurnish* /
Red Right Return *can buoy* /
red rose *red rose* /
redundant negative *irregardless* /
referee *referee* /
referendum *initiative* /
reflecting telescope *reflecting
  telescope* /
Reform Act of 1832 *House of
  Commons* /
refracting telescope *reflecting
  telescope* /
refractory brick *silica* /
refurbish *refurnish* /
refurnish *refurnish* /
regardless *irregardless* /
regardless of *due to* /
regret *regret* /
Relais de Campagne, Route des
  Gourmands *gourmet* /
relation *relation* /
relative *relation* /
relative clause *main clause* /
relative humidity *humidity* /
relative pronoun *main clause /;
  who / that*
relaxation of heart muscles
  diastole /
relief printing *intaglio* /
remorse *regret* /
renovate *refurnish* /
rent strike *strike* /
rep *canvaswork* /
repeated *repetitious* /
repellent *repellent* /

repetitious *repetitious* /
repetitive *repetitious* /
repository *depository* /
Representatives *House of
  Representatives* /
reptile *snake* /
reptile *tortoise* /
repugnant *repellent* /
repulsive *repellent* /
requirement *requirement* /
requisite *requirement* /
residential community *rest home* /
restful *restful* /
restive *restful* /
restore *refurnish* /
restriction enzyme *DNA* /
restriction site *convergent
  evolution /; DNA* /
restrictive clause *that* /
restrictive modifier *descriptive
  modifier* /
retirement home *rest home* /
revenge *revenge* /
review *criticism* /
reviewer *criticism* /
Rh− *Rh-negative* /
rhetorical devices *metaphor* /
Rh-factor *Rh-negative* /
Rhine wine *claret* /
Rh-negative *Rh-negative* /
Rhode Island *North* /
Rhode Island clam chowder *New
  England chowder* /
rhotacism *iotacism* /
Rh-positive *Rh-negative* /
rhyme-scheme *Shakespearian
  sonnet* /
rhythm *alpha wave* /
ribonucleic acid *DNA* /
ribose *DNA* /
ribosomal RNA *DNA* /
ribosomes *DNA* /

Richard I "the Lionheart" (r.1189–99)
  Plantagenet /
Richard II (r.1377–99) *Plantagenet* /
Richard III (r.1483–85)
  Plantagenet /
Richard of Gloucester (1452–85;
  r.1483–85) *red rose* /
Richmond *city* /
Rickettsiae *typhoid* /
riesling *claret* /
rifle *gun* /
rifling *gun* /
"right" and "wrong" language
  purism /
right off the boat *boat* /
right of way at sea *lee* /
rill *river* /
"Rime of the Ancient Mariner, The"
  dramatic poetry /; *either* .. *or* /
risqué *acute* / *grave* /
risus sardonicus *sarcastic* /
rite *rite* /
rites of passage *rite* /
ritual *rite* /
Rivals, The *malapropism* /
river *river* /
rivulet *river* /
RNA *DNA* /
robbery *burglary* /
robbery *homicide* /
roça *acute* / *grave* /
rocaille *baroque* /
rock *icing sugar* /
rock band *band* /
rock candy *icing sugar* /
rock crystal *crystal* /
Rockefeller Center *freehold* /
rockets *turboprop* /
rock sugar *icing sugar* /
rock the boat *boat* /
rococity *neologism* /
rococo *baroque* /
rococo music *baroque* /

Roget, Peter Mark (1779–1869)
  dictionary / *glossary* /
Roget's Thesaurus *dictionary* /
  glossary /
rôle *acute* / *grave* /
rolled gold *solid gold* /
rolled steel joist *beam* /
roller-blind shutter *focal-plane
  shutter* /
ROM *hardware* /
Roman Catholic Church *High
  Mass* /
Roman Catholic dogma *Virgin
  Birth* /
Romance words in English
  grammar /
Roman Emperor *Roman Empire* /
Roman Empire *Roman Empire* /
Roman Empire *Goth* /
Roman Empire, invasions of
  Vandal /
Roman household gods *lares* /
Roman numerals *Roman numerals* /
roman type *italic* /
Rome, fall of *Vandal* /
rook *crow* /
rosé *claret* /
rose engine *motor* /
Rossini, Gioacchino (1792–1868)
  opera /
Rossini, Gioacchino Antonio
  (1792–1868) *grand opera* /
rotating-wing aircraft *autogiro* /
rough breathing (Greek
  pronunciation) *acute* / *grave* /
rounded *phonetics* /
row houses *balcony* /
royal families of England
  Plantagenet /
rRNA *DNA* /
RSJ *beam* /
rubber bridge *contract bridge* /
rubella *measles* /

rubeola **measles** /
rudder fittings **gudgeon** /
rug **carpet** /
Rugby **private school** /
rules of the road at sea **lee** /
run a tight (or *taut*) *ship* **boat** /
running head **page** /
running title **page** /
Russia **Bolshevism** /

S

saddle-wire binding **sewn binding** /
sailing yachts, rigs of **sloop** /
Saite kings of Egypt **Old
    Kingdom** /
Saki **nom de plume** /
salary **salary** /
Salian Franks **Goth** /
Salmonella typhi **typhoid** /
salmon spawning **anadromous** /
salon **salon** /
saloon **salon** /
saloon bar **salon** /
sal soda **washing soda** /
salts **-ate** /
Samoa Islands **Polynesia** /
samurai, weapons and ceremonial
    gear **katana** /
sand crabs **circadian** /
sanserif **serif** /
sans serif **serif** /
Santa Cruz Island **Polynesia** /
Saqqara **Old Kingdom** /
sarcasm **sarcastic** /
sarcastic **sarcastic** /
sarcastic spoof **irony** /
sardonic **sarcastic** /
sardonicism **sarcastic** /
Sarvastivada **Hinayana Buddhism** /
sash window **mullion** /
satellites, active **troposphere** /
satellites, passive **troposphere** /
satem languages **centum** /

satire **irony** /
satyriasis **nymphomania** /
satyromania **nymphomania** /
sauce **gravy** /
Saxe-Coburg-Gotha **Plantagenet** /
scalar quantity **speed** /
scalene triangle **scalene** /
Scarlatti, Alessandro (1659–1725)
    opera /
scarlet fever **bacteria** /
scattering of data **mean deviation** /
scent **perfume** /
Schoenberg, Arnold (1874–1951)
    opera /
schooner **sloop** /
Schutzstaffel **Gestapo** /
science as a term **exact science** /
scientific as a term **exact science** /
scientific naming **phylum** /
scintilla **metaphor** /
scintillation **laurence** /
scorpion **bug** /
Scotch whisky **whisky** /
Scotland **England** /
Scotland **Highlands** /
Scott, Sir Walter (1771–1832) **red
    rose** /
"Scourge of God" **Vandal** /
screw **bolt** /
script for Arabic **Kufic** /
scruple **avoirdupois weight** /
Scylla and Charybdis **Scylla** /
Scythia, invasion of by Huns
    Vandal /
sea grasses **circadian** /
seal **seal** /
sea lion **seal** /
sea mile **statute mile** /
seamount **atoll** /
séance **acute** / **grave** /
seas **lake** /
seasoning **herb** /
seasoning **oregano** /

second *first* /
secondary boycott *strike* /
secondary school *college* /
second degree murder *homicide* /
Second Intermediate Period of Egypt
   Old Kingdom /
second mortgage *first mortgage* /
secret police *Gestapo* /
section *elevation* /; *sewn binding* /
security *bond* /
seed production *circadian* /
self-tapping screw *bolt* /
selling *hard sell* /
Selterser Wasser *club soda* /
seltzer *club soda* /
semantics *lexicography* /
semi- *demi-* /
semi-, the prefix *bi-* /
semiannually *demi-* /
semiautomatic *demi-* /
semicircle *demi-* /
semiconductor *conductor* /
semiconductor *silica* /
semiconductor, intrinsic *conductor* /
semiconscious *demi-* /
semimonthly *demi-* /
Semitic branch *Yiddish* /
Semitic people in Egypt *Old*
   Kingdom /
semiweekly *demi-* /
Senate *House of Representatives* /
Senate *lower house* /
Senators *House of*
   Representatives /
senior citizen community *rest*
   home /
señor *acute* / *grave* /
sensorimotor *ideomotor* /
sensory functions of the brain
   cerebrum /
separatrix *dagger* /; *numerator* /
Sepharad *Ashkenazi* /
Sephardi *Ashkenazi* /

septentrional *austral* /
serenade *sedition* /
serif *serif* /
serpent *snake* /
Sesostris *Old Kingdom* /
sesqui- *demi-* /
sesquicentennial *demi-* /
sestet *Shakespearian sonnet* /
Seti I *Old Kingdom* /
set-in sleeve *set-in sleeve* /
settee *bergère* /
settlements, development of
   Paleolithic /
settling-day *backwardation* /
seventeen-year locust *circadian* /
sewn binding *sewn binding* /
sex and gender *feminine* /
sex chromosome *X chromosome* /
sex hormones *androgen* /
sex of nouns *feminine* /
sex organs *informal* /
sexual acts *informal* /
sexual intercourse *informal* /
sexual recombination of genes
   DNA /
Seychelles *England* /
Shakespeare, William (1564–1616)
   ferret /; *red rose* /; *who* / *whom*
Shakespeare's English *purism* /
Shakespearian sonnet
   Shakespearian sonnet /
shall *shall* /
shape up or ship out *boat* /
share *corporation* /
share certificate *bond* /
shareholder *corporation* /; *cum*
   dividend /
Shaw, George Bernard (1856–1950)
   literally /
sheepskin *parchment* /
sheep, wool from *wool* /
Shelley, Percy Bysshe (1792–1822)
   dramatic poetry /

shelve **table** /
sherbet **ice cream** /
Sheridan, Richard Brinsley
   (1751–1816) **malapropism** /
sherry **claret** /
shinbone **fibula** /
ship **boat** /
ship oars **boat** /
ship of fools **boat** /
ship of state **boat** /
ship of the desert **boat** /
ship, positions / directions on **port** /
ship's company **boat** /
shipshape **boat** /
ship's papers **boat** /
ships that pass in the night **boat** /
ship water **boat** /
shit **informal** /
short story **novel** /
short ton **avoirdupois weight** /
short wave **long wave** /
shotgun **gun** /
should **shall** /
Shrewsbury **private school** /
shrimp **bug** /; **crayfish** /
shrub **bush** /
Shubenacadie river **Acadia** /
sickle cell anemia **endemic**
side-wire binding **sewn binding** /
Sidney, Sir Philip **Acadia** /
Sierra Leone **England** /
sigmatism **iotacism** /
signature **sewn binding** /
silica **silica** /
silicon dioxide **silica** /
silicone **silica** /
silicon oxide **silica** /
Silingian Vandals **Vandal** /
silk **wool** /
silk screen **intaglio** /
silkworm **wool** /
silver, obsolete word for **archaic** /
similar to **metaphor** /

simile **metaphor** /
simple fraction **integer** /; **simple
  fraction** /
simple fracture **simple fracture** /
simple sentence **simple sentence** /
simple sugars **fructose** /
simplified spelling **-or** /
sine **sine** /
Singapore **England** /
singing voices **bass** /
single cuff **single cuff** /
singular **singular** /
sinuses **adenoid** /
sister ship **boat** /
"sitcoms" **high comedy** /
sit-down strike **strike** /
site **locate** /
situate **locate** /
situation **locate** /
situation-comedies **high comedy** /
sixty-fourmo **folio** /
skunk **ferret** /
slander **libel** /
slang **informal** /
slang **style** /
SLANG **purism** /
slash **dagger** /
Slavonic **centum** /
slender build **ectomorph** /
sliced bread **thin** /
sliced thin **thin** /
sliced thinly **thin** /
slight breeze **breeze** /
slipknot **square knot** /
sloop **sloop** /
slowdown **strike** /
sluggishness, seat of **black bile** /
small arms **gun** /
small calorie **calorie** /
small intestine **large intestine** /
smallpox **chickenpox** /
smelt **smelt** /
smolt **smelt** /

smooth breathing (Greek
  pronunciation) *acute / grave /*
smooth muscle *smooth muscle /*
Smyth-sewn binding *sewn binding /*
snake in the grass *snake /*
snooker *billiards /*
snowed under *metaphor /*
snow job *metaphor /*
social bee *wasp /*
socialist state *Bolshevism /*
social psychology *psychologist /*
social science *exact science /*
Society for Nautical Research *port /*
Society Islands *Polynesia /*
soda *washing soda /*
soda pop *washing soda /*
soda water *club soda /; washing
  soda /*
sodium acid carbonate *washing
  soda /*
sodium bicarbonate *baking
  powder /; washing soda /*
sodium carbonate *washing soda /*
sodium hydroxide *washing soda /*
sodium monoxide *washing soda /*
sodium vapor lamp *incandescent /*
soft sell *hard sell /*
software *hardware /*
soigné *acute / grave /*
soil layers, types of *A horizon /*
solar day *ebb tide /*
solar eclipse *lunar eclipse /*
solar wind *interplanetary /*
Solder *braze /*
soldering iron *braze /*
solicitor *barrister /*
solid *fluid /*
solid gold *solid gold /*
solidus *dagger /*
soliloquy *monologue /*
solitary bee *wasp /*
Solomon Islands *England /;
  Polynesia /*

solstice *equinox /*
solution *element /*
somatotypes *ectomorph /*
soon *presently /*
soprano *bass /*
sorbet *ice cream /*
so that *indicative /*
soufflé *mousse /*
sound reproduction system
  tweeter /
sounds, excessive use of *iotacism /*
sounds of English *consonant /*
South *North /*
South Carolina *North /*
South Dakota *North /*
Southeast *North /*
'southern' *austral /*
south frigid zone *Arctic Circle /*
South, the *Confederate States of
  America /; South /*
Southwest *North /*
Soviet Union *Bolshevism /*
space ship *boat /*
Spain *Goth /*
Spain, invasion of by Vandals
  Vandal /
Spanish Inquisition *Ashkenazi /*
Spanish pox *chickenpox /*
sparkling burgundy *champagne /*
sparkling wine *champagne /*
spasmodic *spasmodic /*
spear side *distaff side /*
special police *Gestapo /*
specie *species /*
species *species /*
specious *spurious /*
specious argument *spurious /*
speech *cerebrum /*
speed *speed /*
speed *airspeed /*
speedometer *speedometer /*
spelling reform *-ise /; -or /*

Spenserian sonnet **Shakespearian sonnet** /
sphenoidal sinuses **upper respiratory tract** /
spice **herb** /
spider **bug** /
spinal accessory nerve **cranial nerves**
spinal cord **arachnoid membrane** /; **gray matter** /
spiny lobster **crayfish** /
spire **steeple** /
spirilla **bacteria** /
spiritus asper **acute** / **grave** /
spiritus lenis **acute** / **grave** /
splitting infinitives **grammar** /
spondee **iamb** /
spoof **irony** /
spoon **iron** / **wood**
spoonerism **malapropism** /
Spooner, Reverend W. A. (1844–1930) **malapropism** /
sporadic **spasmodic** /
sports **game** /
spring tide **ebb tide**
spumante **champagne** /
spurious **spurious** /
spurious coin **spurious** /
square brackets **parentheses** /
square knot **square knot** /
squash racquets **racket** /
Sri Lanka **England** /; **Hinayana Buddhism** /
SS **Gestapo** /
stage left **upstage** /
stage right **upstage** /
stalactite **stalactite** /
stalagmite **stalactite** /
St. Albans, Battle of **red rose** /
Stalin, Josef V. (1879–1953) **Bolshevism** /
Stalinism **Bolshevism** /
stallion **colt** /

stamen **dioecious** /
staminate **dioecious** /
stanch **stanch** /
standard **standard** /
standard deviation **mean deviation** /
Standard Time **Greenwich Mean Time** /
stapes **anvil** /
Staphylococcus **bacteria** /
starboard side **port** /
starboard tack **lee** /
starch **fructose** /
starlike symbol **dagger** /
START **abbreviation** /
starter **antipasto** /
Staten Island **city** /
statute law **civil law** /
statute mile **statute mile** /
statute mile **breeze** /
statutory referendum **initiative** /
staunch **stanch** /
stays (in stays) **irons** /
steady-state theory **big bang theory** /
steamship **motor** /
steel **iron** / **steel**
steel **pig iron** /
steeple **steeple** /
steer(ing)board **port** /
Stephen (r.1135–54) **Plantagenet** /
stereophonic **monophonic** /
stern **port** /
Stesichorus, idylls of **Acadia** /
stimulus / *stimuli* **-us, words ending in**
sting **wasp** /
stirrup **anvil** /
St. Kitts-Nevis **England** /
St. Lucia **England** /
stochastic process **Markov process** /
stock certificate **bond** /
stocky build **ectomorph** /
stoic **Cynic** /

stoical **Cynic** /
Stone Age, stages of **Paleolithic** /
stone fence **fence** /
stonewall **fence** /
stoneware **china** /
stone (weight) **avoirdupois weight** /
stop **consonant /; phonetics** /
storm **breeze** /
strake **carvel-built** /
strata **stratum** /
stratagem **strategy** /
strategy **strategy** /
stratosphere **troposphere** /
stratum **stratum** /
Stravinsky, Igor (1882–1971) **opera** /
streak **carvel-built** /
stream **river** /
streamlet **river** /
Streptococcus **bacteria** /
stress **accent** /
striated muscle **smooth muscle** /
strike **strike** /
strike action **strike** /
striptease **exotic** /
stroke **heart attack** /
strong breeze **breeze** /
strong gale **breeze** /
Stuart rulers **Plantagenet** /
stud **beam** /
stuffing **gravy** /
St. Vincent **England** /
style in language **purism /; style** /
stymie **billiards** /
subarachnoid space **arachnoid membrane** /
subdural space **arachnoid membrane** /
subjects, explanations of **dictionary / encyclopedia**
subjunctive mood **indicative** /
sublittoral zone **littoral** /
submarine **boat** /
subnormal **abnormal** /

subordinate clause **main clause** /
subordinate constructions **indicative** /
subspecies **phylum** /
substantial damages **compensatory damages** /
subtopia **utopia** /
suburb **utopia** /
subutopia **utopia** /
succeed **successful** /
success **successful** /
successful **successful** /
succession **successful** /
successive **successful** /
succory **chicory** /
sucrose **fructose** /
suffix **prefix** /
sugar metabolism control **endocrine** /
sulcus **cerebrum** /
sulfate **-ate** /
sulfite **-ate** /
sulfuric **-ate /; -ic** /
sulfurous **-ate /; -ic** /
Sullivan, Sir Arthur S. (1842–1900) **opera** /
summa cum laude **cum laude** /
summerhouse **belvedere** /
Summer Solstice **equinox** /
summer solstice **Greenwich Mean Time /; Tropic of Cancer** /
Sunbelt **North** /
sunken fence **fence** /
supercontinent **Pangaea** /
superfine sugar **icing sugar** /
superior conjunction **inferior conjunction** /
Superior, Lake **lake** /
superlative **positive** /
superlative of adjectives in English **adjective** /
supine **prone** /
surd **rational number** /

surface boundary layers
   macrometeorology /
surprise **amaze** /
suspension **element** /
Swaziland **England** /
sweep under the rug / carpet
   carpet /
sweet marjoram **oregano** /
sweet marten **ferret** /
Swift, Jonathan (1667–1745) **irony** /
Swiftie or *Swifty, Tom*
   malapropism /
switch **toupee** /
sympathetic magic **contagious**
   magic /
symphony **symphony** /
synapse **neuron** /
synonym **synonym** /
synonyms in dictionaries
   dictionary / **glossary** /
syntax **grammar** /
syntax **style** /
syntax of some languages
   adjective /
synthesis **analysis** /
synthesize, synthesise **analysis** /
synthetic **analysis** /
synthetic fibers **wool** /
synthetize, synthetise **analysis** /
syphilis **chickenpox** /
Syria, influence of Egypt on **Old**
   Kingdom /
systemic veins **artery** /
systole **diastole** /

T

table **abstract noun** /; **table** /
table d'hôte **table d'hôte** /
taboo **informal** /
taboo words **obscene** /
tachograph **speedometer** /
tachometer **speedometer** /
tachycardia **bradycardia** /

tack **lee** /
tactics **strategy** /
take **bring** /
takeoff **irony** /
tallboy **highboy** /
tally **lover** /
tangent **sine** /
tangential **sine** /
Tanzania **England** /
tapestry **canvaswork** /
tartan **tartan** /
Tartarus **tortoise** /
tatting **canvaswork** /
taxonomy **phylum** /
Tay-Sachs disease **endemic** /
teacher **educator** /
technology **exact science** /
teeth, kinds of **incisor** /
telamon **atlas** /
telemarketing **direct mail** /
telescopes **reflecting telescope** /
television screen **cathode** /
Tell el-Amarna **Old Kingdom** /
temerarious **timidity** /
temerity **timidity** /
temperament and health, control of
   black bile /
temperature **humidity** /
temperature **zero** /
temperature, body **cold-blooded** /
temperature scales **Fahrenheit**
   scale /
tempo **adagio** /
Tennessee **North** /
tennis **game** /
tenor **bass** /
tenor viol **violin** /
tenseness **phonetics** /
tent stitch **gros point** /
terefah **kosher** /
term to be defined **definiens** /
terrace **balcony** /
terraced houses **balcony** /

terrapin   **tortoise** /
terrine   **pâté** /
Terry, Ellen (?1848–1928)   **literally** /
testes   **endocrine** /
testosterone   **androgen** /;
   endocrine /
tetanus   **bacteria** /
"tetragraph"   **diphthong** /
tetrameter   **iamb** /
Teutonic people   **Goth** /
Texas   **North** /
textiles and earthenware,
   development of   **Paleolithic** /
thalamus / thalami   **-us, words
   ending in**
that   **that** /; **this** /; **who** / **that**
Thebes   **Old Kingdom** /
theft   **burglary** /
The Merry Wives of Windsor
   ferret /
Theravada   **Hinayana Buddhism** /
thermionic valve   **conductor** /
thermometer   **barometer** /
thermonuclear reaction   **nuclear
   fission** /
thermonuclear reaction   **atom
   bomb** /
Thermopylae, taken by Huns
   Vandal /
thermostat   **barometer** /
thesaurus   **dictionary** / **glossary** /
thesaurus, plural of   **-us, words
   ending in**
theta wave or rhythm   **alpha
   wave** /
Thiebaud, Wayne (b. 1920)
   idealism /
thief   **burglary** /
thin   **thin** /
thinly   **thin** /
third   **first** /
thirty-twomo   **folio** /
this   **this** /

thorough bass   **violin** /
thought   **abstract noun** /
thousand million   **billion** /
thromboembolism   **embolus** /
thrombosis   **embolus** /
thrombus   **embolus** /
thrombus   **heart attack** /
thrombus / thrombi   **-us, words
   ending in**
throughput   **input** /
Thutmose   **Old Kingdom** /
Thutmose I   **Old Kingdom** /
Thutmose III   **Old Kingdom** /
thymine   **DNA** /
thymus gland   **endocrine** /
thyroid gland   **endocrine** /
tía   **acute** / **grave** /
Tibet   **Hinayana Buddhism** /
tibia   **fibula** /
tick   **bug** /
tides   **ebb tide** /
tied house   **tied house** /
tiger lily   **tiger lily** /
'til   **till** /
tilde   **acute** / **grave** /
till   **till** /
'till   **till** /
timid   **timidity** /
timidity   **timidity** /
timorous   **timidity** /
-tion, the bound form   **prefix** /
title page   **colophon** /
Tocharian   **centum** /
toilet water   **perfume** /
token   **type** /
tolerance   **tolerance** /
tolerant   **tolerance** /
toleration   **tolerance** /
tolmen   **cromlech** /
Tom Swiftie   **malapropism** /
tone, in Chinese   **accent** /
Tonga   **England** /; **Polynesia** /
tonsils   **adenoid** /

tools, bone **Paleolithic** /
tools, flint **Paleolithic** /
tools, stone **Paleolithic** /
tools, use of **Paleolithic** /
tornado **cyclone** /
torrão **acute** / **grave** /
Torricellian tube or barometer
   barometer /
tortoise **tortoise** /
tortuous **tortuous** /
torture **tortuous** /
torturous **tortuous** /
total eclipse **lunar eclipse** /
totally ordered set **partly** /
toupee **toupee** /
to weather **lee** /
Tower of London, ravens at **crow** /
to windward **lee** /
town **city** /
township **city** /
trachea **alimentary canal** /**; upper
   respiratory tract** /
trademark, publisher's **colophon** /
traditional forms of worship **Low
   Church** /
transcendental number **rational
   number** /
transfer RNA **DNA** /
transformation **toupee** /
transistor **conductor** /
transverse colon **large intestine** /
treason **sedition** /
treble viol **violin** /
tree **bush** /
tref **kosher** /
trefah **kosher** /
trial **singular** /
trigeminal nerve **cranial nerves**
trigesimo-secundo **folio** /
trigonometric functions **sine** /
trigraph **diphthong** /
trillion **billion** /
trimeter **iamb** /

Trinidad and Tobago **England** /
triphthong **diphthong** /
triumphal **triumphal** /
triumphant **triumphal** /
tRNA **DNA** /
trochee **iamb** /
trochlear nerve **cranial nerves**
trópico **acute** / **grave** /
Tropic of Cancer **Tropic of
   Cancer** /
Tropic of Cancer **equinox** /
Tropic of Capricorn **Tropic of
   Cancer** /
Tropic of Capricorn **equinox** /
troposphere **troposphere** /
Trotskyism **Bolshevism** /
Trotsky, Leon (1879–1940)
   Bolshevism /
troy weight (table) **avoirdupois
   weight** /
true north **true north** /
true value **mean deviation** /
Truk Island **Polynesia** /
tsarist regime **Bolshevism** /
Tuamotu Archipelago **Polynesia** /
tuberculosis **bacteria** /
Tubuai Islands **Polynesia** /
Tudor, Henry (1457–1509;
   r.1485–1509) **red rose** /
Tudor rulers **Plantagenet** /
turbinado **icing sugar** /
turbojet **turboprop** /
turbopropeller engine **turboprop** /
turtle **tortoise** /
turtledove **tortoise** /
Tutankhamun **Old Kingdom** /
Tutankhaton **Old Kingdom** /
Tuvalu **England** /
twain **singular** /
Twain, Mark (1835–1910) **style** /
tweeter **tweeter** /
tweeter-woofer **tweeter** /
twelvemo **folio** /

tympanum **anvil** /
type **type** /
typewriter keyboard **QWERTY keyboard** /
typhoid fever **typhoid** /
typhoon **cyclone** /
typhus **bacteria** /
typographic symbols **dagger** /

U

Uganda **England** /
UHF **AM (VHF)** /
uisce beathadh **whisky** /
uisge beatha **whisky** /
Ulanov, Vladimir Ilyich
  Bolshevism /
ulna **radius** /
ultrahigh frequency **AM (VHF)** /
-*um*, plurals of words ending in - **us, words ending in**
-*um*, words ending in **stratum** /
umbra **penumbra** /
umlaut **acute / grave** /
umpire **referee** /
un-, the prefix **amoral** /
unabridged **abridged** /
under, the free form **prefix** /
undertone **overtone** /
UNESCO **abbreviation** /
uninterested **disinterested /; like** /
Union army **Blue** /
Union of Soviet Socialist Republics
  Bolshevism /
Union, the **Confederate States of America** /
united, a before **a** /
United Kingdom **England** /
United Kingdom of Great Britain and
  Northern Ireland **England** /
United States **Confederate States of America** /
United States System **magnum**

United States Trust Territory
  Polynesia /
universal constant **constant** /
university **college** /
unlawful **illegal** /
unliquidated damages
  compensatory damages /
unprincipled **principal** /
unrounded **phonetics** /
until **till** /
untruth **lie / fib** /
unvoiced **phonetics** /
unvoiced **consonant** /
unwarranted **guarantee** /
Upanishads **Buddhism** /
upbeat **downbeat** /
upper chamber **lower house** /
upper house **lower house** /
upper jaw **mandible** /
Upper Middle West **North** /
Upper Midwest **North** /
Upper Paleolithic **Paleolithic** /
upper respiratory tract **upper respiratory tract** /
upstage **upstage** /
uptown **city** /
uracil **DNA** /
uranium **atom bomb /; nuclear** /
urban sprawl **city** /
Ursa Major **austral** /
-us, Latin plurals ending in **-us, words ending in**
-*us*, Latin words ending in **-us, words ending in**
-*us*, plurals of words ending in **-us, words ending in**
-*us*, the ending **-us, words ending in**
-*us*, words ending in **-us, words ending in**
U.S.A. **abbreviation** /
usage **use** /

usage information in dictionaries
   dictionary / *glossary* /
usage of English   *style* /
use   *use* /
use, a before   *a* /
usquebaugh   *whisky* /
U.S.S.R.   *Bolshevism* /
Utah   *North* /
Utopia   *utopia* /

V

vaccinate   *vaccinate* /
vaccine   *vaccinate* /
vaccinia virus   *chickenpox* /
vagina   *informal* /
vagus nerve   *cranial nerves*
valence band   *conductor* /
Valley of the Tombs of the Kings
   Old Kingdom /
vandalism   *Vandal* /
Vandals   *Vandal* /
Vandals   *Goth* /
Vanuatu   *England* /
variable   *constant* /
variation   *true north* /
varicella   *chickenpox* /
varicella zoster virus   *chickenpox* /
variety   *phylum* /
variola   *chickenpox* /
variola major   *chickenpox* /
variola minor   *chickenpox* /
vasoconstrictor control   *endocrine* /
veal   *parchment* /
vector quantity   *speed* /
vegetable   *animal* /; *fruit* /
vehicular homicide   *homicide* /
vein   *artery* /
veinous system   *artery* /
velar stop   *centum* /
vellum   *parchment* /
velocity   *speed* /
velum   *nasal* /
venal   *venal* /

vend   *venal* /
vengeance   *revenge* /
venial   *venal* /
ventral   *anterior* /
venules   *artery* /
Venus's-flytrap   *animal* /
veranda, verandah   *balcony* /
verão   *acute* / *grave* /
verb endings   *adjective* /
verb, forms of the   *conjugation* /
Verdi, Giuseppe (1813–91)   *opera* /
vermiform appendix   *large*
   intestine /
Vermont   *North* /
Vernal Equinox   *equinox* /
vernal equinox   *Arctic Circle* /
verse   *iamb* /
vertebrates (*Vertebrata*) as subphylum
   phylum /
very high frequency   *AM (VHF)* /
vessel, positions / directions on
   port /
Vesuvius   *atoll* /
VHF   *AM (VHF)* /
Victoria (r.1837–1901)   *Plantagenet* /
vicuña, wool from   *wool* /
village   *city* /
vintage port   *claret* /
viol   *violin* /
viola bastarda   *violin* /
viola da gamba   *violin* /
viol family   *violin* /
violin   *violin* /
violoncello   *violin* /
violone   *violin* /
viral disease   *measles* /
Virgin Birth   *Virgin Birth* /
Virginia   *North* /
Virgin Mary   *Virgin Birth* /
virgule   *dagger* /
virus   *bacteria* /
virus   *bug* /
Visigoths   *Vandal* /

vitalism   **dynamism** /
viviparous   **oviparous** /
vocabulary   **style** /
voiced   **phonetics** /
voiced   **consonant** /
voiceless   **phonetics** /
voiceless vowel   **consonant** /
volcanic island   **atoll** /
volcano   **atoll** /
volitive subjunctive   **indicative** /
voluntary manslaughter   **homicide** /
voluntary muscles   **smooth muscle** /
vowel   **consonant** /
vowel   **diphthong** /; **phonetics** /
vowel, fullness of   **accent** /
vulcanology   **exact science** /
VULGARISMS   **purism** /

W

wage   **salary** /
Wagner, Richard (1813–83)   **opera** /
wainscot   **dado** /
wainscoting)   **dado** /
wait for   **wait for** / **await; wait for** /
   wait on
wait for one's ship to come in
   boat /
wait on   **wait for** / **wait on**
wakizashi   **katana** /
Wales   **England** /
wall   **fence** /
wall-to-wall carpet   **carpet** /
War Between the States   **Blue** /;
   Confederate States of America /
warm-blooded   **cold-blooded** /
warm front   **cold front** /
warp   **warp** /
warping   **lie** / **fib** /
warrant   **guarantee** /
warrantee   **guarantee** /
warrantor   **guarantee** /
warranty   **guarantee** /
Wars of the Roses   **red rose** /

washing soda   **washing soda** /
Washington   **North** /
Washington, D.C.   **North** /
Washington, D.C. / Boston   **city** /
wasp   **wasp** /
wasp-waisted   **wasp** /
water, boiling point of   **Fahrenheit**
   scale /
water, freezing point of   **Fahrenheit**
   scale /
waterproof   **waterproof** /
water-repellent   **waterproof** /
water-resistant   **waterproof** /
waterspout   **cyclone** /
water vapor in the atmosphere
   humidity /
Waugh, Evelyn (1903–66)   **irony** /
wavelengths   **long wave** /
weasel   **ferret** /
weather   **lee** /
weather, study of
   macrometeorology /
web   **folio** /; **sewn binding** /
Webster, Noah (1758–1843)   **-or** /
wed   **marriage** /
wedded   **marriage** /
wedding   **marriage** /
wedlock   **marriage** /
weft   **warp** /
weight   **mass** /
weight systems, tables of
   avoirdupois weight /
weld   **braze** /
well   **good** /
well and good   **good** /
well-ordered set   **partly** /
Wells, H. G. (1866–1946)   **style** /
West   **North** /; **orient** /
West Coast   **North** /
West End   **freehold** /
Western Roman Empire   **Roman**
   Empire /

Western Samoa *England /;*
　Polynesia /
West Germany *East Germany /*
West Germany *enclave /*
Westminster *city /; private school /*
Westminster, Duke of *freehold /*
West Virginia *North /*
wetware *hardware /*
wharf *dock /*
wheel, invention of *Paleolithic /*
which *that /*
whiskey *whisky /*
whisky *whisky /*
white belt *white belt /*
white blood cell *erythrocyte /*
white-collar workers or jobs) *blue
　collar /*
white corpuscle *erythrocyte /*
white lies *lie / fib /*
white matter *gray matter /*
white paper *green paper /*
white rose *red rose /*
who *who / that; who / whom*
whoever *whoever /*
whole gale *breeze /*
whole number *integer /*
whom *who / whom*
whomever *whoever /*
whose *who / that*
who / whom *that /*
Wienerwerkstätter *antiques /*
wig *toupee /*
wildcat strike *strike /*
wild marjoram *oregano /*
will *shall /*
William III (r.1689–1702)
　Plantagenet /
William II (r.1087–1100)
　Plantagenet /
William I (r.1066–87) *Plantagenet /*
William IV (r.1830–37) *Plantagenet /*
williwaw *cyclone /*
willy-willy *cyclone /*

Winchester *private school /*
Windermere, Lake *lake /*
window *mullion /*
windpipe *alimentary canal /; upper
　respiratory tract /*
Windsor rulers *Plantagenet /*
windward *lee /*
wine *claret /*
wine bottles *magnum /*
wine, sparkling *champagne /*
Winter Solstice *equinox /*
winter solstice *Greenwich Mean
　Time /; Tropic of Cancer /*
WIPO *abbreviation /*
Wisconsin *North /*
without peer *peer /*
wittold *cuckold /*
wood *iron / wood*
woof *warp /*
woofer *tweeter /*
wool *wool /*
word, definition of *synonym /*
word order *who / whom*
word order in English *adjective /*
word processor *QWERTY
　keyboard /*
words, explanations of *dictionary /
　encyclopedia*
words, meanings of *dictionary /
　encyclopedia*
work-to-rule *strike /*
worship, traditional forms of *Low
　Church /*
would *shall /*
wrack *wreak /*
wrack and ruin *wreak /*
wreak *wreak /*
wreak vengeance *wreak /*
wreck *wreak /*
writing *cerebrum /*
writing surfaces *parchment /*
wrought iron *iron / steel; pig iron /*
Wyoming *North /*

X

X-axis *abscissa* /
X chromosome *X chromosome* /
Xeres *claret* /
xerograph *letterpress* /
x-height *ascender* /

Y

yak, wool from *wool* /
Yap Island *Polynesia* /
yard *statute mile* /
yardstick *parameter* /
yawl *sloop* /
Y-axis *abscissa* /
Y chromosome *X chromosome* /
yclept *archaic* /
year, great *Julian calendar* /
yellow bile *black bile* /
yellowjackets *wasp* /
Yersina pestis *typhoid* /

yew, a before *a* /
Yiddish *High German* /
Yiddish *Yiddish* /
York kings *Plantagenet* /
Yugoslavian, a before *a* /

Z

Zambia *England* /
Zen *Buddhism* /
zenith *zenith* /
Zeno of Citium (c340–265B.C.)
  Cynic /
zero *zero* /
zero, the ending *prefix* /
zero longitude *Greenwich Mean
  Time* /
Zimbabwe *England* /
zoology *exact science* /
Zoser's step pyramid *Old
  Kingdom* /